THE VENETIAN REPUBLIC

ITS RISE, ITS GROWTH, AND ITS FALL

by

W. CAREW HAZLITT

VOLUME SIX
Government and Culture

ISBN 9781652886143

chronicon
books

2020

The Venetian Republic

Agents In America

THE MACMILLAN COMPANY
66 Fifth Avenue, New York

The Venetian Republic

Its Rise, its Growth, and its Fall

A.D. 409-1797

by

W. CAREW HAZLITT

VOLUME II
1457-1797

LONDON

ADAM AND CHARLES BLACK

1915

First Edition (2 volumes) published in 1858.
Second Edition (4 volumes) published in 1860.
Third Edition, (2 volumes) published by A.& C. Black in October 1900.
Fourth Edition (2 volumes) published 1915.

CONTENTS

CHAPTER LV

CHAPTER LVI

CHAPTER LVII

CHAPTER LX

CHAPTER LXI

CHAPTER LXII

CHAPTER LXVI

The Venetian Republic

CHAPTER LV

Municipal Trading Guilds — Their Antiquity Superior to Extant Evidences — List of Some of Their Bodies — Many Unincorporated — The Painters and Tapissers — Gold Cloth Workers — The Tapissers — The Carpenters — The Masons — The Stationers — Glass-Furnaces — Antiquity of the Manufacture — Exportation — Imitations of the Venetian Fabric — Sparing Resort to Window-Glass — Chefs d'Oeuvre in Glass in 1585 — Spectacles.

The early chronicler Marco, to whom we owe so much and whose surname has been lost, enumerates many trades or occupations as existing in the Middle Ages, such as corsers or horse-breeders, saddlers, trainers of hunting dogs and hawks, furriers, carters, shepherds and many others. All of these were loans, in the first instance, from the mainland, and followed the ancient traditions of Venetia Maritima, obeying by degrees the peculiar wants and limitations of their insular settlement. The municipal corporations or guilds (successors of the Roman *collegia*) were instituted for purposes of common protection and welfare, as well as with a view to knit together, on terms of fellowship, members of the same calling.

All these bodies possessed their executive government and their capitulary or *mariegola*, which strictly prescribed their relationship to the state, their obligations to each other, and the nature and limit of their privileges. Many of them attained great prosperity, and were enabled on public occasions to defray the cost of elaborate and imposing spectacles.

Of some the mention recurs more frequently, because, perhaps, the character of the industry lent itself to display. All, however, united in constituting a valuable element in social no less than in commercial existence, and in diversifying the monotony of careers. Of six of the trades or arts the headquarters were long indicated by the names which they conferred on them, the Ruga degli Orefici (1) the Calle dei Fabbri, the Casselleria, the Rio dei Sartori, abutting on which water-way, the Tailors Guild still owned in the last century seventeen houses, the Veriera, and the Riva degli Schiavoni where the alien seamen had their quay, their chapel dedicated to Saint George and embellished by Carpaccio, and their places of abode and public restaurants.

(1)　　In a seventeenth century *Life or History of Mary Queen of Scots* by Caussin, the French Jesuit, the copies of an Italian version are said to be published "in the Ruga d'Oresi in Rialto under the Portico."

Several vocations, even of importance, never attained an independent municipal rank, and we trace them only by casual or indirect references. The Ponte della Fava at the outset indicated the immediate neighbourhood of an emporium for the sale of the sweetmeats called *fave*; the Calle del Scaleter marks the site of a shop for the cakes known as *scalete*; and a comparatively recent (1844) murder reveals a vendor of nails known as *brochetta* in the Calle San Zuane (near the *scuola* of the same name). So the spicer, a leading and very influential guildsman in early London, presents himself here individually, but not corporately.

The repugnance of the poorest Venetian of the older days to mendicity had been, met by the funds appropriated to the relief of aged or distressed members, and, when the guilds declined and eventually disappeared, the government thought fit to take their place in this respect, and provide some easy employment for the superannuated operative. In their prime, their eleemosynary functions were, as in other countries, a conspicuous feature in their constitution and justification.

Some of the companies and schools or *scuole*, which incidentally come under notice are:

　　　　Bakers.
　　　　Barbers.
　　　　Bath Makers.
　　　　Butchers.

Carpenters and Joiners.
Carpet Makers.
Casemakers (*Casselleri*).
Cask Makers.
Ferrymen.
Fishermen.
Fringe Makers.
Fruiterers.
Fur Dressers.
Glass Blowers.
Goldsmiths.
Gold Beaters and Wire Drawers.
Gunners.
Linen Drapers.
Mariners of San Nicolo. (1)
Masons.
Mercers. (2)
Merchants.
Painters.
Printers and Booksellers.
Sausage Makers.
Sawyers (Segatori).
Scavengers.
Sensali (or Agents).
Shipwrights.
Shoemakers.
Silk Cloth Weavers.
Silk Weavers.
Skinners.
Smiths.
Stonecutters.
Tailors.
Water Carriers of San Baseio or San Baseggio.
Wax Chandlers.
Wholesale Druggists.
Wine Merchants.
Wool Merchants.
Woollen Cloth Dyers.
Woollen Cloth Weavers.

(1)   "*Regole et Ordini della Fraternita di S. Nicolo del Marinari in Venetia, dalla sua Institutione anno 1572 sine al anno 1736.*"

Folio manuscript on vellum, with illuminations and arms in blazon. The entries are in a succession of hands.

(2)   At Padua, in 1406, the silk merchants formed one of the four estates of the commune.

We miss several callings such as chemists, locksmiths and plumbers, but it is possible that they may be comprised in others, while the stationer, in the sense of a vendor of literary property, was presumably represented here by the Printers and Booksellers Guild. But this enumeration is of interest, since it proves, what might be otherwise concluded, that there were facilities on the spot for procuring all the necessaries and luxuries of existence.

Among the commoners who subscribed to the patriotic fund for the War of Chioggia, occur a wine merchant and a barley factor. Some estimate may be formed of the immense volume of trade and corresponding demand, when we find as many as seventy-one depots of a single species of costly apparel. The *fabbro* of the *Cronologia Magna* (14th century) may have executed different branches of the craft.

The Gold Cloth Workers enjoyed the monopoly of the trade in vestments of cloth-of-gold and purple dyes, in the form of mantles or *palli* for both sexes; and the profit arising from this industry alone must for centuries have continued very large, as, besides the local demand, large quantities were exported abroad. From the early growth of a passion for sensuous opulence of ornament derived from Indo-Byzantine sources, a large business in gold-leaf or foil for architectural and decorative purposes seems to have existed, even in the earlier half of the fourteenth century, for Ruskin cites, on the authority of Cadorin, an entry in the procuratorial accounts, under the date, the 4th of November, 1344, of a payment of thirty-five ducats, for making foil to guild the lion over the door of the palace stairs on the site of the present Porta della Carta. This tissue may have come from the goldsmiths or gold cloth workers; more probably the latter.

The oldest vestige of a school of painting, which ostensibly combined domestic embellishment and musaic, is a passage in the *Cronaca Altinate*, in which mention is made of Marturius, a master of what is termed *pictura*. The painters were then known as *damarzi*, and probably were of Greek origin. It was not, as we are going to find, till a relatively advanced date, that the clear line of distinction was drawn between the mechanical artisan and the professional producer of landscape and portrait.

In a manuscript in the Correr Museum, appears the Master of the Guild of Carpet Makers or Tapissers, presenting the statutes (*matricula* or *mariegola*), probably about 1440, to the Doge Foscari for approval. A specimen of the work of the fraternity forms part of the illustration; it is a bordered mat with a floral design. The Doge is unattended, and is seated in a high-backed chair in a small apartment with a tessellated floor, but the details are evidently arbitrary.

The art of making carpets of various kinds seems to have originated among the tapestry-weavers; Chaucer mentions the Tapisser in his *Canterbury Tales* (1) and there is no doubt that at Venice, down to comparatively modern days, such an article of domestic use was almost unknown, except for the purpose of suspension on walls or for bed and chamber hangings.

(1)   Chaucer, *The Canterbury Tales,* Prologue, line 362.

The Painters and Tapissers seem to have united to execute articles of ornamental furniture in stamped and gilded leather, formerly so common in ancient houses in all parts of Europe; the former body also charged itself with embroidery and playing-card designs.

This guild presented in its inception a certain inconvenient anomaly, inasmuch as it embraced all handlers of the pencil and the brush, and all were on a footing of fraternity. Twice a year the corporation met in chapter to discuss matters of business, and the members naturally sat together at the same board, from Titian to the man who laid the paint on the portal of his door, or the varnish on the framework of his windows. There was a strong spirit of *bonhomie* in many respects among the different classes, and even the Doge is found condescending at special seasons to mix familiarly with his humbler compatriots, but the artists at last revolted against this form of municipal brotherhood, and erected themselves into an independent *collegio*.

The painters, apart from the artists who thus seceded, consisted of several sections (*colonnelli*); painters, gilders, miniaturists, pattern-designers, broderers or embroiderers; makers of gilt leather, playing cards and masks; decorators of shields and other weapons of defence. But they also included in their undertakings and accomplishments the art of embellishing the interiors of houses, presenting a fusion of the operative with the professional designer, and the walls of the salons and boudoirs of Venice, in the seventeenth and eighteenth centuries, were enriched by the brush of a Tiepolo, with lines and tints and airy fancies worthy of a fitter place and of a more enduring fame.

The art of card making thus seems at Venice to have devolved on the painters; but its exact origin is obscure, and the date at which the industry was introduced can only be surmised from proceedings of the Signori di Notte, under the date, the 20th of January, 1390, in which there is mention of *unum par cartarum a ludendo*. There is also a municipal decree of 1441, prohibiting the import of foreign goods of this description, which were said to have reduced the local trade to decay.

Some of the most ancient specimens of Italian playing cards are engraved by Chatto in his well-known work (1848), and one of them, in the suit of bells, bears the Lion of Saint Mark — an almost indubitable evidence of its origin. Under a notice of Filippo Maria, Duke of Milan, who died in 1447, occasion was taken to refer to his passion for cards, and to the employment of persons about the court in painting them. In the fifteenth century, the Italians appear to have used suits or packs consisting of cups, swords, coins and clubs, and these, with dice and tarots (*tarocchi*) or triumphs, supplied the material for the gambling tables, against which the Church began at an early date to declaim.

There is an engaging passage in the story before us, about a Doge of the seventeenth century, the rich Antonio Priuli who flourished from 1618 to 1623, that, in return for the customary oblation made on behalf of the Fruiterers Guild to the Crown on each accession, His Serenity gave the delegates muscadel wine, loaves, pastry, hams and other salted meats. Going back nearly a hundred years, mention occurs in 1521 of the nature of the offering and of the number of contributors. The Doge then received a lemon from each of the 130 fruiterers in Venice, but his quasi-feudal equivalent does not transpire. A collation of the two records establishes an interesting exchange of amenities between the head of the state, and a body of which excessively little is otherwise known.

Under the term glass-blowers are concentrated an employment and an art of the widest range. But the national manufacture, lace, hardly comes within any of the foregoing categories.

What may be treated as a farther illustration of the gracious flexibility of
the Venetian character was the annual election, by the Free Commune of
Fishermen at San Nicolo dei Mendicoli, of its own Doge, Executive
Board and Chancellor, at which representatives of the central
government were appointed to attend, and the ceremonial visit of the
Doge of the *Pescatori* to his brother sovereign at Saint Mark's,
accompanied by the secretary of his Grand Chancery. (1)

(1)   This was akin to the old usage of electing an annual king among
        the fisherfolk of Galway in Ireland.

It was a day of *fete* and gaiety and friendly union, and constituted one of
the innumerable ways in which the people were taught to stand shoulder
to shoulder, patrician and plebeian, at the advent of a crisis, forgetful of
all but their country. We seem to be reminded of the saying of Goethe,
that the Doge was the grandpapa of all the race, and of the remark of the
Russian prince, *Ce peuple est une famille.* It was so, in a measure, but
these observers were acquainted only with the Doge and the Venice of
their own day. Instances might, however, be multiplied without end of
the peculiar bonhomie, not only of the Venetian but of the Italian
character generally.

There is a singular one, belonging to the last quarter of the fifteenth
century and to the annals of Forli in Romagna, in which a half-witted
bricklayer is permitted to approach the sovereign, to grasp him tightly by
the hand, and to tender his advice. (1) It is not unusual to find at all
periods of history, more especially under despotic governments, this
occasional suspension of ceremony and official etiquette. The means of
resumption were ever at hand, and the parties concerned understood each
other; extremes met.

(1)   Pasolini, *Caterina Sforza,* page 157.

The Printers and Booksellers had been originally incorporated in 1548-
1549, and there is a manuscript copy of their bye-laws, or mariegola, (1)
approved by the Council of Ten in that year, but which was apparently
not officially published till 1567. We have also their minutes for the year
1571. Both these documents exhibit the constitution of the body, its
range of authority, its system of mutual protection and its amenability to
the state. Membership was not obligatory, and it became an important
part of the functions of the governing committee over which the Prior

presided, to watch the interests of the guild, and resist encroachment and other irregularities on the part of outsiders.

(1)   Brown, *The Venetian Printing Press,* page 83-86. The rules are there printed from the Cicogna manuscript in the Marciana.

The Squeraroli or Shipwrights, in their reply to an official inquiry in 1773, stated that they had been constituted in 1610, that they received apprentices up to fourteen years of age, that these might become master-builders in six years and ordinary workmen in two, and that, in order to qualify, each had to construct a craft; if he was going to "*fabbricar di grosso,*" a galley or other vessel; if "*lavorar di sottile,*" a gondola. It may deserve a passing mention that, in the earliest representations of vessels of all kinds in books, the artists had before them as models the designs then in general vogue; but an engraver of the sixteenth century naturally gave to antecedent eras the naval architecture of his own.

The Casselleri or Casemakers, whose quarter was the Casselleria, near Santa Maria Formosa, had the right of taking within Venetian woods material for their trade, free of charge. It was this craft-guild which made the hats long annually brought to meet the Doge, when he came to honour, with his presence, the andata instituted to commemorate the rescue of the Brides of Venice. (1)

(1)   *Il Ratto delle Spose* (the Rape of the Brides) by Istrian pirates in 932. The Casselleri were foremost in the rescue.

The Sawyers peep out, as it were, from one of the archivolts of the Basilica, where they form part of a group of trades typical of the Republic. The Wax Chandlers pursued a calling which for centuries remained as busy as it was lucrative, for it appealed alike to the needs of the Church and the layfolk. The incessant and multifarious demand for lights, (1) in connexion with services, processions and obits, or for domestic purposes, represented an enormous yearly consumption, for even the sole alternative, the torch, was charged with a fusion of wax and resin.

(1)   Molmenti (*La Storia di Venezia nella Vita Privata,* Liber I page 188) gives a fourteenth century illustration, after Giovanni da Bologna, of the peculiar sticks or holders in which the candles were then fixed.

In the account of the visit of Henry III. of France to Venice in 1574, the Sensali of Rialto are noticed as contributories to the pageantry, and as occupying their own brigantine, covered with crimson satin. This body appears to have comprised within its range the functions of providing official couriers, keeping a staff of officers who attended to the security and requirements of strangers, exercising control over hotels, and certifying mercantile agreements. Their bureau was known as the Messetaria, and their jurisdiction was perhaps restricted to the capital. But, in the melodramatic episode of Bianca Cappello in 1563, a *Sensali di casa* and his wife were implicated; and this individual ostensibly discharged a different class of duties not readily identifiable with a domestic post. The name suggests a primary restriction to the duty of attending to visitors who come to the yearly Sensa.

In a mercantile city, of which the houses were constructed for the most part exclusively of timber, the Carpenters and Joiners necessarily formed one of the most numerous and important classes of mechanics; in point of fact, they enjoyed a pre-eminence in both these respects. Of the followers of this calling, there existed within the Dogado two separate and distinct bodies; the one was composed of those who confined their attention to the ordinary duties of the trade; the other consisted of such as were employed in the public arsenal and dockyard in the capacity of shipwrights. The latter occupied, of course, the higher and more eligible position.

Until the period arrived when wood fell into disuse for purposes of building, and a demand arose for some material less inflammable and fitter for making history, bricklayers and stone-masons were in little request; and indeed, till the commencement of the twelfth century, they were rarely employed, except in the construction of cathedral churches or edifices of great pretension. In 827 the Church of San Zaccaria, which had been accidentally destroyed by fire, was restored in stone at the expense of one of the Byzantine Emperors, who sent from Constantinople an architect and a body of operatives, most probably from a desire to adopt in the new structure a style of architecture with which the Greeks were more familiar than the Venetians.

Throughout an almost immeasurable time, the carpenter was an operative of the first consequence, for all buildings, public and private, were long formed wholly or mainly of timber and thatch, and demanded perpetual replacement. Construction in stone must have remained rare down to the great fire of 1106, but external walls may very well have been formed of something more substantial than wood, before the latter by very slow degrees made way for masonry.

The current patronymic Tagliapietra which occurs in 1380 is a sort of clue to the existence of the industry in some shape at a much earlier date, and stone-work for churches became more or less familiar under the beneficent rule of the Badoers from 809 to 830. The masons appear to have been of two classes — the muratori or wall-builders, and the *scarpellini* or stone-cutters.

An industry, not specifically indicated, is that of the plumber who, where such vast quantities of lead were used in the roofing of churches and public edifices, necessarily possessed considerable importance.

In 1585, when the Japanese deputation called at Venice on its way from Rome, among the trades which contributed to the show prepared in honour of the visitors were the Apothecaries who followed a calling of great antiquity. An apothecary named Cicogna was one of the commoners called up to the Great Council after the Chioggian War in 1380, and almost precisely two centuries later, his descendant became Doge in the person of Pasquale Cicogna who reigned from 1585 to 1595. In 1574, when Henry III. of France was at Venice, the Apothecaries were among the bodies who contributed to the pageantry a Turkish rowing-barge of twelve banks of oars, splendidly appointed, and having at the prow the sign of the guild, the Testa d'Oro, and the symbol of a pelican with the legend *Respice, domine*; the Apothecaries at this time had their headquarters at San Bartolommeo.

The stationers, or occupiers of *stazioni* in the public thoroughfares where it was officially judged convenient, were dealers in innumerable varieties of common requisites supplied by the different trades, and had even valuable commodities for disposal. They held a position at Venice almost exactly parallel to the original Stationarii of the City of London. (1)

(1)   Hazlitt III, *The Livery Companies of the City of London,* page 625.

It is believed that the Veneti Primi carried with them into the Lagoon a knowledge of the manufacture of glass, with which both the Greeks and Romans were perfectly conversant. Specimens have been found in the excavations of Ilium and Pompeii and among the ruined cities of the Mississippi, but the origin and development of the art are due to Egypt,

whence it was communicated to the Phoenicians. The first ancient and
the first modern people who attained excellence in this valuable art were
dwellers in a sandy region. It is supposed that the crucifix in the Church
of the Dominicans at Treviso, painted on the glass and bearing the date
1177, is of Venetian manufacture. In many parts of the world where the
means of manufacturing glass itself were absent, we find references to
the use of horn, talc and other semi-transparent substances. (1)

(1)   Saint John, *The History of the Manners and Customs of Ancient
        Greece,* Volume II page 82.

It is easy to understand that, at the outset, Venice did not concern itself
with the question of location; each man set up his furnace where he
listed. Building had not made great progress; space was everywhere
abundant; sanitary regulations, if they existed at all, were diffidently
framed, and often contemptuously disregarded.

But the day arrived, when the metropolis at last began to awake to the
necessity of providing for the health and comfort, and indeed security, of
a swelling population, for the nature of the industry demanded the
incessant maintenance of the fires. Conflagrations in the neighbourhood
were traced to this source, and, on the 8th of November, 1241, a decree
was published, banishing all the furnaces from the city and its environs.

The glass-workers concentrated themselves at Murano, within the
tribunitial district of Torcello, and were constituted an independent
municipality with their own gastaldo. The government had indulgently
signified that such manufacturers as happened to have stock in course of
completion were to be allowed to finish it; but, although a heavy penalty
was attached to disobedience, and the Signori di Notte were enjoined to
enforce it, the official order was imperfectly respected, and, in 1297, a
second appeared to a similar purport. Yet the authorities remained so
languid and unliteral in carrying out the law, that, in 1321, the celebrated
Minorite, Fra Paolino, still possessed a property of the kind in Rialto, and
it was not till the second half of the fourteenth century that the entire
collection of scattered furnaces was transferred to Murano, and that the
latter place became the exclusive headquarters of this industry.

From the wording of a decree which passed the Legislature on the 17th
of October, 1276, the twofold inference is to be drawn, that the
manufacture was then in a flourishing condition, and that the Republic
had become anxious to convert it, as far as might be practicable, into a

monopoly. Among the companies which joined in the procession of the trades in 1268, the Glass-Blowers occupied a distinguished place, and brought samples of their interesting specialities for inspection.

Evelyn has, under 1645, a passage in his *Diary* which partly explains the peculiar merit and success of the product: "It is the white flints," he tells us, "they have from Pavia, which they pound and sift exceedingly small, and mix with ashes made of a sea-weed brought out of Syria, and a white sand, that causes this manufacture to excel." He invested in a supply, and had it sent to England "by long sea." A few years before, in 1635, Lady Miller desired James Howell to procure for her, through Mr. T. Lucy who was then at Venice, "a compleat Cupboard, of the best Crystal Glasses Murano can afford, by the next shipping." In 1621, when Howell visited the city of Alicante in Spain on behalf of the English Glassworks in Old Broad Street, we hear of the export of barilla or salt-wort to, Venice, for use in the glass-manufacture there. (1)

(1)   Howell, *Familiar Letters,* Book II, Letter 27, Book I, Letter 25; also Wheatley, *London Past and Present: Its History, Associations, and Traditions,* Volume I page 278, Volume II page 115.

The richer classes at home became munificent patrons; so large was the demand for the article in the metropolis alone, that, in all the better neighbourhoods, every thoroughfare had at last its own glass-warehouse which mainly depended for patronage on the tenants of the few mansions spread along on each side of it. At Murano itself in 1567, we hear of the Rio dei Vetrai, the manufacturers along which had customers in various parts of the Peninsula.

The furnaces were, in the old days, in unremitting activity day and night; there were relays of hands, and the workman alternated six hours of labour with six hours of sleep, snatching his meals as best he could. Saturday was a whole holiday, and there were numerous festive oases. The gastaldo and a bench superintended all the arrangements, and took care that the regulations laid down in the capitulary were strictly observed. This board of control, again, was responsible to a department of the executive.

It bespeaks the usual pioneering and paternal policy of Venice in nearly all that she devised, on the one hand for the protection of the state and the observance of order, and on the other for the well-being of her subjects, that, in such processes as demanded a resort to mercury or lead, child-labour was interdicted in the statutes of the guild which were approved by the government.

Objects in glass and alabaster occur in the inventory of the effects of the Doge Marino Faliero taken in 1355, but whether the former was of local origin or antique is not stated. Glass and earthenware were exported from Venice to England in the fourteenth century, and one of the last acts of Richard II. was a grant of safe-conduct for these goods, dated thirteen days before his abdication. About 1550, Venetian operatives were brought over to England, and the manufacture of glass on the Italian model was pursued till late in the following century. The same may be said of the Low Countries and Germany, where a vast quantity of articles must have had their origin, and where the Venetian manufacture sometimes received the finishing touches to suit the local taste or requirements — perhaps the addition of the armorial bearings (1) of the buyer — and became distinguishable with difficulty from the true prototype; at the same time, the latter remained in great request.

(1)   There is a lamp with the Tiepolo cognizance of undoubted originality. Molmenti, *La Storia di Venezia nella Vita Privata,* Liber II page 172.

In 1580, Queen Elizabeth was induced to grant a patent to a Venetian whose factory was situated in Crutched Friars, London, for making glasses in the style and material adopted by his countrymen at home. The concession awakened a certain amount of jealousy and hostility on the part of the Glass Sellers Association in London, but no farther tidings of it come under notice; we owe a knowledge of the circumstance to the representations of the aggrieved parties to the civic authorities or to the Crown. In 1575, the Glass House in Crutched Friars had been burned down, but that was possibly a different concern.

When the Japanese envoys visited Venice in 1585, one of the shows planned for their entertainment was under the charge of the School of San Giovanni dei Vetrai of Murano, and consisted of a castle and an organ made entirely of glass; but unfortunately the exhibition could not be completed in time to join the procession. Its ponderous character must also have created difficulties, as the other features were susceptible of treatment in more portable material.

The Glass Makers were formed into a guild only in 1436, when they commenced their Libro d'Oro, and had their governing body and their distinctive cognizance — a cock with a worm in its beak. The capitulary, periodically reviewed by the Proveditors of the Arts, was their constitution. In the Capitulary of the Council of Ten, 1578, the twenty-fifth clause wholly concerns this body, but merely lays down the rule and law that they shall not leave Venice or communicate their secret methods to strangers.

The coronation oath of 1229, which does not forget the rights and immunities of the guilds, but refers to both as matters of ancient usage, shews that the Glass Makers had been preceded in the enjoyment of corporate privileges by several of the other trades. By degrees, extraordinary perfection was reached, and the furnaces of Murano diffused over the world (1) an infinite variety of objects for ornament and use, exhibiting the most ingenious combinations of colour and form.

(1)   In one of the show-cases at the British Museum, are two examples of decorated objects of fanciful form, seeming to indicate a trade in ornamental glass with Servia, and an imitation of the fifteenth century German patterns. Both are in the Waddesdon room — one, a cup, has a Servian inscription on the foot; the other has armorial bearings and the date 1518.

Readers of the *Bravo of Venice* recollect the poisoned glass poniard which the bandit chief gave to Abellino; on the other hand, it has been alleged that the drinking goblet could be made so sensitive, that it would immediately betray by fracture the presence of poison. If in this manufacture they did not, like one of the early Egyptian kings, extend their efforts to the production of coins in glass, they soon comprised among their staple commodities measures and weights and all descriptions of fanciful and decorative knick-knacks, which the correspondents of the English East India Company repeatedly mention as in great request by the Great Mogul and his harem.

We see from a letter of Sir Henry Wotton, English envoy at Venice, to a noble friend in London, that he was on good terms with the artificers at Murano, and that he proposed to send his correspondent by the first ship a chest of Venetian glasses of his own choosing. When Thomas Coryat visited the works in 1608, the authorities permitted him to make a specimen with his own hands.

The output here became sufficiently large to supply the majority of European markets, and, in the time of Charles II. after the incorporation of the Glass Sellers Guild in 1664, large consignments of claret, sack, beer and other glasses, with or without covers, some choicely enamelled, speckled and clouded, and of mirrors, necklaces, toys, were made to London, whence they found their way all over the country, and formed one of the attractions at the great fairs. The correspondence of a firm in the Poultry, London, between 1667 and 1672, admits us to an acquaintance with the class of goods which their source of supply at Murano was periodically shipping to them. The letters of instruction are very precise as to quality, kind and measurement; and there are occasional complaints of the arrival of cases in bad order, as if they had been left, after being packed, in the rain. We hear of various sorts of looking-glasses, some for coaches; and the English house represents that Venice mirrors were to be had in London more cheaply than Signor Alessio of Murano invoiced them to that town.

Signor Alessio is begged to be very particular as to how he describes the goods, in order to lighten the heavy customs tariff; to smuggle into the packages a few extra pieces, and to remember to forward the bill of lading in duplicate. This is rather a late glimpse of so ancient and so long-established an industry, but it seemed to offer a few points of interest and curiosity, inasmuch as certain items specified in the orders sent out must have been equally in local use, although the lists comprise articles to be made to English measure and, again, such things as brandy tumblers. The directions to the Venetian, in regard to packing of the wares with layers of dry weeds, and the hooping, nailing, marking and numbering of the chests, are most minute, and he is to see, in the first place, that the receptacles are strong and seaworthy.

Sometimes it unfortunately occurred that there were losses, either on the side of the shippers or the consignees. Sir Thomas Roe, writing to Mr. Kerridge at Surat on the 6th of December, 1617, says: "The Venetians [i.e. mirrors] have sold here, two feet square, cost £20 sterling in Venice, for sixty rupies;" he adds that many other pieces are in hand which will never yield money. (1)

(1)   (compilation) *Letters Received by the East India Company From Its Servants in the East,* Volume VI page 223.

Lassels, writing some time before 1670, says:

"An other day we went to Murano againe, to see the glasse houses which furnish amost all Europe with drinking glasses, and all our Ladyes cabinets with Looking glasses. They utter here for two hundred thousand crownes worth a yeare of this brickie ware; and they seem to have taken measure of every nations belly and humour, to fit them with drinking glasses accordingly. For the High Dutch, they have high glasses, called Flutes, a full yard long, which a men cannot drink up alone, except his man, or some other, hold up the foot of this more then two handed glasse. For the English that love toasts with their drink, they have curious tankards of thick crystal glasse, just like our sylver tankards. For the Italians that love to drink leasurely, they have glasses that are almost as large and flat as sylver plats, and almost as un easy to drink out of. And so for other nations. In one shop they were makeing a set of glasses for the Emperor, of five crownes every glasse; They were drinking glasses with high covers made like spred eagles, and finely guilt." (1)

(1)   Lassels, *The Voyage of Italy,* Part II page 423-424.

He proceeds to speak of ships, organs and castles which were occasionally made of this material, and we know that such had been the case a century before when the Japanese visit was paid to the city. The author of *The Worth of a Penny*, published in 1641, reports the objects in crystal as things to be tenderly handled.

Imitations of the Venetian fabric existed, we perceive, prior to the establishment of the English Glass Sellers Guild in 1664, which put forward, in fact, as a plea for its foundation, the irregularities then committed in the trade. Evelyn, writing in 1676, expresses the opinion that the works at Lambeth, under the auspices of the Duke of Buckingham, made looking-glasses better and larger than any that came from Venice. (1)

(1)   The Casa Salviati has revived the glass musaic work. See Howells, *Venetian Life,* Volume II page 47-49.

The mention of the absence of glass from the windows at the Casa Foscari in 1457, and the intention to supply the deficiency before the abdicating Doge took possession of premises which he had owned ten years, seem to import a practice of movable window-frames which might be stored when not required, leaving only the ordinary *schiavine* or blinds. An indifference which at present seems strange was clearly long manifested in regard to the protection of premises from the weather by means of glazed casements, and, in England in the Elizabethan time, the hall of a leading City guild (1) is said to have no glass and to be exposed to the rain.

(1)   Hazlitt III, *The Livery Companies of the City of London,* page 275.

But, as still continues to be the case, the Venetians of the humbler classes, as well as those who occupied premises devoted to commercial purposes, resorted very sparingly to the glazier. Every population, in its architectural economy, naturally has recourse, not only to the material which is most accessible, but to the forms which seem most convenient. (1) In a city where narrow and dark courts abounded, either open longitudinal bars or Venetian blinds, as we call them, were apt to prove more airy and more secure than glass windows. Even the casements of some of the old prisons under the colonnade of the Palace were known as *schiavine,* and were made on a similar principle, so as to serve the double office of a window and a grating. Glass was, in general, reserved for ecclesiastical and palatial edifices; but even in churches they had, in early times, as in the cathedral at Torcello, substantial Venetian shutters (*scuri*), revolving on massive stone hinges and opening outward on the street. (2)

(1)   Of this the singular sliding shutters of a kind of mother-of-pearl at Manila supply an illustration; and the same principle manifests itself in the material used for hedging at Penrhyn in North Wales, at the Cape of Good Hope, and among the African ivory-gatherers.

(2)   Molmenti, *La Storia di Venezia nella Vita Privata,* Liber I page 73. In Madeline Anne Wallace Dunlop's *Glass in the Old World,* London, 1883, there is an interesting and useful account of the Venetian manufacture (page 142-144). Molmenti devotes several pages to it (Volume I 303, et seqq., and Volume II 169-175).

Artificial aids to sight were already in use in the fourteenth century in England. Eye-glasses occur in the inventory of a London haberdasher's stock in 1378, and the biographer of Carlo Zeno, who died at the age of eighty-four in 1418, expressly states that he never wore spectacles — an indirect proof that such appliances were available at Venice about the same period. Allusions to such matters are not unnaturally rare, and we do not know whether the optician was a salesman or merely manufactured for a retailer. In the large engraving of 1782 which depicts an historical scene at the San Benedetto Theatre, several of the spectators hold opera glasses, (1) but lorgnettes mounted in gold are illustrated in Molmenti, and telescopes for naval and military purposes must have been as familiar and early here as anywhere.

(1)   See the large folding plate [not included in this Chronicon edition] in the pocket of the present work.

A very gracious and winning side of the earlier Venetian life presents itself to our consideration and view in those numerous *scuole* or sisterhoods under holy patronage, which arose and multiplied in various parts of the city, and had their independent homes and special places of worship. From the thirteenth century at latest, these associations were established on a charitable and philanthropic basis, somewhat cognate with the underlying principle of the guilds, and their members dedicated their lives and labour to the relief of the poor and the exercise of religious offices, for which some of them had their own rituals.

From the latter and from their *mariegole*, the work of eminent artists, a delightful glimpse is obtained of phases of their daily routine and costume; and, for many centuries, throughout the most prosperous and the purest epoch of the nation's history, these institutions formed a beneficial and characteristic element. In their possession and use were service-books embellished with drawings by the first masters of the day, in which the discipline and ceremonial of the body were vividly portrayed, and these volumes received bindings of corresponding splendour. (1)

(1)   Molmenti, *La Storia di Venezia nella Vita Privata,* Liber I page 178-184.

CHAPTER LVI

Organ-Building — Bells — Iron Foundries — The Bell as a Time-Keeper — Early Clocks — Computation of Time — Earthenware and Porcelain — Majolica — Lace — Alien Corporations — Turks, Armenians — Florentine Association — Fondaco dei Tedeschi — Cries of Venice — Puppet-Shows — Tobacco — Guides — The Compagnia della Calza.

The introduction of organ-building, which implies a familiarity with the art of working in metal, is traditionally assigned to a certain priest Gregorio, who is said to have brought in the eighth century a knowledge of the mode of construction from Constantinople where the science was even then in high repute. The art which the Venetians had thus apparently acquired from the Greeks they were not remiss in turning to a lucrative account, for Eginhard, the secretary and biographer of Charlemagne, relates that, in 826, there came with Baldrico a certain priest of Venice, named George (perhaps the aforesaid Gregorio), who said that he knew how to construct an organ, and that the Emperor (Louis le Debonnaire) sent him to Aachen, and desired that all the necessary materials should be given to him.

From this date, the manufacture of instruments so essential to religious services, alike in the church and in private oratories, doubtless increased in extent and in excellence, although these matters have, from the absence of specific records, to be judged by inference and from accidental allusions. The organ employed by Matthias Corvinus was made in Venice, and was afterward in the possession of Caterino Zeno who might have acquired it in the course of his travels.

But at Florence, and arguably here also, chamber-organs were in vogue in the first half of the fifteenth century; and, at the social gatherings in which the great Cosimo de' Medici so much delighted, one of his daughters was in the habit of playing on such an instrument. This was the *regale* or regal, which is noticed in the procession of the schools at Venice in 1585 in honour of the Japanese ambassadors, and of which Bacon speaks. But a far more remarkable example might have been the organ, entirely constructed of glass, which was to have been sent from Murano, and which was excluded from the spectacle just mentioned, because it was not ready for delivery.

Under 880-881, the ducal chronicler Dandolo writes: "About the same time, the Doge Orso Badoer was made a Protospatarios by the Greek Emperor; and, in recognition of the honour which he had just received, he sent to Constantinople, as a gift to Basilios, twelve large bells, and from this time forth the Greeks used bells." We are thus to understand that, if Venice owed her acquaintance with organs to the east, she requited the obligation by imparting to Constantinople a discovery, or rather a revival, at least equally valuable and practically still more important. It is surmisable, on the contrary, that Dandolo was under a misapprehension in supposing that the Greeks owed this service to his countrymen, and the present of bells in 881, beyond its commercial value which must have been considerable, could only have furnished the Byzantine prince with evidence of the progress of the Republic, in an art almost unquestionably derived from the east, and in all likelihood from his own Italian subjects. For, in the contemporary or nearly contemporary account of the visit of the Exarch Longinus to Venice in 567-568, it is distinctly stated that, on his arrival, he was received with the sound of bells and musical instruments which almost deafened him; and these, while they were not necessarily, or even probably, of national manufacture, were then obviously familiar objects, procured, perhaps, from the Greeks of the terra firma, partly to meet growing ecclesiastical wants. Nor is it very hazardous to conclude that there was a fairly prompt transition from the stage of importation to that of local fabrication.

The passage from Dandolo, coupled with the other evidences which we have placed side by side with it, satisfactorily establishes the existence toward the end of the ninth century, not merely of a foundry at Venice, but the arrival at a fair state of working efficiency; and the members of this art were bound to work a fixed quantity of metal annually, as their assessed quota of direct taxation. Nor, indeed, viewed in connexion with the manifold uses to which iron might be made applicable at home, and the extensive and increasing demand for the article itself in its wrought and manufactured state, which the Venetians had, so far back as the epoch of the Badoer dynasty, from the Saracens and many other warlike nations, will the antiquity thus claimed for the Venetian foundries appear unreasonable. In later times, the Corporation of Ironfounders acquired social influence and note by its importance and number; it had its peculiar franchises and its own Prefect or Gastaldo.

Comparatively speaking, the iron trade opened to the Republic during the Middle Ages the same source of profit as it at present affords to the English nation, but, apart from any relative increase in the demand and supply of the article, a wide discrepancy exists between the position of the two countries in this respect. At Venice, iron was simply a manufacture, not a product, and the Venetians did not possess facilities for converting the trade into a monopoly. The probability is that, when the present of twelve bells was made to the Byzantine court in 880-881, the art was in a somewhat advanced stage of improvement; it was only a few years later that the general structure of the celebrated Campanile was brought to completion (888-900), and that the tower was made ready to receive the great bell. The latter, the metal of which was expressly cast for the purpose, was of stupendous bulk and diameter in the estimation of that age, and there can be no doubt that it long continued to be accounted one of the wonders of the city. It was viewed by the saunterers on the Piazza in the days of Pietro Tribuno (888-912) with intelligible feelings of pride and admiration.

The Mediaeval employment of bells for civil and ecclesiastical purposes has been referred by some writers to a period considerably anterior to that here indicated; but this point is more or less doubtful, and, certainly, even among the priesthood, their use was at first curtailed by the cost and difficulty of purchase, and the old fashion of striking a board to announce the hours of devotion or repast was long generally retained from necessity, if not from a conservative or indolent option. (1)

(1)   There is a picture of a very ancient bell at page 213 of *Les Arts au Moyen Age et à l'Epoque de la Renaissance*, by Lacroix, 1869. It is the representation of a handbell or *tintinnabulum*, ascribed to the ninth century and copied from a manuscript.

Prior to the general introduction of clocks, the bell played a much more important part in our daily life than we can at first sight believe to have been possible. It was the universal timekeeper and summoner, and it is a point deserving of careful investigation, whether its employment as a factor in the early social system did not precede its adoption by the Church, first for the mere purpose of announcing the hour of prayer or devotion, and subsequently as a moral and religious agency.

In the absence of household clocks, the division of the night into bells was ingenious and indispensable, for the two or three clocks erected in the metropolis itself were valueless after dusk, and all social arrangements depended on this primitive notation of time. Indeed, in an age destitute of culture and education, and among a nautical people, the progress of the hours was long ascertained in chief measure by the courses of the sun and moon and the rise and fall of the sea, as certain islanders in the Pacific still regulate the calendar by the ripening of the yam. We are too prone to see in our method of calculating the hours the sole possible one; the world grew into middle age, and made some excellent history, clockless. It is noticeable that in 1756 Casanova casually remarks that the Terza bell then rang at different times, according to the season of the year; he is writing under the 3rd of July, and it sounded, he tells us, at twelve.

As chanticleer was the sole clock of the primitive villager — the "early village clock" of Shakespeare — the bell was long the only machinery for marking the divisions of the monastic day; elsewhere its function at the auction mart has been recorded. It is of those things which already half belong to the past, perhaps in all its purposes, certainly in its ecclesiastical; for while horology was in its nonage, and places of worship were filled by more scattered congregations unprovided with timepieces, the bell became and remained a valuable auxiliary, whereas at present it seems to be somewhat of an anachronism.

The traditions are familiar enough, which carry back the invention of water-clocks or *clepsydrae* to the third century of the Christian era, and of instruments with metallic works and an index or hand acting on a striking-bell, to the eleventh if not to the ninth. Horology which properly ranked among the discoveries of Archimedes was speedily regained in the renascence of civilization, but it was brought to perfection by the moderns very slowly and gradually. The clocks which existed in England, France, Germany and Italy in the first moiety of the fourteenth century were sufficiently primitive in their mechanism. They seem to have been uniformly diurnal, to have had one hand only, and to have sounded, through the medium of a bell, the hours but not the halves or the quarters. That at Glastonbury, manufactured in 1325, had stone weights. The famous astronomical clock at Padua, made by Jacopo de Dondis, belongs to the same epoch — a few years later; and the middle of the fourteenth century witnessed the erection of the even more remarkable one at Dijon in Burgundy, surmounted by two human figures which the striking process set in motion — an artifice which in different forms was soon to be seen in France, Italy, Germany, and even Sweden. As to watches, Peter Henlein (1480-1542) is credited with having, in the sixteenth century, invented a pocket clock or watch, known as the Nuremberg Egg. We do not hear of the set larum in Venice, but it was in use in England in the time of Queen Elizabeth; Philip, Earl of Arundel, had one in the Tower.

The instruments which were set up during the same century at various places in England, such as Westminster, Dover, Glastonbury, Wimborne, Exeter, Peterborough, were all alike remarkable for their cumbrous machinery and the costliness of their production. Some may have been the work of ingenious and leisured ecclesiastics, but for the most part they proceeded from the hands of secular experts who are to be commended for their initiatory skill, not for a moment to be blamed for having executed what time and experience only transformed into anachronisms and historical monuments. All these clocks were automatons, but they demanded unceasing attention, were perpetually out of repair, and entailed incredible expense. Charles V. of France instituted, after 1364, a special office for the superintendence of the Horologe, and the holder was styled "the Governor of our Palace Clock at Paris."

The absence of any specific testimony of the existence of timepieces at Venice itself anterior to 1310 cannot be accepted as a proof of an ignorance of them. On the contrary, taken in connexion with the advanced state of Venetian civilization in other respects, it indicates that the invention was too familiar and of too ancient date to become subject of particular record. On the institution of the Decemviral Council in 1310, one of the earliest decrees promulgated by that tribunal was directed against the practice of traversing the streets by night, a custom which the recent Quirini-Tiepolo conspiracy had rendered suspicious, and it was ordered, "That no person whosoever shall be suffered, without special licence, to walk abroad after the third bell of the night." This edict undoubtedly alluded to the bell which formed, in the infancy of horology, a substitute for the striking clock, and which, in the Mediaeval clocks of larger size adapted for churches and other public buildings, was of corresponding dimensions and compass. We yet retain at sea, and in ports or other places where clocks are absent or invisible, the practice of sounding the hour-bell, and in a Venetian political letter of 1515, the old method of computation is used; the hour-bell used to be rung in the city of London, at all events down to the time of Edward II. Under 1332 there is a notice of the eleventh bell before noon, and similar reckonings occur elsewhere. (1)

(1)   (compilation) *A Chronicle of London*, page 47.

It is documentarily established that, prior to 1393, a magistracy resembling that at Paris existed here, and that large sums were expended on the construction and repair of chronometrical instruments. In the year mentioned, a report was addressed to the government on the state of the old clock of San Giacomo di Rialto. It appeared (1) that this timepiece, weighing six hundred pounds, was clumsy, ponderous and unserviceable; that its bell, from some flaw in the action of the hand, emitted a sound which was barely audible, and that it was, at the same time, a great charge upon the Treasury. In these circumstances, the procuratorial department sanctioned a proposal laid before them by a mechanical engineer of the day, to replace the instrument by a new one which should be of lighter materials and on an improved model, and, as regards the tone of the bell, of three times the compass.

(1)   Romanin, *Storia Documentata di Venezia,* Volume III page 349.

The computation of time and the necessity for regulating the movements of public bodies, of calculating the dates of the arrival and departure of ships, and of providing for future arrangements in commercial and other affairs, suggested in 1488 a recourse to an ingenious expedient on the part of one Salomon, probably a Jew, in the shape of a perpetual calendar. Earlier issues are possible; this is the first which has been so far recovered, and it forms a folio broadside, having at the foot in the right-hand corner: *Stampata per Nicolo ditto Castilia.* (1)

(1)   Reproduced in facsimile by Molmenti (*La Storia di Venezia nella Vita Privata,* Liber I page 433).

In or about 1496, the clock tower on the left of the Basilica was first erected on its present site opposite the Campanile. Its original form probably differed from that with which we have grown familiar, and the entire mechanism of the timepiece was undoubtedly primitive and imperfect. The tower is not distinguishable in the painting attributed by collateral testimony to 1494, in which the procession of the *Corpus Domini* occupies the foreground. Evelyn notes under 1645:

> "Over this porch stands that admirable clock, celebrated next to that of Strasburg for its many movements; amongst which, about twelve and six, which are their hours of Ave Maria, when all the town are on their knees, come forth the three Kings led by a star, and passing by the image of Christ in his Mother's arms, do their reverence, and enter into the clock by another door."

He also alludes to the bell at the summit, on which two wild men strike the hours with their hammers, and states that the man who superintended it had recently been killed by failing to avoid the blow as it descended.

Abundant evidence exists to shew that at Venice, down to the eighteenth century, the principle of dividing the civil, as distinguished from the natural, day into two terms of twelve hours each was not generally recognized, and that the clocks registered continuously from 1 to 24. When a Doge took office in 1457, the contemporary official memorandum says: *"feliciter eadem die hora XXII. regimen ducatus intravit,"* or in other words, he assumed his authority at ten o'clock at night, having been elected, according to the same record, at fifteen and a half o'clock, or half past three in the afternoon. In 1755, Casanova speaks of hearing *"vingt une heure"* strike; the same system probably prevailed throughout Italy. We see from several passages in the *Life of Cellini* that it did so at Rome, and from Pasolini that the same principle was followed at Forli. In a letter to his brother in 1621, from on shipboard before Venice, James Howell states that he heard a clock from Malamocco strike twenty-one hours. (1)

(1)   Howell, *Familiar Letters,* Book 1, Letter 27. The railway system in Italy still follows this method.

When we note in the *Travels* of Marco Polo from 1270 or thereabout till 1295, that he witnessed in the Chinese province of Fo-Kien, at the city of Ting-chau or Tingui, the processes by which the inhabitants already made utensils of porcelain, and saw cups and dishes of that ware on sale, it is difficult to believe that it was not till the fifteenth century that the material and manufacture were introduced into Venice. The truth appears to be that objects in porcelain were long regarded in Europe as luxuries or ornaments; and the more richly and artistically decorated examples, produced by the Chinese themselves, do not date back beyond the sixteenth century, that and the seventeenth being accounted the finest period of fabric and design; it may therefore be the case that the Italians did not recognize in the ruder work an appreciable advance on their own domestic appliances in wood, earthenware or metal. Articles of porcelain, not oriental but of local origin, are mentioned, however, in a letter of 1470, as then brought to perfection, and also as being modelled on the oriental style to which the writer considered it superior. Ordinary pottery had probably been in use much earlier, first as an import from the east, and finally as a home product; but majolica is not supposed to have been an article of Venetian manufacture prior to the fifteenth century, when a certain Mistro Agustino of Venice seems to have executed this description of work.

A plate is said to be still in existence bearing the inscription; "*1530 fato p. M. Agustin in Venetia.*" The earlier records of the porcelain and majolica works in Venice are apparently very obscure and incomplete, notwithstanding the Campori, Piccolpasso and Drake papers of which Chaffers had the use (1) As early as 1520, Titian figures as negotiating a supply of majolica and Murano glass for the Duke of Ferrara, but the pavements of certain ecclesiastical buildings are mentioned at an anterior date as formed of majolica, though there is a disposition to attribute this to Siena.

(1)   See also Drake, *Notes on Venetian Ceramics*, 1868. The most remarkable assemblage of Italian majolica, including a large number of utensils designed for professional purposes and originally belonging to the Dukes of Urbino, is preserved in the Santa Casa at Loreto. The collection had come from the medical dispensary attached to the palace at Urbino. Chaffers, *The New Chaffers: Marks and Monograms on European and Oriental Pottery and Porcelain with Historical Notices of Each Manufactory,* page 148.

The manufacture of majolica and earthenware continued during the sixteenth and seventeenth centuries, that of ordinary pottery much later. Mistro Lodovico occurs in 1540 as the salesman of majolica at a shop on or adjoining the bridge leading to San Polo; the same depot was in existence in 1568, a painter named Domenigo working for it. There is some ground for the opinion that Faenza (whence comes the term *faience*) was the inspiring source of the Venetian school of ceramic art, as the products of these two places bear a striking resemblance to each other. In the second half of the eighteenth century, a revival of the industry took place at Murano under official protection; but it did not succeed.

Immense quantities of earthenware for domestic and pharmaceutical use were doubtless made here, as well as at Padua and other cities on terra firma, from the fifteenth century onward, and the trade was largely in the hands of the Bocaleri Guild which enjoyed the usual privileges and exemptions. But, alike in regard to pottery and porcelain, if not also majolica, Venice is shown to have been an extensive medium for the distribution in Europe of eastern wares, before the Republic started as a maker or imitator.

The regular manufacture of true porcelain is ascribed to the Vezzi family (1) who commenced their operations about 1720 at Lido. The business was soon converted into a company, with a capital of 30,000 ducats, to which Carlo Ruzzini, Doge from 1732 to 1735, belonged, and which rented the premises of the family. The main difficulty arose from the need of obtaining the kaolin from a distance, but the industry continued with more or less success down to 1812, and both sorts of paste were made. The marks were numerous, including the creeper or fish-hook which differed from the Chelsea anchor, although the latter may have been suggested by the Venetian symbol found on the Chelsea work of the second period, attributed to Venetian hands.

(1)   For some account of Francesco Vezzi, goldsmith and jeweller, born 1651, see Drake, *Notes on Venetian Ceramics,* page 19. Giovanni Vezzi, the father of Francesco and Giuseppe, was a follower of the same business at the Golden Dragon in San Zuane, in Rialto.

Chaffers draws attention to the resemblance borne by the English china to its Italian prototype, not merely in gilding and painting, but in the method of preparation; as a matter of fact, a comparison of the same object — such as the figure of Justice — made at the factory at different periods prompts the suggestion that the Italian style is the later one. He engraves the mark on a Venetian cup and saucer, "Ven. A.G. 1726," which is taken to be the most ancient example with a date. The marks on the majolica are of course infinitely more varied, and usually comprise the name of the artist and that of the salesman, with his address, whence comes the information that majolica was made in Castello and Murano, as well as in Venice itself There is a dish bearing the inscription: "*Fatto in Venezia in Chastello. 1546.*" Both majolica and porcelain were made at many places in the Venetian territories outside the Dogado, particularly at Bassano, Verona and Treviso. A peculiar kind of white china, long assigned to Capodimonte, is now pronounced to be Venetian.

A customary wedding-gift in the eighteenth century was a service of china in a leathern case or box bearing the arms of the family or families. One with the coat of the Semiticoli is mentioned as having been in the Cavendish-Bentinck collection. (1) There is elsewhere a mention of the dessert-service of fine porcelain, painted with mythological subjects, presented by the Queen of Portugal before 1784, to Angelo Emo, the famous Venetian admiral.

(1)   Litchfield, *Pottery and Porcelain,* page 305.

Lace does not appear to have entered into any of the programmes of the guilds, unless it fell within the province of that of the Fringe Makers, the Scuola dei Passamaneri. But it was an object of extensive manufacture in nunneries and private dwellings, and ladies of the highest rank dedicated a portion of their time to this accomplishment. Two Dogaressas of the fifteenth and sixteenth centuries, Dandolo Malipiero and Morosina Morosini Grimani, and the noble Viena Vendramin Nani zealously encouraged it. To the last, Cesare Vecellio inscribed his *Corona delle nobili e virtuose donne* in 1592, which closely and suspiciously corresponds with a volume published by Gianantonio Tagliente in 1560, *Ornamente delle belle e virtuose Donne.*

The production in private houses continued down to the latter part at least of the seventeenth century, for De la Haye notices that, when the ladies are at home, they commonly entertain themselves in making their *Punti in aria,* which are the *Points de Venise* so much valued in France, and sometimes improperly claimed and described as *Points de France.* Mention has been made of a volume of German, French and Italian designs by Pagano, published at Venice in 1525; but this book seems to belong to a later date — about 1560 — and has no note of issue. (1) In 1530, Zoppino published his *Book of Patterns Ancient and Modern,* (2) and the varieties became very numerous and the application of the art more and more extended, the Church sharing with the house and the person the benefits of this charming invention.

(1)   Paganino, *Raccolta de Tvtti i Ritratti & Disegni di Riccham,* with many engravings and a representation on title of women at work.

(2)   Zoppino, *Esemplario di Lavori, Dove le Tenere Fanciullealtre Donne Nobile Potranno Facilmente Imparare il Modoordine di Lavorare, Cusire, Raccamare, Finalmente Far Tutte Quelle Gentilezzelodevoli Opere, le Quali Po' Fare Una Donna Virtuosa con Laco [!] in Mano, con li Suoi Compassi, Misure.*

Both sexes made lace a part of their ceremonial attire, and, even at a date prior to any distinct records of the export of the material to foreign countries, the fame of the Venetian fabric must have been well diffused, for it is thought that the lace worn at the coronation of Richard III. of England was obtained from this source. The Venetian Lace and Linen Books were, during half a century or so, constantly reprinted, yet complete copies are naturally of very rare occurrence. In 1414, the horses in a state procession at Venice are said to have housings of the material, but it was probably not in ordinary use for female costume till the seventeenth century. Gold and silver lace was largely employed in the vestments of ecclesiastics, and in the robes of ceremony and state worn by both sexes. In a contemporary account of the rich costume of the Dogaressa Mocenigo in 1763, the petticoat (*sottana*), partly shewn beneath the outer mantle of cloth-of-gold, is described as covered with flowers in gold lace.

The manufactory of Burano claims the distinction of having invented the *coupe* and the point in relief. It is difficult to decide what credence is due to the tradition that the germ of this beautiful fabric is to be sought in the art of the net-maker, or in the seaweed. It was the same principle as that of the net, differently applied and more delicately handled. But a species of seaweed known as *Alcyonaria* also bears a strong likeness to lace, and examples of lace coral have been found at considerable depths in the Antarctic Ocean. The noble Italian ladies often distinguished themselves by their skill in needlework and embroidery as well as in lace-making. In 1502 we find Battista Riario thanking Madonna Caterina of Forli for seven shirts which she had made him.

The cosmopolitan tendency and attributes of the Republic involved, almost as a necessity and beyond mere tolerance, the admission into the city of traders of all the most prominent nationalities of Europe and Asia. The Greeks, the Turks, the Jews, the Armenians, the Germans, the Swiss were not only welcomed, but were accommodated in a suitable and convenient manner, subject to strict conformity with the laws as well as with special regulations framed in the interest of general tranquillity. All these strangers were originally at liberty to reside where they pleased;

but it was discovered to be inconvenient on different grounds to allow persons of heterodox faith the free range of the capital and its suburbs, and separate and special quarters were successively assigned to the Jews and the Turks, the former occupying the Ghetto, the latter, subsequently to 1621 when the ancient Valmieri Palace was converted to this new use, being restricted to the precincts of the Fondaco dei Turchi on the Grand Canal, where the government caused all the approaches to be closely guarded and watched after sunset, and interdicted visits from women and young boys.

The building has in our time been reconstructed, and now holds the famous Correr Museum. In 1507, three women of the town were whipped through the Merceria, for having been found within the precincts and having lain with Turks. (1) Of the most ancient foreign fraternity we perhaps hear the least. The Armenian merchants were already in 1178 established here, and by his will the Doge Sebastiano Ziani, who had in earlier life resided in their country and probably accumulated part of his wealth there, left to the company one of his houses in the Street of San Giuliano. (2)

(1)   Molmenti, *La Storia di Venezia nella Vita Privata,* Liber II page 603.

(2)   Filiasi, *Ricerche Storico-Critiche da Giacomo Filiasi,* page 137.

An element in the system of foreign domestication at Venice, which differed from the others in one respect, was the colony of silk weavers from Lucca which, in the first half of the fourteenth century, was driven from its home by tyranny, and sought an asylum in the Lagoon, where it formed itself into a sort of fraternity, and built for its use the Church of Volto Santo of which some remains were recently visible near the ruins of that of the Servites. In the often-quoted oration before the Pregadi in 1423, the Doge Mocenigo lays heavy stress on the benefits which accrued to the Venetians from the Lucchese settlement.

The Florentine Association dates even farther back than that of Lucca, for it appears in the light of an important and wealthy body in 1313 during the course of the negotiations for a settlement of the Ferrarese difficulty, and the government is found putting some pressure on its members in order to facilitate an exchange of Venetian for Tuscan money. In 1425, one of the provisions of a treaty to which Florence was a subsidiary party placed this body on an equality with the German Guild, as a means of indemnifying the Tuscans for disappointment in other directions. At this point of time, Giovanni de' Medici was a member, and acted in a diplomatic capacity on behalf of his country during its unequal struggle with Milan. There is a distinct indication that, at a much later period, the Tuscan colony at Venice remained numerous and influential, for, in 1621, funeral honours on a splendid scale were paid by the Florentine residents here to Cosimo II., Grand Duke of Tuscany. (1)

(1)   Ciotti, *Esequie Fatte in Venetia dalla Natione Fiorentina al Serenissimo D. Cosimo II Quarto Gran Duca di Toscana Il dì 25 di Maggio 1621.*

On the Campo dei Frari at a relatively late date, the Milanese were permitted to establish themselves, and, in immediate contiguity to their hall, to have a chapel in the Frari Church where they were at liberty to use the Ambrosian liturgy. It is scarcely probable that this event happened prior to the middle of the fifteenth century — perhaps after the Treaty of Lodi, when the political relations between Venice and Milan had become more friendly through the death of Filippo Maria Visconti in 1447. The altar-piece in the chapel was not completed till 1498.

Every country in the world, having diplomatic or commercial relations with Europe, and more especially northern Italy, was adequately represented at Venice. Ambassadors, consuls, agents or factors, bankers, abounded through the whole of the flourishing and strong period. The Italians of the terra firma, the Germans, the Swiss, the French, the Spaniards, the English, had their delegates, and the utmost facilities for trade and personal protection. It was to the obvious interest of the Republic to encourage, by every legitimate method, all those who conduced to promote its mercantile welfare, and to maintain its dignity and rank as one of the family of European states.

Of all the establishments erected for the benefit of foreigners, the Fondaco dei Tedeschi, previously in succession the Casa Pesaro and the palace of the Dukes of Ferrara, is probably the most familiar to the eye of the modern traveller, since it has survived every revolution, and is to be seen at the present day on the Grand Canal — a splendid shell, for it has long ceased to answer the purpose for which it first rose from the lagoon; indeed its palmiest days preceded the advent of the Hollanders to the front rank for a season. Within those precincts, even the princely house of Fugger of Augsburg once thought it desirable to have a branch of their bank to meet the convenience of German traders and financiers, till that power gave way before the wave of Dutch ascendancy.

Coryat saw the Fondaco dei Tedeschi, and speaks of it as the Fontigo of the Dutch merchants. "They say," he tells us, "there are two hundred severall lodgings in this house; it is square and built foure stories high, with faire galleries, supported with prety pillars in rowes above each other." (1) Over the entrance there was an inscription in stone; *Leonardi Lauredani Inclyti Principis Principatus anno sexto*, which seems to indicate the restoration in 1507-1508 after the disastrous fire of 1505. The exterior of the old building had been decorated with frescoes by Giorgione and Titian. So far back as 1268, the German Guild was under the superintendence of three Visdomini, and at all times the Venetian executive regulated the whole external economy of the institution, which was at once a boardinghouse, a restaurant and a club.

(1)   Coryat, *Coryat's Crudities,* page 245-246.

In the eighteenth century, on the decline of the chartered trading associations, arose a considerable number of licensed itinerant hawkers. Gaetano Zompini has left evidence of sixty callings, represented in this way, in his illustrated *Cries of Venice* (1) and possibly there were others. Part of the value of the book lies in the fair assumption that the condition of affairs depicted by Zompini might be equally applicable to the earlier years of the century, if not to the preceding one, for the Venetians were inimical to change. The author has etched for our benefit the Vintner, the Cooper who equally officiated as a shop-fitter, the Cobbler, the Tinker, the Knife Grinder, and the peripatetic Glazier who carries in his arms a whole window frame, the Coal Higgler (who is made to say that there are only two authorized by superiors, although five or six are discernible in the picture), the Quack who offers his miraculous balsam, the Slop Seller, the Wood Dealer from Friuli, who is depicted, hat in hand and tools on shoulder, making a bargain with a customer who smokes a long pipe, and the Chair Mender from Cadore which yielded, after all, something more than Titian. In an early engraving belonging to another work, the chimney-sweep, with his long broom and the sack for the soot, is in a street parleying with a woman from an upper casement. (2)

(1)   Zompini, *Le Arti che Vanno per Via nella Citta di Venezia.*
(2)   Molmenti, *La Storia di Venezia nella Vita Privata,* Liber III page 188.

Two vocations which modern judgment has separated appear to have been possessed by the same individual, who was at once your gardener and your dustman; he would even attend to your vineyard. A pretty industry, followed by a later Autolycus, was the street traffic in small wares, needles, pins, laces and ribbons. We perceive that people of the Grisons were specially licensed to vend buns, that the man with the performing monkey was a Piedmontese, that there were dancing-dogs of unrecorded origin, and that the seller of singing birds for casements found his business briskest in March.

In one plate there is a puppet show, and in another some sort of kaleidoscope, where a boy, mounted on a stool, has paid a *soldo* for a peep. The dealers in comestibles are numerous and persuasive. There are for the fortunate persons at hand with money in their pockets black puddings, hot puddings buttered and seasoned with cheese, plum fritters, *polentina* or hasty pudding, and snails; the last, properly dressed, are particularly recommended for children and invalids. In the cut in which the fritters are on sale, a lady and gentleman, the former holding a fan, appear to be contemplating an investment. The dealer in *polentina* has, as his clients, three hungry and eager boys, who regard the covered dish, laid on a basket turned upside down, and evidently deprecate delay in coming to terms. The merchant who supplies Easter eggs is not forgotten; and we are reminded in the text that there was the egg game, in which the victory was to whoever played longest with an egg without breaking it. In one of the plates, there is a statement which we cannot guarantee, that the price charged by the pedlar was lower than that asked in shops. It is numbered 29, and the letterpress verses beneath are:

> *"Da tutte le stagion mi vendo fruti*
> *Piu a bon marca de quei delle boteghe,*
> *E per la baza ghe ne compra tuti."*

The ingenuous vendor is weighing the quantity ordered, and one of two women holds out her apron to receive it. A phase of Venetian life, familiar enough down to the close, if even yet obsolete, was that shown in Number 43 of the present series, in which a fortune teller and palmist is holding a levee of persons of both sexes and of different ranks. From the most remote age, necromancy and all the cognate arts had had their votaries at Venice.

The collection of which we have made use more immediately depicts the later life, and does not seem to approach exhaustion; for, in a similar one for Rome of 1646, which is evidently a reprint of an earlier issue, an examination readily detects numerous industries which must have been common to other places — sulphur matches, pure ink, locks and bolts, melting ladles, straw hats, hornbooks, rat pills and spindles. There is a third publication of correspondent type, purporting to illustrate the trades of Bologna as they were in the time of Annibale Caracci. (1)

(1)   Caracci, *Le Arti di Bologna Disegnate da Annibale Caracci ed Intagliate da Simone Guilin.* There are editions of 1608, 1646, 1776. So early a knowledge and use of the lucifer match seems to have escaped Fournier, *Le Vieux-Neuf: Histoire Ancienne des Inventions et Decouvertes Modernes,* Volume I page 120-121. There are also the glimpses of the broom seller in 1443, whom we meet, as it were, as we go down the Street of Santi Gervasio e Protasio, talking to a woman at a casement above on an October day about some passing matter, and of the woman who sells eggs, who is introduced by Titian into a picture of the Presentation at the Temple. Molmenti, *La Storia di Venezia nella Vita Privata,* Liber II page 453.

      In the *Cries of Bologna*, we encounter the cheesemonger from Piacenza, the chair mender, the house painter, the gardener with rake and grapes, the architect, the picture dealer, the cat's meat man, the pork butcher and the vendors of sieves and clogs.

Besides the ordinary puppet-show, there was the cheap theatrical spectacle, where the proprietor was not precluded, on certain special occasions, from erecting in the principal thoroughfares a temporary scaffold, whence the performer or company might operate without obstruction, generously relying on voluntary fees. A similar method was pursued even by the astrologer and the cheap or charlatan tooth drawer, who conducted their respective callings in the sight of the admiring crowd.

We do not precisely know in what places of business, unless it was at the apothecaries, tobacco and snuff were on sale, and still less the boxes for holding them, but we encounter the man in the street in the eighteenth century, with his stock of tobacco on a covered stall. It grew into a habit among ladies in a certain sphere or of easy manners, to take pinches of snuff out of men's boxes as a pretty or gracious compliment. We have in the *Cries* the fellow smoking a long pipe, probably of clay; a German traveller observed the same thing in London in 1598, yet as a novelty, at least to him.

An occupation which probably engrossed the services of a sufficiently large body of respectable and trustworthy hands was the constant duty of guiding parties at night to the theatre, the masquerade and the dinner or evening party; this phase of humble industry is reflected in the pages of the volume before us, where the lantern bearer (*codega*) precedes two masked and cloaked figures bent on some errand of pleasure. One of the prints indicates that keys to the opera house were publicly sold; a vendor is seen in the foreground holding a bunch in his hand.

Allied to the guilds, merely in a ceremonial and festive sense, was the peculiar organization, the Compagnia della Calza with its numerous branches. It was a rich and brilliant fellowship of gallant and debonair young aristocrats, devoted to the pursuit of pleasure in all its healthier forms. In every fashionable wedding, in every gala, regatta, tournament, masquerade, its members took a distinguished part, and generously contributed to the attendant expense. The association was wholly non-political, and did not interfere with the government, nor the government with it. The preparation of its sumptuous programmes in connexion with periodical entertainments, their successful issue and the agreeable survey in retrospect went far to engross the time and thoughts of these superb triflers, to make topics for gossip and opportunities for harmless intrigue, and to save the Signory the trouble of curbing a bevy of hot and restless spirits.

The uniform of the society (1) consisted of a striped parti-coloured stocking (*calza*) worn on the left leg, reaching to the hip, drawn over tight breeches, and embroidered with quaint figures of quadrupeds and birds; a doublet of velvet or cloth-of-gold with open sleeves and facings displaying the shirt-frill, a flowing mantle of silk or other costly texture, thrown back on the shoulder in such a manner as to shew the emblematic stocking richly worked on the lining, a black or red bonnet with a jewelled apex, and long pointed shoes studded with precious stones. Many of the female members of the aristocracy were honorary associates, and on festive occasions the latter wore a dress bearing on the sleeve the mystical device of the Calza.

(1)   Romanin, *Storia Documentata di Venezia,* Volume IV page 6-7.

The Company had its own statutes and bye-laws. At a subsequent date, its numbers increased, and it was divided into several branches of which the Immortals, the Royals, the Ethereals, the Accesi or Gays and the Peacocks were the most noted. (1) Nor was there a peremptory limit of age when a personage at once eminent and popular desired to join. There were also foreign honorary associates; in 1476, Lodovico III., Marquis of Mantua, was admitted on his visit to Venice to the fellowship as a distinguished stranger.

(1)   Morelli, *Delle Solennita e Pompe Nuziali Gia Usate Presso li Veneziani,* page 14-16; Mutinelli, *Del Costume Veneziano Sino al Scolo Decimosettimo Saggio di Fabio Mutinelli;* Malespini, *Dvcento Novelle,* Part 1, Number 41.

Apart from the Calza which wearers of the Orders of the Bath, the Garter and the Thistle need not undervalue, the Venetians had two methods of bestowing marks of their appreciation on personages of merit; admission to the rights of citizenship, which was very frugally dispensed and was, of course, limited to foreigners including crowned heads, and the diploma of the unique knightly Order of the Patron Evangelist, which was open to all. (1) In a few instances, knighthood was conferred by foreign sovereigns on the diplomatists accredited to them by the Signory, and eminent Venetians have been so honoured by the English kings from Henry VII. to George III.

(1)   In 1662, Andrea Rossini, a faithful public servant and Master of the Mint, received this distinction. The diploma occupies thirteen lines on a single sheet of parchment, and is engrossed in large characters in black and gold, with a broad illuminated border displaying the winged Lion of Saint Mark. The seal, silk cord and tassel are still attached to the document.

CHAPTER LVII

The Coinage — Obscurity Attendant on the Most Ancient Currency of the Republic — Lengthened Poverty of the System — Fifty or Sixty Varieties of a Mediaeval Silver Denaro Recovered — Payments Calculated by Weight — Foreign Money Recognized — Bills of Exchange — The Silver Grosso — Sterling Coinage — The First Gold Ducat (1284) — The Legends — Earliest Pieces With the Likeness of the Doge — The Practice Promptly Abolished — The Scudo d'Oro (1528-1530) — The Silver Ducat (1559-1567) — The Doppia d'Oro — The Giustina (1571) — The Scudo della Croce — Colonial Currencies — Money of Necessity — Convention Money — Oselle or Ceremonial Pieces — The 100-Ducat Piece of Luigi Manin.

There is, on the whole, no portion of an historical task on which so much labour attends, as an attempt to trace the beginnings of a nation's coinage. (1) The right to strike money, by its own authority and on its own soil, is one which every country has been anxious to claim and to cherish, and even this jealous solicitude has increased in great measure the embarrassment of the historian. For the legitimate interest and curiosity which have always been manifested in this subject since the revival of literary tastes, have led to an immense fabrication of false pieces which have formed the material on which credulous and inconsiderate persons have built false theories and opinions.

(1)   "I must first thank your Serenity for sending me the money with your imprint. I will take it home with me to shew to His Majesty, who will be pleased, as the excellency of the money is one of the chief evidences of the greatness of princes." Sir Henry Wotton,

British envoy to Venice, addressing the Doge in Council, 18th December, 1618.

From this form of danger and mischief Venice has not enjoyed an exemption. At Padua in 1818, an attempt was made to present a complete view of the currency in circulation under the consuls, and this so far differed from ordinary impositions that it was entirely unsophisticated by authenticity. It is certainly remarkable, however, that, in the continual process of dredging the lagoons under government inspection in the days of the old Republic, numismatic relics should not have been exhumed even in abundance; and it is extremely likely that excavations undertaken on the spot would bring to light some valuable and authentic examples of the primitive coinage.

When we look at the coins struck in the darkest ages by nations infinitely less advanced than the Republic, they almost compel a belief that Venice must have had some sort of money, several generations before the probable or approximate date of any now known. In the first quarter of the sixth century, the Prefect Cassiodorus, writing *Tribunis Maritimorum*, in which term it may be allowable to suppose that the Venetians were embraced though the hypothesis is not vital, describes those whom he addresses in the name of his royal employer as striking *moneta victualis quodammodo*. In other words, a traveller who had commercial relations at that time with Venice and her neighbours was expected and bound to accept in payment any symbol which he knew or believed to be officially recognized. Perhaps at the very first outset, strips of leather as among the Russians, or tablets of salt such as Lord Valentia mentions as circulating in Hindustan and to which the Frankish Veneti themselves are also alleged to have resorted, were received here on the authority of certain accredited marks or characters, as equivalents for smaller parcels of goods and in ordinary daily transactions.

It seems beyond belief and possibility that any state having, like Venice, a free existence from the middle of the fifth century, should have neglected for a very great length of time to organize some more or less distinct monetary system, but the hypothesis that one which was from the outset so emphatically commercial should or could do so is simply inadmissible. In the eighth century, at all events, the Republic was making war and concluding treaties on her own account. At the commencement of the ninth (810), the Emperors of the East and West joined at Aachen or Aix-la-Chapelle in pronouncing her independent of either.

A community, increasing yearly in wealth, power and estimation, possessing its own sovereign, governed by its own laws, was not likely, when it wanted nothing else essential to its political life, to be without a currency of its own, however imperfect and rude, or without some more or less efficient substitute for it. In the earlier half of the ninth century, *monetario* or moneyer had found its way into the Venetian nomenclature. It is perhaps not too rash to infer that, before it became the name of a family, it was that of an established vocation. Unfortunately, as to the date of settlement of the *monetarii* in the lagoons we are at fault, nor do we seem to hear of them any more — they were possibly foreigners.

According to a passage in the chronicle of Dandolo, Rodolph, King of Italy, in the year 926, "declared that the Doge of Venice had the power of coining money, because it appeared to him that the ancient Doges had continually done this." (1) Now, it is excessively important to remember that this is not a licence to strike money, but a declaration that the Doges (according to the information afforded to Rodolph, rather than possessed by that prince) had long done so, and had the right. The mere sanction of a weakly established German potentate, such as his majesty, might not have been of much real utility, when an extended recognition of a currency was even more important to the Republic than the leave to issue one on her own account. The question arises. What was this money which the ancient Doges issued? The answer must be. We do not certainly know.

(1)   *"Declaravit Ducem Venetiarum potestatem habere fabricandi monetam, quia ei constitit antiques Duces hoc continuatis temporibus perfecisse."*

The Venetians, entitled from the sixth to the ninth century to the privilege of a separate mint, had a comparative abundance of models before them. They might have copied and improved the Lombardic types as Charlemagne did. It was open to them to imitate the Byzantine coins, like the Merovingian moneyers; or, with regard to the old Greek and Roman pieces in all metals, there was no difficulty in reproducing them with a few necessary changes of detail, and it was almost impossible that such reproductions should have been worse than the efforts of the Gauls and the Britons in the same direction.

A series of coins of the Frankish type in about fifty-five varieties, from the time of Louis le Debonnaire to that of Henry IV. or V. — a period extending over two centuries and a half — appears to be the whole salvage of tons upon tons of metal, impressed with recognized characters at various mints including even Paris. The series embraces silver *denarii* of the Otto Imperator type and with the name of the Emperor Berengarius II., both of the tenth century and bearing the word "*Venecias.*" Other coins of the same rulers were struck independently for Verona, which may tend to shew that those inscribed *Venecias* were limited in their circulation to Venice and the more or less immediate confines. (1)

(1)   The present opportunity may be taken of noting that the various and able works of Count Papadopoli on the coins of Venice render more than a general view superfluous.

Under a democratic government, it is especially probable that, the pattern once approved, the coin was reproduced year after year without material alteration; and the extant specimens may represent what was issued during the ninth and following centuries by hundreds of thousands. The *denaro* occupied the same position in the primitive monetary system of Venice as the *denier* among the Franks and the silver penny in England. It was the only circulating medium in Venice till the twelfth century, in France till the Carolingian era, and in England till the reign of Edward III. But in all these countries, though in the Republic to the largest extent, a great amount of Byzantine and other foreign money was freely taken in payment; we have, besides, to consider that the Mediaeval system of taxation and trade had a tendency to retard, rather than to stimulate, the development of a metallic currency.

The so-termed galley halfpence or *suskin* and *bodkin*, of which casual notices present themselves, were probably small billon pieces of various origin, which were long accepted in payment from the Venetians and other foreign visitors arriving in the port of London, but their precise monetary value was apparently uncertain, and at length the Venetians at least were ordered, under penalties by Acts of Parliament 13 Henry IV. and 4 Henry V., not to bring or tender them. They were, however, still occasionally offered and accepted. (1)

(1)   Hazlitt III, *The Coinage of the European Continent with an Introduction and Catalogues of Mints Denominations and Rulers,* page 236-237. Galley Row was between Hart Street, Crutched Friars and Church Lane.

The translation of the remains of Saint Mark to Venice took place in the year 829. From that date and that circumstance, an inference has been drawn which we shall content ourselves with describing as rather a bold one. Taken in connexion with the absence of any mention of the new patron saint on the *denaro*, the arrival of the holy relics is presumed to have been posterior to the issue of the coin, or, in other words, the *denaro* has been pronounced older than 829. In this superior antiquity there is nothing improbable; the type and character themselves are not sufficiently pronounced or distinctive to fix the origin of the coin within a century, but the argument is of no validity. We should prefer to describe the piece of money as apparently the earliest Venetian coinage yet discovered, and as the only traceable currency of local mintage in the Republic from the sixth to the ninth century.

The public and private collections of England and the Continent are seldom without specimens of this sort of *denaro*, unmistakably emanating from a Frankish or German mint, with the name of the reigning prince on one side and *Moneta Venecias, Venecias,* or *Venecia* in one or two lines on the other. These pieces are generally accepted as having been intended for the province rather than the city of Venice, and are presumed to have been *denari* specially struck for currency in the Peninsula by the Kings of Italy. They do not go farther back, it seems, than the reign of Louis le Debonnaire, with whose name two types are extant, and, during the continuance of the Carolingian rule, they must have passed habitually through the hands of Venetian traders and travellers. In general appearance they are not dissimilar from some of the Anglo-Saxon pennies, but they more immediately resemble in fabric much of the earlier Imperial money on which they were doubtless modelled, as well as the autonomous coinages of Trieste, Aquileia, Mantua and Genoa. They may be seen in all their modifications and varieties in the Papadopoli monographs. The association of the name of the reigning emperor with that of the local government had its precise analogy in the other Italian currencies of the Middle Ages, including that of the Popes from the tenth to the thirteenth century.

The game of problems, however, is not quite terminated; we do not yet come to firm ground. Schweitzer (1) and Padovan (2) have included in their series two billon coins, one of eight, the other of ten grains, (3) with the name of one of the emperors styled Henry on one side, and of the ordinary Imperial type, but, what is surely very remarkable and speculative, having on the reverse S. MARCVS VENE and the effigy of the saint. Both writers seem to concur in thinking that the Henry meant is

Henry IV. who was crowned only in 1084. Henry III. became emperor in 1039. Whichever it may have been, the date might be the same within about fifty years; it was a piece struck in the eleventh century. With every desire to keep within cautious limits, we will go so far as to add a belief that this other *denaro* was issued at Venice for circulation in the Italian territories of the third or fourth Henry, with the Imperial name as a mark of complimentary distinction, and the name of the tutelary saint as a proof of local origin, somewhat on the same principle as the continental convention money from the thirteenth to the eighteenth century.

(1)   Schweitzer, *Serie delle Monete e Medaglie d'Aquileja e di Venezia.*

(2)   Cecchetti and Padovan, *Sommario della Nuininografla Veneziana Fino alla Caduta della Repubblica.*

(3)   The weight slightly varies in specimens equally unworn, the preparation of the flans of metal having been imperfect. Of course, friction and use are other powerful agencies in the decline from the mint standard.

There is an analogous case in a coin of the same epoch struck for West Friesland. There the name of the Emperor Henry III. is associated with that of Count Bruno III.; Venice, being a republican government, might have preferred the introduction of the tutelary saint. Delepierre speaks of a Count of Flanders in the seventh century; but, at any rate, the provinces of the Netherlands severed themselves at an early date from the German yoke, and were practically as independent as the Republic herself.

Count Papadopoli (1) has described and engraved types of the Venetian piece with and without the name of Saint Mark. On the whole, the ancient coinage, although it was scanty from a modern point of view, was not more so than the contemporary coinage of such countries as England and France.

(1)   Papadopoli, *Le Monete di Venezia Descritte ed Illustrate.* See Molmenti, *La Storia di Venezia nella Vita Privata,* Liber I page 155-166.

Yet, even when the Republic had fairly begun to establish its own coinage, and to reduce the operations of the mint to a system and a science, the process was slow, and the results unimportant. It was long before the currency acquired any considerable proportion or volume. The truth is that the *denaro* continued to be the staple, if not the sole, medium. Just as the English were six or seven centuries without possessing any higher denomination than a penny in silver, the Venetians mechanically reproduced the *denaro* from generation to generation, and relied, for coins of higher value and in the more precious metals, on the specie which came to them from various directions, more or less regularly in the way of business or tribute, and which was tacitly recognized and accepted.

The moneys of all countries were probably at one time by sufferance legal tender; and among the Italian republics generally the coinage was apt to acquire an international character. A merchant merely asked in payment of his goods something tangible which would enable him to go back into the market and enter into new purchases. Thus it happens that in ancient documents foreign currency is mentioned just as familiarly as if it had been that of Venice itself. At the same time, precautions were necessary in the reception of more or less considerable sums in foreign specie, to secure proper weight and genuine money; and from a rather obscurely worded clause in the coronation oath of Giacomo Tiepolo (1229), it is not very dangerous to infer that some system of assay was carried on by a department of the executive, to check abuses in importations, and to regulate the standard at home.

In the remarkable account of benefactions of Fortunatus, Patriarch of Grado, about A.D. 825, the property described is estimated by *romanati*, *mancusi* or *mancosi* (marks) and *librae*. Of these three denominations, the first was simply the Byzantine *solidus* of gold, which varied in weight and value, but may be approximately set down as worth ten shillings of English money; from the coronation oath of Tiepolo (1229), we learn that the yearly tribute from Veglia to the treasury was paid in *romanati* — the ordinary currency of the locality. The mark was not a coin, but money of account, and represented about 13s. 4d. The *libra*, so often named by Fortunatus, must be interpreted as a measure of weight — there was no money so called at the period or till very long after; and where we see some costly object appraised by the patriarch at so many pounds, it is to be concluded that they were pounds of *denari* or *lire di piccoli*, unless they are specified as being of gold, in which case an equal bulk in Greek *solidi* is presumably implied.

Muratori speaks of *Libre Veneticorum* as current in the middle of the tenth century, but he does not tell us what they were, and in 1088 we meet with an equally vague reference to *librae auri*. A clause in the coronation oath of 1229 goes a step farther, in referring to the cloth-of-gold to be presented by a new Doge to the Church of Saint Mark, which was to be worth twenty-five pounds of *denari* of Venice (*librae denariorum Venetiarum*) or upward. The *denari* might be large or small, but the calculation was by weight or in bullion; the *libra Venetiarum* was not a coin.

The close intimacy between weight and early currency is illustrated by the *oncia* or *onza* of some European states as well as of Chili and Peru, the *peso* of South America in *genere*, the *peseta* of Spain, and (to a certain extent) the *drachma* and *obolos* of ancient and modern Greece. In an account of the English towns of Warwick in Norman times, we similarly hear of *librae denariorum* — evidently a computation by weight. (1)

(1)   Hazlitt III, *Blount's Tenures of Land,* page 356.

Of foreign money, in addition to what we have enumerated, there were three other varieties which Venice, from lack of a sufficient supply of her own manufacture, acknowledged and accepted during the earlier centuries. These were the Arabic *dirhem* of silver which conveniently adapted itself to current requirements, being equal to two Lombard or Frankish *denari*; the *perpero*, and the *bezant* or *byzant*. The last certainly, if not both that and the *perpero*, existed in two metals, gold and silver; and it is particularly noticeable that, in the time of the Doge Domenigo Contarini (1043-1071), the *byzant* passed commonly current in the Republic on Saturday market days. Whether this was the gold or the silver piece is not stated; perhaps it was both; and we may observe that, in the important treaty between the Republic and Armenia in 1201, the *byzant* is the only coin named, the gold and silver of the document being pretty clearly bullion, like the three hundred pounds which King Tarquin gave for the Sibylline Books, and the silver which the patriarch Abraham paid for his field. The silver *byzant* was known as the *byzantius albus*, just as the Venetians subsequently had their *quattrino bianco* and the French their *blanque*, and was received in England in 1395 as equivalent to two shillings. (1) In the phraseology of Mediaeval codices and deeds, *alba firma* usually stands for silver or bullion currency. In the same manner as the *denaro*, the *perpero* was treated also as money of account, and value was occasionally calculated by *lire di perperi*.

(1)   Hazlitt III, *Blount's Tenures of Land,* page 247.

With reference to the right of circulation accorded on Saturdays to the *byzant* of one or both metals, it is perhaps a notion apt to occur to the student that, so far from this being the original form of the privilege or licence, it was probably a limitation of a wider acceptance or recognition, a transition from a general to a special reception of the coin of another government.

In addition to the *lira* or *libra*, regarded as a measure of weight, and the other artificial expedients of the same sort already mentioned, there were two species of money of account in use — the *libra grossorum* or *lira di grossi*, and the *libra parvulorum* or *lira di piccoli*. In a work giving an account of a sale of galleys by auction in 1332, the realized values are uniformly computed by the *lira di grossi*.

All these devices for obviating the inconvenience arising from a scanty currency might, however, have failed to provide any adequate remedy for the evil, if trade had not been largely conducted on a basis of exchange, and payments in kind had not long remained in universal vogue. Bills of exchange were already well known in the fourteenth century at Venice, and the broker who conducted such transactions was a familiar figure on the Rialto and in Lombard Street. The names of several of them have come down to us. (1)

(1)   The terms for the cession of Padua to the Signory in 1405 comprised in pecuniary payments 5000 ducats in bills of exchange on Florence. In 1481 a bill for 2000 ducats was registered by Thomas Kyffyn, citizen of London and notary public, at his house in Lombard Street. (compilation) *Calendar of State Papers Relating to English Affairs in the Archives of Venice,* Volume I page 143.

The earliest Venetian bill so far recovered belongs to 1394; in numerous cases they are recorded in the archives in the shape of protests or errors. The rate was reckoned at the current value of the gold ducat from day to day, and was, so far as London or England was concerned, from 46 to 53 silver pence. An immense volume of business was done for centuries in these securities, and it is to be more than suspected that, in the civil commotions and troubles in England and Scotland, the Venetian traders suffered at intervals in a pecuniary direction, through the uncertainty and the vicissitudes of fortune incidental to the wars of the Plantagenets and their royal successors.

The practice of making payments in this manner arose from the constantly increasing amount of business between parties at a distance, and the different monetary standards in vogue. Default was doubtless a not unusual incident, and we encounter protested bills as early as 1442 — such documents may very well have existed long before. We have an actual document of 1326, immediately belonging to Milan, but it is the counterpart and sample, beyond doubt, of thousands or hundreds of thousands which once existed up and down commercial Europe. It is in the subjoined terms, and points to a practice of giving six months' credit, or, as it is now expressed, of drawing at six months: "*Pagate per questa prima letera a di ix Ottobre a Luca de Poro, Lib. xlv. Sono per la valuta qui da Masca Reno al tempo si pagate e ponete a mio conto, e che Christo vi guarde! Bonromo de Bonromei de Milano, ix. de' Marzo 1325.*" (1)

(1)   From a transcript in (compilation) *Notes and Queries*, more than possibly an inaccurate one. There was a large find of *bianchi* of Ziani, Malipiero and Enrico Dandolo in 1901.

The promissory note, which seems in the first instance to have been simply an undertaking to perform an act, not necessarily to make a payment, must impress us as an institution and resource as absolutely indispensable as the bill, and both were long drawn by clerical or other scriveners in the absence of a general conversance with the art of writing.

The memorandum book, at first, no doubt, rudimentary enough, and somewhat analogous to the English writing-tablets, was made in later days of costlier material. In special cases it was clothed in a sumptuous binding, if a wealthy trader or traveller, perhaps accompanied by his wife, visited Venice, and recorded in this manner his experiences, expenses, or transactions. It was a method of assisting the recollection, which descended to us from ancient times and was the companion, not of merchants only to note the rate of exchange and similar matters, but of authors, playwrights, artists and persons of various callings, and was prone to early destruction when its temporary use had been served.

Even when facilities arose for possessing printed books of this class, the manuscript form still held its ground, as it does to the present day. A dainty little oblong duodecimo volume, which appears originally to have belonged to a family at Nurnberg, and possesses realistic portraits of the owner and his wife, with their arms, all excellently done, may have subsequently passed through other hands, and yet retains the richly gilt black morocco binding centre-pieces and clasps of the sixteenth century beautifully preserved.

Prior to 1156, the old *denaro*, first without, and then with, the name of the patron saint, had been reinforced by a second coin representing the moiety of it, the *denaro minore* or *piccolo*. This new piece, which some have confounded with the *marcuccio*, to be presently noticed, was of billon, and weighed from eight to ten grains. On the obverse appears a cross, with the pellets in a double indented circle, and the legend D. MAVR. DVX (Domenigo Morosini); the reverse exhibited the bust of Saint Mark, with the glory or nimbus and the inscription S. MARCVS VEN. The circulation of *denari* was, for some unknown reason, suspended from 1205 to 1268, or, at least, no examples are known of the reigns comprised within those years.

DENARI OF SOME TWELFTH-CENTURY DOGES

SEBASTIANO ZIANI
1172-1178

ORIO MALIPIERO
1178-1193

ENRICO DANDOLO
1193-1205

Where the purchasing power of money is extraordinarily great, the fractional divisions of the coinage seem to be almost infinitesimal. In the reign of Vitale Michiele II. (1156-1172), the idea was conceived of striking a *bianco* or *bien* of mixed metal and weighing eight grains; it had, on the obverse, a crosslet in a double circle, with the legend V. MICH DVX, and, on the reverse, a full-face bust of Saint Mark and the legend S. MARCVS VNE. Sebastiano Ziani and Orio Malipiero, the two next Doges (1173-1192), added the double, or *denaro piccolo*, in more than a single variety. These pieces, which, with some modification of type, had a duration of two or three centuries, led to endless trouble, on account of the difficulty of giving change in small transactions or the tendency to evade it, and numerous cases present themselves in the official registers of penalties inflicted on tradesmen, for imposing on customers by withholding the difference or part of it. This was constantly occurring down to the fourteenth century or later; and many particulars are preserved. (1) The punishment was not infrequently remitted when the culprit was poor or was thought to have acted inadvertently.

(1)   Papadopoli, *Le Monete di Venezia Descritte ed Illustrate,* page 63.

But the first clear step of an important character was the introduction of the *grosso*, during the administration of Arrigo or Enrico Dandolo (1192-1205). It was of fine silver weight 44 grains in proof condition, and of Byzantine pattern. It was the prototype of the French *gros* and the English groat, and was originally worth 26 *piccoli*; it was subsequently raised to 28 and 32 *piccoli*, and eventually merged in the *grossetto*. Its value in English computation was about 5d. On the obverse were represented the erect figures of the Doge and Saint Mark, face to face, the latter with the *nimbus*, and tendering the standard for which a flag-pole does duty; the legend is DVX H. DANDOL. S. M. VENETI. On the reverse, the Saviour with the glory is seated on a decorated throne, His right hand extended in the act of benediction, His left holding the Gospels, and the letters IC. XC.

This handsome coin was also known as a *matapan*, and was so called from the cape of that name between Zante and Cerigo. The reason for the denomination is uncertain, unless the exigencies attendant on the unexpectedly protracted expedition to Constantinople in 1202 led to the local coinage of a special issue for immediate use. There is a farther difficulty as to the precise date at which the *grosso* first appeared, for, while the historian Andrea Dandolo assigns it to the year 1194, and Marino Sanudo to 1192, Martino da Canale who lived nearer to the time distinctly speaks of it as introduced to pay the operatives engaged in the preparations for the voyage to the east. But Da Canale, according to the text of his *Chronicle* handed down to us, also makes Enrico Dandolo contemporary with the ducat, not coined till nearly a century later, and aggravates the mistake by describing it as of silver, (1) in which metal no such money existed before 1559.

(1)   Papadopoli, *Le Monete di Venezia Descritte ed Illustrate,* page 81.

One clue to a solution of the difficulty may be the form of the title of the Doge which, in lieu of the Christian name alone, adds the family or surname, a practice not observed on the *quartarolo*. This may therefore have been a piece not originating till late in the reign — possibly 1202 or thereabout. The *grosso*, which had a run of at least two centuries (we have specimens struck by the Doge Foscari 1423-1457), with its divisions in its own metal, has the appearance of having been the earliest distinct aim, on the part of the mint, at the establishment of a standard. It fluctuated, indeed, in weight three or four grains under successive Doges, but it was far from being so irregular and capricious as the groats of the English Edwards. There was not the same inducement.

The word *sterling*, in relation to the coinage and currency, is found in documents of the thirteenth and fourteenth centuries, and must be understood to mean standard metal, in contra-distinction to mixed or billon of which much of the Mediaeval money was composed. On the 9th of October, 1274, the Great Council directed the Mint to cast bars of silver of sterling standard, for the convenience of merchants trading with Bruges; it was a medium which, in the absence of paper money, was immensely serviceable in large transactions.

The *grosso* or *matapan* of or about 1192 was the first piece struck which can be said to have been of a fixed weight and fineness. From 1356 to 1368 there was no coinage of *grossi*, and when it was resumed under Andrea Contarini (1368-1382) the pattern was altered.

Grosso of Reniero Zeno, 1253-1268.   Soldino of Marino Faliero, 1354-1355.

Lira Tron or Trono of Nicolò Trono, 1471-1473.

Gold Scudo of Andrea Gritti, 1523-1538.   Soldo of Dalmatia and Albania.

Silver Ducat of Luigi or Alvise I. Mocenigo, 1570-1577.

Osella of Luigi or Alvise I. Mocenigo, 1570-1577.

VENETIAN COINS

An exceptional and almost insuperable difficulty arises at this time and stage of the inquiry, in regard to the identity of the *soldo* specified as equivalent to eight *denari grandi* in the coronation oath of 1229; and the question directly concerns the *grosso* immediately under notice, because it is open to conjecture or hypothesis, that the *soldo* is the same as that more usually known under the other name, and that the *soldino*, otherwise the little *soldo*, presently to be introduced, was the moiety of it or of the *grosso*. The point is, that no silver coin actually recognized as a *soldo* is found in the numismatic records of Venice, and yet it is perfectly possible that at first, and down to 1229, the denomination more generally known as a *grosso* may have been accepted and officially described under the other term. It strikes us as singular that, while the Republic possessed the *grosso* and the quarter *grosso*, it did not strike the half till so many years later, for Count Papadopoli (1) apprises us that the denomination was first ordered in or about 1332; but the same authority states that the public records are imperfect for the immediately prior years.

(1)   Papadopoli, *Le Monete di Venezia Descritte ed Illustrate,* page 158.

The reign of Dandolo also witnessed the foundation of a copper currency. Somewhere about the close of the twelfth century, the Mint coined the *quattrino* or fourth of the *grosso*; the legends E. DADVL. DVX, and cruciformly within a circle the four letters V N C S for *Venecias*. The government of Pietro Gradenigo (1289-1311) ordered a double *quattrino* of copper or half-*grosso*, but we hear no more of it.

The successor of Dandolo, Pietro Ziani, continued, during his reign of twenty-four years (1205-1229), to strike all the pieces now in circulation; but he added to the wealth of the coinage nothing but a small copper piece called the *marcuccio*, or little mark, of five or six grains, with a cross having in the angles triangles in lieu of pellets, and the legend P. ZIANI DVX. On the other side occur Saint Mark with the glory in a double circlet and the legend S. MARCVS VE. Giacomo Tiepolo (1229-1249) issued the *grosso* in two states, with and without a mint-mark, and that valuable emblem of distinction here makes its first appearance. It presents itself in the form of a triangle enclosing three pellets under the mantle of the enthroned Christ. Andrea Contarini (1368-1382) altered the pattern by placing the figure of the Doge in profile, and his successor made farther changes.

Reniero Zeno (1253-1268) made an experiment of an entirely novel kind; for, as a companion to the silver *grosso*, he produced one in copper of 40 grains, with the Doge's name and S. M. VENETI on one side, and the usual seated effigy of the Saviour on the other. In the field to the left is a small globe which may be a mint-mark. Zeno also struck the silver *grosso* in six types, weighing from 38 to 40 grains, and the next Doge coined one of 40-1/2 grains. But the copper *grosso* does not seem to have met with favour; although it was larger than the silver piece and varied in other respects, the similarity of denomination, in an illiterate age, made it perhaps too open to the ingenuity of the plater, and it was permitted to drop.

Thus, toward the close of the thirteenth century, the Republic found herself provided with a currency in silver, copper and billon. It was reserved for Giovanni Dandolo (1280-1289) to venture a step farther, and to meet the increased demand for money, owing to the development of trade, by striking the famous ducat in 1284. After the removal of the Mint to the Giudecca, which in the Venetian dialect was called Zecca (1) the ducat was better known as the *zecchino*.

(1)   In Latin documents the word is corrupted into *cecha*.

The coin of Dandolo was of fine and pure gold, and was equivalent to 8s. 8d. English currency, although Coryat states that it was seldom reckoned in England at more than 7s. Of money of Venice it originally represented 20 (subsequently raised to 24) silver *grossi*. In its character it displayed no prodigality of invention, following very much the same lines as the *grosso*. On the obverse we see the Doge in costume, kneeling before the patron saint who delivers to him the banner, with the legend IO. DANDVL, and S. M. VENETI. The reverse portrays the Saviour with the nimbus, full length in a stellated oval. His right hand extended as usual, and His left holding the Gospel. The legend is SIT. T. XPE. DAT. Q. TV. REGIS. ISTE. DVCAT. (1)

(1)   *Sit Tibi, Christe, datus, quem tu regis, iste Ducatus.*

Like the *grosso*, the ducat shewed a tendency to copy the Byzantine style of art, and, in fact, the moneyer had doubtless before him the earlier coin as a model or point of departure. The long familiarity of the Republic with the Greek currency predisposed those who presided over such matters, to borrow the patterns and ornaments engrafted by that nation on the Imperial coinage of Rome.

In the figure of the Doge, as he appears in an attitude of genuflection, the portrait is more or less conventional; but it, as well as that of the Redeemer, suffered an essential change in the time of Andrea Dandolo (1343-1354), under whom also the Ducal bonnet or berretta first assumed the shape of the corno.

That familiar head-dress dated from the ninth century, and had been originally presented to the Doge Tradenigo by the nuns of San Zaccaria. The value of the piece was nowhere expressed; the probability is that it was proclaimed, as usual, by cry. But its peculiar freedom from alloy and the strict maintenance of the standard procured for this, as for all the other sterling money of the Republic, in common with that of Florence and Verona, an immense celebrity and a wide circulation throughout the Peninsula and throughout the world (1) Such a demand necessitated a large annual issue; in or about 1420 it is said to have been a million in ducats alone, of which the greater part was exported. Vasco da Gama found the ducat current at Calicut in Malabar; Bruce saw it in Abyssinia; it is still occasionally discovered in Egypt. But reconversion into bullion and other causes have rendered the whole series of ancient ducats more or less scarce, especially pieces in fine preservation and of certain reigns.

(1)   In Shakespeare, *The Comedy of Errors,* Act IV Scene 1, Angelo the goldsmith speaks of a transaction in which a gold chain is made up to a certain value by the addition of three ducats, but it is open to question whether the poet exactly understood the current value of the piece or its relation to bullion.

There is a *sequin* of Pierre d'Ambusson, Grand Master of Rhodes (1476-1503), which is a copy of that of Venice, except that Saint John is substituted for Saint Mark. The Republic, as far back as 1423, had intimated its displeasure at this practice, which was not confined to one locality or power. Nor was Rhodes the earliest offender. From 1314 to 1341, the feudal lords of Foglia Vecchia are found copying the style and costume of the Venetian piece, even to minor details, the legends, of course, varying to suit the circumstances, and the standard being probably lower.

In 1357, a communication was addressed by the Genoese, at the instance of Venice, to the Signore of Mytilene, remonstrating with him for the output of a gold type, resembling that of the Republic but of inferior standard. In 1370, the government of Venice insisted on the discontinuance of this piracy by the authorities at Ephesus. Other places whence issued about the same period these more or less inferior copies were Chiarenza, Scio and Pera, and at a later period the Prince of Dombes in France added himself to the roll of culprits, and incurred the reproof of the Doge.

While Genoa and its dependencies were temporarily under Milanese rule, Filippo Maria Visconti issued a gold *sequin* for Chio, closely following the Venetian pattern. There were even Indian *contrefaçons* which are said to have been treated as phallic symbols. All these imitations surely regarded the general acceptance of the Venetian original rather than its artistic merit. They led the government in 1447 to make a regulation that the employment of engravers at the Mint should be restricted to Venetian citizens, by way, at least, of modifying the abuse.

The Gauls and Britons had struck gold coins at a remote epoch, some in grotesque imitation of the Greek staters, others in the later Roman taste. Specimens exist, not only of pieces in the same metal issued by the order of the Merwing dynasty in France, but of a similar type struck in Holland, Germany and many other parts of Europe. In Sicily, the Norman Duke of Apulia, Roger II., introduced, about 1150, a gold coinage suggested by that of the Arabs; and, in the same or following century, the German princes Henry VI. and Frederick II. struck the *augustale* and its half on the model of the Roman Imperial *solidi*. We have also the gold money of Louis IX. (1226-1270), and the so-called gold penny of Henry III. of England (1216-1272), but both are probably posterior to the Florentine piece. It may well be doubted, again, if either of these had much width of circulation or were in general use; the English one is ordinarily treated as an unpublished essay.

With the exception of the *fiorino d'oro* of Florence, which claims a priority of about thirty years (1252), and was equally designed as a practical trading medium, the Venetian ducat of 1284, which a great commercial people would have at once the means of applying to practical purposes and had long been wanted, may be entitled to rank as the oldest gold currency established in Mediaeval Europe.

In 1313 when the Republic paid the Holy See a sum by way of indemnity, the Pontifical government stipulated that it should be delivered in Tuscan currency, but, in 1422, the Florentines unsuccessfully attempted to procure the acceptance in Egypt of their own gold *florin*, on the same footing as that of Venice, pleading that, of the two pieces, it was slightly the heavier and finer. Twenty years later, they practically retracted this declaration by issuing ducats of Venetian weight for their oriental trade. The Tuscan coin, however, was not usually received on the same footing, and did not obtain the same universal recognition as the ducat, which, in one sense, strikes us as more analogous to its distant prototype, the Lydian heavy stater of Phoenician weight. An influential motive to preserve the standard was the need of successful competition with the oriental currencies in the same metal, which were generally of great purity.

Beyond the issue of a double *quattrino* or *mezzo-grosso* of copper, with the name of the Doge Pietro Gradenigo (1289-1311), the Mint paused a little after its introduction of the *zecchino*; nor was it till the administration of Francesco Dandolo (1329-1339), that the Venetian moneyers reproduced the old forms in a new combination in the *soldino* of silver, also the moiety of the *grosso*, and the piece to which allusion has already been made. On the obverse was the Doge with the bonnet on his head and the standard in hand, encircled by the legend FRA. DANDVLO DVX; on the reverse, Saint Mark as usual.

A second and distinct type which was popularly called the *cenoghelo* represents the Doge kneeling, and, on the other side, in lieu of the saint, the lion rampant holds the flag-pole in his claw; the legend, S. MARCUS VENETI. The numismatists allege that these pieces fluctuated between 22 and 10-1/2 grains, but the truth is that this wide discrepancy has resulted from testing specimens in different states, as the old Venetian money has descended, for the most part, in a far from satisfactory condition. The *soldino* is almost undoubtedly the moiety of the piece which we sometimes find described as the *soldo*; and, as mention of the latter occurs in a state-paper of 1229 and in other documents, it may reasonably be surmised that, as in a few other cases, the original issues have perished, more especially as the very Doge (Arrigo Dandolo. 1192-1205) who published the *grosso*, also published the *quattrino* or fourth of it.

It is perhaps fair to question whether the *soldino* was ever struck otherwise than in silver, although Schweitzer seems to draw a distinction between the original piece and a later one which he specifies as the *soldino d'argento*; the only difference may have been in the smaller proportion of alloy. In the series of *soldini*, a comparative examination leads to the discovery of a differential individuality, which, if it could be taken to have an authoritative source or character, would possess this feature of interest and importance, that in some cases — nearly all — we should gain an approximate idea of the personal appearance of the Doges, including Marino Faliero; the same remark may be thought to apply to other coins bearing the ducal effigy. The long series of silver *soldini* appears, in common with all the Venetian coins of professedly pure metal, to have always preserved its reputation for standard, and, in 1493. when the Duke of Saxony was preparing to visit the Holy Land, he succeeded in obtaining a special issue of these pieces for his petty expenses. It is supposed that an example exhibiting the Redeemer rising from the Sepulchre is a solitary survivor of this coinage.

Possessing already the double *quattrino* and the *soldino*, the government under Andrea Dandolo (1343-1354) thought proper to create a third equivalent for the *mezzo-grosso* in a silver coin called the *mezzanino*, weighing 14 grains and a fraction. On the obverse we have the Doge, Saint Mark and the flag-pole; but the reverse shews a light stroke of originality in the figure of Christ rising from the tomb, with the legend XPS. RES VRESIT. The mint-mark in one example is a sword, but the same Doge sanctioned several varieties of the *mezzanino* with distinguishing mint-marks after its original issue in 1346, and, in 1354, the coin of the Doge Francesco Dandolo was reproduced with technical alterations under the name the *soldino nuovo*.

The copper *grosso* had been a failure and did not remain in circulation; its place was successively supplied by the double *quattrino*, the *soldino* or *soldo*, and the *mezzanino*; the first in copper, the two latter in the same metal as the *grosso* itself, but Andrea Dandolo seems to have approved of a second trial piece in the shape of a ducat in copper of 30 grains. The experiment was, perhaps, not carried out, and the specimen which exists is presumed to have been one of the patterns submitted to the government.

The business of the Mint at the end of the fourteenth century began to grow heavy and responsible. Even when no new dies were in preparation, the ordinary issues of coins in standard use from year to year were sufficient to keep a large staff in employment, more particularly at a period when the various processes were not very expeditious. It is said that in 1423 the yearly coinage, independently of a million gold ducats, extended to 800,000 pieces — a total of nearly two millions. When, therefore, we have to traverse six reigns (1354-1382) without meeting with anything fresh to report, we are not to conclude that the moneyers were idle. The Doge Celsi who sat on the throne from 1361 to 1365, although he apparently added nothing to the numismatic series, often gave a morning to the Mint which he, no doubt, invariably found a scene of interesting activity.

A billon piece, called the *grossetto*, and resembling in character and design the *grosso* which it seems to have supplanted, but having on the reverse the legend TIBI LAVS & GLORIA, made its first appearance under the Doge Veniero (1382-1400), and, at a later period, we find the half-*grossetto* (1523-1538). The *grossetto* weighed nine carats. A triple *grossetto* which is said to exist is supposed to be an essay, but such an inference seems to have no better foundation than its alleged uniqueness. The *piccolo* or *denaro* had been, continued under the majority of reigns from the twelfth century. In 1442, we first find the *lagattino* in billon for some of the provinces.

The inconvenience of possessing no currency intermediate between the *grosso* and the ducat must, at the same time, have soon been felt, and Francesco Foscari (1423-1457) struck two types of a silver coin, equal to eight *soldi* or *soldini* and styled a *grossone*. On the obverse, the Doge stands with the national banner in his hand; the legend, FRANCISCVS FOSCARI DVX. The reverse has a full-faced bust of the Evangelist, and SANCTVS MARCVS VENETI. In the second variety the Doge kneels.

Two pieces of money which possess rather a special interest are the *gazzetta* and *gazzetteno*. The latter, which it may appear justifiable to treat as of later introduction, is said to have originated during the dogeship of Leonardo Loredano (1501-1521), but Romanin states that the *gazzetta* itself was not struck prior to 1528. At first of billon or a low standard of silver, it degenerated into a roughly struck copper coin of two values — the *gazzetta* and double *gazzetta*; and the name is so far remarkable, that it lent itself to the synonymous periodical news-sheet which spread over Europe, representing, no doubt, the price of issue. But, whatever may have been the true date of birth of the *gazzetteno*, it is eminently probable that the *gazzetta* preceded it. The Venetian synonymous publication is named by Howell in a letter of 1623 to Lord Colchester, as inclosed in a letter which he is sending to his lordship from London, so that it was probably a broadsheet of which there is an extant series.

The numismatic annals of Venice resemble a stream which, in its earlier course sluggish and narrow, expands into a swift and broad torrent. We are arriving at a time when an extraordinary development took place in the currency of the Republic, and the Venetian coinage was, within a short period, to manifest a variety and profusion, strangely contrasting with the indigence of former days, and with the advised simplicity of modern monetary economy. But, in the absence of paper, and with the constant demand for heavy amounts in specie to pay troops and meet the unceasing expenses of the Arsenal, the parallel employment of several coins of large and nearly identical denominations becomes tolerably intelligible, and, where the value was expressed on the face of the piece as in a few exceptional cases, it was not particularly inconvenient at the time.

As regards the form given to the legends on the money, we observe that, at first, there was no indication on the face of coins that they were destined for the city of Venice and not for the province of Venetia. The earliest movement in the direction of localizing the currency and denoting its actual source was the insertion of the name of the patron saint, in addition to that of the Emperor for the time being. During the eleventh and twelfth centuries, a few pieces of small module occur, with the Christian name of the reigning Doge abbreviated in lieu of the Imperial title, as V. MICHE. DUX, SEB. DUX, AURO. DUX, OR ENRIC. DUX, for Vitale Michiele III., Sebastiano Ziani, Orio Malipiero and Enrico Dandolo; but, although such an expression is commonly employed in public documents, the coinage never exhibited the *Dei Gratia* introduced into nearly all the monetary systems of Europe from the ninth century.

The activity of the Mint may be said to have had its real commencement in the middle of the fifteenth century. The copper *bagattino* and *doppio bagattino* of copper and billon, and the silver *lira* and *mezzalira* which were ushered into the world with a well-executed likeness in profile of Nicolo Trono (1471-1473) were the earliest attempts to transfer to the coinage a realistic and professed resemblance of the reigning Doge. The *lira* which represented 20 *soldi* was an important step in the direction of making the silver coinage more comprehensive. Of the *bagattino* there are four known types, including those struck for Verona and Vicenza, and Bergamo; the *doppio* was a billon piece of a different pattern, and appears to be of the utmost rarity, the unit being unrecorded. This *doppio* was ordered by the government in 1520, and an example was discovered among the ruins of the Campanile in 1902. But the usage of giving a portrait of the Doge in office on the money was soon superseded by another less obnoxious to the oligarchical taste.

After the death of Trono, the only Doge in whose reign the experiment had been permitted, a decree of the Great Council, pursuant to the recommendation of the Correttori, forbad its continuance, and a copper piece of his immediate successor, Cristoforo Moro perhaps struck prior to the settlement of the new order, and at present of the first rarity, brought the short-lived usage to a close. Yet, not only in the likeness of the reigning Doge, said to be discernible in the small kneeling figure on the sequins and other pieces coined throughout the sixteenth and seventeenth centuries, but the kneeling figure on the *grosso* of the second type of Francesco Foscari (1423-1457), and the seated object at the top of the column on an *osella* of Francesco Morosini (1688-1694) certainly seem to be intended for portraits. The repugnance of the aristocratic government, however, was probably awakened by the presentation of the features of the chief magistrate, in the same prominent manner as those of the heads of professed monarchies. It did not interfere with a few cases in which the Serenissimo or even his consort transferred his or her lineaments to a medal, which might, in common perhaps with the *osella*, have been viewed as outside strictly political lines.

It seems that dissatisfaction was now beginning to make itself felt at certain irregularities in the processes of coining, and in the adjustment of the weight of pieces, and the government treated it as a public scandal that the currency should be suffered to deteriorate in character or decline from the original standard. It is interesting to mark such a solicitude, but, on the part of a mercantile community which had lifted itself to the height of power and renown, nothing could be more natural or more sagacious. On the 11th of November, 1457, a decree was promulgated against this evil, shewing that the blame rested, not with the moneyers, but with the workmen and overseers at the Mint, who neglected the instructions delivered to them for the verification of the weight and alloy.

The multiplication of small pieces of a low standard gradually entailed trouble and loss through the extensive output at home of counterfeit money, and, in and about 1473, this abuse prompted the Council of Ten to nominate two changers to station themselves on the Piazza of Saint Mark and the Rialto, as a check on utterers of false or light coins. Representations were made to the authorities at Ferrara and Bologna, in regard to the surreptitious and illegal imitation of Venetian types, and many persons, even of rank, were severely punished at Venice for connivance at the circulation of this spurious specie within the dominion. (1)

(1)   Papadopoli, *Le Monete di Venezia Descritte ed Illustrate,* Parte II, page 21, 22.

It is a curious circumstance that, at this date, the accumulation of very small coins of correspondingly trifling values had led to a practice, obviously prone to abuse, of carrying specified amounts of such money in purses or *cartocci* whereon the sum inside was recorded in writing, and offering the collection in payment as it stood, without inquiry by the recipient, as we accept a bag of gold or silver from our bankers. Such a plan seems, in 1458, to have been tried sufficiently long to prove to the authorities the expediency of its disallowance.

The *mezzalira* coined during the government of Nicolo Marcello (1473-1474) was christened the *marcello*; and again, on its reissue by Pietro Mocenigo (1474-1476), the *lira*, which had passed under the name of the *lira tron*, became popularly known as the *mocenigo*. (1) It was a method of associating a piece of currency with the reigning Doge, while his likeness upon the money was from political motives forbidden. The *marcello* presented, on the obverse, the Doge on his knees accepting the standard, and, on the reverse, Christ on a throne of a more richly decorated character than before; the legend was also changed. Schweitzer quotes four types; it appears to have been known under the same name as late as 1509. A somewhat later Doge, Marco Barbarigo (1485-1486), issued a copper sesino of 25 grains, but without a portrait, and we soon meet (1486-1501) with a half-*marcello* struck for the colonies. It is an illustration, one among so many, of Italian adherence to ancient names and usages, that the *lira tron*, popularly known as the *tron*, as well as a second piece called the *marchetto*, continued, in some parts of the old Venetian dominion down to the close of the nineteenth century, to be recognized and cited under their original appellations.

(1)   In 1477, a silver piece called the *massenetta*, equal in weight to the *lira* but otherwise not correspondent, was struck by the Duke of Ferrara. It was equivalent in value to 5-1/2 *quattrini*.

Agostino Barbarigo (1486-1501) added the *bezzo* or *quattrino bianco* of silver, the moiety of the *soldino* (one of the most popular pieces current in Venice) and the fourth of the old *grosso* or *matapan*. Its obverse offered nothing beyond the hackneyed flag-pole with the kneeling Doge and the upright Saint, and, on the reverse side, Christ erect, with the new legend LAVS TIBI SOLI. The most curious feature in connexion with this piece, however, is the coinage of multiples of it in silver, distinguished as *da Quattro, da Otto, da Dodici* and *da Sedici*, which must have assisted in making the currency still more intricate than before.

In the time of Leonardo Loredano (1501-1521), the idea seems to have occurred of issuing the half of the gold *sequin* of 1284. The quarter did not come into use till 1577-1578, and is a piece of the rarest character, although specimens survive, both of that and the half *sequin*, belonging to the latest era of the Republic. The legend on the reverse is altered to EGO SVM LVX MVNDI. The half and quarter *sequin* represented in modern English money about 4s. 9d. and the moiety. The weight of the ducat underwent slight variations in the sixteenth century, and fluctuated between 120 and 124 *soldi*; the former was known as *ducato mozzo* or *ducato a moneta*. But the *ducato corrente*, otherwise described as *ducato d'oro in oro* preserved its standard; and, to render the payments in the highest metal additionally unexceptionable, a customer might demand ducats *venetiani d'oro novi di cecha* (in mint state), as the freedom from alloy involved an early deterioration.

Under Andrea Gritti (1523-1539), the Mint produced a remarkable novelty in a *scudo* or crown of gold and its half, in addition to the *sequin* and half-*sequin* already in existence. The new pieces were possibly suggested by the French *ecu* and *demi-ecu*; they were worth 6 *lire*, 10 *soldi* and the moiety respectively. (1) These newcomers were not designed for commercial purposes, but for the pay of troops and other general matters, as they fell below the standard of the ducat. The *scudo* and its half did not extend, however, over more than two or three reigns, and examples are of some rarity; yet, after a long interval, the *doppia* of gold, equal to two of these *scudi*, made its appearance (1618-1623). The *doppia* was, in fact, a double crown, and was estimated at about 12 *lire*; it was the highest denomination ever in regular use. In the return of the expenses of the Venetian diplomatic representative in France in the second half of the seventeenth century, some of the amounts are set down in *doppie*.

(1)   This is probably the piece intended by the proclamation of Elizabeth of England, 2nd November, 1560, in which it is misdescribed as a *pistolet*, and allowed currency.

At the same time, a method, which, in the absence of paper money, was apt to be useful, was devised, by which two or three of the large silver coins — the silver ducat, the *scudo della croce* and the *giustina* of 140 *soldi* — were struck in limited numbers, no doubt in gold, to pass for four, eight, sixteen and twenty ducats, the divisions of the pieces in the lower metal answering for the inferior values. These issues were known as *da Quattro, da Otto, da Sedici, da Venti,* respectively, although they retained on the face their silver equivalents, and were independent of occasional outputs of multiples of the ducat in the more precious metal, under some of the later Doges.

Since the launch, in 1429, of the *grossone,* a piece of eight *soldini,* the Republic had made little progress in the silver currency. A coin representing about three shillings in modern English money was still the largest piece known in this metal, but, during the government of Girolamo Priuli (1559-1567) there came into existence the ducat of silver, worth 124 *soldi,* or 6 *lire* 4 *soldi,* and the half and the quarter. The need of affording ampler facilities for commercial and other monetary transactions was at last finding a response. The Mint did not rest here, for, a few years later (1571), it brought out the *giustina* of silver, valued at eight *lire* or 160 *soldi,* and its divisions. Ere long (1585-1595) succeeded the *giustina minore,* corresponding in value with the silver ducat, as well as the half and the quarter.

The Doge Marino Grimani (1595-1606) added to these mediums the *scudo della croce* of 140 *soldi,* and his two immediate successors (1606-1612) completed this extensive series by a new variety of silver *zecchino,* current for ten *lire,* with its divisions (1606-1615). The sixteenth century may thus be regarded as the epoch at which, above all others, Venice provided herself with a metallic currency, eclipsing in richness and capability anything of the kind achieved before or since.

The only supplementary feature in the numismatic chronicle was the substitution (1606-1612) of a gold ducat, diverging in design and circumference from the original *sequin* of 1284. It was a broader and thinner piece, of analogous type and nearly identical weight; the size is precisely that of an English sovereign. The ground for the change is not obvious, but the Venetian Zecca was evidently partial to new experiments, and, besides the productions which were admitted into circulation, Schweitzer and others record numerous trial-pieces or patterns which found their way into private cabinets, but were not adopted by the executive. Of these essays France has, in the same way, the honour of possessing a singularly large assemblage, submitted by her own Mint for approbation and ultimately abandoned.

The silver ducat of 1559-1567 exhibited Saint Mark on the obverse, seated and tendering the standard to the Doge; while, on the reverse, occurs the winged lion passant with the book of the Gospel in his fore-claw. This piece remained in vogue down to the end; of the Doge Alvise Mocenigo (1763-1779) there is a double ducat. The silver *giustina* (1578-1585) presented the patron saint and the Doge on the obverse, but, on the other side, for the first time in the annals of the coinage, we meet with a complete novelty, in the standing figure of Santa Giustina and the lion reposing at her feet, with the legend MEMOR. ERO. TUI. IVSTINA. VIRGO, in grateful reference to the Battle of Lepanto, fought on Saint Justina's Day, the 7th of October, 1571 — that holy martyr whose name was so tenderly bound up with one of the most ancient of Venetian traditions.

There was a certain unusual originality, again, in the treatment of the two other silver pieces (1) which have just been mentioned as belonging to the same period; the *giustina minore* which was reckoned 40 *soldi* or 2 *lire*, and the *scudo della croce* which passed for 140 *soldi*. The latter, which balances in the scales about 5s. 6d. in modern English silver currency, bears, on one side, an elaborate cross with the name of the Doge in the legend, and, on the opposite side, the winged lion, with the glory enclosed in a shield and encircled by the title of the patron saint. The silver ducat, the two *giustine* and the *scudo* of silver, with their fractions, seem to stand alone in expressing the value in *soldi* at the foot of the reverse, but a ducat of a later type, while it expresses the denomination, omits the value. In the lower left-hand corner, occurs a small view of Saint Mark's, for which space has been made by removing the book of the Gospel from the lion's claw. Of the *giustina maggiore* and the *scudo della croce* examples struck in gold are known; they were probably intended as *pieces de plaisir*. On the other hand, there is the quarter of the *scudo*, also struck in the higher metal, which may have been intended to represent four ducats; probably the *scudo* itself in gold was accepted as equivalent to sixteen.

(1)   Thomsen, *Les Monnaies du Moyen-Age,* Number 4484.

Thomsen (1) cites a bracteate of base metal or of copper of the Mediaeval time, with the winged lion as part of the type; he ascribes it to the Abbey of Reichenau in Suabia. When Venice borrowed the notion is slightly uncertain, except that the lion might be taken to have some affinity with Saint Mark, but the symbol is absent from the earlier numismatic productions of the Republic, The winged bull of Egyptian mythology and sculpture differed in its significance from the lion of the ancient Greek moneyers.

(1)   Thomsen, *Les Monnaies du Moyen-Age,* Number 4484.

Subsequently to the commencement of the seventeenth century, the Mint or Zecca of Venice, which was erected in 1536 from the design of Jacopo Sansovino and had its independent staff and administrators, shared the languor and narrowness of her later political life. The currency responded with speed here, as in Poland and everywhere else, to the declension of the state. No new monetary issues of any consequence marked the interval between the date to which we have carried the history of the coinage and the fall.

The administration of Marcantonio Memo (1612-1615) made farther subdivisions of the silver currency by the issue of the *soldone*, and still more by the introduction of a coin, dated 1614, of an entirely novel type; but it is not unlikely that the coin was a re-issue of the *osella*; Antonio Priuli (1618-1623) added the double and the half *soldone*. The *soldone* series was equal to twenty-four, twelve and six *soldi* respectively; they were alike of pot-metal. Of the Doges Nicolo Contarini and Francesco Erizzo (1630-1646), there has been a recent find, in unused state, of copper *bagattini*.

The number of coins of all metals in contemporary circulation at Venice, after a hundred years of unexampled activity at the Zecca, exceeded the number concurrently in circulation in any other country in the world, at that or any other time. Many of the types which answered the wants of the Republic in earlier years had silently vanished, including all the pieces of Imperial or foreign origin and of dubious authority. Although, at the severely critical juncture which arose from the European coalition of 1509 against the Republic, a scarcity of specie seems to have necessitated for some time (even so late forward as 1550 or thereabout) the admission of certain foreign money at a stipulated tariff, (1) her rulers had no longer, as a rule, a motive for utilizing the specie of their neighbours and allies, or for issuing money under the countenance of emperors, and, indeed, the government was incessantly striving to discourage the circulation of foreign currencies, as the practice, in fact, involved a vast amount of labour and inconvenience, on account of the disparity of standards and values.

(1)   Papadopoli, *Una Tariffa con i Disegni di Monete Stampata a Venezia nel 1517;* Papadopoli. Facsimiles. The same *Tarifs Vénitiens Avec Dessins de Monnaies du XVIe Siècle.* Facsimiles. This practice seems to have been common to other European states. See (compilation) *Ordonnances, Statutz & Instructions Royaulx,* 1538, folio 128, where the acceptance of foreign currencies was notified by cry. There is a tariff of this kind belonging to Lorraine, 1511. In the printed broadsheet displaying the coins to be taken in payment at Venice in 1564, it is stated that the proclamation was published both on the steps of Saint Mark's and at the Rialto.

But what is apt to strike the student of Venetian numismatic art is the poverty of invention, and the servile and monotonous republication of the same design, with the slightest possible pretence to variation or novelty. The first school of moneyers had their cross with its pelleted angles; the second, the tutelary Evangelist and the Doge in different positions, and the flag-pole. The *grosso* or *matapan* of the twelfth, and the ducat or *zecchino* of the thirteenth century were creditable performances for the time; but, with one or two reservations, the genius of the Mint appears to have been capable of nothing more. Except the *lira*, and the copper *bagattino* and double *bagattino* with the portrait of the Doge, the two *giustini* and a few other productions spread over centuries, all the coins were unfruitful seedlings of the same germ.

A laudable feature of the numismatic economy of the most flourishing period was the solicitude of the Decemvirs, to provide a constant and copious supply of small change for the convenience of the poor and of the dealers in cheap commodities; and, throughout all that time, a usage prevailed, to obviate a monopoly of the banks, by which the Mint received the gold bullion direct from merchants and others, and delivered it back to them in coins of the prescribed weight and fineness, subject to a fixed discount for coinage.

Of the engravers who were employed first at the Ducal Palace itself and subsequently at the Zecca we possess, through the studious preservation of archives, exceptionally considerable and consecutive knowledge, (1) and the names of a long series of moneyers have come down to us, with the terms on which they worked; for instance, Francesco Marchiori, who appears to have presided over the Mint in the time of Arrigo or Enrico Dandolo (1192-1205), and to have coined the first *grosso*. We cannot be quite sure whether the differential token which, after a certain date, is observable on the pieces is a mint-mark or a moneyer's symbol. Our conversance with the ruder artificers who worked in some of the Mediaeval European mints arises from the occasional registration of their names on the. money — a practice, however, unknown to Venice, beyond the employment of initials. Here and there we casually learn the terms on which those engaged at the Mint worked, and they strike us as extremely moderate; in many cases the employment passed from father to son. In 1484, the salary of the chief moneyer was 50 ducats a year, and that of his assistants 20.

(1)   Papadopoli, *Le Monete di Venezia Descritte ed Illustrate*, Appendice ii.

A view of the Venetian coinage is, perhaps, chiefly striking by comparison; and by comparison it is very striking indeed. The Republic was, of course, a commercial country, and, for purposes of trade, the introduction of as ample and complete a medium as possible was imperative, as soon as the world had emancipated itself from the primitive system of barter and exchange. A survey of the numismatic economy of other peoples, even at a later period, will leave an advantage on the side of Venice. The English, prior to the reign of Edward III., had merely the silver penny. Till the time of Louis IX. (1226-1270), who added the *gros tournois* and certain gold pieces, France possessed nothing but the Carolingian *denier* and its half. A similar or greater dearth of coin existed in Germany, the Netherlands, Poland and Italy itself.

A volume (1) has been devoted by an enthusiastic inquirer to the provincial and colonial coinage of Venice alone; and it may be expedient to add a schedule of the possessions among which it circulated:

Padua.	Ravenna.
Verona.	Scutari in Albania.
Vicenza.	Trieste.
Treviso.	The Ionian Isles.
Brescia.	Morea.
Bergamo.	Candia.
Rovigo.	Negropont.

Dalmatia (with Zara) and Spalato.	Cyprus.
	Nauplia or Napoli di Romania.
Albania	Friuli.

(1)   Lazari, *Le Monete dei Possedimenti Veneziani di Oltremare e di Terraferma.*

It appears that no separate currencies for the territories of the Republic, outside the original Dogado, had been attempted prior to the commencement of the fourteenth century. (1) In 1282, considerable dissatisfaction was felt at the systematic imitation of Venetian types, more especially the *grosso*, by the Ban of Rascia, which led Dante in his *Paradiso* to couple him with Philippe le Bel of France (*Le Faux Monnoyeur*) as a sufferer in another world; the inconvenience was aggravated by the wide circulation of these coins throughout the Venetian dominions, and their acceptance on an equal footing with the legitimate currency. The consequence was that, on the 3rd of May, 1282, the Great Council decreed that all holders of these pieces, and all officials into whose hands they should fall, were to surrender them, that they might be broken up; the regulation was also made applicable to the provinces. (2)

(1)   Count Papadopoli has produced a copiously illustrated monograph on the extensive series of coins, without ruler's or Doge's name, for the most part in billon or copper and in the lowest denominations, struck by Venice for its several possessions in the Peninsula and elsewhere. The volume is entitled; *Le Monete Anonime di Venezia dal 1472 al 1605.*

(2)   Lazari, *Le Monete dei Possedimenti Veneziani di Oltremare e di Terraferma,* page 45.

The government found incessant vigilance requisite to protect the national interests in this direction. In 1476-1477, a report was circulated and reached the ears of the Ten, that a Genoese association, with a capital of 50,000 ducats, contemplated the absorption of all the *tornesi* of Venetian origin, with a view to the extraction of the silver, and orders were forthwith given to the governors of all the colonial provinces concerned, to stop the exportation of these coins in large or small numbers, beyond their respective frontiers.

The difficulties attendant on these matters and on the general administration of the Mint doubtless had, in or about 1514, a juncture, when political conditions still remained more or less critical after the capital episode of Cambrai, to the transfer by the Ten to themselves and the Giunta of Fifteen, of the supreme control and management of the whole business, and, six years later, we find them quashing a decree of the Senate relative to an illegal issue of *tornesi* for the Levant. We are induced to conclude that the objection and hostility to foreign specie was its deficient weight and standard, quite as much as its places of origin, for the periodical tariffs comprehend a very large and wide assortment of external coinages which, probably after being officially tested, were receivable at a fixed rate.

A noteworthy feature in the Great Council minute regarding the false *grossi* is the direction, to all holders of stalls or counters (*stationes*) in Rialto and their assistants being over twelve years of age, to discover any which they might find, on pain of losing ten per cent, if they were detected with such in their hands. Half the fine was to go to the informer, and half to the government; no penal cognizance was taken of young children.

This imitation of models was by no means uncommon, and, to a certain extent, it establishes the fact, that the money of the Republic was viewed as holding an exceptionally high rank among the earlier European currencies. Two of the Kings of Servia, Stephen V. and VI., 1275-1336, also copied the *grosso*; a coin of the latter ruler is, with the exception of the legend, a counterpart of the Venetian; the two figures originally designed for Saint Mark and the Doge answer equally well for Saint Stephen and the King.

In 1354, a decree prescribes the suppression of a foreign coin termed a *frisachesa*, illegally introduced into the Republic; and, similarly, on some of the *zecchini* of the Knights of Saint John of Jerusalem, the figures do duty for Saint John and the Grand Master, while, on the reverse, the Venetian legend remains unaltered. In 1603, the Signori of Frinco in Piedmont issued counterfeits of Venetian types, and were cited to appear at Venice in answer to the charge, or, in default, to be (with their moneyers) condemned to death. As they were beyond jurisdiction, however, a price was set on their heads — 10,000 ducats for each of the principals, and 2000 for each of their agents, dead or alive.

We find the *fiorino d'oro* of Florence adopted in the same flattering and servile manner by half the states of Europe. In 1618, a case occurred in which false English twenty-shilling pieces found their way to Venetian ships where they might not be detected, and the Venetian ambassador in London puts his government on its guard against them. (1)

(1)   (compilation) *Calendar of State Papers Relating to English Affairs in the Archives of Venice,* 1617-1619, Volume I page 217.

On the other hand, as late as the eighteenth century, the Venetian copper money (*marchetto* and half-*marchetto*) are represented as having unfairly encroached on the German currency on the Austrian side, and we find an order, proceeding from Vienna in 1748, to put into circulation, more regularly, the *soldi* and half *soldi* struck at various mints in the provinces since 1733.

Elsewhere another kind of anomaly had arisen, for the Prince of Achaia and others, who owed their possessions to the operation of the same causes, coined *tornesi*, which not only served as currency within their regular limits, but were as much the ordinary circulating medium of the Venetian dependencies as the money struck by the Republic. In 1305, the government of the Doge at length tried to find a remedy for this state of affairs, by the proposal to issue at Koron and Modon a new type of money for local use; but of this currency no examples seem to be recognizable; possibly the idea was relinquished. (1) But, although it was the provincial neighbours of Venice who had set the example of intrusion and encroachment by pirating her numismatic models, another century elapsed before a special coinage for the trans-Adriatic districts was undertaken.

(1)   Papadopoli, *Le Monete di Venezia Descritte ed Illustrate,* page 141.

Between 1410 and 1414, the Venetian government, partly under the advice of the notary Bonisio who enjoyed the advantage of local knowledge, struck money for Dalmatia (including Zara) in the form of billon *soldi* with a shield on one side, supposed to be that of the Suriani family. From 1436 to 1442, and perhaps during a longer term, silver *grossetti* were struck for Scutari in Albania which had been at least a feudal dominion from 1395, with the effigy of Saint Stephen on the obverse, and, on the reverse, the Lion of Saint Mark. These pieces were probably struck at the castle of Scutari by the Venetian governor. There is a disposition to appropriate to Dalmatia under Venetian rule a *doppio scudo d'oro*, a copper foil is of Byzantine type, and a *quattrino* of the same metal, all of the more ancient autonomous Rascian type and current between 1420 and 1638.

The arrangements for Friuli, Ravenna and the Lombard provinces appear to have varied; the coins were usually struck at home, and, so relatively late as 1605, there is the signal case of a gentleman, named Carlo Ruiniscalco, of the tower at Zevio in the Veronese, who was convicted of issuing pieces modelled on the Venetian pattern, and who, on his flight from justice, had all his property sequestrated, a price set on his head, and his house razed to the ground with an injunction that it should never be restored.

In the case of Treviso which had belonged to Venice since 1339, there was a sort of attempt to reconcile foreign control with financial autonomy, if we may judge from a *bagattino* of 1492, evidently struck for the Trevisano, with S[TATUS] LIBERATUS TARVIXI on one side, and, on the other, S. MARCVS VENETI. This judicious concession to local sentiment was in harmony with the attitude which the Venetians thought it wise to maintain, as a rule, toward their dependencies, and had not they themselves known very well a time when S. MARCUS VENETI on a chip of metal was welcomed with pride? At a later date, the same pieces and others, such as the *gazzetta*, worth two *soldi* and originally introduced in 1528, were issued for Dalmatia and Albania; and, in course of time, a similar principle was applied to the Morea, Candia and Cyprus.

Under the Doges Antonio Priuli and Giovanni Cornaro (1618-1623, 1624-1630), pieces in copper for 15, 30 and 60 *tornesi* were struck for Candia, and some of the coins of the same metal of the *gazzetta* type bore Candia on the face. The Venetian currency for Candia is classifiable into the normal coinage in gold and copper or billon, and money of necessity struck between 1646 and 1650, during the siege of the capital by the Turks. The former comprised a gold *perpero*, of which there seems to have been only a single issue, a *soldino*, a *gazzetta* and double *gazzetta*, and a *soldo*. The *soldino* was equal to 4 *tornesi*; the *soldo*, half a *gazzetta*. The money of necessity included pieces of 10 and 5 *lire*, dated 1650, 10 *gazzette*, and 2-1/2) *soldini*; the 10 *gazzette* pieces bore the name and arms of Giambattista Grimani, the Venetian commander. This coinage covered the period from 1618 to 1669, when Candia was abandoned.

Of Cyprus there are, besides countermarked Venetian and Spanish money for local use, small billon coins denominated *carzie*, modelled on those in use under the Lusignan dynasty, and extending from 1515 or thereabout to 1570, although (1) examples of some Dogates have apparently yet to be recovered. This was the ordinary colonial series for the island; but, during the siege of Famagusta in 1570, pieces of the *soldo* type were struck in base metal in more than one variety.

(1)   Papadopoli, *Les Plus Anciens Deniers ou Carzie: Frappes les Venetiens pour Chypre: 1515-1518.*

A piece of five *gazzette*, struck in base metal for Corfu, bears the winged Lion of Saint Mark on the obverse and the blundered date 1081. It appears to be the only coin issued of this denomination and value, and was probably money of necessity. We have examples of such a coinage for both possessions, notably, one piece of 1570 issued during the siege of Famagusta, and one of 1650 struck during the defence of Canea by the Venetian commander. Both of these are of copper, and when in fine preservation are highly desirable. Thus the Signory, in its money, as well as in its principles of government and in its laws, aimed at spreading, wherever the sword or diplomacy had opened the way, its name and its influence.

The employment of occasional money by the Republic in early days was extremely rare, and it was limited to three objects; siege-pieces, largess distributed at the investiture or coronation of a Doge, and convention money with certain Swiss cantons. In 1123, the want of some medium for paying the troops engaged in the Syrian war obliged, it is said, the Doge Domenigo Michieli, who commanded there in person, to authorize the mintage of leathern money, impressed on one side with the figure of Saint Mark, and, on the other, with his own family arms. The incident of the loan to his allies, which had produced the drain on the Venetian finances, and the publication of this leathern siege money, may be corroborated by the circumstance that the Michieli subsequently carried on their escutcheons, as a memorial of the event, a ducat of gold. (1) But the story belongs to a class which the judicious student treats with distrust, (2) although the name *micheletto* has been traditionally handed down as that of the piece.

(1)   Dandolo, *Chronica Venetorum, Liber IX page 270*
(2)   Compare Calogera, *Spiegazione della Moneta del Doge Domenigo Michieli in Soria,* with Lazari, *Le Monete dei Possedimenti Veneziani di Oltremare e di Terraferma,* page 3, and see supra Volume One page 213.

The fairly intimate commercial relations with Switzerland led at two different intervals to the issue of a special currency; in 1603 under a concordat with Graubunden, and, in 1706, under one with Zurich and Berne. But both measures seem to have been little more than experiments or essays, although of the piece of 1603 two varieties occur. Examples are rare, particularly of those of 1706. In the latter year, a commemorative medal was struck in honour of the renewal of a monetary concordat with the Swiss.

Osella of Morosina Morosini-Grimani, 1597.   Bagattino of Francesco
                                              Erizzo, 1631–1646.

Giustina or Justina of Giovanni Cornaro, 1625–1629.

Osella of Francesco Morosini, 1688–1694.

Osella of Silvestro Valieto, 1694–1700.

VENETIAN COINS

The money struck at Venice on ceremonial occasions, though principally at the investiture of a Doge or Dogaressa, forms the subject of an interesting monograph by Giovanelli. That writer (1) commences his series with a Doge who reigned in the first moiety of the sixteenth century; but Antonio Grimani is so far from having been the earliest who distributed these tokens, denominated *oselle* or *uccelle*, that, in the revision of the coronation oath before his accession, it is stipulated that, by reason of the difficulty experienced in having a proper supply to present to all the public officials at Christmas, a new piece of money equal to a quarter of a ducat shall henceforth be struck instead.

(1)   Giovanelli, *Illustrazione delle Medaglie Denominate Oselle.* There is a later work on the same subject by Count Leonardo Manin; *Illustrazione delle Medaglie dei Dogi di Venezia Denominate Oselle: Edizione Seconda con Correzioni ed Aggiunte.*

This new regulation, however, did not interfere with the issue of the *oselle* in all metals, and double *oselle* by the Doge and (in two or three instances) by the Dogaressa on their accession, or in memory of some notable incident in their reign. Thenceforward the custom was followed at intervals down to the very fall of the Republic; but, in 1543, the Council of Ten limited the presentation to nobles, as it had then become the fashion to give the *osella*, at all events in the lower metals, to minor government officials.

The Venetians had perhaps borrowed the idea from the ancients, who commonly struck money in commemoration of particular events and allowed it to be current, and the practice soon grew familiar throughout the continent of Europe. To this category we ought, perhaps, to refer the 100 ducat piece in gold struck by the last of the Doges; it was what the French designate a *piece de plaisir*.

But centuries prior to the *oselle* engraved by Giovanelli, a case is known in which a Doge resorted to this practice. (1) In 1173, before his coronation, it is averred that Sebastiano Ziani circulated among the people certain money, stamped with his own name and struck by his order for the express purpose on the preceding day. It is perhaps singular that, among the many resuscitations of Mediaeval curiosities, this largess has not descended in the form of a unique specimen snatched from the ooze of the lagoons; but the circumstance itself is not unlikely, more especially as money of the ordinary type, bearing the name of Ziani, is extant.

(1)   Mutinelli, *Annali Urbani di Venezia dall'Anno 810 al 12 Maggio 1797*, page 49.

With the fewest possible exceptions, the money of the Republic bears no superficial evidence of the period of issue, but a certain chronological code, intelligible to the contemporary authorities, is discerned in initials placed in the exergues of the coins of the later period.

The peculiar rarity of the earlier currency, especially in all its varied types, arising from its flimsy character or from the practice of constantly calling in light and defaced pieces, renders it something like an impossibility to form a consecutive series. As an example of the enormous destruction of the low denominations, it has been pointed out that the *bagattino* of 1478, found in the ruins of the Campanile in 1902, is the sole surviving representative of an issue of nearly three million pieces.

In Count Papadopoli's *Table of Commercial Values*, none of the prices rises to any very serious figure, except here and there — perhaps in a dozen instances — in which from 200 to 400 *lire* are computed as the purchasing equivalent. The rarity of the gold ducats is very unequal; that of Marino Faliero takes the lead at 400 *lire* or £16, while many are set down as procurable for 15 *lire*. Next to the Faliero ducat in appreciation is the *grosso* of Michele Morosini, reckoned as worth 200 *lire*.

A piece of criticism which applies to the entire series of currencies is their liability, in chief measure at political and financial crises, to debasement of standard or artificial inflation of value by order of the executive. The pages of Count Papadopoli vividly reflect this normal feature of monetary economy; and, again, we meet here, as everywhere, with moments or intervals of severe tension, when foreign specie was temporarily suffered to pass at a stipulated tariff.

Another point, worthy of commemoration, is the fairly early resort at Venice to the practice of receiving back at the Mint, at a valuation, coins worn and defaced by use. In 1472, the Council of Ten called in all the false or light money then in official and private hands, and made it good if it was forthcoming within eight days of the date of the decree (the 15th of May). At a later date (1608), we find Coryat, the traveller, earnestly admonishing his readers to beware of the light Venetian gold, and to take by preference what was due to them in silver *lire*.

He visited the Mint, and describes it as "A goodly edifice, and so cunningly contrived with free stone, bricke, and yron, that they say there is no timber at all in that whole fabricke, a device most rare." He proceeds to say that all round the court is pointed diamond work, and that there are ten doors, the upper part made of iron, leading out of it. A well was in the centre, and inside there was a gallery along the whole extent of the court with white stone pilasters. The writer saw a large number of chests hooped with iron, some of them with seven locks, and he computes the value of the coins in these, with forty-two more in two chambers at the Rialto, at not less than 40 million ducats, that is, 100 million sterling of the present day.

Every aspect of commercial life was assiduously studied and encouraged. Tables of weights and measures, to facilitate dealings in Venetian and other goods, were doubtless obtainable in some form, long prior to the first publication by Bartolommeo di Pasi or Paxi of Venice of his *Tariff of Weights and Measures in 1503*, (1) and the work was one likely to be kept in print for the use of the mercantile world, and many editions may have disappeared. The undertaking was professedly, of course, designed as a boon to buyers, and possibly it appealed to contemporary understandings; but to an untechnical modern eye it is a puzzle.

(1)   There are later issues of 1521, 1540, 1553 and 1564, but there was unquestionably a continuous series. The impression of 1553 is in agenda form, so as more readily to be carried in the pocket. There is a woodcut of the Holy Family on the last leaf.

CHAPTER LVIII

Chamber of Loans — Loan of 1160 — The Monte Vecchio and Monte Nuovo — The Funds — Division of Opinion on the Movement — Competition of Investors Abroad for Places on the Roll — Private Banks — Profitable Business in Loans to Foreigners — Bankrupt Estates — Prohibition of Fictitious Partnerships — Bank of Venice — Principle of Honouring Drafts by Owners of Current Accounts — Rent-Rolls, 1365-1425 — Value of House-Property and Land — Large Prices Paid for Mansions — Costly Internal Embellishments — Resources of Venice After the Commencement of Its Decline.

On the 4th of June, 1160, the government borrowed of half a dozen merchants the sum of 150,000 silver marks. (1) From this transaction dated their origin the national debt and the Monte Vecchio, the latter the germ and foundation of the Bank of Venice. It was not till twelve or thirteen years later, that a Chamber of Loans with its staff of functionaries was called into existence, and that the Funding System was made a branch of the political economy of the state. The confidence which was almost universally felt in the stability and good faith of Venice encouraged an extensive resort to the Monte Vecchio, and afterward to the Monte Nuovo. Foreign princes and capitalists of all nationalities deposited their money in the Funds, as the securest investment which could be made; the right to hold Venetian scrip was a privilege which could not be obtained without legislative sanction, and the sums registered in 1428 represented an aggregate of 9,000,000 ducats of gold, (2) the interest upon which, paid half-yearly at Lady Day and Michaelmas, was 130,000 ducats.

(1)   Romanin, *Storia Documentata di Venezia,* Volume IV page 94.

(2)   Gallizioli, *Delle Memorie Venete Antiche, Profane ed Ecclesiastiche,* Liber I Capit 13. In twenty years from that time the amount had risen to thirteen millions.

The subjoined table shews the fluctuations in the interest paid upon the debt from 1386 to 1398:

Year.	Amount in Ducats.
1386	146,690
1387	239,830
1388	228,180
1389	220,870
1390	211,480
1391	236, 230
1392	218,000
1393	241,190
1394	193,589
1395	217,669
1396	197,310
1397	188, 950
1398	195,500 (1)

(1)   Gallizioli, *Delle Memorie Venete Antiche, Profane ed Ecclesiastiche,* Liber I Capit 13.

Between 1341 and 1352, as has already been stated, the rate of interest charged on loans fluctuated between 2 and 38 per cent, the lowest rate being found in 1350.

Venice, even in the thirteenth century, was the favourite depository of any sums of money, the payment of which was awaiting the result of some negotiation or contingency. The marketable value of the Funds was liable to rapid variations; at one time (1440) they were as low as 18-1/2. So far as can be ascertained they were never higher than 59, at which figure they stood during a few months in 1409; but before the end of the year they had sunk to 45; in 1425 they were again at 58. It can scarcely be matter of surprise that the fluctuations were so frequent and so violent, when each ship which entered the Lagoons brought tidings of the prospect of a new war with Milan or Hungary, or the report of a fresh revolution at Genoa or Bologna. Our astonishment must be rather that, at such an epoch and in such a cycle of the world, any state should have succeeded, even imperfectly, in establishing a Funding System, and in imparting to it a moderate degree of equilibrium.

The loan of 1160 (1) was under a bond, and was redeemable in eleven years; the security was a mortgage of the dues of the Rialto, and among the subscribers were the Doge himself and many of the leading mercantile houses. The rate of interest is apparently not specified; it seems to have been the first debt of the kind that was contracted. But twelve or thirteen years later, new financial difficulties, arising from the lax and imperfect method of collecting the taxes, obliged a second resort to extraordinary expedients, and a bureau was established, entitled Camera degli Imprestidi, under the superintendence of three Camerlenghi del Commune. This institution charged itself with the duty of raising a forced loan, amounting to 1 per cent, on the estimated aggregate property of every individual liable to such a call. The Chamber kept a register of names and addresses, and books of accounts, and engaged to pay 4 per cent, half-yearly on the amount realized, till redemption became feasible.

(1)   The text of the document is printed *in extenso* in Sanudo, *Diarii,* Volume I page 497-499.

Among the moderns, these steps taken by Venice were perhaps the earliest recourse to that great and vital System of Funding, which became, at a later period, a recognized branch and feature of the political economy of nations. The circumstances which attended the transaction of 1160 present that system in its most rudimentary and experimental aspect; the whole question of banking was then in its infancy and on its trial.

Many politicians looked askance at the principle. They were alike ignorant of its value, of its working and of its peculiar function, and nothing, perhaps, was more remote from their intention, than the imposition of a burden upon their posterity by the creation of a national debt. The earliest subscribers to the Monte Vecchio were not unwilling to receive their half-yearly dividends, but they were far more anxious, in all probability, to recover their advances. The latter were guaranteed to them on substantial security within a limited term, and the Fund was then doomed to extinction, until another emergency arose, and another public credit was taken by the government.

In an age when specie was not abundant, and in a country where the number of capitalists was comparatively small, it was barely likely that this new class of investment would meet with much favour, or, so long as it remained optional, would be largely embraced. Nor was it reasonable to anticipate that a merchant would deposit in the Treasury, at 4 per cent., money which was possibly yielding in the course of business quintuple returns. Hence it may have been that, in 1173, resort was had to compulsory assessment. Yet we are to witness throughout the present history a constant, if not a relatively increasing tendency to lean on private and voluntary subsidies in the presence of critical circumstances, and it may have been the inadequacy of the resources of the Doge and his fellow patricians in 976, when a complication of burdens arose, which led to what seems to be regarded as the earliest levy of a tenth or tithe (1) as a special measure.

(1)   Romanin, *Storia Documentata di Venezia,* Volume I page .

It gradually acquired the attribute of a concession for any foreigner to be admitted as a stockholder. It was a political question on which the executive reserved the right of decision, even when the object was philanthropic. In 1376, the Bishop of Cremona, and, in 1383, the Cardinal of Ravenna, solicited and obtained permission to hold 6000 and 12,000 ducats for the endowment of poor girls and the part-maintenance of the Studio of Padua respectively. Other instances occur in 1386-1387, when the Duchess of Milan invested by leave 100,000 ducats in the Funds; and in 1389-1390, when Don Manfredo di Saluzzo was allowed to invest 3000 ducats for purposes of poor relief. In the next century, we find the great and unfortunate general Carmagnola placing the bulk of his fortune in Venetian securities.

Beside the official Chamber of Loans, there were numerous banks belonging to private individuals, including Jews, where money could be deposited or borrowed at interest. The rate was fixed by the government, as well as the amount which might be advanced. In the case of two foreign Jews in 1389, the firm was required to put 4000 ducats into the business and to limit its loans to 30; and persons of the Hebrew nationality were only admitted by special licence, and, as it were, till farther notice. The house just mentioned, that of De Vult, however, was one of modest pretensions and of small capital, and private banks of all classes had ever to contend against the public Camera degli Imprestidi, which did business with persons all over the world to any amount, proper security being forthcoming.

In 1397, 15,000 ducats were lent to Henri and Jacques de Bourbon, great lords of France, on their undertaking not to quit Venice till the sum was repaid. In 1398, the Commune of Perugia borrowed 5000 ducats. In 1399, the Duke of Norfolk effected with a Venetian merchant or banker a loan of 750 ducats while he stayed in the city on his way to the Holy Land; but the Duke died at Venice, and probably his creditor never saw his money again, although a strong representation was addressed to the English government on the subject.

Bankruptcy was, of course, a more or less frequent incident of Venetian commercial life, and the arrangement of insolvent estates devolved on the Consoli de Mercatanti. On the 15th of October, 1355, it was resolved by the Pregadi that Ser Marino Baffo of Santa Maddalena and Ser Marco Trevisano, bankers, having absconded with 20,000 ducats, be tried, and that whoever shall lead to their conviction by delivering them into custody shall have 550 *lire*. In 1390, the private bank of Ser Antonio Contarini failed, and was wound up by order of the Council of Pregadi. It was among the domestic troubles and embarrassments of the Doge Foscari that the bank of Andrea Priuli, his father-in-law, suspended payment about 1440. In 1502, the general inconvenience produced by insolvencies led to the institution of the Proveditori Sopra Banchi.

There is a provision dated 1535, (1) by which no person engaged in business was at liberty to pose as forming one of a company or firm, or as having a partner, unless he could satisfy the authorities that there was absolute *bona fides*; the names of the parties were to be registered in the proveditorial books, and to be communicated to all likely to be affected by the transactions of the said house. This piece of legislation was professedly aimed at a long-standing abuse.

(1)   (compilation) *Statuta Veneta, 1729,* page 142.

The Bank of Venice underwent several developments and changes of nomenclature. It was successively known as the Monte, the Monte Nuovo (1580), the Monte Novissimo (1610), and the Banco del Giro (1712). At the last-named date, its statutes were revised and additional facilities were afforded, agreeably to the more modern principles then gaining general acceptance, for keeping and paying private and other accounts, side by side with adequate arrangements for the accommodation of customers in need of temporary advances, and for the investment of surplus capital at remunerative interest.

The rate customarily paid for the use of money had been in the fourteenth century and later, 20 per cent; in 1549, it is represented by a contemporary English authority — Thomas in his *History of Italy* — that Venetian nobles could then get 10, 12 and 15 per cent for their spare resources, but such rates must have been exceptional. Four per cent for six months, on the security of a house, is mentioned in a document of 1176; probably transactions were regulated on their own merits. There is no doubt that ten per cent long remained an average claim between private parties. Half that amount was found by the official department — in ordinary circumstances — sufficient to meet with acceptance in the fourteenth and fifteenth centuries, but when the bank was reconstituted on a new and broader footing in 1712, the rate had probably fallen much below the minimum amount.

The practice of depositing liquid securities in private banks for current use had, however, evidently been familiar long before, and we find the written order on the banker already in fashion in the fifteenth century, for, in or about 1433, Cosimo de' Medici is found handing to some one a slip of paper, directing the principal of the Hospital of Santa Maria Nuova where he apparently kept an account, to pay the bearer 1100 gold florins. (1) In some places it was called a *polizza*; such a system remained in England down to the nineteenth century before the regular cheque was introduced. It seems to have been about 1715 that the London banks began to deal with private customers and to open current accounts; the House of Child was probably the earliest in the field; the members of the family were originally linen drapers. The first Earl of Bristol (1665-1751) was one of their earliest customers, and mentions in his *Diary* that he kept his banking-account or one of them there.

(1)   Machiavelli, *History of Florence and of the Affairs of Italy From the Earliest Times to the Death of Lorenzo the Magnificent,* page 195.

The practice of framing Rent-Rolls is named in a public document of 1207 as an established institution. In 1365, the Old Rent-Roll or Catastero Vecchio had been rendered, by the expansion of the national wealth, obsolete and unserviceable, and, in 1367, a fresh survey was authorized.

The *Catastero Nuovo* exhibited the results which follow:

Ward	Number of Parishes	Total Rental in Gold Ducats.
San Marco	16	799,180
Castello	12	456,960
Cannaregio	12	485,230
San Polo	8	490,270
Santa Croce	9	281,280
Dorsoduro	11	368,800

In this tabular statement, a few trifling inaccuracies exist which it is no longer possible to rectify. The correct total for the six Wards is 2,880,818 ducats of gold. (1)

(1)   Romanin, *Storia Documentata di Venezia,* Volume III Document Number 5, *Estima delle Case di Venezia nel 1367,* from the *Cronaca Magna.*

Another, perhaps the next, survey was made in 1425, and the roll of 1367 became in its turn the Old Roll. It is said (1) that the new survey exhibited a total of 3,253,042 ducats of gold, being in excess of the former by 372,224 ducats; in 1469 the figures are given as 4,558,490 ducats. (2)

(1)   Romanin, *Storia Documentata di Venezia,* Volume IV page 500.
(2)   Romanin, *Storia Documentata di Venezia,* Volume IV page 551.

These statistics furnished the government with the basis for an estimate of the rateable property of the city and state, but, unless many intervening records are lost, material changes necessarily occurred, almost from year to year, in the financial position of individuals. Again, at Venice that peculiarly oligarchical spirit, which, with the direction of affairs, accepted many of the burdens of government, rendered a descent to the lower scale of incomes or fortunes less imperative than it was, or was made to be, elsewhere. The reluctance to exact, in the absence of necessity, even the legitimate quota of taxation, or to press payment of dues to the state, formed part of the diplomatic tenderness toward the community at large, which distinguished Venice and conciliated the lower classes. But it had not always been so, for the old chronicler Marco tells us, that the tax-gatherer in his time (the thirteenth century) was nicknamed an *orso*, because he cuffed and struck those who would not or could not pay. *Orso* might be either a bear or a paring-tool.

Two circumstances which supplied an indication of the growing prosperity of Venice at the close of the fourteenth and the commencement of the fifteenth century were the increase in the population and the rising value of house-property. It is supposed that, in the last quarter of the twelfth century, the population of the whole Dogado, including persons in holy orders, did not exceed 70,000; but the difficulties necessarily attendant upon the verification of a census, in a city in which the absentees were constantly numerous, warn us against the reception of this class of statistics in too exact or literal a sense. In 1336, the official returns shewed 40,100 males between twenty and sixty, representing, by comparison with other tables, an aggregate of nearly 150,000. In the last decade of that century, the numbers fell little short of 200,000, and, by a census taken in 1367, it is established that the heads of noble houses in that year were no fewer than 204.

Occasional documentary glimpses are obtainable of earlier valuations, at all events of land, and they offer the same powerful contrast to more modern figures, as is almost universally the case where fundamental changes have occurred in the demand for space. In 1031, the Veniero family sold a plot of ground in Chioggia for four *denari*. Probably it was a small one, for, in 1088, they and certain coparceners obtained for another property five *librae* of gold. But there was an antecedent time when areas were allotted to settlers on a feudal basis for a more or less nominal service, and, from 1310, the Rossi family held in perpetuity of the Procurators of Saint Mark a house in one of the most central thoroughfares — the Merceria — at a rent of fifteen ducats; but this was professedly a peppercorn rate in merely exceptional circumstances.

The mansions which studded the Grand Canal and other leading thoroughfares ultimately fetched enormous sums. The possessor of a more or less moderate fortune, the Doge Francesco Foscari was not, relatively speaking, a rich man; yet the house at San Pantaleone, in which he lived before his accession to power, and also for a few days in October 1457 after his retirement, cost him 20,000 ducats. A large number of residences on or near the Rialto were estimated at 10,000 and 15,000 ducats, and 5000 or 6000 ducats was quite an ordinary figure. The house which was purchased by the Commune so far back as 1348 for Jacopo da Carrara, grandfather of Francesco Novello, cost 5000 ducats. In 1413, among the rewards of Pandolfo Malatesta, Captain-General of Venice in the Hungarian War, was a dwelling for which the Procurators of Saint Mark paid 6000 ducats, and, in 1429, the Palazzo Giustiniani at San Pantaleone was bought for the Lord of Mantua, ex-

Captain-General of the Signory, for the sum of 6500 ducats. In the same year, the government, desirous of doing honour to the Waiwode of Albania, a Venetian citizen, procured for him the house of the patrician Nicolo Morosini, at an outlay of only 3000 ducats.

The prices demanded for shops in the choicer and more fashionable localities were, at the same time, exorbitant. The smallest counter on the Rialto itself did not let for less than 100 ducats a year, and, for the Bell Hotel at the Pescheria, with a frontage of little shops, the Sanudo family received annually 800 ducats. Tenements which, at the beginning of the fourteenth century, used to let for fifteen or twenty ducats, had become, in the fifteenth, according to their situation and their proximity to the Ducal residence, worth six, eight, ten or even twelve times as much. In the more sumptuous of the private edifices in and about the Foscari period (1423-1457), there were not infrequently single apartments, upon the decoration of which 800, 1000, or 2000 ducats had been expended by the proprietor, principally in gilding, musaic or carving, marble and glass.

In the presence of several political and national crises of the most acute and exhaustive character, when Venice was thrown for months on her own internal resources and was left without an ally, it becomes highly necessary to inquire what enabled a city so situated to live, and, again, what is in a sense still more important and remarkable, to feed her people and uphold her independence, during all that prolonged period when her eastern trade had shrunk to the slenderest proportions, and her grasp of the terra firma was immensely relaxed. Even when the Republic was no longer, either what she shewed herself at the epoch of the Fifth Crusade — a maritime and commercial power capable of contracting for the equipment of the expedition to the east and of governing its movements, or what she became in two centuries forward — a first-rate European state, with a ruling voice which was audible far beyond the Italian frontier, the Venetian economic system rendered it possible to support a considerable population and a luxurious minority during centuries of political decadence.

Venice was almost to the last severely protectionist, and the city from its happy topographical site was a sort of reservoir for an enormous amount of goods imported from various directions, and also the seat of numerous profitable manufactures. Imports and exports alike paid duty; a stringent excise guarded all points of ingress or egress; and even the members of the craft guilds contributed a certain quota of their gains in addition to the entrance fees.

Mention occurs elsewhere of the thousands of persons who derived a livelihood from the woollen trade, mainly through the large and continual demand of the staff of the Arsenal and of seafarers, and the Salt Office was at all times a source of revenue which the state jealously guarded and on which it could implicitly rely. In 1454, it was estimated that a tenth of the public income came from this industry, on which the Praetorian Prefect Cassiodorus, in the fifth century, is already found felicitating the Islanders as more precious than mines of gold and silver.

The principle of taxing every object of ornament or use and every article of consumption was in harmony with the commercial ideas of the passed centuries; it recommended itself to the later Venetians by the peculiar nature of many of their home products, which yielded a wide margin of emolument and of which they were long enabled to keep the monopoly; and no effort or encouragement was spared to prevent industrial specialities from leaving the lagoons. The glass trade in all its branches was alone a rich field of employment and profit. Altogether the internal resources of Venice, nearly down to the close, were, even if deficient in the old amplitude and elasticity, by no means contemptible, and it was not to the blame of the constitution, but of the natural course of external events, that the volume of trade decreased, and that with it the voice of the country dropped to a lower key.

For, as in the naval department, all ships were for the common use, subject to certain necessary restrictions of the executive and of individuals, of war and commerce, so, while the days of monopoly lasted, and until the opening of the Cape of Good Hope route reduced the Mediterranean to secondary importance and value, the Venetian patricians shared with the Cittadinanza the advantages of practical business as merchants and bankers, while they were precluded, by rigorous self-imposed checks and counterchecks, from irregularly or mischievously interfering in a government of which they were constitutionally hereditary members.

Thus, the more modern Venice, as it came under the notice of observers in the eighteenth century, had parted with the spirit and genius which, with favouring conditions, enabled it to rise to a height of power and glory almost without a parallel in history, but it still remained a self-supporting community on the old-fashioned commercial lines, and, even in its declining strength and opulence, occasionally, on a great emergency or under some Mocenigo or Morosini, astonished the world by a momentary revival of its pristine vigour and heroism.

The elaborate measures which the government concerted for the official supervision of the arts or guilds were part of the entire system of paternal control. Those bodies were, as we have noted, under the jurisdiction of a department of the executive, which kept registers (*mariegole*) of all names and duplicate copies of the statutes. The ruling aims were to preserve the efficiency of the craft, and to prevent its arcana or secret methods of production from being divulged. The administrative committee of each guild was qualified to make provision for the sick and aged, for widows and orphans, and for the admittance of new members, but all these steps were subject to the approval of the state. The latter exacted a *taglione* or poll-tax, and an *ad valorem* commission on working profits.

This was therefore an appreciable element in the fiscal budget, when we consider the costly nature of many of the articles of luxury made by the guilds; and it was, besides, an incidence of revenue to the end, helping to prop up the constitution when certain other contributions began to fail. Taking the latter half of the sixteenth century when we enter on the period of decline, the annual sale of silks alone represented half a million ducats, while, in 1582, it was reckoned that there were not more than 187 beggars in Venice.

It was so in a far less important degree, as time progressed, with the income arising from government loans to states and individuals, and with the amounts deposited by foreigners in the Funds, for both these sources of revenue were unfavourably affected by the competition of other markets, and by the political decline of Venice itself. The former inducement to invest here was the sense of security and the rate of interest. The Republic, in short, when her wonderful fortune deserted her, fell back on her realized capital, her local industries and her position as a general entrepot.

Moreover, the normal expenditure of the state itself, as distinguished from that incurred by private munificence, was comparatively moderate; the Civil List was kept within fairly frugal limits, and was carefully audited; there was no standing army, and the Navy was so handled that its cost to the country was minimized. Again, there was ever that prominent factor in all perilous junctures and moments of financial pressure — the devotion of the private citizen, who never failed, so long as the means existed, to bring his money or material of war to the government as a free patriotic oblation; and, if we must admit that outrageous sums were habitually spent on luxury and ostentation to the very end of the scene, we must also allow that such things tended to occupy and distract general attention, and to conciliate certain classes.

While Coryat is tolerably eloquent in praise of the Venetian patricians, he admits that, in one respect, they did not bear comparison with his own noble countrymen, for he observed that, although they owned and maintained splendid mansions, they not only kept no retinue of servants and displayed no hospitality, but contented themselves with a frugal table. The author of the *Crudities* was informed that this course was necessitated by the sumptuary laws which limited expenditure, and it is not unlikely that the practice and temper were an inheritance from the old feudal times, when the aristocracy could never be sure how much they might be required, in their private capacities, to contribute at any moment to some public object. Yet, down to a period when the ancient purity of manners still more or less survived, there were members of the aristocracy who, in place of voluntary and gratuitous contributions to the national expenditure, lent their surplus income to the government, at a rate of interest which Shylock might have been prepared to entertain.

CHAPTER LIX

*The Arts and Sciences — Geographical Knowledge and Discovery —
Early Venetian and Other Travellers — Preparation of Charts and Maps
— Map of Marino Sanudo Torsello (1306) — Planisphere of Andrea
Bianco (1436) — The Crusaders — Sir John Mandeville — Marco Polo
and His Relatives — Marco's Chequered Career — His Return Home
About 1295 — Graphic Narrative of Ramusio — His Misfortunes —
Second Return in 1301 — Some Account of Marino Sanudo — His
Important and Interesting Correspondence — His Interview With the
Pope — Apparent Want of Friendly Relations Between Sanudo and Polo
— The Zeni — John And Sebastian Cabot — The Collection of Ancient
Charts in The Marciano — The Mariner's Compass — Mechanics and
Medical Sciences.*

At Venice, the arts and sciences were assiduously and affectionately
cultivated. Those to which the Republic directed its attention with the
greatest earnestness, perhaps, were astronomy and astrology,
mathematics, trigonometry, chemistry, botany, alchemy, history, sacred
and profane, physics and metaphysics, painting and sculpture. Some of
these studies were of essential service in the mastery of geography and
navigation. During the most prosperous times, no labour, no cost was
spared to render the standard of knowledge as high and complete as
anywhere in the world, and it is remarkable that, in the eighteenth
century, when the political rank and weight of the Republic had visibly
begun to decline, a distinct, if a tardy and futile, movement arose in the
direction, not merely of political and commercial reform, but of science
and culture. In other days, the Venetians had found it possible long to
deliberate before they acted, but they had failed to gauge the new forces

which the French Revolution liberated, and ruin overtook them before they had fully realized the peril.

Venice was one of a group of states which, in the divided condition of the Peninsula, contributed during many ages, amid all kinds of political distractions and anxieties, to foster the liberal arts, while it created its own schools of painting, sculpture and architecture, and was one of the earliest possessors of an important public library. The union of Italy under one government is a modern necessity, but the days of noble and rich performance were those of many centres regally emulous of each other; societies in which the fiercest passions and the darkest crimes went hand in hand with the most intense appreciation of beauty and the most perfect homage to nature, in which the god and the devil were so often blended in an individual, that local independence and local fame were at length thought worth bartering for general freedom and tranquillity.

The standard of geographical knowledge was not higher in any part of the world than in Venice. The discoveries of the three Poli in Tartary, China and the East Indies; of their contemporary, Marino Sanudo detto Torsello, in Armenia, Palestine and Egypt; (1) of Nicolo and Antonio Zeno, about 1390, on the coasts of Scotland and in the direction of the American continent toward Labrador and Newfoundland, the latter not reached by the elder Cabot till more than a century later; (2) of Ca' da Mosto, on the African continent; and of many others whose names and narratives have alike perished, were continually swelling the stock of information. In the ordinary course of trade, the subjects of the Republic, men of character and education, naturally contributed to advance the cause, nor was it in commercial life alone that the intercourse with remote regions was maintained and Venetian influence extended. As early as the first half of the eleventh century, we find Gherardo Sagredo, who was martyred in 1046 and eventually canonized, acting as Bishop of Chonad or Csanad in Hungary, and a favourite of the King, himself hereafter to become a saint and the founder of the Holy Roman Empire.

(1)   See also Filiasi, *Ricerche Storico-Critiche da Giacomo Filiasi,* page 137; Zurla, *Di Marco Polo e degli Altri Viaggiatori Veneziani Più Illustri Dissertazioni del P. Ab. D. Placido Zurla;* Foscarini, *Della Letteratura Veneziana,* page 497; Morelli, *Operette Ora Insieme con Opuscoli di Antichi Scrittori,* Volume II.

(2)   Zeno, N., *Dei Commentarij del Viaggio in Persia di M. Caterino Zeno il K. & delle Guerre Fatte nell' Imperio Persiano*. This book is very far from being what it professes to be, but is perhaps not quite so bad or so thoroughly disingenuous as the most recent critics seek to maintain. It seems to have been compiled nearly two centuries after the presumed date of the voyage or voyages, from papers no longer known to exist, and is accompanied by an apocryphal wood-cut map which is reproduced in the edition of Ptolemy, 1561. See the interesting monograph by F.W. Lucas, 1898.

The charts which were published at intervals helped importantly the same object, and the practical experiences of observant and more or less educated travellers tended to create two broad divisions or schools; the one which gave to the world the fruit of hearsay and guesswork, such as the Zeno volume above mentioned, and the other to which we owe the prototypes of our modern system of cartography. Some of the primitive *mappae mundi*, executed in the cloister or in the study or on the wall of a building, such as the map alleged to have been painted for Henry III. in Westminster Hall, seem to have no claims to authority, and when we have before us a work performed by some scribe, under the immediate dictation of a personage who had newly come from the regions which he sought to describe and delineate, and who, to fortify his memory, had brought in his hand sketches, even of a rough kind, made on the spot, we easily perceive the vital difference.

It is scarcely susceptible of doubt that, on his return from his travels in 1295, Marco Polo brought with him a plan more or less perfect and accurate of the latitudes which he had visited. In 1321 (1) the scarcely less illustrious Sanudo presented to the reigning Pontiff his celebrated book On the *Faithful of the Cross*, with four maps. (1)

(1)   Bongars, *Gesta Dei per Francos*.

In 1351, a traveller, supposed from internal evidence to have been a Genoese, designed a chart of the Black Sea. (1) The production is jejune and meagre enough, but it is valuable and interesting as the most ancient delineation of that region and littoral. The Doge Marino Faliero possessed among many other valuable curiosities, some of which had belonged to Marco Polo himself, a brazen *sphoera mundi*, formerly the property of Antonio, an astrologer. In 1357, a map of the world, perhaps based on that of Sanudo, was made by Francesco and Domenigo

Pizzagano of Venice, (2) and other contributions to nautical science appeared in 1368, 1380, 1426, 1436 and 1448. (3) The map of 1436, which proceeded from the pencil of Andrea Bianco of Venice, was the most perfect which had hitherto been seen, but not even the parallels of latitude were marked upon it. About the same time. Bianco produced a planisphere, (4) which preceded by some years that which the celebrated Fra Mauro prepared by commission for Alfonso IV. of Portugal, and which was transmitted to Lisbon in 1459. (5) Some of the details are sufficiently grotesque, and the designs of men and places are primitively quaint, but, on the whole, it is executed with an elaborate skill and with a delicacy of manipulation which entitle Bianco to the warmest eulogy. It is easy to conceive that it procured the draughtsman no common applause.

(1)   Serristori, *Illustrazione di Una Carta del Mar Nero del 1351.*
(2)   Romanin, *Storia Documentata di Venezia,* Volume III page 366.
(3)   Morelli, *Dissertazione Intorno ad Alcuni Viaggiatori Veneziani Eruditi Poco Noti,* Volume I; Morelli, *Operette Ora Insieme con Opuscoli di Antichi Scrittori,* Volume I.
(4)   Formaleoni, *Saggio Nautica Antica de' Veneziani,* page 16 et seqq.
(5)   Foscarini, *Della Letteratura Veneziana,* page 445 Number 2.

The labours of modern geographical experts and specialists have somewhat contributed to overlay the state of the question as it remained down to comparatively recent times. The spirit of commercial enterprise among the Italian republics, especially Venice, indirectly fostered that of religious enthusiasm, when the reports were brought to western Europe of the profanation of the holy places by the enemies of Christianity. These accounts, not a little exaggerated, found the feudal system and the principles of chivalry beginning to develop themselves in France and England, and an eager desire to redeem the Sepulchre and Palestine generally from the Mohammedan invaders, not only actuated the soldier at home in offering his services and embarking on the vessels hired from Venice and other maritime powers, but set numerous persons at work, in different parts of Europe, to construct, for information and curiosity, charts of the region which the Crusaders proposed to visit and liberate.

These draughts were principally executed at second-hand in the closet or the cloister, from report or from rough indications furnished by practical travellers deficient in literary and artistic skill. They range from the eleventh to the fifteenth century, and those which we possess must be regarded as only a salvage. As they emerge from merely speculative empiricism, they become interesting, as shewing the very gradual acquisition of any exact knowledge of localities. Their imperfection and poverty, however, were aggravated and prolonged, by the absence of capable cartographers to commit to paper the discoveries and communications of those who were acquainted with the ground, but were incompetent to delineate what their eyes had seen, as well as by the almost unavoidable want of concert among such few as then employed themselves in these inquiries.

The state of the case may be summed up by saying that the charts, *mappae mundi*, planispheres and portolani which survive in public libraries do not represent the full contemporary experience enjoyed by actual navigators and travellers, but as near an approach as rude draughtsmen could accomplish, from intercourse with direct observers without culture and without due appreciation of the importance of accuracy. We do not even know, whether the map of Marino Sanudo was made by himself or by some one else better versed in such work, or, again, whether it was prepared prior or posterior to his return home in 1306, but he had personally, in common with his contemporary and countryman Marco Polo, studied the geography of many regions, and was a man of considerable literary ability, and, if he was not an hydrographer, he was far better qualified than most explorers to direct the hand of another.

From the eighth century, at all events, a succession of pioneers, chiefly actuated by religious zeal or the spirit of adventure, but almost without exception illiterate, had contributed to build up a body of traditional and more or less vague information respecting distant localities, their features and products. Even when they left narratives behind them, however, these necessarily survived in unique manuscript copies, usually prepared from the roughest memoranda, or even from memory by third parties gifted with some share of clerical skill, and hidden in private repositories where they were forgotten; each individual started afresh, as it were, with the bare knowledge that certain regions presented objects of interest or advantage. (1)

(1)   See Tajir, *Ancient Accounts of India and China, by Two Mohammedan Travellers Who Went to Those Parts in the 9th Century.*

One of the concluding paragraphs in the ordinary editions of Sir John Mandeville's more or less apocryphal *Travels* (1322-1356) tends to corroborate the view, that the ancient charts (1) from various sources which we possess were more or less habitually based on a study of the manuscript narratives, brought home by travellers or drawn up by them from their notes on their return, which might leave the way open to many serious divergencies from facts and to empirical, or at least secondary records; in fact we know that the fruits of the explorations of Marco Polo were dictated to a French amanuensis, partly perhaps from notes, partly from memory.

(1)   The earliest English impression of Mandeville with a map and illustrations appears to be that of Wynkyn de Worde, issued in 1503. But editions in French, German and Spanish, with similar cuts, appeared between 1480 and 1531. No early Flemish translation has yet occurred to notice; nor indeed does Delepierre recognize the Liegeois version as such (*Sketch of the History of Flemish Literature*, 1860). The chart and engravings in all the historical issues just referred to were from a German source, and from a hand as imaginative as that of the writer of the text. The pseudo-Mandeville, however, enjoyed at least as great a popularity as the authentic Polo.

The *Mandeville* was, it is to be suspected, the work of a doctor of Liege, Jean de Bourgogne, or, as he is called in one place, Master John ad Barham, who, while he temporarily absented himself from his own country in order to avoid prosecution for homicide, may have visited Egypt, Palestine and Syria, and that, on his return, a traveller and countryman, about 1355, found him again at home, and joined with him in compiling an account of their common experiences and observations with a certain measure of embellishment.

Master John, perhaps, found it convenient to pass under an assumed name, and adopted that of Mandeville, the narrative in course of time successively passing as the work of Messire Jean de Mandeville and of Messire Jean de Mandeville Chevalier. He seems to have permanently renounced his original designation, and a lapidary, of which there were several printed editions, bears the name probably assumed by himself in the supposed circumstances and the rank wrongly bestowed on him by others. The original printer of the *Lapidarium* (about 1500) doubtless accepted without misgiving the personal credentials of the *soi-disant* Mandeville, his claim to spurs inclusive.

Polo, who profited by the previous observations of his father and uncles, had been preceded by others to some extent; and others, again, extended their travels farther than any of the Poli; but the labours and researches of Marco, occurring at a period when the world was beginning to awaken to an appreciation of the arts and industries of the far east, and enhanced in value by his practical training, cultivated mind and opulent circumstances, did more than those of any antecedent traveller from Europe to advance western civilization; and some of the Mediaeval Venetian customs, such as the notation of time by bells, suggest our indebtedness to his oriental experiences. (1) At the same time, we must not be surprised to find that later travellers, down to quite modern days, have had it in their power to rectify many erroneous or imperfect statements by a writer labouring under all the difficulties attendant on the pioneer. Such has been quite lately the case with the book of Major Sykes on Iran, in which he finds it possible to correct Yule in several particulars.

(1)   Beazley (*Prince Henry the Navigator*) pays a high tribute to the geographical services of the Poli.

Polo, after his return home in or about 1295, volunteered to fit out a galley at his own cost for the war against Genoa, and was taken prisoner in the disastrous battle of Curzola in 1298. Among his fellow captives or visitors at Genoa was Rusticien de Pise, translator from Latin or Italian into French of the Arthurian romance of *Meliadus de Lionnois*. Rusticien took peculiar pleasure in the society of the Venetian, and at length he even went so far as to propose, as a means of passing the tedious hours, that his friend should dictate to him a methodical account of his travels in Tartary, China and India. This proposition was accepted; the undigested memoranda, which Polo had left at his father's house at San Giovanni Grisostomo, were transmitted from Venice with the concurrence of the Genoese executive, and the work was henceforth continued from day to day, until it was brought to completion.

Polo lingered in captivity, mitigated by these circumstances, till 1301, and there was ample opportunity for making duplicate copies of the narrative; the original text was in French; translations into other languages were successively undertaken; an abridged version in the Venetian dialect appeared in 1496, and in English in 1579, but no authentic Italian edition seems to have been produced prior to 1827. The French narrative is stated to have been circulating shortly after 1298, and we are informed that the author or his amanuensis presented a copy to the King of France; (1) it is said that copies were then already circulating among the curious. The *Travels* of the great Venetian in the hand of Rusticien would now be cheaply purchased at a hundred times their weight in gold; the author has been acknowledged as the Herodotus of modern times; his book has been rendered into nearly all the languages of Europe. Honoured in his lifetime at the Chinese court, he was placed after his death among the Five Hundred Gods of Canton, and the name of the contemporary of Dante and Petrarch has become a household word.

(1)   Filiasi, *Ricerche Storico-Critiche da Giacomo Filiasi,* page 126. A text of the Latin compendium was printed from a fourteenth century manuscript in facsimile at Stockholm, quarto, 1782.

The influence of his Genoese acquaintance was exerted in the ineffectual attempt to restore him to freedom; a large ransom was offered to no purpose by his family with this object, and an advantageous marriage, which the elder Polo had had in view for his son on the return of the latter from abroad, was in consequence indefinitely postponed. It is supposed that he was liberated in 1301, but it is not known with certainty in what year he died. His will which forms the sole clue was made in 1323, and from this circumstance an inference may be drawn that his decease did not occur much later than 1324 or 1325; he left only two daughters — Moretta and Fantina. In the fifteenth century, by failure of male issue, the family merged in that of Trevisano, but a share of the personality of Polo passed by some means into the hands of the Doge Marino Faliero, and is included in the extant inventory of his estate (1355).

There is a tale that, on his death-bed, he was exhorted by certain persons to expunge from his *Travels* many passages upon which discredit had been cast in some quarters, and that the dying man treated the insulting proposition with merited scorn, exclaiming that "so far from being fairly chargeable with exaggeration, he had omitted to record countless extraordinary matters, to the truth of which he could have borne ocular testimony." (1)

(1)   The portrait of Polo accompanying Sir Henry Yule's *The Book of Ser Marco Polo,* 2nd edition, 1875, is almost certainly supposititious, but, in a copy of Marsden's book, 1818, was inserted a fine coloured drawing from some early manuscript. far more likely to have resembled the traveller.

It is Ramusio who preserves from the traditional anecdotes handed down by his father and his grandfather to a friend, the distinguished senator Gasparo Malipiero, that graphic and singular account of Marco Polo and his two kinsmen returning home in 1295, dressed like Tartars, and so much altered in their features by exposure and privation, that even their own family and their most intimate friends did not recognize them. The old historian produces the parallel case of Ulysses, and that of the Dutch discoverers of Spitzbergen in 1597 will be remembered. The interest of the little narrative is immensely enhanced by the distance of the period and the celebrity of the central figure; they had even forgotten the Venetian language.

On proceeding to the Casa Polo at San Grisostomo, they found the house in the occupation of relatives who thought them dead, and it was with great difficulty that they made these understand who they were. (1) They hereupon resolved upon an expedient by which they might make themselves known to their family and connexions, and at the same time to the whole city. A splendid banquet was arranged, and to it were bidden all the members of the House of Polo and their friends. When the guests had assembled and were seated at table, the three travellers entered, attired in robes of crimson satin down to their feet, "as the custom in those days was." Water was brought to them, and, having immersed their hands, they bade the company to be seated. They then divested themselves of their satin garments, and arrayed their persons in similar ones of crimson damask, ordering the satin dresses to be cut up and distributed among the servants.

(1)   In Sir Henry Yule's *The Book of Ser Marco Polo*, edited by Cordier in 1903, is a representation of the arrival of the voyagers at the house, the doors of which are closed against them. It is as destitute of authority and value, I apprehend, as the German likeness just referred to, which Cordier unfortunately again reproduces. It probably resembled the Venetian as closely as that at Canton.

Then Marco Polo, his father and his uncle joined their friends and kinsfolk in the repast, and when they had partaken of some of the dishes, they rose once more, cast off the damask, and had others of crimson velvet brought which they donned in the presence of all, the servants, as before, receiving the damask as a perquisite. The same lot, at the conclusion of the feast, befell the velvet suits, and finally the Poli appeared in woollen like the rest. (1)

(1) This incident reminds us a little of the concluding story in the *Thousand and One Nights*, in which the two heroines change their attire several times (*Lady Burton's Edition of Her Husband's Arabian Nights Translated Literally From the Arabic by Sir Richard Francis Burton*, Volume VI page 201). The period approximately suits the supposed composition of the *Nights*; it is a pure orientalism; but, as Sir Harry Johnston mentions in his *Nile Quest*, the early Venetian explorers and merchants habitually, from motives of security, adopted the costume of the regions which they visited.

This series of incidents naturally created much surprise, and Marco, as the youngest, having ordered all the servants to quit the hall, and the mantles being removed, fetched from one of the apartments the coarse clothes in which they had returned home. Taking a knife, he unripped the linings and pockets, and laid out before the astonished visitors all the precious stones which he had sewn up in this ingenious manner, because it would have been dangerous and difficult to carry so much gold. When those present beheld this extraordinary treasure, they marvelled exceedingly, and no longer doubted that the strangers were indeed what they professed to be.

The news spread, and crowds flocked to the Casa Polo to embrace the long-lost travellers, to see the wonders which they had brought with them, and to hear from their own lips of the strange regions which they had visited, and the fabulous wealth of the Great Khan. It was Marco's fashion of reckoning by millions the riches of the princes whom he had seen, that won for him the name Messer "Marco Milioni," and two centuries and a half later when Ramusio wrote, the Casa Polo or Corte Sabbionera (of which Sir Henry Yule gives an illustration) was still popularly called La Corte dei Milioni. Of the residence of Polo only the archway survives, the remainder having been destroyed by fire. It is not known where he was buried, except that it may be conjectured that it was at San Lorenzo, among his ancestors and immediate descendants.

Under the administration of seven Doges and contemporary with Polo, a gentleman of ducal and tribunitial family dwelt at Venice in the Street of San Severo Confessore, who was ennobled by his contributions to literature and science as well as by his extraction. His name was Marino

Sanudo Torsello. He was one of the four sons of Marco Sanudo Torsello
by his wife Maria; (1) his brothers were Filippo, Tommaso, and
Giovanni, and it seems that he was connected by the ties of
consanguinity with Nicolo, son of Guglielmo, son of Marco Sanudo, first
Duke of Andros (2) and nephew of Arrigo Dandolo.

(1)   SEPULTVRA D. MARCI SANUDO TORSELLO ET D.
          MARLAE VXOEIS EJVS ET HEREDVM DE CONFINIO S
          SEVERI. IN QVA REQVIESCIT JOANNES FERATE EORVM
          FILIVS. CVJVS ANIMA REQVIESCAT IN PACE. AMEN.
          ORATE PRO EO.

          The foregoing inscription is reported by Agostini, *Notizie degli
          Scrittori Viniziani*, Volume I page 441.

(2)   Sanudo di Torcello, *Epistolae* in Bongars, *Gesta Dei per
          Francos,* passim.

It is surmised that the Sanudi and the Torselli, who were more anciently
known as the Basaniti, (1) had intermarried, and that thence arose the
hereditary cognomen which was common to all the children of Marco.
The precise date of the birth of Marino has not been ascertained, but he
was probably the junior of Polo by some years; the event may be
assigned, without the chance of serious error, to 1260. From his youth an
ardent enthusiasm for the diminution of Turkish preponderance shared
with a thirst for geographical discovery his time and attention. The rank,
talents and affluent circumstances of the Venetian gradually procured for
him the acquaintance and esteem of many distinguished personages of
the age, and of more than one crowned head, and of his access to the
French court he unceasingly availed himself to urge the organization of a
fresh crusade against the Osmanlis. If his counsel had been followed, the
destiny of Europe might have been changed, and neither Nicopolis nor
Lepanto would have been fought.

(1)   Dandolo, *Chronica Venetorum*. Liber VII page 156.

In an undated memorial to the King of France (1) written in French and
assignable to 1321, Sanudo demonstrates that it will only cost His
Majesty or Christendom ten galleys, carrying 2500 men, 300 horse and
1000 infantry, to guard Armenia. (2) He recommends him to seek the
concurrence of the Pope and the friendship of the Venetians, and to
appoint some competent person Captain of the Host; if the King does

these things, he makes no doubt that other European powers will co-operate. (3)

(1)   *Sanudo Torsello, Ramembranze a la Royale Maieste faite humblement et devotement par Marin Sanud, dict Torzel, de Venise,* Bongars, *Gesta Dei per Francos,* Liber II page 5.

(2)   In another place he says: "If any one were to ask me, how many men,, I answer reverently, I, Marinus Sanutus, dictus Torsellus, that with 300 horse, 1000 foot, and 10 galleys, well armed, not only Armenia, but Romania itself could be protected." Bongars, *Gesta Dei per Francos,* Liber II page 7.

(3)   "*Et si vostre haulte Seigneurie faict ceste chose, je ne doubte pas, avec layde de Dieu, que le Roy Robert, le Roy Frederic de Secille, et l'Empereur de Constantinople, seront obeissants a vous en toutes choses, qui seront razonnables.*"

Like the majority of Venetians, Sanudo was a citizen of the world. The greater part of his active and useful life was spent in foreign countries. His travels, which were chiefly prosecuted between 1300 and 1320, extended over the whole coast of the Mediterranean, Egypt, the Holy Land, Armenia and Arabia Felix. In one passage, which it must be premised is not free from the suspicion of being an interpolation, (1) he speaks of the smaller islands lying about England, Scotland and Ireland, "the names of which are unknown to me," and it is clear at least that he is not to be understood to have visited personally the northern latitudes, but simply to be quoting some other traveller, who may have forestalled even the Normans (2) in their discovery of Iceland, Greenland and Newfoundland.

(1)   Sanudo di Torcello, *Liber Secretorum Fidelium Crucis,* page 287.

(2)   Rafn, *Découverte de l'Amérique par les Normands, Rapports des Normands avec l'Orient.*

In March 1306-1307, we find Sanudo at home, in the Street of San Severo in Rialto; he had returned from some of his oriental voyages, and, in that year and month, (1) he began to commit to writing the fruits of his labour and experience. The first book only of the work so celebrated as *The Secrets of the Faithful of the Cross* was finished at that time and place.

(1)   *"Anno a nativitate D.N.J.C. 1306, mense Martii, inceptum est
       hoc opus, quod per Dei gratiam Marinus Sanudo aliter dictus
       Torsellus, filius D. Marci Sanudo,"* et cetera. Sanudo di Torcello,
       Liber Secretorum Fidelium Crucis, page 21.

In this division (1) which comprises five parts, he exhibits the method by
which, in his opinion, it was possible to compass the destruction of the
infidels; in fact, it is nothing more than the memorial subsequently sent
to Paris in a more elaborate form. The second book of the *Secrets,*
composed at Chiarenza in 1312 and 1313, (2) enters into statistical and
arithmetical detail touching the recovery of Palestine; his estimates for
manning and victualling fleets and armies are curious but rather prolix,
and he lays peculiar stress on the preparatory conquest of Armenia.

(1)   *"Incipit Liber Primus Operis Terrae Sanctae, continens
       dispositionem ac praeparationem ad Terram Sanctam
       recuperandam."*
(2)   Sanudo di Torcello, *Liber Secretorum Fidelium Crucis,* Page 34.
       34. "I began to write it in the month of December 1312 at
       Chiarenza."

Of the third and concluding section, which is devoted to a speculation on
the means of preserving the Holy Places when they should have been
won back, (1) and is partly occupied by genealogical trees of Noah and
other not less extraneous topics, the chronology is obscure; but it was
certainly posterior to 1324, and as certainly antecedent to 1326 when, in
a letter to the Duke of Lorraine, (2) he expressly says:

> "Your Highness must be aware that from my infancy I have
> (neglecting all other business) devoted myself to the
> advancement of the glory of Christ, to the service of the Faithful,
> and to the extinction of the Pagans; and in order that my labours
> might be made known to Kings and Princes, and might not pass
> into oblivion, I have digested into one volume the work of which
> the title is *Secrets of the Faithful of the Cross,* being not only for
> the preservation of the Faithful, but for the conversion or
> annihilation of the Misbelievers, and for the safe holding of the
> Holy Land and many other countries. (3)

> "That book I have presented to our Lord the Pontiff, to the Kings
> of France, England and Sicily, to the Cardinals and many other
> Prelates, to the Count of Hanover, and to several of the French

Counts (including the Comte de Clermont); and seeing that your progenitors, in whose happy footsteps you are beginning to tread, strenuously bestirred themselves in the affairs of the Holy Land ... I send you with these presents the Prologue, Rubrics and Chapters of the aforesaid book, and some other matters. I am ready to transmit to you the whole work, with the maps of the world, should you express a desire to possess it."

(1) *"Incipit Liber Tertius ejusdem Operis, continens infallibilem et veram doctrinam conservandi ac tenendi ac possidendi Sanctam Terram Promissionis."*

(2) Sanudo di Torcello, *Epistolae,* Letter Number 14 in Bongars, *Gesta Dei per Francos,* Liber II page 303.

(3) *"Et tenendam Terram Sanctam et alias multas terras."* Sanudo di Torcello, *Epistolae,* Letter Number 14 in Bongars, *Gesta Dei per Francos,* Liber II page 303.

Of such a performance, exhibiting his skill at once as an hydrographer and geographer, the author had just cause to be proud. It was welcomed with applause, and by competent judges it was warmly approved. Sanudo must be allowed to speak once more for himself: (1)

"On the 24th of September 1321, I, Marino Sanudo, called Torsello, of Venice, had an audience of the Pope, to whose Holiness I presented two books on the recovery and preservation of the Holy Land, one of which was bound in red, and the other in yellow. I presented to the same four maps, the first being of the Mediterranean, the second of the Sea and the terra firma, the third of the Holy Land, and the fourth of Egypt.

"The Father benignly accepted all these things; and he ordered some of the Prologue, some of the Rubrics, and other portions besides, to be read in my presence. From time to time he put questions to me, which I answered. At length he said, 'I wish to have these books examined'; to which I replied, that I should be very happy, provided that the persons were trustworthy.' 'Have no doubt of that,' he rejoined. Then he sent for the undermentioned Frati; Fra Boentio di Asti, of the Order of Preachers, Vicar of Armenia; Fra Jacopo de Camerino, a Minorite, who wears a beard, and who had come to the See on behalf of his brethren in Persia; Fra Matteo of Cyprus, and Fra Paolino of Venice; (2) and he gave them the volume bound in yellow, and desired them to look into it, and to report to him their opinion.

"The said Frati hereupon withdrew into the house of Fra Paolino, and diligently and faithfully investigated the Book; and they were unanimous in its favour. On the thirtieth day after the commencement of the examination — it was on a Saturday evening — he (the Pope), who was most affable to me, inquired of the Frati repeatedly, when we were together, whether they were of accord; and they assured him that they were. Other remarks were made on both sides. At last the Pope observed; 'The hour is late; you will be so good as to leave the report in writing with me, and I will inspect it, and afterward send for you.' And so," concludes Sanudo, "the book and the report remained in his possession."

(1)   Sanudo di Torcello, *Liber Secretorum Fidelium Crucis,* page 1 et seqq.
(2)   This was perhaps the same who wrote the (anonymous) *Treatise De Recto Regimine*, dedicated to the Duke of Candia in 1313 or the following year, and who owned glass works in Rialto as late as 1321.

The letters of this benevolent and enlightened Venetian, of which all that are known, being two and twenty, were printed as a supplement to the *Secreta* in 1611, (1) abound with interesting matter, and occasionally contain curious scraps of gossip. They purport to have been written at Venice, and range in date from December 1324 to October 1329. It is obvious that they represent only a fragment of his correspondence.

(1)   Sanudo di Torcello, *Liber Secretorum Fidelium Crucis,* page 289-316.

i.   to the Pope John XXII., December. 1324.
ii.   to the Cardinals.
iii.   to the Archbishop of Capua, Chancellor of Sicily.
iv.   to the Bishop of Nismes.
v.   *ad diversos.*
vi.   to Leo, King of Armenia.
vii.   to And. Palaeologos, Emperor of Constantinople.
viii. to the Bishop of Caiaphas.
ix.   to And. Palaeologos, Emperor of Constantinople.

x.   to Stefanos Simpolos, Turcoman of the same.
xi.   to the Archbishop of Capua.
xii.   to And. Palaeologos.
xiii.   to Stefanos Simpolos.
xiv.   to the Duke of Lorraine.
xv.   to the Archbishop of Ravenna.
xvi.   *ad diversos.*
xvii.   to the Cardinal Legate.
xviii. to the Archbishop of Capua.
xix.   to the Cardinal Legate.
x.   to the Archbishop of Capua and another,
xxi.   to Pietro de la Via, the Pope's nephew.
xxii.   *ad anonimum.*

There is no more remarkable fact connected with the life of the author of the *Secreta*, than the circumstance that he does not seem either to have been personally known to Marco Polo who was living in a street adjoining San Severo after 1301, or to have inspected any of the numerous transcripts of the *Voyages* in Tartary, China and Tibet which appear to have been circulating in Europe prior to 1300, but such absence of contact does not seem to have been very unusual, strange as it may impress us to-day; although, for example, Petrarch and Boccaccio lived side by side, as it were, and were even together at Venice at least once as fellow visitors, it was not till the year prior to his death, that the former saw a manuscript of the *Decameron*.

Where, in his own narrative, he has occasion to treat more or less at large of the latitudes visited by Polo, Sanudo, overlooking the more recent authority, falls back on preceding and probably far less accurate observers; nor is Polo among those who are mentioned as recipients of presentation copies of the *Secreta*. (1)

(1)   Pier Angelo Zeno, in his *Memorie de' Scrittori Veneti Patrizi Ecclesiastici e Secolari,* attributes to Torsello, besides his *Secreta* and a *Book of Letters*, a *History of the Morea*.

It is as curious as it is perhaps regrettable that our early European travellers and geographers worked independently, and left to a distant posterity the sometimes difficult task of collating and reconciling their accounts. The impediments to intercourse might often be the source of this phenomenon, and men who wandered thousands of miles from their homes in quest of knowledge grudged the labour of comparing notes with cooperators, residing, not in a neighbouring country, but in a neighbouring street of the same city. The general apathy in respect of such matters down to the nineteenth century is too clearly established by the long want of any complete and authentic Italian version of Polo, and the burial of the excessively important and fascinating narrative of his fellow countryman and contemporary in an illegible Latin folio.

But, just at the precise point of time when Sanudo was compiling and illustrating with charts his *Secreta Fidelium Crucis*, a Frenchman, named Pierre Dubois, of whom the Venetian knew far less even than of Polo, was at work on his treatise *De Recuperatione Terrae Sanctae*. The chronological data are so singularly correspondent, that it becomes a natural question, which borrowed from the other. Dubois does not profess to have been a traveller; Sanudo commits to paper the fruit of his own experiences, and a copy of his narrative, perhaps more than one, was sent to France. The views and recommendations of both are, to a main extent, identical; it is in the sources from which the material was obtained that the vital difference seems to lie.

There is the farther point that, if Dubois was not immediately and almost exclusively indebted to his Venetian contemporary, we scarcely know whence he derived his information. There were certainly earlier travellers over the same ground, but their narratives would not have served the purpose. It is fairly clear that Sanudo multiplied copies of his manuscript for distribution in promising quarters, and Philippe le Bel of France, with whom Dubois was in more or less frequent communication down to 1308, was one of the earliest recipients. (1)

(1)   Other charts, portolani, et cetera, have come down to us. In 1875-1581 Ongania of Venice published five, dated between 1318 and 1554, of which two, those of Visconte of Genoa, 1318, and Laurenziano-Gaddiano, 1351, belong to the fourteenth century and fall within the Sanudo period.

A career, not very dissimilar in its earlier stages from that of Marco Polo, was that of a later explorer on a more contracted scale, Fra Francesco Suriano, who was born at Venice in 1450, and accompanied his father in his first Mediterranean voyage as a boy of twelve. Between 1462 and 1475, he pursued his vocation as a merchant in conjunction with his father, but, on the attainment of his twenty-fifth year, he relinquished commerce, and took holy orders in which he attained considerable distinction.

But in two instances his old maritime experiences proved signally valuable, for in 1484, on his return home from the Holy Land, the ship was twice overtaken by storms, and was saved only by Suriano who, to the astonishment of all on board, tucked up his sleeves, assumed the command, and brought them safely to port. After his return to Italy, he wrote, at the request of his sister, an account of his travels which passed through many editions. He led a busy and useful life, and attained an advanced age, but we lose sight of him after 1529.

The fortunes of Nicolo and Antonio Zeno, brothers of the greater Carlo, were remarkable. After the War of Chioggia, the former equipped a vessel and embarked on a voyage of discovery round the French and English coasts. But, having been overtaken by a tempest, he was thrown upon one of the Shetland Isles, where he was hospitably received by Henry Sinclair, Earl of Orkney and the Faroe Islands, and Admiral of Scotland under Robert III. (1390-1406). (1) Sinclair invited his guest to remain with him, and the Venetian was subsequently joined by his brother.

(1)   There is no adequate ground for questioning that Zeno actually visited the Orkneys and was received by Sinclair, and a Venetian, if he did not commit to writing at the time a name strange to him, may have carried away in his memory a distorted form of it.

Antonio, however, did not long outlive his arrival in Shetland. After his death, Nicolo remained in the service of the Earl, and, treading in the footsteps of the Norman pioneers, he (as we are asked to believe) extended his explorations westward so far as Newfoundland. Zeno is said to have seen Iceland and Greenland, and to have touched the eastern point of Labrador. According to the account printed in 1558, it was in the winter season that he reached Newfoundland (Terra Nuova), and he had proposed to pursue his travels in the spring, but his crew mutinied, and he was obliged to abandon his plan.

A chart of the route which Nicolo Zeno took was prepared by the two brothers, in all likelihood before their departure, and, so recently as the sixteenth century at least, this relic was in existence. In 1558, it was published by Caterino Zeno as an appendix to his own *Travels in Persia*, and bears the date 1380. Nearly a century after the era of the Zeni, the Venetian seaman, Cadamosto, who enlisted himself in the service of

Prince Henry of Portugal, laid claim to the discovery of the Cape Verde group of islands. This was in 1458, about two years before Prince Henry's death.

The tendency of modern geographical research, however, has been to throw discredit on the posthumous narrative of the achievements of the Zeni, so far as a title to the distinction of having ascertained the existence of land in the direction of the North American continent is concerned. (1) The details purport to have been derived from family papers, and, seeing the uncertainty of much that is even yet advanced on this subject, it may be premature and unjust to characterize and dismiss as fabrications the particulars first published so long after the events. On the contrary, considering that the explorers started from Shetland under the auspices of Sinclair, who figures in the sixteenth century text as Prince Zimchni, that they belonged to a particularly adventurous family, and that the volume was brought out presumably under the eye of a descendant, himself a distinguished traveller, it is quite probable that they may have approached the region in question.

(1)   Beazley, *John and Sebastian Cabot,* page 23.

The real fact seems to be, that the merit of the Portuguese and Spaniards has been equally misunderstood and overstated. Although the existence of a new continent was not actually ascertained, or the scanty anterior knowledge had been lost, the tradition as to the acquaintance of navigators with such a thing, centuries before Columbus, could hardly have perished, and whatever honour is due to the Zeni is probably due to them, merely in the same kind of suggestive and contributory measure.

With the careers and fortunes of John and Sebastian Cabot, Venice has no more than an indirect concern. The former had settled at Chioggia at least as early as 1461, and, on the 29th of March, 1476, the Senate conferred on him by decree, possibly for the second time, the privilege of citizenship for fifteen years (as usual) at home and abroad (*de intra et extra*) (1) But the elder Cabot, to whom it now seems that we should ascribe the chief part of the honour due to the geographical services of father and son, was a Genoese by birth, while Sebastian is generally thought to have been a native of Bristol, where his father is indeed found residing in 1499.

(1)   (compilation) *Calendar of State Papers Relating to English Affairs in the Archives of Venice,* Volume I page 136. A facsimile of the original entry is given.

The older Cabot had been commissioned by Henry VII. in 1497 to proceed on a voyage of discovery, and after three months' absence he returned with an account of his experiences. Henry VII. promised to furnish him with the means of equipping another expedition, and made him a present of money, with which his wife and himself created a great sensation; he dressed in silk, and, says Sanudo the diarist, "these English run after him like mad people, so that he can enlist as many of them as he pleases and a number of our own rogues besides. The discoverer of these places planted on his new found land a large cross with one flag of England and another of Saint Mark, by reason of his being a Venetian, so that our banner has floated very far afield." (1)

(1)   (compilation) *Calendar of State Papers Relating to English Affairs in the Archives of Venice,* Volume I page 262.

Except, therefore, the political interest and importance attached to the explorations of the Cabots, they hardly enter into the category of Venetian heroes and benefactors, beyond the initial fact that the father was a naturalized subject of the Signory when he first comes under notice; indeed, from a Venetian standpoint, he was immediately instrumental in one of the discoveries which dealt a fatal blow to the commercial welfare and national vitality of the land of his adoption.

It is almost impossible to avoid the conclusion that the Republic was imperfectly sensible of the vast and permanent bearings of the labours of such men as the elder Cabot and Columbus, or, at a point of time when money was far more abundant at Venice than in London, Madrid or Lisbon, a monopoly of both at any cost would, as is natural to suppose from the habitual generosity and foresight of the government, have been secured. Yet, so late as 1521, when Henry VIII. and Cardinal Wolsey applied to the Corporation of London for the means of sending out Sebastian Cabot to America, the proposition was rejected on the ground that the authorities considered Cabot to be a pretender. A protracted correspondence and inquiry indeed took place, and the representatives of the Signory were most assiduous in reporting all that came within their knowledge and hearing. (1)

(1)   (compilation) *Calendar of State Papers Relating to English Affairs in the Archives of Venice,* Volume III page 276.

In September, 1522, a very elaborate dispatch from Gasparo Contarini, the ambassador in Spain, contained intelligence derived from letters received from the Indies, and more was promised when the master of the expedition arrived, but Magellan was murdered in the Philippines. It was in the same month that a Ragusan introduced himself to the Council of Ten on behalf of one Sebastian Cabot who was residing at Seville, and who had been employed by Charles V. as his pilot-major for voyages of discovery. The Ten at once instructed their ambassador in Spain to ascertain all that he could, and intimated a readiness to see Cabot, although they did not entertain great hope of any useful result.

In this case, the Venetians permitted themselves to be no more than parties when they should have been principals, and when it was too late to repair the capital error — down to 1551 or thereabout — the matter was yet under discussion. Venice ought to have been foremost in planting stations and depots; not have wasted precious years in writing letters and considering reports.

The efforts of Charles V. of Spain in 1553 to regain the services of the younger Cabot were a tribute to his geographical and nautical value. But there were, of course, serious difficulties and complications, arising from the fact that other foremost powers began more correctly to appreciate the advantages of trade, and that the opportunity supplied by geographical enterprise of carrying it on with facilities had so vastly increased. For, in the last-mentioned year, England sent out, through the Muscovite Company, an expedition of discovery and conquest under Chancellor and Willoughby, and, in 1555, the government of Edward VI. granted a charter of incorporation to that body under the control of the younger Cabot. Perhaps it was during this voyage that he executed or ordered the set of maps, mentioned by Sir Humphrey Gilbert as to be seen in 1576 in the Queen's Majesty's privy gallery at Whitehall.

Contarini, one of the most capable of Venetian diplomatists, who afterward performed excellent service in the difficult negotiations with Charles V. and other princes during the troubles succeeding the battle of Pavia in 1525, writing home from Valladolid on the 31st of December, 1522, reported progress and furnished particulars of a conversation which had just then taken place between himself and Sebastian Cabot. The latter professed every sort of devotion to the Republic, and mentioned that he had already told the ambassadors of the most serene Signory in England how anxious he was, for the love which he bore to the country of his birth (Venice), to do what he could for it in regard to the newly-discovered lands.

His interviewer had some gentlemen to dine with him, and brought the meeting to a close for the moment, letting Cabot understand that he was in possession of all the facts of the case so far as it had gone. They met again on the same night, and remained closeted together for some time, the navigator supplying Contarini with an outline of his life and career, including his experiences in England, and his conferences, about three years before (he thought), with Wolsey, whose offer of employment, he said, he had declined because he was in the Spanish service.

He spoke of a talk which he had had there with Franceso Sebastiano Colonna who said to him: "Messer Sebastiano, you are doing great things to benefit other countries; do you not remember your own? Would it not be possible that it might derive some good from you?" Cabot, according to Contarini, was equally communicative and, so far as words went, patriotic; but nothing came of it, although Cabot declared his readiness to proceed to Venice, wait on the Signory, and, if they could not agree, come back, all at his own expense.

Contarini advised his government on the 7th of March, 1523, that he had seen Cabot several times, and that he expected to be able to go in three months to Venice to lay his services at the feet of the Signory; but nothing farther is heard of him, till he is reported the commander of a fleet of twenty-eight sail which was to have left Seville in October, 1525, but did not actually do so till April, 1526. It is manifest enough that, when Contarini saw him, he had already been bought by Spain. He merely signified to the envoy that he had recently devised some new method of ascertaining by the compass the distance between two points from east to west. (1)

(1)   See Molmenti, *La Storia di Venezia nella Vita Privata,* Liber II page 232, for a portrait of Sebastian Cabot, derived from Samuel Seyer's *Memoirs Historical and Topographical of Bristol and It's Neighbourhood: From the Earliest Period Down to the Present Time,* the original, attributed to Holbein, having perished in a fire in 1845.

The Venetians both at home and in London had watched with interest and solicitude the progress of geographical enterprise under John Cabot and his son, on whom they might not unreasonably look as pursuing a course unbecoming naturalized subjects of the Republic, however much they might be gratified by the indirect honour to their country.

The small folio volume in which the planisphere of Andrea Bianco (1436) is preserved belongs to the Marciana. It contains eight other drawings which merit a passing notice. There were originally, in all probability, as many as thirteen charts in the collection, but the first, second and fifth have disappeared, and the last is nothing more than an illustration of the *Geography* of Ptolemy. (1)

(1)   Formaleoni, *Saggio Nautica Antica de' Veneziani;* Zurla, *Di Marco Polo e degli Altri Viaggiatori Veneziani Più Illustri Dissertazioni del P. Ab. D. Placido Zurla.*

The first chart in the present order, or Number 3, consists merely of a series of mathematical designs, demonstrating the laws of the winds and the phenomena of the tides, with a catalogue of instructions to navigators, and a table for measuring distances at sea.

Number 4 represents with striking precision and accuracy the Euxine, the Crimea, the Sea of Azof and the adjacent parts. Number 6 is devoted to the eastern section of the Mediterranean, and includes the Archipelago. In Number 7 and Number 8 the remaining sections of that sea are given. Number 9 exhibits the shores of France and Germany, and comprehends the Scotish and Irish littorals. In Number 10 we see the Baltic, the Gulf of Bothnia, Norway, Iceland, Friesland and (under the name Stockfish conjecturally) Newfoundland. Number 11 is simply the reproduction of some of its predecessors in miniature; and lastly, at Number 12 we find the planisphere of Bianco, (1) which is presumably indebted to anterior sketches now lost. In the Ambrosian Library at Milan is the later planisphere executed by Bianco in 1448. (2) It has been suggested that all these productions are founded on anterior prototypes no longer known.

(1)   Formaleoni, *Saggio Nautica Antica de' Veneziani.*
(2)   The planispheres of 1436-1448 have been reproduced in facsimile at Venice, 1871-1881, obl. quarto, and are inserted on a smaller scale in the (compilation) *Calendar of State Papers Relating to English Affairs in the Archives of Venice,* Volume I.

Considerable interest seems to have been taken in England in the progress of maritime discovery, and the privy purse expenses of Henry VII., 1491-1505, contain numerous entries of sums paid to persons concerned in the settlement of Newfoundland.

It may be worth noting that, in the fire at the Palace in 1479, a *mappa mundi* executed by an ecclesiastic perished, and that, in 1509, there was, for the use of the government and councils, a map of Italy (doubtless on a largo scale) painted on one of the walls of the Senate House.

From the sixteenth century onward, dated the series of collections of maps and plans in book form for general information and guidance. The oldest which we have seen is a volume, apparently issued in separate sheets, some of which bear the date 1571, and comprising nearly ninety charts and views of countries, districts and fortified positions, almost exclusively in the Venetian territories, but including Africa on the one hand and England, Scotland and Ireland on the other. America does not occur. (1)

(1)   Camocio, *Isole Famose Porti, Fortezze, e Terre Maritime Sottoposte alla Ser. Ma Sig. Ria di Venetia.*

The first systematic attempt by a Venetian to execute a complete geography was made by Livio Sanudo or Sanuto, a name honourably associated with learned and scientific researches since the fourteenth century. He not only failed to complete his scheme, but did not live to publish that portion (Africa) which he had succeeded in finishing, and for which he himself designed twelve maps or charts. After his death, the work was published at Venice in 1588 (1) under the editorship of Damiano Zenaro, with the maps engraved by the author's brother Giulio, and an engraved title by Giacomo Franco. Such a production must have been received with a warm and admiring welcome, as something novel and distinct from all the contributions to geographical knowledge so far available for study and reference, and one is bound to judge it to-day, independently of its technical value, as a monument of the industry, taste and accomplishments of a noble and ancient Venetian family.

(1)   Sanutus, *Geografia di M. Livio Sanuto Distinta in XII. Libri. Ne' quali, oltra l' esplicatone di molti luoghi di Tolemeo, e dalla Bussola, e dell' Aguglia, si dichiarano le prouincie, popoli, regni, città, porti, monti, fiumi, laghi, e costumi dell' Africa: con*

XII tanole di essa Africa in dissegno di rame: aggiuntini di pin tre indici da M. Giovan Carlo Saraceni.

Nor was the desire for geographical exploration restricted to the aristocracy, for we find a Venetian jeweller, Gaspare Balbi, who had doubtless proceeded to the East Indies on some business connected with his calling, and who seems to have been absent from home eight or nine years, signalizing his return by the publication of a narrative of his travels between 1579 and 1588. (1)

(1)   Gaspare Balbi, In a small octavo volume published in 1590: *Viaggio dell' Indie Orientali.*

No school of navigation appears to have been in existence, at least under official patronage and supervision, until 1683. At that time captains of vessels were recommended not to accept as able seamen any who had not undergone an apprenticeship or training; but it was thought a good plan to draft on board, in subordinate capacities at half-pay, any strong young fellows who had no employment at home, and were an incumbrance on their relatives or their parish.

It is indisputable that the Mediaeval Venetians were conversant with the polarity of the needle, and it is even probable that they were aware of its liability to declination. In a monograph on *Antient Marine* (1) the author justly ridicules and ably confutes the superficial prejudice respecting the insignificance of the old Venetian Navy, and claims for his countrymen, with some reason, not only the honour of having been the first to apply trigonometry to nautical science, but of having developed the theory of tangents and the decimal division of the radius. Sanudo the Elder confidently speaks of the compass as in use in his day, and it thought to have been introduced from the east about that time by Flavio Gioia of Amalfi, although Marco Polo might well have seen it in use among the Chinese. Sebastian Cabot claimed it as an original discovery, but Columbus, not many years before, is believed to have been aware of it.

(1)   Formaleoni, *Saggio Nautica Antica de' Veneziani;* Nicolas (*History of the Royal Navy,* Volume I) cites passages from two poems of the beginning of the fourteenth century, in which the loadstone is mentioned.

Prior to the invention of such an instrument, birds were frequently employed as guides by their flight to the direction of the nearest land, as we perceive in the Noah myth, but this method has been improved down to modern times.

It is an ascertained fact that the Venetians, in and before the thirteenth century, employed a chart of navigation, and were acquainted with a fixed system (*martelojo*) of sailing tactics. It seems to be one of those points which are self-evident, that a people who visited Egypt, the Euxine and even the Sea of Azof, so far back as the ninth century, could not have remained ignorant, till the twelfth or thirteenth, of the properties of the magnet, which seems to be specified by Alexander Nickam in his *Treatise De Utensilibus* in the twelfth century, and by more than one writer in the thirteenth. (1) But naturally the apparatus was, at the outset, in its form as a compass, rudimentary and imperfect; mariners were long obliged to content themselves with the most primitive appliances, and by night the steersman largely relied on astronomical observation. The variations of the compass have not, even yet, been exhaustively ascertained, for almost obvious reasons.

(1)   Wright, *A Volume of Vocabularies,* page xvii-xviii.

So late as 1603, a gentleman of Languedoc, Guillaume de Nautonnier, published at Venice and Toulouse, for the use of seamen, astrologers, geographers and others, a large and elaborate work, entitled *The Mecography of the Loadstone*, with tables of longitudes, French and English editions being separately printed for the convenience of buyers. But such English as occurs savours of a north British parentage, as though this part of the business had been intrusted to one of the numerous Scots who frequented Venice in those days.

The mechanical sciences were directed principally to hydraulic purposes, to the manufacture of clocks, and to the development of the powers of the lever, and the Republic, notoriously liberal toward those who had it in their power to serve her in some important direction, naturally enjoyed the refusal of many valuable improvements in naval and military science. Even Leonardo da Vinci, better known to us to-day as a painter than as a mechanical engineer, tendered his services, and had some of his experiments tried at Venice, and it is far from improbable that he was concerned in the introduction of the floating batteries employed by the Republic on the Po about 1480. (1) Of those who submitted plans for the Rialto Bridge about 1525, long before the work was carried out, Michael Angelo was one.

(1)   Compare Fournier, *Le Vieux-Neuf: Histoire Ancienne des Inventions et Decouvertes Modernes,* Volume I page 301-302.

The knowledge of the lever was introduced by the Lombard Barattiero, who, from 1173 to 1178, superintended various works of drainage and architectural improvement at Venice, and who, at his own suggestion, performed the feat of raising, on the Piazza of Saint Mark, the two monoliths subsequently known as the notorious Red Columns. There can be no hesitation in concluding that the Venetians themselves soon successfully exerted their imitative talents in emulating the ingenuity of the stranger, nor is it easy to believe that so great a commercial people remained long in ignorance of the use of cranes. In connexion with the internal improvements under the Doge Soranzo (1312-1328), we have referred to the erection of windmills in various parts of the city and its environs.

The studies introductory to a military career as well as to a naval one formed a branch of the education offered and obtained at Padua. For centuries the distinguished men who fought under the Venetian flag in all divisions of the service by land and sea were, as a rule, pupils of this famous seminary, and foreigners availed themselves of its superior advantages. Sir John Reresby tells us that he learned the art of fortification here under a Venetian instructor from November, 1657, to the following spring, and that his master presented him, perhaps as a parting gift, with a manuscript treatise on the subject embellished with original drawings.

What Coryat the traveller terms the "manuary" arts are probably to be referred to the present section. He notes that he saw in a painter's shop in 1608 an absolutely perfect facsimile of a hind quarter of veal and a picture of a gentlewoman, an automaton whose eyes moved up and down.

The science of medicine, though confined to a limited class, was diligently prosecuted. It was almost an occult science; its professors occupied a high social position, and enjoyed many rare privileges; they were lightly taxed; they carried themselves like lords; they were permitted to dress themselves as they pleased, (1) and to wear as many rings on their fingers as suited their taste. They were at liberty to order of their tailor pantaloons of Alexandrian velvet, to use white silk stockings and shoes of morocco leather with gold buckles and jewelled points, to trim their coat-sleeves with Valenciennes lace and cover the garment itself with rich brocade, and to buy hat and gloves in keeping.

(1)   *Legge sul Lusso*, May 21, 1360, *Avogaria di Comune*; Romanin, *Storia Documentata di Venezia*, Volume III page 6.

If the individual was skilful, he was handsomely remunerated; if he proved himself a quack, he was not allowed to practise. No sumptuary law touched the doctor; no luxuries were denied to him. The best March wine and the maraschino of Zara were to be seen at his table; there was no dainty which he could not command; he was in a position to eat his dinner with a double-pronged fork.

The names have been preserved of the physicians who attended Paolo Sarpi, and the Doges Giovanni Bembo and Marco Foscarini. During a visitation of the plague in the sixteenth century, a preference was given to the local practitioners over those of Padua. At the same time the physician was required to comply with the official rules prescribed for his use and control, of which we possess a text compiled in 1258. (1)

(1)   Romanin, *Storia Documentata di Venezia*, Volume VII page 541.

The seventeenth century saw Venice in possession of such medical and sanitary appliances as hot and vapour baths, some apparently not dissimilar from the Turkish principle, and, what was equally important, of safeguards against the sale of spurious drugs, and the preparation of medicines by apothecaries uncertified by a physician.

The Republic, in 1324, retained in her pay twelve general practitioners and twelve surgeons, at a salary of twelve *lire grosse* each, or 120 ducats. In 1310, if not earlier, a free residence was assigned to these functionaries at the office of the Chamberlain of the Commune, and it was shortly after that a College of Physicians was instituted, and followed, in 1368, by an Academy of Medicine. At this important and learned society, monthly meetings were appointed at which all professional persons were invited to be present, and to lay on the table, or deliver orally, reports of all the remarkable cases which had come under their notice since the previous assembly.

The examination of medical students was confided to the new Academy, which seems wholly to have superseded the old Hall of Physicians established earlier in the century, and any foreigner who might be desirous of practising at Venice applied to it for his diploma.

At San Giacomo dall'Orio was a School of Anatomy; and at San Giovanni in Bragora, the College of the Liberal and Physical Sciences, upon which, in 1470, Pope Paul II., formerly Pietro Barbo, a Venetian and a native of the parish, conferred the privileges of a university. (1) In the provinces of the terra firma, and wherever the Venetians extended their beneficent and humanizing sway, institutions similar to these, and endowed for the most part with similar privileges, were founded in the fourteenth and fifteenth centuries. (2)

(1)   Romanin, *Storia Documentata di Venezia,* Volume IV page 500.
(2)   At Zara in 1409. See Romanin, *Storia Documentata di Venezia,* Volume IV page 500-501 note 5.

Provision for mental infirmities was probably made, in the first instance, in the ancient Hospitium for Incurables. The available records do not establish the existence, under the old Republic in its more flourishing days, of an institution dedicated to this specific object on its modern humane basis, but, in 1715, a lunatic asylum was founded at San Servolo by the Hospital Father of Saint John, and gradually acquired the reputation of a model house of the kind.

As comparatively late as 1611, Gasparo Despotini, a Venetian physician who had attracted the notice of Sir Henry Wotton, was sent by him and his chaplain William Bedwell to England, and attended James I. during a serious and alarming illness. He became a naturalized subject, and established a practice at Bury Saint Edmunds.

Of the philanthropic surgeon Gualtieri and his parent Physic Garden of 1334 mention has been made elsewhere. In 1499, or perhaps earlier, the *Fasciculo de Medicina*, a folio volume with a profusion of woodcuts, represented the knowledge and experience of the day on subjects connected, not only with medicine itself, but with such cognate subjects as anatomy, parturition, the diagnosis of the urine, phlebotomy and safeguards against the plague. There were editions in 1513 and 1522, all from the Venetian press. These theses went far to constitute the old-world cyclopaedia of medical and surgical experience and practice. Wine had probably been recommended and employed when a tonic was deemed judicious, at a date long anterior to any specific record; we find it mentioned in the last illness of Paolo Sarpi in 1622.

Side by side with the explorer, who treated geographical discovery as his principal, if not sole, aim, were the enthusiasts who travelled abroad in the interest of science, and we hear of those who visited distant regions in quest of ancient coins and inscriptions, to view the remains of Carthage, or to measure the Pyramids. (1)

(1)   Molmenti, *La Storia di Venezia nella Vita Privata,* Liber II page 233.

The trade of the apothecary comes to the surface in 1379, when Marco Cicogna, a member of that vocation, qualified himself for the Great Council by his patriotic sacrifices during the Chioggian crisis.

It was prescribed to physicians at an early period that, when an illness was deemed serious, the patient should be forewarned, in order that he might take testamentary and spiritual precautions. It is hardly necessary to mention that, here also, the universal belief in the diagnosis of the urine existed in full force, and, as early as 1483, we find an elaborate treatise issuing from the Paduan press, in which medical students or professors might acquire an exhaustive knowledge of the subject.

CHAPTER LX

System of Education — Private Tutors — Arithmetic — Book-Keeping — Mercantile Education — Hand-Writing — Latin Grammar — Female Education — The Venetian Dialect — Great Families — Origin of Their Names — Places Whence They Came — Their Palaces — Christian Names — University of Padua — Its Curriculum — Paduan Students — Galileo.

The system of education, which ascends to the Gothic era when from slight documentary references we augur the institution of schools and schoolmasters, consisted of three divisions; the seminary, the finishing school and the university. There were pedagogues to whom boys were sent when they had learned their alphabet and christ-cross-row at home, to acquire a knowledge of arithmetic, grammar, writing and psalmody, as well as, if the pupil was of a good family, an elementary acquaintance with the classics. Such was the master who taught little Carlo Zeno his first lessons in Latin and Greek, and who put into his hands the *Book of David the King*, which delighted the child so much. There were other masters, generally barristers or advocates of standing, who undertook to prepare the sons of the nobility for college, and who initiated them in the principles of law and jurisprudence, without which the education of no Venetian gentleman was deemed complete.

Such was that Riccardo Malhombra, who directed the studies of Petrarch's friend, the Doge Andrea Dandolo; but that very distinguished man also acquired a proficiency in French. In the following century, Giorgio Alessandrino and Benedetto Brognolo prepared students for the bar, and gave lectures, at the public expense, on forensic eloquence as well as on poetry. There was also the divinity tutor who lived in the house, and who, if a person of sensitive temper, was not apt to relish the treatment which he received from an inconsiderate employer who compelled him to take his meals in the kitchen, and to sleep on a common mattress in the servants' quarters.

Judging from a work printed at Venice in 1484, and perhaps the earliest of its kind (1) in Italy, posterior to the *Abaco* of 1478 which appeared at Treviso in the Venetian territories, it was part of the training, at all events in schools intended for the education of the mercantile classes, to qualify pupils to calculate the value of money, and to reduce higher denominations to lower, or *vice versa*. The science of book-keeping among the early Venetians was hampered by the complex character of the currency, and the acceptance of that of nearly every other country, either at par or at a discount. Toward the end of the sixteenth century, the Italians seem to have retained the leadership, and to have found disciples of their system in the Netherlands and in England. (2)

(1)   Borgi, *Qui Comenza la Nobel Opera de Arithmetica*, 1484; later impressions 1488, 1491, 1501. Piero Borgi may have been related to Luca Paciolo de Borgo, who in 1509 published at Brescia his *Divina Proportione*, in which some of the designs are ascribed to Leonardo da Vinci. His work comprises, in a Venetian edition of 1494, the principles and uses of algebra. See Filippo Calandri, *Trattato di Arithmetica*. The most ancient work on this science is probably the German *Ars Numerandi*.

(2)   Petri, *The Pathway to Knowledge*.

In the first quarter of the sixteenth century, Giovanni Antonio Tagliente or Taiente kept, under official patronage, an academy where reading, writing, arithmetic, book-keeping, and probably other branches of learning, including elementary groundwork, were taught and acquired; and he was assisted in some of his scholastic labours by a colleague or usher, Alvise de la Fontana, whom he terms *carissimo campagno*. Of his text-books we have seen four, which deal with calligraphy, spelling and accounts; they bear the dates 1524 and 1525, and the name Fontana occurs on the title-page of the manual of book-keeping.

The Primer (1) or Grammar is to some extent of the ordinary type, and ascends from the alphabet to words of two and more syllables, but it rather unusually comprehends models of letters and aids to the art of versification. This apparent incongruity arises from its professedly dual function of instructing, not only adults and children, but ladies; in fact, it is specifically introduced as a miscellany or composite work. The writing-book is on the same plan as those with which we are familiar; its importance is due to its apparent priority to any noticed by bibliographers.

(1)   Tagliente, *Libro Mistevole. Opera nuouamente stampata del M.D.xxiiii. in Venetia la quale insegna maistreuolente con nuouo modo & arte a legere a li gradi et piccoli & alle Donne ...* quarto. The works of Tagliente passed through several editions, and enjoyed a fairly long vogue. An impression of the Grammar (*Libro d'Abaco*), printed without date by Lucha Antonio di Uberte at Venice in octavo, is described as probably the third.

In the thin volume on the art of keeping accounts and ledgers, which Tagliente designates *Luminario di Arithmetica* and which was printed with the privilege of the government in 1525, there are incidental notices of names and customs intended as practical illustrations of the subject-matter, and supplying hints indirectly serviceable to the student of ancient manners and opinions.

In 1527, Giovanni Tagliente, probably in co-operation with a relative, perhaps a son, produced his monograph on mercantile education and practice, entitled; *Opera Nova che Insegna a Fare ogni Ragione di Mercantia*, which comprised arithmetic, geometry, money tables and other cognate matters serviceable to traders, and it passed through three or in more impressions. It introduces to us Hieronimo Tagliente as a part-compiler of the work, and was illustrated with woodcuts. Great obscurity hangs over the literary history of the two Taglienti, and the circumstances in which they worked, and all their publications, from their popular character, are of signal rarity.

Of the invaluable art of calligraphy, which so greatly affected the preparation and transmission of records of all kinds, the origin, so far as Venice is concerned, is uncertain. It was long confined to the priesthood who equally discharged the duties of scribes and notaries. Even in the fourteenth century, official documents were drawn up by these ecclesiastics, and certified, not by the signature of a ruler or other principal, but by his seal. The earliest writing-books were by Italian professors, but the series does not commence till about 1520. Toward the close of the eleventh century, the Doge Ordelafo Faliero Dodoni, who died in battle in 1117, subscribed a state paper, according to Zanetti, in a sort of rudimentary uncial hand of which he furnishes a facsimile; there are other numerous examples.

The successive styles of writing for official, diplomatic and ordinary purposes were the Gothic with uncials, the *minisculo antico*, the *minusculo regolare*, and the *corsivo* or running hand, but, of course, individuals fell into special mannerisms, and created numerous schools. The surviving specimens of the sixteenth century demonstrate that public men and persons of station, at all events, learned to acquire, not only a legible hand, but what the earlier English masters distinguished as the Italian style.

The diffusion of a knowledge of hand-writing among the laity raises an inquiry, at what epoch we are to fix the most ancient autograph manuscripts of literary works, and how many masterpieces of genius, produced during the Middle Ages and early Renaissance, are necessarily clerical copies, or, at best, manuscripts dictated by authors to professional scribes. Probably there never existed holograph texts of the works of such writers as Marco Polo, the so-called Sir John Mandeville, Dante, Petrarch or Boccaccio; and if some became competent to trace their names and even alter a sentence, it was a more difficult task to commit to paper or parchment a more or less lengthy narrative in prose or verse, in characters available for purposes of reference or of recitation.

The art of calligraphy was, as we see, part of the curriculum of the Tagliente establishment concurrently with grammar and arithmetic. But there were seminaries, as well as manuals, of instruction for such as desired to acquire a knowledge of special classes of hand-writing for commercial and legal purposes; and we meet with a bipartite work by Lodovico Vicentino, which he defines as an *Operina* for students of chancery letter or character and for initiation in the proper method of mending the quill pen. This appeared about 1523 at Venice, and was claimed as a new invention. It exhibited a series of ornamental alphabets by Eustachio Celebrino. This side or branch of the educational movement, while it was in advance, perhaps, of anything so far produced in France or England, rather tardily arrived to the succour of persons of business and culture, when it is considered that, at that date, the Republic at least had more than attained her highest point of prosperity and grandeur, and that all that she was and all that she owned, had been won and held, mainly by men restricted and accustomed to the most rudimentary principles of learning and the most archaic machinery for transacting business, either from a political or mercantile point of view. Their training had been in large if not exclusive measure monastic.

Contemporary with Tagliente were, of course, many other teachers, and the first half of the sixteenth century shews a large survival or continuance of activity in the system of general education, more especially in those branches which dealt with the requirements of commercial and maritime life. In 1565, Francesco Tomaso da Salo published, in a small octavo volume, his *Art of Writing*, with the engraved text inclosed within ornamental borders, and with examples of artistically designed initials. (1)

(1)   Two pages are given in facsimile by Molmenti (*La Storia di Venezia nella Vita Privata*, Liber II page 273).

These manuals and primers are occasionally illustrated in a style quite superior to anything attempted at the same date in western Europe, nor did the series limit itself to objects associated with trade and navigation. We meet with the *Casselina*, or word-book for the Holy Scriptures, and, again, with a treatise on grammatical rules, containing examples taken from Dante and Boccaccio. Even the more purely technical compilations are found to possess an indirect value and curiosity, where they enter, as several do, into tariffs, prices of common necessaries, and details of the Italian domestic costume of the time.

The first principles of instruction in elementary schools were evidently the precursors and models of those which were followed and recognized in England and France during the earlier half of the sixteenth century, and which strike us as so unfavourable to the speedy or satisfactory acquisition of the groundwork of learning. In common with the numerous primers published in London, they inspire us with wonder how pupils of average capacity learned what was set before them.

One at least of the earliest text-books for the use of the Venetian youth was the *Latin Grammar* of Francesco Nigro, a priest, which was repeatedly printed, and of which a revised edition, from the press of Jean Petit of Paris, 1507, lies before us. Nigro was admittedly the source of more or less of the material employed by Robert Whittinton the English grammarian, and there is slight doubt that the latter founded his labours on those of the Venetian, which had appeared and become famous long before his day — as far back, in fact, as 1480.

A second work of this class issued in 1508 by Cantalycius, who maybe judged from the laudatory notices before his volume to have been a personage of eminence at Venice, (1) expressly purports to be designed "*pro rudibus pueris*," and the preface points to an antecedent and incorrect text, as having been published at Florence, without leave, from a manuscript copy obtained at Foligno, for the author had been unwilling to have his book committed to the press, lest his special methods should be pirated or forestalled.

(1)   Cantalicio, *Summa Perutilis in Regulas Distinctas Totius Artis Grammatices et Artis Metricae.*

The two primers alike contain testimony, on the part of those most nearly concerned, that they were not by any means so obscure and puzzling as we are apt to deem them. Cantalycius was encouraged by the public reception of his labours to recommend the scheme to his fellow teachers. The system of tuition everywhere was long, at all events, identical, and we meet, in the primers of Italy, with the primitive arrangement observable in the engravings which accompany many of the early English and French works; in both cases the preceptor alone holds the book, and the pupils repeat after him, even when the nature of the lesson might seem to render such a process difficult and ineffectual.

The introduction of pictorial school-books is assigned to an epoch which preceded typography, and the earliest examples combine a series of drawings accompanied by explanatory indications and a connecting manuscript text. The *Cronologia Magna* in the Marciana at Venice is, in fact, more than the title conveys, for it comprises delineations of various callings and pursuits from the King and Queen to the tailor, and here occurs probably the oldest suggestion of the aspect of the Mediaeval notary.

The progress of culture and scholarship among women was as slow and casual as elsewhere, and the few names of learned ladies of Venetian birth which have descended to us are associated with gifts and undertakings of relatively insignificant value. Broadly and generally speaking, the sex was, down to the close of independence in 1797, profoundly illiterate, although a slender minority in the eighteenth century attained a certain proficiency in painting and poetry, and shone in social accomplishments and even as correspondents, while, for the former, teachers of deportment and elegance and of such arts as music, singing and dancing sufficed, and, for the latter, a qualified intimacy with grammar and composition long remained too widely diffused a trait to attract criticism or awaken disrespect.

The educational curriculum for men was superior, and in a commercial state they profited by the abundant opportunities of contracting knowledge and information. But, throughout early societies, the employment of professional secretaries and amanuenses, as well as the delegation of all domestic concerns to a special functionary in the higher class of households, relieved the master of the necessity of writing letters and keeping accounts. The higher mental training of women of family did not enter into the constitutional scheme of the Venetians, who contented themselves, until the New Thought peremptorily interposed, with those superficial and specious qualities which enabled them to fill with propriety and dignity their allotted stations.

We cannot be perfectly satisfied, of course, that we have received all that the early Venetian press yielded in an educational direction, and we may be almost sure that the most ancient productions, especially those of a purely elementary character, have disappeared. But from existing evidences there is sufficient to convince us, that the Republic neglected little in this way calculated to be serviceable in all social and commercial respects. With the first quarter of the sixteenth century, the art of engraving on wood was freely introduced here in educational literature, as a recognized aid to the pupil to comprehend and follow his teacher, and even the latter was furnished with the means of pronouncing correctly the difficult words in liturgical works, when he, as often happened, united the functions of a schoolmaster and a priest. (1)

(1)   (anonymous) *Casselina, Sive Compendiolum Sacre Scripture de Brevibus et Longis Syllabis Distinctis cum Suis Accentibus.* There was also the *Ecclesiastical Vocabulary* in Latin and Italian, 1522.

The Venetian dialect, in which Mr. Theodore Bent in his able paper on the Estradiots finds many proofs of Hellenic influence and descent, was remarkable for its habit of eliding or rejecting the terminal syllable in proper nouns, as well as for other more arbitrary modifications of Italian forms. A name mournfully famous passed through the stages of Faletrus, Faledro, Faliero, Falier. But in another case, as in *tafora*, from the Greek μεταφορά, the first syllable in lieu of the concluding one was sacrificed to the exigencies of pronunciation. Shakespeare's Iago is Venetian patois for Jacopo, and the form Arrigo for Enrico is found in Venetian publications and also in early German nomenclature, as in the version of the *Decameron* printed at Ulm in 1473.

During the Mediaeval time, while the men of culture were developing by selection and adaptation a language which was to become the Italian tongue, and while at Venice this was being adopted among the better classes, subject to local influences and colouring, those to whom education was unknown probably expressed themselves in a jargon which would have puzzled even Petrarch and Boccaccio on their occasional visits, and which stood at as great a distance from modern Italian as it did from the idiom which Cicero employed.

The spoken language of the Republic, in common with that of the rest of Italy, was strengthened and enriched by her intercourse with the Goths and the Franks. The invader blighted with one hand and fertilized with the other. Of the freedom and property of the Italians he took as much as they had to lose of either, while he communicated to them his speech, his arts, his institutions and his sentiments.

The makers of Italian borrowed from the right and the left, and imported into their work material from all available sources, as the Greeks and Romans had done before, and as the English have done since. Of the composite structure which thus grew up into what the revivers of learning found it, the Venetian was a provincial dialect, more Hellenic in its phraseology, more quaintly attractive, perhaps, to the ear, but more Teutonic in some of its inflections, and, to the grammarian, less acceptable than the purer and softer forms heard on the Arno and the Tiber.

Perhaps sufficient stress has not usually been laid on the historical value of the archaic forms of the names of places and persons, and, in yielding a preference for what is most familiar, we are apt to lose sight of the nomenclature which was employed by the very people themselves whom we have made it our business to describe, and which carries on the surface its origin and its meaning. The locality, which the Italians call Chioggia and the Venetians Chiozza, was known in the Middle Ages as Clugia. Caput Aggeris is lost to us superficially (as it were) in Cavarzere. Nor do we at once recognize in Malipiero the transition from Magister Petrus and Mastropiero. A Venetian boatman called his son his *fiol*, and he would have referred to the Doge Pietro Polani as Ser Pier Boldu. But some uniform standard is essential in a homogeneous narrative; and those forms which are generally intelligible are to be preferred on the whole to such as are less corrupt, yet more obscure. The nomenclature long remained unsettled and capricious, and in certain public documents and on some coins the text is found to be a medley of Latin and the vernacular.

The following lists, taken from Boerio and Mutinelli (1) will enable the reader to form some idea of the general peculiarities of the Venetian dialect.

(1)   Boerio, *Dizionario del Dialetto Veneziano;* Mutinelli, *Lessico Veneto.*

I. Proper Names

Italian	Venetian
Adige	Adice, Adese
Angelico	Anzelico
Angelo	Anzolo, Anzo, Anso
Angioletta	Zanze
Antonietta	Tonina
Antonio	Toni
Arsenale	Arsanal, Arzana'
Aureliaco	Oriago
Badoero	Baduario
Bartolommeo	Bortolo
Basilio	Baseggio
Benedetto	Beneto
Biagio	Biasio
Brenta	Brinta
Broglio	Bruolo, Brolo, Broio
Caterina	Catina, Cate
Chioggia	Chiozza
Domenico	Menego
Elena	Nene
Enrico	Arrigo, Rigo
Epifania	Empifania
Erasmo	Rasemo
Eufemia	Fumia
Eustachio	Stadi, Stai, Stae
Federico	Ferigo
Francesco	Checo
Gemello	Zemelo

Geminiano	Zeminian
Gennaio	Zenaro, Zener
Giacomo	Zacco
Giammaria	Zamaria
Giobbe	Giopo, Agiopo
Giorgio	Zorzi
Giovambatista	Zambatista
Giovanni	Zuane, Nane
Giovedi	Zioba
Girolamo	Moniolo
Giudecca (Iudaica)	Zuecca
Giudeo	Zudio
Giugno	Zugno
Giuliano	Zulian
Giuseppe	Isepo
Guglielmo	Vielmo
Iubanico	Iubenigo, Zobenigo
Jacopo	Iago
Leonardo	Lunardo
Leone	Lio
Lodovico, Luigi	Alvise, Lovigi
Luglio	Lugio
Maggio	Mazo
Marziale	Marcilian
Matteo	Matio, Mafio
Melchiorre	Marchio'
Natale	Nadal
Paolo	Polo
Puglia	Pugia
Rivo Alto	Rialto
San Giovanni Decollato	San Zan Degola
San Giovanni in Oleo	San Zani Novo
Santi Gervasio e Protasio	San Trovaso
Santi Giovanni e Paolo	San Zannipolo
Sebastiano	Bastian
Stefano, Stefanino	Stin
Teodoro	Todaro
Teresa	Gegia
Tommaso	Tomado, Tomao, Toma', Tomio
Ubaldo	Baldo, Boldo

Venezia	Venetia, Venecia, Venesia, Veniesia, Veniexia
Zecca	Cecca

II. Common Words

Italian	Venetian
Alloggiare	Alozar, Lozar
Ambasciatore	Ambassador, Imbassador, Imbassaor
Argento	Arzento
Arringo	Arrengo, Rengo
Ascensione, Ascenso	Sensa
Avuto	Abu'
Avvocatore	Avogador
Baciare	Basar
Beato	Beao
Bestemmia	Biastema
Biada	Biava
Biglione	Viglion
Canapa	Canevo
Capitale	Cavedal
Capo	Cao
Carico	Cargo
Casa	Ca', Caxa
Castaldo	Gastaldo
Chiesa	Clesia, Gesia, Giesia
Ci, Ce, Ne	Ghe
Cio	Zo
Consigliere	Consegier
Consiglio	Consegio
Cortigiana	Cortesana
Cosi	Cossi, Cussi
Da poi che	Daspuo'
Desinare	Disnar, Zirnar
Deve	Die
Doge	Dose, Doxe
E, sei, sono	Xe
Elleno, Loro	Ele
Figlio	Fiolo, Fio
Fondaco	Fontego, Fontico
Fu	Fo

Gente	Zente
Gentiluomo	Zentilomo
Ginocchio	Zenochio
Giorno	Zorno
Giu	Zo
Giudicare	Zudegar
Giudice	Zudeze
Giungere	Zonzer
Giunta, Aggiunta	Zonta
Ingegno	Inzegno
Insieme	Insembre
Invece	Impe'
Io so	Soi
Li	I
Maestro	Mestro, Mistro
Maggiore	Mazor
Matricola	Mariegola, Marigola
Medesimo	Medemo
Metaphora	Tafora
Miglio	Megio, Mio
Modo	Muo'
Moglie	Mugier
Moneta	Moneda, Monea, Munea
Monsignore	Bonsior
Ne il	Nil
Ne meno	Nianca
Niente affatto	Neche
Nipote	Neodo, Nievo, Nezzo
Notaio	Nodaro
Orafo	Orese
Portico	Portego
Pregati	Pregadi, Pregai
Purche	Previo
Quegli, Colui	Lu
Ragione	Rason
Se tu	Sti
Selciata	Salizada
Sii tu	Siestu
Sopra	Sora
Sorella	Suor
Suo	So, Soo
Talvolta	Talfie

Traffico	Trafego
Trinita	Ternita
Tuo	To
Uccello	Oselo
Vergine	Verzene
Vigilia	Vegia
Voglio	Voi
Voi	Vu
Zecchino	Cecchino

Santi Giovanni e Paolo, Santo Stefano, Santo Eustachio and Ascensione almost disappear in Zannipolo, S. Stin, S. Stae, and Sensa, but certainly the great printer Theobaldo Manutio can scarcely be traced in Aldo. The familiar British *ditto* is nothing more than the *detto* of Venetian invoices and bills of exchange, and *el peron* stood for *il padrone*, which seems to have been an eighteenth century colloquialism for "the governor." One of the local forms of *ambasciatore* is precisely the English ambassador, and *mistro* (for *maestro*) draws close to our Mister, the modern pronunciation of Mr. which is really an abbreviation of Master.

In the comparatively early decree by which it was ordered that all legal and legislative proceedings should be conducted in the Venetian tongue, the solicitude of the Republic was apparent, not only to remove the inconvenience of a Low Latin vocabulary, but to give dignity to her peculiar patois. The latter was not merely the language of ballads and pasquinades, of street-cries and popular songs, but it was, after a certain period, the language which was spoken from the bench and in the Senate. Nevertheless, by the better historical writers it was largely if not altogether eschewed. The more ancient historians, like the pseudo-Sagorninus and Dandolo, composed their works in Latin, or, like Da Canale, in Norman-French. Sanudo wrote his voluminous *Diaries* for the most part in Venetian, but of some of his other works he left versions both in that and in Latin.

It is not surprising that, at the outset and long subsequently, different dialects should have existed among the inhabitants of the capital and those of the more distant insular townships, but we should not be prepared to suppose or believe without proof, that such variations have been observed by modern visitors and are familiar to local students. They seem to be attributable partly to physical causes, and to the conservatism which has retained in these places the descendants of early colonists from more or less distant points. The more popular compositions in the vernacular are very numerous, and of no mean value as illustrations of manners and tastes. They are chiefly of a poetical or metrical cast, and have been collected by Gamba. (1)

(1)   Gamba, (in fourteen volumes, duodecimo, 1817).

The Venetian families, apart from political distinctions, were of two classes: 1. Those which merely migrated into the islands; and 2. those which were of a purely insular origin, and were founded subsequently to the rise of the Republic. The population, in common with the language, was a blend or fusion which, as had been the case at Rome, and as was subsequently the case in England, proved eminently beneficial to the national calibre and genius.

Infinitely numerous were the localities from which the immigrants came. The Orseoli, Quirini, (1) Cornari (Cornelii), Marcelli, Valieri (Valerii) and Michieli, pointed to the Eternal City as the cradle of their race. Vicenza gave the Grimani, Capua the Cappelli, Candia the Calergi and the Gezi, Pavia the Badoeri, Altino the Dandoli and the Orii, Fano the Falieri, formerly known as Anastasii, Forli the Ordelafi with whom a Faliero intermarried in the eleventh century, Ravenna the Caloprini, Aquileia the Gradenigi, Trieste the Barbari whose original name was Magadesi, Messina the Foscari, Loredo the Loredani, and Friuli the Vezzi and the Manin families.

(1)   Symonds, *Days Spent on a Doge's Farm,* page 18.

The Gritti, the Zeni, the Tiepoli, the Venieri sprang from Greek stocks; in the veins of the Giustiniani flowed the blood of the Heraclian dynasty. The Pisani were furriers in the city to which they owed their name, but settled in Venice in the earlier years of the tenth century. The ancestors of the Contarini, whose original name may have been Contadini, (1) are said to have been Lombard peasants, but a member of the house is traditionally said to have been one of the conclave of twelve who elected the first Doge in 697. The Memi, who survived down to a late period and retained their social standing, gave a Doge to the Republic in the tenth century in the person of Tribuno Memo, a case in which the name of an office developed into a patronymic.

(1)   In the first half of the thirteenth century, a member of this family, a naval commander, bore the name Romeo.

The families entitled by birthright to a seat in the Great Council comprised, especially those with branches, so many individuals of the same name, that it often became requisite for identification, to distinguish them by their place of residence or the precise line to which they belonged. We therefore meet with the expressions Dandolo of San Moise or Contarini della Casa Maggiore (or Ca Mazor), and here and there even a personal peculiarity was brought into service, such as *Nasone, Collo torto* or even *Guercio*, or an agnomen such as Marino Sanudo Torsello. The father-in-law of the celebrated Doge Foscari was known as Andrea Priuli del Banco.

A different principle is apparent in such an appellation as Cane, which occurs as an honourable distinction in two successive generations of the ducal house of Dandolo in the fourteenth century, and has the air of having been borrowed from Verona where the form is found side by side with Mastino, both ostensibly signifying a tenacious and loyal courage typical of the mastiff. But we miss the Italian Maria as the name of a man usually found as an adjunct to another, as in Filippo-Maria; the fashion was even adopted by English Romanists as in the case of Anthony Maria Browne, Viscount Montague, in the time of Charles I.

The families which belonged to the second category, and which may be described as indigenous, were those of Da Canale, Da Ponte, Da Riva, Spazza-Canale, Tintoretto, Dalle Fornaci, Dalle Contrade, Molino, Tagliapietra, Monetario, Tribuno, Ducato, Veneto, Malipiero (Mastropiero), Engegniere, Marini, Premarino and others; the origin of these is mainly traceable to employments and places of abode. The painter Tintoretto was the son of a dyer called Robusti.

If we watch with attention the occurrence of names from age to age, old ones disappear, new ones rise up. Many, however, remain to the end, and almost form a link between the last days of the Roman Empire and the French Revolution. There is a curious parallel between the English saying which ascribes special qualities to certain great houses, and the Venetian adage *"Ne Mocenigo povero, ne Erizzo pietoso, ne Balbo ricco."*

The pride of descent among all nations or societies of men appears to arise from antiquity of blood, rather than magnitude of achievement. The Venetian houses were pleased to point to ancestry which had occupied the same estate or patrimony from time immemorial, and strove to refrain from behaviour derogatory to men and women before them who carried back their traditions to the laying of the first stones in the dark past, as the citizen of the United States who can prove his consanguinity with the pilgrim fathers is a greater man than he who owns millions in oil or in steel.

But neither here nor elsewhere has intellectual genius ever served as a passport to the recognition which military, naval or political distinction commands. Wealth and titles have everywhere been freely lavished on the heroes of the hour, and their successors have treasured the remembrance of their great deeds by sea and land, in politics and in diplomacy, but no parallel solicitude has been evinced to establish a connexion with men who have glorified the arts. In Italy a statue, a pension or a small gratuity suffices for Dante, Michael Angelo or Ariosto, as it does in England for Milton or Defoe — nay, for Shakespeare.

The population of Venice long remained incontestably scanty, and never attained such proportions as might have been expected. The periodical ravages of epidemics, coupled with the roving propensities of the people, were opposed to its increase. It is true that, in the course of time, natives of all countries from Brittany to Bohemia settled in the city, and acquired by the prescribed term of residence, varying from ten to fifteen years, the enjoyment of civic rights, but it is unlikely that any of these distant emigrations were accomplished till the twelfth century. It was not till after the events of 1204 that a Calergi of Crete and a Lippomano of Negropont made the Republic their adopted country. It was only about one hundred years before, that the family of Polo quitted Dalmatia and sought a new home on the opposite coast. The influx of Greeks from Constantinople is commonly assigned to the reign of Vitale Michiele III. (1170), nor can the establishment of the Brici of Saint Jean d'Acre and other orientals be referred with much probability to an epoch anterior to the First Crusade (1096).

From Brescia came the Bontempelli; from the Bergamasque the Cuccina, Persici, Albrizzi, Muti, Tasca, Gozzi, Castelli, Maccarelli; from Lucca the Angelieri; from Piacenza the Fontane. Among members of the plebeian order who attained wealth and won social aggrandizement were the Bonomi, the Cuccine and the Labie. The Bresciano and Bergamasque yielded the most valuable accessions to the industrial strength and moral tone of the community. Many or most of them came to the city very poor, and by almost penurious frugality accumulated large fortunes.

Bartolommeo Bontempelli of Brescia was originally a mercer; he subsequently established a bank, associated with him his relative Graziano Bontempelli, and was able to negotiate loans to crowned heads. At the same time he spent, when he had grown rich, considerable sums on the erection or restoration of churches and hospitals, leaving ample legacies to charitable objects.

Giuseppe Persico, a Bergamasque, was, at the outset, an assistant at a silk merchant's in the Street of San Lio, and was employed in drawing water for his master's kitchen and in other menial offices. He, in course of time, opened a depot on his own account, and eventually entered the Great Council on payment of 100,000 ducats. Even in comparatively early days, the sumptuous residences of these successful adventurers changed hands. The palace of the Angelieri passed to the Marcelli, and that of the Muti to the Baglioni. The stately Papodopoli mansion on the Grand Canal has successively belonged to the Cuccina of Brescia and to the Tiepoli.

Fontana of Piacenza settled here in 1577 as a trader, and was able to erect a palace at San Felice on the Grand Canal; one of his sons was appointed Governor of Caserta Vecchia by the Duke of Guise in the following century. In 1646, the House of Labia bought its nobility for 10,000 ducats, and acquired a splendid palace at San Geremia (1) where its guests were served on gold plate. The diamonds of the ladies of the family are described by the President de Brosses, who was here in 1737 and 1740, as one of the sights of Italy.

(1)   See Molmenti, *La Storia di Venezia nella Vita Privata,* Liber III page 116, where the building is shewn. The President de Brosses was unfavourably impressed by the Ducal Palace and the Basilica. The former he characterized as "*vilain, massif, sombre et gothique du plus mechant godt,*" and the latter as "*sombre, impenetrable a, la lumiere, d'un gout miserable.*"

In 1716, the brothers Giuseppe and Francesco Vezzi, who had done much to advance industrial and commercial interests, especially in the manufacture of porcelain, were similarly admitted by a large majority on payment of the same sum, and we learn that, on election, two nobles officiated as their sureties or guarantees in respect of identity, and presented them to the Advocates of the Commune with a view to the registration of their names in the Golden Book. (1)

(1) Drake, *Notes on Venetian Ceramics,* page 20.

The Christian names were borrowed principally from the Scriptures and the Martyrology. The passion of the Venetians for this class of appellation occasioned the speedy transfer to their baptismal nomenclature of such names as Zaccaria, Giovanni, Paolo and so on. A love of Roman prototypes gradually naturalized Amulius, Ascanius, Priam, Hector, Troilus, Cornelius, Lucretius, Camillus, Fabius, Octavian, Justinian, Aemilius, Valerius, Fabricius, and Livius.

Among women, Felicia, Buona, Clara, Agnes, Joan, Lucretia, Margaret, Mary, Anne, Catherine, Justina, Benedicta, Julia, Constance, Romana were favourites. After the Lombard conquest of 568, Froiba, Archielda, Marchesina and many names, found neither in the Pentateuch nor in Eusebius nor in Dion Cassius, were of more or less frequent occurrence.

Subsequently to the rise of the Norman power, it was not unusual to meet with Robert, Bohemond and Godfried. A not uncommon name in the earlier centuries was Diodato, or Given of God, the equivalent of the Greek Theodores; the second Doge of the family of Orso, who reigned from 742 to 755, was thus christened. It was perhaps merely given in the peculiar circumstances of an unexpected blessing. We recognize the identical principle and notion in the French form Dieudonne.

At a later date, at all events, it became customary for women of high family to retain their patronymic on marriage, and thus, when a Morosini, a Dandolo or a Quirini espoused a Grimani, a Priuli or a Valier, the bride was thenceforth known as Morosini-Grimani, Dandolo-Priuli, or Quirini-Valier. There was a reluctance on the part of an historical house to lose the recollection of its origin; it was a usage which became general throughout Europe. When, in 1579, Bianca Cappello espoused the Grand Duke of Tuscany, she obtained or assumed the right to style herself Bianca Cappello de' Medici; and, at a much anterior date (1339-1349), a member of the Fieschi family, on becoming the wife of the Duke of Milan, became known as Isabella de' Fieschi Visconti.

The *Fasti* of the *Studio* or University of Padua under Venetian auspices display to our view an imposing and brilliant array of names, in every department of human learning and science, not only of Venetians but of foreigners. It was toward the middle of the sixteenth century that this institution attained the height of its prosperity and importance, and the Senate, acting in the strictly conservative spirit of those days, decreed that no degrees other than those of Padua should be recognizable. Upward of a hundred professors were engaged at this period in giving instruction and lectures on the entire range of educational knowledge, and their salaries were such as might tempt the most capable and distinguished scholars to offer their services. In 1498, a Sienese, Giovanni Cambezo, was appointed Reader in Civil Law at a net salary of 1100 ducats. (1) Indeed, many of the names are those of wealthy patricians or disinterested enthusiasts to whom the pecuniary consideration was indifferent.

(1)   Sanudo, *Diarii,* Volume I page 965.

The subjects taught embraced nearly all branches of human learning then studied and recognized, and the Venetian Senate was ever ready to remunerate on the most generous scale its professors, of whom the one who gave instruction in medicine was the recipient of the highest pay. In 1629, the earliest year for which the prospectus seems to be extant, the courses were:

> Theology.
> Holy Scriptures.
> Metaphysics, in which Aristotle, of course, occupied a prominent
>   rank.
> Philosophy. Aristotle again.
> Philosophy Extraordinary. *De coelo et de mundo.*
> Mathematics. The elements of geometry and of the globe.
> Belles Lettres (Greek and Latin). *Horatii Opera,* particularly the
>   *Epistola ad Pisones* (the *Ars Poetica*).
> Anatomy.
> Medicine, Theory of.
> Medicine, Practical.
> Medicine, Theory of, special or extraordinary, aphorisms of
>   Hippocrates.
> Medicine, Practical, extraordinary.
> Medicine. Fevers.
> Simples in Physic.
> Surgery, Ordinary. Tumours.
> Lectures on the Third Book of Avicenna.

In addition to these studies, were those connected with law, jurisprudence and the long most prominent and lucrative vocation of the notary public, who, in ages of general illiteracy, was required to discharge a multifarious variety of functions at once important and confidential.

From the period of the revival of learning in Italy, it seems to have been usual for students to attend lectures and to read books with their special tutors when they were able to engage them. The Doge Andrea Dandolo had, as a youth, enjoyed the benefit of the services of Riccardo Malhombra about 1330, in acquiring a knowledge of jurisprudence. Others, when Padua became more widely celebrated under Venetian management, came there to study divinity, philosophy, poetry and the rest of the curriculum. Some took up special lines; some went through the whole regular course. In the last decade of the fifteenth century (1491-1492), we trace the Nurnberger Wilibald Pirkheimer, subsequently so distinguished as a scholar and bibliophile, reading Horace and Cicero with Calphurnius of Brescia, one of the professors or tutors at Padua. The copies which he employed are still extant; they are all Venetian editions then current.

The University of Padua directed the course of public instruction throughout the entire Venetian dominion in Italy, and the head of it, termed the Reformer, was invariably a patrician of approved accomplishments, both in an administrative and an intellectual sense. The whole establishment was under his supreme sway, subject to the approval of the Senate.

The system of granting diplomas was not restricted to Padua, but was shared by the College of Physicians and the Pharmaceutical College at Venice, and numerous documents are extant illustrating the old practice, and recording the names of successful candidates. Englishmen included. In the ceremony of admitting a Doctor of Medicine, the ring, the cap and the kiss of peace formed the staple features. One of the diplomas (the earlier have probably disappeared) was in favour of Robert Ley of London, son of the *praeclarissimus Dominus* Robert Ley of London, Englishman, 1696. Nearly seventy years ago, the library of the University is described (1) as containing more than 70,000 volumes.

(1)   Galibert, *Histoire de la Republique Venise,* page 324.

Padua was not exempt from the consequences of being, like Oxford and Cambridge, the centre to which converged a great number of young men in the enjoyment of high animal spirits, and we hear of the town-and-gown rows and fights, nocturnal frolics, and even sanguinary conflicts, which have everywhere signalized such phases of life. In 1560, the reformers of the University were clothed with judicial powers of a limited and weak character, and were required to submit grave cases to the ordinary tribunals. One fruitful source of discord and tumult was the friction between the members of the Jesuits College (subsequently suppressed) and those of the University; but the usual butt and victim of academical licence was the peaceable citizen whom those hot-headed roisterers delighted to annoy.

The authorities on the spot and at home might be fairly indulgent to these delinquents, unless the offence was of a nature requiring exemplary punishment, but the strictest discipline was maintained within bounds, and the Rector or Reformer himself was liable to dismissal and degradation if a breach of duty or gross misconduct was proved.

The students at Padua are represented by Evelyn the diarist as being very unruly and dissolute when he was there in 1645. He says: "The students themselves take a barbarous liberty in the evenings when they go to their strumpets, to stop all that pass by the house where any of their companions in folly are with them. This custom they call the *chi vali*, so as the streets are very dangerous, when the evenings grow dark." Before Evelyn's time, about 1580, Montaigne speaks of a member of the University as having accustomed himself to the noisy situation of the college square, and says that the continual tumult helped his studies.

Among others who were attracted hither by the reputation of the place and the excellence of its methods, was John Tiptoft, Earl of Worcester, translator of Caesar and Cicero, and one of the earliest benefactors of the Bodleian Library at Oxford, who occupied a professorial chair in the fifteenth century. He was a nobleman of liberal feeling, whom we find paying a visit to Florence, and accepting the guidance of the famous bookseller Vespasiano de' Bisticci. Here also Columbus came in due time from Genoa, his native city, to complete his education. In 1622, the two sons of Thomas Howard, Earl of Arundel, Earl Marshal of England, were members of the University. (1)

(1) See Volume Four, page 203.

The most signal and most honourable trait in the relations of Venice with the University of Padua was its attitude toward the illustrious and unhappy Galileo, who, in 1594, under the Rectorship of Marcantonio Barbaro, was invited to occupy the mathematical chair at a yearly stipend of 1000 ducats, a sum, as Galileo informs a friend, twice as much as he had previously received at Pisa from the Medici.

Galileo quitted Venetian patronage and protection to visit the Holy City, where he narrowly escaped the resentment of the Inquisition on account of his heretical opinions. He must have looked back with fond regret on the days which he had spent at Padua, among a people warmly and flatteringly appreciative of his genius and valuable scientific services. What other European power would, in 1609, have invited a man of such advanced ideas in astronomy, to deliver at Venice itself, before the Doge and the Signory, a lecture on his discoveries, so momentous, not merely for astronomy but for navigation? The text of his discourse is preserved, and the medal exists, struck by order of his entertainers to commemorate the occasion.

English scholars and artists resorted in the sixteenth century to models and material outside the Studio itself. In 1535, an anonymous translator (probably William Marshall) rendered from the Latin, with a Prayer for Queen Anne Boleyn, the *Defence of Peace* by Marsilio Menandrini of this city, and, in 1591, the designs executed by Girolamo Porro of Padua for the *Orlando Furioso* were copied by William Rogers for the Elizabethan version of Sir John Harington.

At a later period, when a long series of continental wars and the decline of trade had impoverished the Republic, one of the unfavourable symptoms and results was the inability of parents, through reduced incomes, to send their sons to Padua, and, as we see elsewhere, a second academical centre was established for the convenience of the Istrian population at Lesina.

CHAPTER LXI

*Literature — Account Written in The Eighteenth Century by the Doge
Foscarini — Venetian Historical Literature — Its Secular Complexion —
Official Historiographers — Independent Annalists — The Two Schools
of Writers to be Consulted — Minuteness of Many of The Older
Historians — Theology — Natural Philosophy — Alchemy — The
Trevisano Family — Botany — The Barbaro Family — Logic — Free
Thought — Petrarch's Curious Experiences — Ethics — Geometry —
Public Lecturers — Hebrew — Poetry — A Friend of Dante —
Introduction of Tuscan Melodies by the Fugitive Silk-Weavers of Lucca
in the Fourteenth Century — Provencal Poetry Naturalized by a Noble
Venetian — Sacred Poetry — Fugitive Verses on Current Events — The
Battle of Lepanto — The Giustiniani — Marino Sanudo the Diarist and
Historian — Some Account of His Career — His Remarkable Library —
Marcantonio Barbaro — Paolo Sarpi — Sketch of His Life — The So-
Called Admirable Crichton — Antiquities — Folk-Rhymes.*

The earliest and long the sole historian of the literature of the Republic
was Marco Foscarini who filled the ducal throne in 1762-1763. The book
amounts to little more than notice of the principal writers in
chronological order; but it is one of those efforts at which we are
prompted to look with indulgence, when we consider the circumstances
of production, and the laudable interest manifested by the noble author in
such a subject. The Doge lived only to publish the first part.

With one or two exceptions which occur in the earlier stages, the
historical literature of the Republic is in its origin secular. To the
monkish chroniclers of western Europe we meet with few counterparts;
there is nothing correspondent with the Scandinavian saga, the Saxon

minstrel or the Norman *trouvere*. No country perhaps can shew such a long series of historians or writers of an historical cast as England. It is traceable back to the commencement of the era of the Heptarchy, but the names which constitute it are the names of ecclesiastics.

Venice cannot be said to have produced any narrative, pretending to elucidate or describe the sources of her existence and her power, till the second half of the tenth century. The earliest native essayist upon her *fasti* was John the Deacon, who fortunately contented himself, for the most part, with telling us what he knew and saw, rather than what he had heard or what he thought. (1) His account comes to a close in 1008, but he was the pioneer of other writers of whom some, such as Martino da Canale and Lorenzo de Monacis, followed the same narrow yet valuable lines as himself. A third whose surname has not reached us we know only as Marco; others, like Andrea Dandolo, Marino Sanudo and Bernardo Giustiniani, not content to put into writing their own impressions of contemporary events, planned their labours on a broader and more ambitious scale, and not only resorted to records and evidences of antecedent times, that indispensable helpmate tradition included, but even brought to their work a certain share of critical discrimination. Giustiniani founded his work on a chronicle written by Abbot Zeno in the eleventh century.

(1)   The chronicle is commonly known as that of the ironmaster Johannes Sagorninus.

But the Venetians had no Beowulf or Wace, no William of Malmesbury or Henry of Huntingdon, no *Domesday Book* or *Great Charter*. That the Republic possessed chronicles of a date anterior to any now known is exceedingly probable, nor is it much less so that those chroniclers were churchmen, of whose productions their immediate successors in the same literary field might have had the use. The frequent fires which desolated the city, and the fragile material of which its public buildings were long composed keep us here within the limits of conjecture, for the citations which occur in the pages of such civilians as Dandolo, Sanudo and Navagiero from historical manuscripts preserved in the monasteries do not refer, as a rule, to compilations long anterior to their own epochs, and are not explicitly described as of local origin.

But, if the admission is made that the most ancient writers belonged to holy orders, it does not rob of much of its force the view just now propounded that, in her historical literature, Venice enjoyed a singular and wholesome exemption from clerical influence. Whatever the piece of guesswork about primeval annalists of whom no vestige seems to survive may be worth, it does not in the least degree militate against the fact that the Venetian temper and taste, from the moment when the Republic might be said to have had a definite constitution and a distinct national life, were in this, as in all other things, emphatically lay.

In forming an estimate of other countries, the student is referred to compositions which emanated from the cloister, but he finds to his satisfaction that here, from the very commencement of any sort of culture in the ranks of the laity, men of the world, often personages of the highest position, undertook to communicate to the ages to come what they thought to be important in passed or current transactions. Where, as at the outset, local authorities fail him, there come to his succour lay-folk beyond the verge of the Islands; the Prefect Cassiodorus (523), the Exarch Longinus (568), Eginhard, one or two Lombards and certain Byzantines, with whom he may lay out his hours more profitably than with the harvest of the monastic scriptorium. Moreover, whether or not the Republic once possessed certain annals from the pens of ecclesiastics, there is no doubt that the earlier secular authors had recourse to a large assortment of original papers which have since partly perished, and that they have (like the English martyrologist Fox) transmitted their substance and frequently their very text to us with a fidelity far from commensurate, perhaps, with modern literary canons, but much more satisfactorily and veraciously than analogous monuments elsewhere produced under the eye of the Church.

The official historiographers of Venice whose performances are sufficiently well known date from 1505. They wrote in Latin, and their consecutive narratives, which are, for the most part, dry and jejune to excess, were formed into a uniform series in the last century. Independently of them, the Council of Ten in 1551 resolved that, in order to put and keep men in possession of the events of passed ages as a method of avoiding error, the annals should be recorded, not in Latin, but in the vernacular, by persons selected from time to time from the Order of Secretaries. To what extent this direction was pursued we do not know; it was possibly abandoned as superfluous. But, even before the wider diffusion of historical records through the medium of the press, manuscript copies were multiplied for the use of public men and for libraries, and it is not unusual to meet with cases in which speakers refer to incidents belonging to antecedent centuries, and display a sense of their bearing and value as lessons and precedents, when the printed book was still unknown.

The importance and interest of the official school of writers are mainly limited to a faithful registration of facts which came within their personal knowledge, and their style is usually academic and dry. They do not possess, on the one hand, the picturesqueness and naivete which render a few early annalists, even in the Venetian series, so attractive and valuable, or, on the other, the philosophical temper which might have led them to enter into a comparative investigation of original archives, and to draw their own conclusions. But their pens were naturally hampered by their official engagement, and although Nani, one of them, affirms that he deemed it his duty to place on record a full account of all transactions within the dates assigned to him (1613-1671) (1) it is absolutely certain that, if the world had depended on these narratives, its knowledge of Venetian history and institutions would have remained singularly imperfect.

(1) Nani, *Storia della Repubblica Veneta.*

Apart from the official historiographers and the critical productions of later times, no nation has done more toward writing its own history, or has written it with less bias and more ability. As a sufficient warrant, we have but to mention:

1. John the Deacon, author of *Chronicon Venetum Nunc Primum Editum, ad Annum 1008,* published in Venice, 1765.
2. Martino da Canale, author of *Cronaca Veneta, ad Annum 1375,* begun in 1267; published in *Archivio Storico Italiano,* Liber VIII.
3. The anonymous Marco, author of *La Cronaca Veneta detta Altinate di Autore Anonimo in Latino.* This work was written about 1292 and published in *Archivio Storico Italiano,* Liber VIII. He is also the author of the *Juxta Codicem Dresdensem,* published in *Archivio Storico Italiano,* Liber V.
4. Andrea Dandolo (*Chronica Venetorum*) apud Muratori, *Antiquitates Italicae Medii Aevi sive Dissertationes,* Volume XII. The prooemium is: "*Ego Andreas Dandolo proposui sub brevi compendio provinciae Venetiarum inicium et ipsius incrementum, et prout sub ducibus constitutis notabilia facta fuerunt, summatim enarrare;*" and his three contemporaries, the Grand Chancellor Raffaello Caresino

also in Muratori Volume XII, Nicolo Trevisano (*Cronaca Trevisana*, manuscript), one of the Chiefs of the Council of Ten; and Lorenzo de Monacis, Grand Chancellor of Candia (1428), historian, ambassador and poet (*Laurentii de Monachis civis Veneti et Magni Cretae cancellarii, qui floruit anno 1428, Chronicon de Rebus Gestis Venetis* in the Additional Manuscripts section of the library of the British Museum, Manuscript 8574, or a quarto edition published in 1758.)

5. Pietro Bembo, author of *Dell'Istoria Veneziana*, Venice, 1552.
6. Donato Contarini, and Gasparo Contarini, author of *Dei Magigistrati e della Repubblica Veneta*, Venice, 1563.
7. Bernardo Giustinini, author of, *Dell'Origine della Citta di Venezia*, Venice, 1545, Pancrazio Giustinini, and Pietro Giustiniani, author of *Storia de' Fatti de' Veneziani*, Venice, 1676.
8. Giovanni Tiepolo.
9. Paolo Morosini (*Storia della Citta e Repubblica di Venezia*, Venice, 1637), and Antonio Morosini.
10. Nicolo Zeno, *Origine di Venezia*, Venice, 1558.
11. Giorgio and Pietro Dolfino.
12. Giovanni Giacomo Caroldo, Secretary of the Ten.
13. Marino Sanudo the Younger (*Vitae Ducum Venetorum*, apud Muratori, Volume XXII, and *Diarii*.), historian and diarist, of whom an account will elsewhere occur.
14. Andrea Navagiero.
15. Pietro, son of Antonio Marcello.
16. Domenigo Malipiero.
17. Nicolo Contarini, subsequently (1630-1631) Doge, who compiled an elaborate history of his own times from 1597, *Delle Historie Venetiane et Altri a Loro Annesse Cominciando dal' Anno 1597 et Successivamente, di Nicolo Contarini Doge,* 4 folio volumes in Phillipps Manuscripts, Numbers 386 to 389, with the bookplate of Lorenzo Antonio da Ponte.
18. And numerous anonymous chroniclers whose contributions to the literary annals of their country remain unprinted and even unidentified. The value of many of these compositions may be said to be due, to some extent, to the circumstance that they were not written with a view to the press, and that

their tone and matter were consequently more likely to be impartial.

The two classes of writers on Venice, principally to be regarded and followed, are the coeval or, at least, early chroniclers, and the modern critical and documentary essayists or compilers, if indeed both do not practically belong to one family and category. There is hardly any great people whose history has so gravely suffered from inadvertent and wilful misrepresentation, nor is there any which has found, in modern days, a larger number of enthusiastic and enlightened contributors to the task of undoing the mischief produced by spurious material and imperfect research.

Certain among the historical writers, official or otherwise, have shown an almost excessive tendency toward minuteness, even in treating events of remote date and secondary consequence. There has been no attempt to conceal or extenuate the long series of crimes and errors perpetuated by a succession of despotic rulers of various types, and even if we owe such candour to an inability or disinclination to view those transactions with our eyes and feelings, our gain and our gratitude remain undiminished, as we are thereby often admitted to disclosures and confidences (1) which we would have missed, at the hands of authors more critical in the selection of their material, and less disposed to leave posterity to form its own opinion.

(1)   Romanin, *Storia Documentata di Venezia,* Volume IV page 500.

A collateral aspect of the earlier schools of historical research and belief is furnished, by the meagre and exceptional opportunities enjoyed by ordinary Venetian readers and students of forming an accurate judgment of passed events, since the works of reference at their disposal were either uncritical compilations or narratives produced under official sanction. No use seems to have been made of the national archives, down to comparatively modern days, and still less was there any attempt to analyse and discriminate. Those who desired to acquire some knowledge of the anterior history of their country, to learn the causes which had operated in raising it to so marvellous a prosperity and power, and to become acquainted with all the great personalities who had contributed to make it and keep it what it was, could be referred only to meagre sketches and outlines, to casual records covering particular periods among private manuscripts, or to traditional report. Any one, therefore, who addressed a public assembly and appealed to the patriotism of those present, citing the great and glorious actions of their ancestors, appealed, as a rule, to hearers incapable of supporting or contradicting him; and, in the libraries of the wealthier families, as time elapsed, sumptuous bindings were bestowed on historical volumes which have long been discarded as waste paper.

It was not till the middle of the eighteenth century that we met with an effort to place the Venetian student, traveller or inquirer in a position to ascertain the condition and character of the rest of the known world, after three centuries had elapsed since maps and globes were introduced for the use of the professional navigator. In 1740, Signor Salmors commenced at Venice the issue of a series of volumes, embellished with engravings, and furnishing, in a sectional form, a view of the current state of all countries so far as they had been explored or discovered, and the result was a sort of library of instructive knowledge, rudimentary enough from a more modern standpoint, yet a welcome addition to many a scholar's stores. (1) The cyclopaedic spirit and movement manifested itself about the same time in a different manner, when the patrician Francesco Foscari defrayed the cost of the publication, extending to fifty-four folio volumes, of the *Thesaurus Antiquitatum Sacrarum* and the *Bibliotheca Veterum Patrum*. This was a new and modern departure.

(1)   Salmon, *Lo Stato Presente di Tutti i Paesi, e Popoli del Mondo Naturale, Politico e Morale.*

In theology, the Venetians were quite on a level with their contemporaries. Already, in the eleventh century, San Gherardo Sagredo, a bishop and subsequently a martyr, had produced A commentary on the *Song of the Three Children*, the *Praises of the Blessed Virgin*, *Quadragesimal Sermons*, and *Homilies* (1) The first, which is divided into eight books, is a folio manuscript on parchment, said to be preserved in the library of Frisingen. (2) During the reign of Pietro Gradenigo (1289-1311) flourished Bartolomeo Falvero, Patriarch of Constantinople, who wrote on the *Merits of the Holy and Immaculate Virgin*, on the *Celebration of Saints' Days*, and several orations. About 1321, Teodoro Memo, a Franciscan, compiled biographies of Saint Francis and of Saint Clara d'Assisi. In the latter half of the fourteenth century, Domenigo Leoni was a voluminous writer of glosses on the Scriptures and on profane authors, and, about the same time, Ricardus de Mediavilla, an English Franciscan, compiled his *Comment on the Fourth of the Sentences*, a work existing in manuscript, and printed by Valdarfer in folio without date, but about 1475. Both the latter and a fine manuscript.

before the writer present us with what purport to be portraits of the author — the one a small full-length, the other a figure seated at a table. But this writer also produced a *Commentum Super Librum Secundum Sententiarum*, of which a folio manuscript. has descended to us with the probably apocryphal tradition of once having belonged to Petrarch.

(1)   Zeno, P., *Memorie de' Scrittori Veneti Patrizi Ecclesiastici e Secolari,* in voce Sagredo.

(2)   Agostini, *Notizie degli Scrittori Viniziani,* Volume I Preface.

In 1372, Nicolo Muzio, of the Order of Preachers, dedicated an edition of the *Works of Saint Gregory* to the reigning Pontiff, Gregory XI.; and (it is alleged) the manuscript is still to be seen in the public collection at Toledo. Angelo Corraro or Correr, afterward Gregory XII. (1) (1406), and Gabriele Condolmiero, afterward Eugenius IV. (1431), (2) the latter of whom penned a philippic against the Hussites, (3) were both persons of admirable erudition in sacred writ. It was to Eugenius (4) that Blondus of Forli dedicated, about 1450, his *Italia Illustrata*.

(1)   Muratori, *Annali d'Italia,* Volume IX folio 34.

(2)   Muratori, *Annali d'Italia,* Volume IX folio 142.

(3)   Zeno, P., *Memorie de' Scrittori Veneti Patrizi Ecclesiastici e Secolari.*

(4)   Blondus, *Italia Ilustrata.* The same writer inscribed his *De Origine et Gestis Venetorum* to the Doge Foscari.

Contemporaneous with these distinguished Churchmen were Marco Giorgio, the author of two tracts, one upon ecclesiastical liberty, the other against simoniacs; Alberto Alberti (1381) who left to posterity a volume of divers orations; Tommaso Strozzi who gave to the world an *Exposition of the Apocalypse, the Psalms, and the Gospel of Saint Mark*; Domenigo Bollani who composed a disquisition on the purity of the Virgin; Luigi Bollani who annotated the Epistles of Saint Paul; and Andrea Trevisano, a metaphysician, who commented upon *Genesis*. (1)

(1)   Zeno, P., *Memorie de' Scrittori Veneti Patrizi Ecclesiastici e Secolari.*

Somewhat later, Fantino Dandolo, a grandson of the Doge Andrea and Archbishop of Candia, compiled for the use of the clergy a *Manual of Sacerdotal Discipline and Instruction*; (1) and in 1509 there is from the Venetian press a *Vocabulista Ecclesiastica* or *Word Book of*

Ecclesiastical Terms. Dandolo died in 1459 in his eightieth year; his performance has been printed. In 1472, the well-known writer, Antonio Cornazano of Piacenza, addressed to the Doge and the Venetians a treatise on the faith and life of Christ, and in the ensuing year Paolo Morosini published at Padua *De Aeterna Christi Generatione.* In or about 1510, while the Republic was still only gradually rallying from the troubles of the League of Cambrai, Hieronimo Donato, who had been nominated Venetian ambassador to the Vatican, compiled a monograph on the schism between the Greek and Latin Churches, which he had intended to present to the Pontiff Julius II. Owing to the troubles throughout Italy, he thought fit to withhold it, and it was subsequently dedicated to Leo X. by Filippo Donato, son of the writer, who in 1525 committed to the press, and inscribed to Clement VII., his father's *Apology for the Papacy.* The elder Donato was regarded as an eminent Hellenist. (2)

(1)   *"Incipit Compendium Reverendissimi in Christo patris Domini Fantini Dandolo Archiepiscopi Cretensis pro Catholice fidei instructione;" sine ulla nota, 8vo.*

(2)   The identical manuscript. offered to Leo X is thought to have been abstracted from the Vatican, and to be No. 234 described in (compilation) *Catalogus Librorum Manuscriptorum in Bibliotheca d. Thomae Phillips, Bt.*

A collection of 129 sermons, various letters, a pamphlet on benefices, and other pieces of current interest are also ascribed to this learned divine who became Bishop of Padua. (1) A manual for the use of the confessor, entitled *Modo Generale di Confessarsi*, by Fra Marino Baldo, exists in an impression of the sixteenth century, but is construably of much earlier origin. It provides for all contingencies; even if the confessor has to challenge tailors and shoemakers on their commercial doings.

(1)   1. *Sermones Fantini Danduli Protonotarii Apostolici, Postea Archiepiscopi Cretensis;*
       2. *Constitutiones Sanctae Synodi Celebratae April. 27, 1457, editae, et cetera;*
       3. *Fant. Danduli Epistolae (sex);*
       4. *F.D. de Beneficiis;*
       5. *Ejusdem Responsio Quaedam Juridico.*

Agostini, *Notizie degli Scrittori Viniziani,* Volume I page 34 et seqq.

About the same period (1400), Nicolo Condolmiero, not improbably a relative of the Pontiff Eugenius IV., contributed to philology *Observations on the Meaning of Words*, and to miscellaneous literature a volume entitled *Consilia*. (1) A very early essay on economics, ascribed to 1304, was the discourse by Fra Paolino on the *Government of the Family*, in which he enters into the details of domestic management and expenditure, and exhorts husbands to exercise a proper control over their wives, who are always jealous of the acquisition by other women of dress and jewellery superior to their own. He declares that, when the good man has done his best, his partner wrings her hands and deplores her ill-luck, finishing up with "What have you brought me from the Rialto?"

(1)   Zeno, P., *Memorie de' Scrittori Veneti Patrizi Ecclesiastici e Secolari.*

In natural science, the most eminent name was Bernardo d'Iseo, who, in his seclusion at San Francesco della Vigna, consumed the better part of his life and his entire patrimony in chemical and alchemical experiments. Fortune, however, was kind to him at last. He made money by his researches, and, having quitted his country when his purse became low and friends were lukewarm, he spent his declining days abroad and died a German Count. His book on alchemy is still extant, and it concludes with the words: "Here ends the book and treatise composed by Master Bernard, Count of Tervisia, who acquired the countship and jurisdiction of Neige, in Germany, by this precious and noble art." (1)

(1)   *"Hic finit liber et tractatus compositus per Magistrum Bernardum comitem Tervisianum, qui aquissivit comitatum et ditionem de Neige in Germania per hanc artem pretiosam et nobilem."* Romanin, *Storia Documentata di Venezia,* Volume III page 367.

Iseo was followed by Bernardo Trevisano who flourished about 1366, (1) and who was accounted one of the leading chemists of the age. He composed a treatise on the transmutation of metals, which has been printed more than once. (2) About the same time, Paolo Veneto of the Augustinian Order of Hermits wrote a *Summary of Physics*, which still exists in a contemporary manuscript., dated 1373. It is a folio of 171 leaves, and the writing is in small cursive Gothic characters. (3) Paolo

Veneto also produced a work *Super Posteriora Analytica Aristotelis*, which was printed at Venice in 1491.

(1)   Zeno, A, *Lettere di Apostolo Zeno,* Volume I page 183-185.
(2)   Romanin, *Storia Documentata di Venezia,* Volume III page 367-368.
(3)   Sold at Sotheby's auction rooms, 28th July, 1904, Number 34.

Three other members of the Trevisano family attained celebrity in other walks of literature and learning. Marco of the Parish of San Marziale wrote, for the edification of his son Luigi, an elaborate dissertation called by him *Macrocosmos, sen de Majore Mundo.* It appears that this gentleman was engaged (1) in this labour during the last ten years of his life, yet, at his death in 1378, he left it unfinished.

(1)   Zeno, A, *Lettere di Apostolo Zeno,* Volume I page 183-185.

Andrea Trevisano, of the Order of Servi, occupied for three years the Chair of Metaphysics at Tubingen. Zaccaria, the fourth Trevisano, who was born in 1370 and died in 1413 in the flower of manhood, (1) was one of the most accomplished men of his time, as an orator, a scholar, a politician and a soldier; of his orations only three are extant. (2)

(1)   Blondus, *Italia Ilustrata,* sign. H1; Agostini, *Notizie degli Scrittori Viniziani,* Volume I page 310 et seq.
(2)   Trevisani, *Oratoris Illustrissimi Ducalis Dominii Venetiarum ad Gregorium XII, Pontificem prò Unione S. Ecclesia Dei Conficienda Oratio*; Trevisani, *Ejusdem ad Dominum Ariminensem pro Integratione Ecclesiae*; Trevisani, *Ejusdem in Refutatione Officii Capitanae Almas Civitatis Paduae.*

In botany, Venice boasts the eminent physician and philosopher Benedetto Rinio. In the Marciana may be seen at the present day the original manuscript. of his *Book of Simples* (*Libro di Semplici*), illustrated with 443 drawings of plants, with their names beneath in several languages. Those drawings were probably made from specimens furnished by the author to the painter Andrea Amadio, and they bear the date of 1415. But, long prior to that date, a Physic Garden had been established on the Rio di Castello by the surgeon Gualtieri, and in the eighteenth century the Farsetti, of whom there were three who attained eminence, founded, at their villa at Sala, a new botanic garden which long enjoyed the reputation of being the richest in Europe.

To the fourteenth and two following centuries belong many other names — the unfortunate Jacopo Foscari, a distinguished Hellenist and a collector of Greek and Latin manuscripts; and of Francesco Barbaro, (1) the defender of Brescia, illustrious alike in letters and in war, and six later representatives of this great family, so remarkable for the versatility of its intellectual gifts and political services; Pietro Loredano, hero of Motta and Gallipoli, the Venetian Marcellus, a gentleman not less renowned for his cultivated taste and his literary acquirements than for his feats of arms; and the immortal Zeno, soldier, sailor, scholar, orator, diplomatist, the Scipio and Camillus of a second Eternal City.

(1)   A treatise by Barbaro, *De Re Uxorid*, is well known, and obtained at the period of its first appearance a wide reputation. An English version by "a person of quality" appeared in 1677; there are French translations by Martin du Pin (1557) and Francois Joly (1679).

It was about this date that Domenigo de' Domenichi expounded the principles of logic at Padua, where the patricians Lauro Quirini, Ermolao Barbaro, (1) Francesco Contarini and Antonio Cornaro, as well as Nicolo Leonico, successively taught ethics. The *Morals* and *Analytica* of Aristotle were favourite text-books, and Leonico is said to have been the first to redeem the writings of the Stagyrite from the interpolations of Averroes and others.

(1)   Barbaro is specifically named in the prolegomena to the *Geniales Dies* of Alexander ab Alexandro of Naples; folio, Parisiis, 1532.

The testimony of Petrarch may warrant the deduction that, in his time, scepticism and free thought had made considerable ground in the Republic, and the famous adventure of the poet with an alleged atheist shews that, among a certain class probably not very numerous, that deplorable affectation was in vogue. The Aristotelian theories, seen through a false and misleading medium, were the great delight of the young Venetian collegians down to the age of the erudite Leonico. It was impossible, Petrarch tells us, to listen to these silly wranglers without a sensation of nausea. His feelings may be imagined when a knot of these exquisite coxcombs constituted themselves a jury upon his literary merits, and concluded by pronouncing him a gentleman of upright purpose enough, but of manifestly neglected education.

A work upon Ethics, entitled *Rettor, Seu de Recto Regimine*, (1) was dedicated about 1314 by Fra Paolino the Minorite to Marino Badoer, Duke of Candia. (2) It was written in the Venetian dialect, and its purpose was to demonstrate the four cardinal virtues which help to form the perfect ruler.

(1)   Romanin, *Storia Documentata di Venezia,* Volume III page 367.
(2)   Cornelio, *Creta Sacra, Sive, de Episcopis Utriusque Ritus Graeci et Latini in Insula Cretae,* Liber II page 307.

Among the earlier teachers of geometry were two contemporaries, Marco Sanudo and Fra Luca Paciolo, a Minorite. The latter was the author of *A Summary of Geometrical Arithmetic*, which he edited, perhaps, merely for the use of his own pupils. In 1449, Paolo della Pergola kept a school of philosophy, geometry and arithmetic, and at his death his chair was assumed by Domenigo Bragadino, a Venetian patrician. (1)

(1)   See Chapter LX.

Near the Church of San Giovanni Evangelista in Rialto stood, about the same period, a house where, every morning and afternoon, public lecturers, salaried by the government, delivered readings in philosophy and theology. One of the most distinguished lecturers was the noble Antonio Corraro, whose love of literature and intellectual attainments gave him the highest reputation in his own time. At Saint Mark's, in the immediate neighbourhood of the Campanile, there was a school or academy where humanity was taught without any fees; among the earliest professors at that establishment were Giorgio Valla and the historiographer Sabellico.

From the twelfth century, the more highly educated Venetians were usually masters of Latin and Greek. In 1170, Pasquale, Bishop of Equilo, was appointed by Vitale Michiele III. as one of his ambassadors to the Byzantine court, on account of his peculiar conversance with Greek, and this circumstance, while it may indicate the rarity of the accomplishment, establishes its existence. The Romans themselves had been very imperfectly acquainted with the literature of their predecessors in power and in culture, until they extended their conquests and rule into eastern Europe.

The unhappy son of the unhappy Doge Foscari was a zealous phil-Hellenist and a collector of Greek and Latin manuscripts. The language generally employed at Venice was Latin, and, among the lower orders, a dialect or patois of which some account has been given. The general ignorance of Hebrew necessitated the perusal of the Scriptures in the Vulgate, and it was this necessity, more than any other cause, perhaps, which led to the acquisition of the former. In the first half of the fifteenth century, there were several scholars, among whom were Marco Lippomano (1) and Daniele Reniero, who were competent to read the Bible in the original.

(1)   Blondus, *Italia Ilustrata,* sign. H2.

Not only were the Latin, Greek, and Hebrew tongues studied, understood and spoken at an early date, but even Arabic, of which the most ancient printed examples, however, appeared, not here, but at Fano, from the press of Gregorio de Gregoriis, a Venetian subject, and one of two brothers who subsequently established themselves at Venice.

In the first moiety of the sixteenth century, Sebastiano Erizzo, a member of the Council of Ten, an antiquary and numismatist, delivered readings at Padua University on the fruitfulness of the study of ancient coins. Erizzo was born in 1522 and died in 1585.

About the same time we hear of Giorgio Colonna as a miniaturist, just before the period when Titian and Veronese arose to execute on a larger scale likenesses of some of their countrymen and countrywomen, so many of which must have perished or remain unidentified.

A department in which the Venetians publicly shone was poetry. (1) An ancient poem entitled *Leandreis,* on the mythological loves of Hero and Leander by an anonymous Venetian coeval with Petrarch, (2) introduces Dante speaking of the Venetian bards of his day:

> *Dirove alquante nobele person e,*
> *E primo e Zuan Quei-in, che mi fo amicho*
> *In vita; e l' altro, che appo lui si pone,*
> *Zuan Foscharen.* (3)

(1)   Morelli, *Dissertazione Sulla Cultura della Poesia Presso li Veneziani.* In Alfani, *Poeti del Primo Secolo,* there is not a single Venetian Poem. The editor has not even included the sonnet of

Antonio Cocco to Sacchetti, which is found in Allatius, *Poeti Antichi*, and of which the first stanza is here given:

(2)   Morelli, *Dissertazione Sulla Cultura della Poesia Presso li Veneziani.*

(3)   Agostini, *Notizie degli Scrittori Viniziani*, Preface page xv.

> *Ame e gran gratia, Francho, aver udito*
> *La fama, che di voi nel mondo corre;*
> *E questa e stata fondamento e dorre*
> *A durmi qui sanz' aver altro invito.* Allatius, *Poeti Antichi.*

Quirini, whom Dante here claims as his friend, addressed a madrigal to an acquaintance, Matteo Mattivilla of Bologna, (1) in which he begs the latter to transmit to him a copy of the *Acerba* of Cecco d'Ascoli, containing strictures on the *Divina Commedia*, and declares himself prepared to vindicate Dante.

(1)   Morelli, *Dissertazione Sulla Cultura della Poesia Presso li Veneziani.*

A production, belonging (if genuine) to an earlier epoch than the *Leandreis*, and equally anonymous, is called *A Lament for the Absence of a Husband at the Crusade in the East*. The author who was perhaps a lady may be no other than "Dona Frisa" herself:

> *Responder voi a Dona Frisa,*
> *Che me conseia en la soa guisa.*
> *E dis ch' eo lasse ogni grameza,*
> *Vezando me senza alegrezza;*
> *Che me mario se n' e andao,*
> *Ch' el me cor cum lui a portao;*
> *Et eo cum ti me Deo comfortare.*
> *Fin ch' el stara de la da mare.* (1)

(1)   Gamba, *Raccolta di Poesie in Dialetto Veneziano d'Ogni Secolo*, page 1-2.

Besides Giovanni Quirini (1) and Giovanni Foscarini, the *Leandreis* mentions Bernardo Foscarini and a second Quirini, Nicolo, Rector of San Basso and a participator in the Quirini-Tiepolo conspiracy of 1310, (2) some of whose effusions are in the Biblioteca Barberina at Rome.

(1)   This poet must not be confounded with another of the same
        name who wrote in the sixteenth century, some of whose pieces
        are preserved by Gamba.
(2)   Allatius, *Poeti Antichi,* Indici.

So far back as 1268, the Merchant Tailors had recited in the streets of the
capital, in honour of the accession of the new Doge Lorenzo Tiepolo,
ballads and scraps of roundelays, either extemporized or committed to
memory. It is not hazardous to conclude that these melodies belonged to
the rudest school of composition. There is some reason to suppose (1)
that the silk weavers of Lucca, when they forsook their native looms and
fled from the hand of persecution to Venice between 1315 and 1320,
introduced to their adopted countrymen the ditties which they had so
dearly loved in happier days, and that this event, while it was fraught
with utility to the Republic in a commercial respect, was also
instrumental in imparting to Venetian poetry a certain Tuscan element.

(1)   Tommaseo, *Canti del Popolo Veneziano Raccolti,* page 8.

But it is certain that, long before the Lucchese migration, a great reform
was wrought in poetry by Bartolomeo Giorgio, a patrician, and almost a
contemporary of Tiepolo. By profession, Giorgio was a merchant, and
his taste for the lyric muse was acquired during his residence at the court
of the Count of Provence, (1) where he tells us that many other Italians
had congregated for the purpose of studying the literature of the
jongleurs and troubadours.

(1)   Foscarini, *Della Letteratura Veneziana,* page 50 Number 2;
        Taylor, (*The Lays of the Minnesingers,* page 101) mentions him
        as a gentleman of the city of Venice, evidently quoting from a
        description of Giorgio or Zorzi elsewhere.

Giorgio or Zorzi, no doubt in his commercial capacity, visited other
countries, and he is stated to have composed a funeral dirge or anthem on
the death of Conrad II. of Sicily, in or about 1268. On his return home,
the Venetian composed certain songs or *canzoni,* similar to those which
he had heard in Provence, and a revolution was gradually operated in this
branch of the liberal arts. The bard had subsequently, in every probability
during the arduous struggle between his own country and Genoa, the
misfortune to be taken prisoner by the enemy, and it seems that he
remained in their hands seven years, during which space he possibly
wrote many pieces now lost. At all events, of his *canzoni* or *serventesi,*

seventeen (1) only survive in the Vatican; of these five were rendered into prose by the Abbe Millot.

(1)   Foscarini, *Della Letteratura Veneziana,* page 50 Number 2.

For the use of church-choirs a musical compendium entitled *Cantorinus* was printed in 1513, and purported to embrace within its covers all necessary and available information for learners and students.

The custom of lightening toil by some sort of rude vocal melody had been very familiar to the Greeks, and was widely diffused over Mediaeval Europe. Each trade had its own peculiar compositions handed down from father to son, from mother to daughter. The Venetian craftsman beguiled the monotony of a sedentary employment, like the Huguenot weavers of Spitalfields, by singing to traditional airs words the author of which he, perhaps, could not have named; and the gondolier in the good old days of autonomy made the canals echo with their favourite fragments of popular effusions, caught by ear or inherited from generation to generation. Looking back through the vista of years and of ages, we already in the thirteenth century discern at Venice a school of national music and song among the operative classes, which naturally found freer scope and a fuller throat amid the exuberant gaiety of the independent holiday life.

In the latter half of the fourteenth century, flourished Marino Dandolo, Gabriele Bernardo, Maffeo Pesaro, Antonio Cocco, whose sonnet to Franco Sacchetti has been mentioned as having been printed by Allacci, Marco Piacentino some of whose metrical trifles are in existence, and Filippo Barbarigo, an imitator of Petrarch. During the reign of Andrea Contarini, Pietro di Natali, Bishop of Equilo, composed in *terza rima, The Visit of Alexander III. to Venice* (in 1177), (1) which has escaped the ravages of time, and, about 1381, Marco Giorgio the theologian finished a *Life of the Blessed Felix Benci of Florence* in heroic verse. (2) In the succeeding reign, Lorenzo de Monacis, Grand Chancellor of Candia but better known as an historian, dedicated to Mary, Queen of Hungary, consort of Sigismund, (3) *A Poem of Charles of Hungary, called, the Little, with a pious description of the miserable haps of the Illustrious Queens of Hungary.* This performance (4) is supposed to have seen the light about 1385.

(1)   Morelli, *Dissertazione Sulla Cultura della Poesia Presso li Veneziani.*

(2)   Zeno, P., *Memorie de' Scrittori Veneti Patrizi Ecclesiastici e Secolari.*

(3)   Mary died in 1392, according to Bonfinius, *Res Ungaricara Decades Tres,* page 383.

(4)   It will be found at the end of Flaminio Cornaro's edition of the Monacis, *Chronicon de Rebus Venetis.*

Toward the end of the century, it is said that an Olivetan monk, Matteo Routo, was engaged in turning the *Divine Comedy* into heroic verse, but it seems to be doubtful whether the work was ever completed. (1) A few decades posterior to Routo, Maffeo Pisani, a priest, produced (1453) a *Lament for Constantinople* in verse, still preserved in print. (2)

(1)   Morelli, *Dissertazione Sulla Cultura della Poesia Presso li Veneziani.*

(2)   See Cicogna, *Saggio di Bibliografia Veneziana.*

Nor was it long before sacred poetry grew into fashion. The famous Minorite, Fra Jacopone da Todi, author of the *Stabat Mater Dolorosa,* found zealous disciples in Jacopo Valaresso and Leonardo Pisani, (1) both of whom, under the Contarini and Veniero administrations (1368-1400), occupied their leisure with spiritual offerings to the Muse. In or about 1399, the Cavaliere Jacopo Gradenigo, Podesta of Padua, whose family had intermarried with the House of Carrara, (2) put a finishing hand to *A Concordance of the Four Gospels,* in *terza rima,* of which a transcript was among the manuscript treasures of an eminent antiquary and scholar of the eighteenth century. (3)

(1)   Agostini, *Notizie degli Scrittori Viniziani,* Preface.

(2)   Morelli, *Dissertazione Sulla Cultura della Poesia Presso li Veneziani.*

(3)   Zeno, A, *Lettere di Apostolo Zeno.*

A little later, the two sons of Bernardo Giustiniani (1) trod worthily in the footsteps of Valaresso and Pisani, the pupils of Da Todi. The elder, Lorenzo, successively Prior of San Giorgio in Alga, Bishop of Castello and Patriarch of Venice, comprised, among the thirty-six works on various subjects which proceeded from his prolific pen, (2) a small garland of *Spiritual Rhymes.* (3) The future Metropolitan, who was subsequently canonized, was born in 1380; (4) the composition of these rhymes may therefore be assigned, without particular hazard, to some period between 1400 and 1410.

(1)   Agostini, *Notizie degli Scrittori Viniziani,* Volume I page 135.
(2)   Zeno, P., *Memorie de' Scrittori Veneti Patrizi Ecclesiastici e Secolari,* in voce Giustiniani.
(3)   Zeno, P., *Memorie de' Scrittori Veneti Patrizi Ecclesiastici e Secolari*e. In 1494 his *Doctrina della Vela Monastica* was published at Venice, and it was accompanied by an engraved portrait of Giustiniani copied from an original painting by Gentile Bellini.
(4)   Agostini, *Notizie degli Scrittori Viniziani,* Volume I page 136.

Leonardo, who was the junior of San Lorenzo by about eight years, and pronounced in 1418 the funeral oration on his friend (1) Carlo Zeno (2) had written in his younger days a volume of *Poesie Volgari* of a profane cast; (3) but at the persuasion of his brother he eventually abandoned this school of poetry, and became the author of *Laudi Spirituali,* which were received with applause, and were printed at Venice in 1474. (4) In the following year, they were reproduced at Vicenza, and such was their reputation, that the printer, Leonard of Basle, ventured to take off 1000 copies. (5)

(1)   Bernardo Giustiniani, writing to Giacomo Zeno, the nephew of Carlo, says: *"Vetus ilia necessitudo et amicitia, quae inter praeclarum virum Carolum avum tuum Leonardumque patrem meum fuit."*
(2)   *"Viri Patricii Leonardi Justiniani Veneti oratio habita in funere Caroli Zeni concivis sui,"* presso Giustiniani, B., *Epistole di Bernardo Giustiniano (suo figlio),* Venice 1492, folio; frequently reprinted.
(3)   Blondus, *Italia Ilustrata,* sign. H1.
(4)   *"Incominciano le devotissime et sanctissime Laudi le quali compose el Nobele e Magnifico Messer Leonardo Giustiniano."*
(5)   Agostini, *Notizie degli Scrittori Viniziani,* Volume I page 165.

The family of Giustiniani was rarely gifted, and boasted the heraldry of genius as well as of birth. The celebrated Ciriaco de Pizzecolli of Ancona, addressing Leonardo in a sonnet which was printed for the first time by Agostini, says:

> *Se stencle fino al Ciel con care piume*
> *La fama del valor Justiniano.* (1)

(1)   Agostini, *Notizie degli Scrittori Viniziani,* Volume I page 154.

According to the testimony of a contemporary, (1) this gentleman was not only one of the most conspicuous orators of the age, but a passionate musician. After filling several responsible posts under the government and attaining the Procuratorial dignity, he died in 1446 in his 58th or 59th year. His *Poesie Volgari* were still in manuscript when the *Laudi* were given to the press in 1474, but the former also appeared in 1482, and were republished a few years later, with additions. (2) The metre of the *Canzonette* is irregular, and occasionally rugged and inharmonious.

(1)   Blondus, *Italia Ilustrata,* sign. H1.
(2)   Giustiniani, L., *Comincio il Fiore delle Elegantissime Cancionete del Nobile Messere Leonardo Justiniano.* The colophon is; *Il fine delle elegantissime cancionette di Messere Leonardo Justiniano quivi in Venetia con ogni diligentia impresse per Antonio di Strata a di nove Marzo MCCCCLXXXII,* in quarto.

To miscellaneous literature, Leonardo Giustiniani contributed from Plutarch translations (1) of the biographies of Cimon, Lucullus and Phocion, a life of Saint Nicholas the Confessor, Bishop of Myra, (2) containing a prefatory dedication to his brother Lorenzo, then Bishop of Castello, at whose suggestion he had undertaken the labour; numerous letters, printed in 1492; some elegiac verses on the death of Victorino of Feltre; and a book, entitled *Liber Philologicus,* of which little seems to be known, except that it was seen by Montfaucon in the choice library of Bernardo Trevisano. (3)

(1)   Giustiniani, L., *Canzonette e Stramhotti d'Amore Composte per el Magnifico Miser Leonardo Zustignano di Venetia.*
(2)   Printed by Aldus, with other opusculi, in 1502.
(3)   Agostini, *Notizie degli Scrittori Viniziani,* Volume I page 174-175.

Aesop seems to have acquired popularity among some of the educated class. A whimsical case is cited, in which the shops were ransacked for forty-one copies of the *Fables,* because a member of the Quarantia had, during a suspended sitting, called for the book to beguile the time, and it was thought necessary to observe impartiality by placing a copy in the hands of each of the councillors.

In 1409, the wife of Leonardo, reputed to have been Maria Quirini, (1) bore her husband a son, who was christened Bernardo after his grandfather. This Bernardo was destined to attain the highest distinction as an orator and historian. He was thirty-seven when his illustrious parent died, and was inconsolable for the loss. He immediately called on his uncle Lorenzo the Bishop, who told him to be of good cheer: "for," said he, "your father is in the path of salvation." "How can you tell that?" responded the young man. "Never mind," persisted the other: "be assured that he is on the way to heaven, and for the rest do not concern yourself!" (2)

(1)   Agostini, *Notizie degli Scrittori Viniziani,* Volume I page 36.
(2)   Agostini, *Notizie degli Scrittori Viniziani,* Volume I page 162.

After the death of San Lorenzo, his nephew became his biographer, and the *Life of the Patriarch* was among the earliest productions of the Venetian press. It appeared in 1475, (1) and was prefixed to the *Works of the Saint* published at Brescia in 1505. The other performances of the same writer are a funeral oration on the Doge Foscari, (2) which he delivered in 1457, and a *History of the Origin of Venice*, bringing down the annals to the year 809 — both in Latin. In the latter, which was translated into the vernacular by Lodovico Domenichi and printed in 1545, Giustiniani has introduced a variety of particulars not seen elsewhere. The genuineness of the narrative is largely established by the circumstance, that it is expressly stated to have been partially founded on the *Chronicle* of Zeno, Abbot of San Nicolo del Lido (3) from 1070 to 1100. Bernardo, whose life has been written by Antonio Stella, a Venetian priest, and published in 1553, left a son Pancrazio who in his turn won literary renown.

(1)   Foscarini, *Della Letteratura Veneziana,* page 324 Number 1.
(2)   Foscarini, *Della Letteratura Veneziana,* page 316.
(3)   Romanin, *Storia Documentata di Venezia,* Volume IV page 502-503.

The universal practice of commemorating notable and glorious events in verse or prose was by no means unknown. It seems to have commenced in the fifteenth century, and, when facilities for printing effusions of this kind were given by the multiplication of presses, an historical landmark like the Battle of Lepanto in 1571 was bound to evoke an abundance of patriotic ephemerides. We have before us a list of between sixty and seventy poems written on that occasion, principally anonymous.

In a sphere of usefulness totally different from that of his predecessor and namesake, a second Marino Sanudo, son of Leonardo Sanudo, a distinguished public servant, by his wife Letizia Venier, was born on the 22nd of May, 1466, in the Street of San Giacomo dall'Orio. He lost his father when a boy of ten, and was taken by his mother to the Castello di Sanguinetto in the Veronese, where he was placed under competent tutors. Amid other calls both of a public and private character, he, at the age of thirty, conceived and began to execute the design of commemorating the transactions of his country on a principle entirely new. From day to day or at brief intervals, Sanudo registered in a folio volume every incident which came under his observation, as he attended the meetings of the Great Council, or sauntered on the Broglio or the Exchange, or met with the recipients of news from outlying districts and abroad. He even prevailed on the Council of Ten to permit him to examine public documents under their charge or control, and he lived to see his notes and collections fill fifty-eight volumes, and include certain papers nowhere else preserved.

The work was compiled on a scale which renders their use and quotation, even to a moderate extent, in a general work, a sheer impossibility, inasmuch as they represent a daily record of the transactions, not of Venice or even Italy, but of Europe, as they progressively unfolded themselves.

The *Diaries* or *Ephemerides* are written throughout in the Venetian patois, except here and there where the author diverges into normal Italian or Latin. They concern external affairs almost to a larger extent than those of Venice itself, but they very preciously illustrate the foreign interests and policy of the Republic during the thirty-three years which they cover. The diarist appears to have gained the earliest and exactest knowledge of the meetings and compositions of the several councils and their agenda, and to have been permitted to take notes (1) of their proceedings and decisions. The diction of Sanudo occasionally strikes one as careless rather than idiomatic as where he uses such a form as Elemagna for Germany, and uses indifferently the forms Puglia and Puja, *ozi* and *hogi*.

(1)   The original manuscripts were removed to Vienna at the dissolution of the Republic, but were restored by the Austrian government in 1868 with other papers.

He omits nothing, forgets nothing; even when he is arrested for a small debt, owing to his absorption in his employment and neglect of his affairs, he mentions where the tipstaff met him, and how long he was detained in the sponging house. He speaks of it as "*l'orribil casa.*" But, on the whole, the autobiographical element is by no means conspicuous, and he does not register, as a rule, petty, local or current incidents. In one place, however, he cited a case in which a man was hanged for a theft of jewellery, and a suspected accomplice failed to confess under the cord, which he characterizes as a notable matter, whereas assuredly it must have been a by no means unusual occurrence. In another way, under the date, the 18th of December, 1531, he lets us understand that a mob of women (he puts it as 7000 or 8000!) had a few weeks before sallied from London with the intention of killing Anne Boleyn, "*l'amata del Re d'Inghilterra,*" who was supping in a summer-house on the Thames, and that she was forewarned of the danger and escaped in a wherry.

This monumental work not only survives in its integrity, but a careful transcript of it was actually made for the historiographer Francesco Donato, with a view to a work on the subject in the eighteenth century; and now the Italian government has generously presented us with the whole in type (1879-1903). The series is as unique as Venice itself, yet the two cyclopaedias, printed at the cost of a private individual during the period of independence and extending to fifty-four large volumes, almost eclipse it in magnitude, if not in permanent importance.

During the life of Sanudo, little or nothing was known of his incessant application to what he made his career, and after his death the whole work and its author were equally forgotten. It is fortunate that the manuscript volumes escaped all accidents, and can be added to the grand trophy which the Republic has erected to its own memory and honour.

Besides his *Diaries*, Sanudo left *Lives of the Doges*, incorrectly printed by Muratori, a description of the magistrates of Venice, a treatise *De Bella Gallico*, which may be what he describes in the commencement of his *Diary* as "*La Guerra Francese in Italia,*" a *Commentary on the War of Ferrara*, privately issued in 1829, and an *Itinerary of the Venetian Terra Firma* in 1483, with original sketches of places visited and inspected by him; this was printed in 1847, accompanied by facsimiles of the illustrations. Thus justice has been done, only in our days, to a man whose exertions and sacrifices in the cause of learning were so exceptionally great, and whose sole personal reward was the affectionate ardour with which he followed his favourite and self-chosen path.

Sanudo seems to have been brought into the world for the express purpose of accumulating records of the proceedings and careers of others, for the benefit of an unknown posterity which too tardily awards him recognition and thanks. From his boyhood, he evinced an enthusiasm for antiquities and historical inquiry, and, at a period of life when many have not yet quitted school, he was an author. When he was a child of about eight, he started on his mission by transcribing the inscriptions, then beginning to fade, beneath the portraits of the Doges in the Council Chamber. This must, from collateral evidence, have been in 1474, and the realization of the small fissure at work is not a little interesting. At seventeen he produced his *Itinerary*, and entered into every variety of technical and financial detail. But the central and crowning labour was the stupendous and invaluable *Diary*, extending over seven and thirty years (1496-1533).

That it is an arid register of events and a repository of dull archives is true enough; it is equally the case that it preserves to us, at the hands of a man of rank and culture, the history, not of Venice alone, but of Italy and Europe during many momentous and eventful years, interspersed with occasional glimpses of the personal history and experiences of Sanudo as a youthful lover of the peerless Gemma, as a statesman whose views generally found him in opposition, as an indifferent economist who was sometimes reduced to financial straits, and as a book-collector.

The social position of the diarist afforded him immense opportunities for obtaining information, and facilitated intercourse with the best Venetian and Lombard families. He fell in love with a maiden at Rovigo, probably during his tour in 1483, visited the family, and composed songs in honour and praise of Gemma; (1) but he remained single, and devoted himself to his writings and his library which included many charts and topographical drawings, and amounted in the aggregate to 6500 volumes, printed and in manuscript, of which he drew up a catalogue with his own hand. This was a larger assemblage of literary monuments than the combined public libraries at that time in London, Oxford and Cambridge.

(1)   It is slightly uncertain whether this is a real or a poetical name. It was the name of the lady whom Dante married about two centuries before.

Sanudo had completed some of his works, and had by him versions both in Latin and Venetian for the benefit of learned and unlearned, when

Aldus inscribed to him one of his publications in 1498; the *Itinerary* and *Commentary on the Ferrarese War* were also probably in existence, and the *Diary* in progress. In 1498 he was two and thirty, and he pursued all these literary occupations and his public duties, amid continual interruptions from visitors desirous of seeing him and his treasures. Sometimes he consented to receive them; sometimes he declined, even when it was a prince. But he lived to witness the day when great personages presented themselves at Venice, and were told that there were three things worth seeing — the Arsenal, the Treasury of Saint Mark, and the Sanudo Library. Sanudo was Treasurer of Verona when Anne de Candalles, accompanied by the Marchioness of Saluzzo and a French retinue, passed through that city on her way to Venice, where she was to meet the delegates of her future husband the King of Hungary, and proceed thence to Alba Reale. He informs us that he tendered his services to the two ladies, and made their stay at Verona agreeable; it was for him almost a unique experience.

The diarist died poor on the 4th of April, 1536. He had been repeatedly disappointed in his wish to obtain the post of Historiographer, but the Council of Ten, in consideration of his literary labours, allowed him for many years an annuity of 150 ducats, which, as he truly observes, was a mere nothing; the sale of his books and other effects must have realized an appreciable amount. Yet it is not unnatural that he should have been angry at the preferment of others to an office so peculiarly congenial and appropriate, and that even the Council of Ten should have found some difficulty in prevailing on him to allow Cardinal Bembo to make use of his material. The *Diaries*, however, were appropriated by the Council of Ten, and had been kept in a private apartment where they were lost to sight; they were regarded as having perished, until casually recovered in 1784 by Francesco Donato.

He was evidently a many-sided man, to whom study and knowledge were the greatest charms of life. He was a genuine collector who could not refrain from dwelling over a bargain, even if it resulted from the pressure of bad times, for, in his will, dated the 4th of December, 1533, he expressly tells us that many of his acquisitions had been made at seasons of great public distress; we should, however, recollect that it was long his intention to make the Republic his heir.

Besides Sanudo, there were two other patricians about the same stirring and critical period who compiled similar records of their observations and impressions — Girolamo Priuli and Marcantonio Michiel. Priuli carried on his notes from 1494 to 1512, and Michiel from 1512 to 1545. The *Diary* of Priuli extended to eight volumes, and two manuscripts of it exist, both unfortunately incomplete, but the two form a perfect set, save in the third volume; it seems to be questionable whether either is the original copy.

The distinguished statesman Marcantonio Barbaro, to whom Yriarte has dedicated a monograph, was, among his multifarious public functions, employed by his government to delimit the Friulan frontier in conjunction with the representative of the Emperor, in order to preclude any farther disputes. Barbaro received from the Senate on the 15th of December, 1583, the fullest and clearest instructions. He was to have an exact chart drawn up of the territory, shewing not only every town, river, mountain, but the number of inhabitants, the character of the soil and a variety of other minutiae. He was to have two hundred golden ducats a month as pay, and not to be accountable for his disbursements to any one. But it is to be concluded, that this eminent and trusty public servant had a confidential charge to report on the question of points in Friuli toward the Imperial or Austrian lines which it might be expedient to strengthen, for we find, sixteen years before, a fortnight's debate in the Senate, in which Barbaro held his ground against a heavy majority and won the day, arguing that it was of no use to establish fortresses in the interior of a province, unless the frontier was protected, since an enemy could pass the former.

The discussion had lasted at least since 1544, and did not terminate till 1593, when the Senate allowed Barbaro to follow his own ideas and furnished him with the means. The fortification of Friuli proved of importance, both against the Germans and the Turks in course of time, but unhappily the vitality of the Republic was ebbing, and a few strong heads could accomplish less and less against the inevitable issue.

At the very period when Barbaro was distinguishing himself by his versatile abilities, another Venetian, Fra Paolo Sarpi, discovered an even higher genius for learning, and an even wider diversity of accomplishments. (1) The mother of Paolo was a tall, fair, gentle lady, but his father is described as a little man with a touch of the bravo. There was also a daughter of the marriage, who, with her mother, withdrew into a convent after the death of Francesco Sarpi. Young Paolo was brought up by his maternal uncle, who seems to have educated many other distinguished Venetians. At the age of twenty, he had begun to acquire a knowledge of the classics and the sciences, and he gradually became proficient in Greek, Latin, mathematics, theology and canon law, as well as in astronomy, chemistry, anatomy and every other branch of human learning which his retentive memory enabled him to store up and utilize on occasion. At twenty-six he was elected Provincial Master of his order. In person he was small, but he is described as having had plenty of pluck or fight in him; he seldom bought books, and relied on those lent to him by his friends, particularly by his worthy acquaintance Bernardo Secchini to whose shop he was a constant visitor.

(1)   Farther particulars of this eminent personage may be found in antecedent chapters (Chapter XXXVI et seqq.).

In 1574, when Sarpi had reached his twenty-second year, his enemies, of whom he had already so early the honour of possessing many, raised a cry that he did not believe the inspiration of the Holy Ghost, and that he was in correspondence and league with Jews, the latter charge arising from the fact that Sarpi jocularly quoted, in reference to a very estimable French Jew whom he met in a shop, the sentence: "*Ecce vere Israelita in quo dolus non est.*" (1) The Inquisitors dismissed the whole accusation as absurd and malicious.

(1)   John, *The Gospel According to Saint John,* 1:47.

It was his intimacy with Camillo Olivo, secretary to Cardinal Gonzaga, which probably gave Fra Paolo his earliest insight into the policy of the Roman Curia, and led him to qualify himself for the task of championing his native country against the pretensions of the Holy See. He was essentially, more or less in common with many Italians of that age, a man of the most varied acquirements, and endeavoured to render himself familiar with all branches of human knowledge; but in canon and civil law he was a specialist, and there he was best able to serve the Republic which learned to entertain for him the highest respect and affection, when the rupture with Paul V. occurred in 1605.

Although so formidable an antagonist, Sarpi had inherited from his mother a nature which won him friends wherever he went. He was welcome alike at home, at Mantua, at Milan and in the Eternal City, and, previously to the schism with Venice in which he played so prominent a part, he remained on the most friendly terms with successive Pontiffs. When the day arrived for him to put on his armour and stand forward to fight the cause of the Republic, he had acquired, no less in public life than in the closet, all that ripe culture which made him so excellent and so unanswerable an advocate, and which prompted the most jealous of governments to confide to his hands a task beyond the reach and compass even of Venetian diplomatists.

It was while Sarpi was side by side, as it were, with Barbaro, yet in a different way, completing himself in his studies (1572-1600), that he was, perhaps unconsciously, making ready to stand forth as the advocate of the Republic in the struggle with the Spanish faction at Rome, which used as its tool the reigning Pontiff, and betrayed him into the issue of the famous interdict of 1605. This admirable personage, this earlier and greater Magliabecchi, whom it is out of the question to rank with Paul V. in the controversy, and who could see behind His Holiness the real authors of the movement — the wire-pullers inspired from Naples and Milan, this genuine Master of Arts, would have attained distinction in any calling; but to us he is realized as the daring polemical opponent of the Holy See, who relied, and safely relied, on the unflinching support of his own government in resisting the Pontifical claims, at the very moment when a knot of Romanists was nearly successful in England in destroying king and parliament.

The writings of this illustrious Venetian remain standard. His *History of the Council of Trent* is his most esteemed production. But in no instance, perhaps, is it more true than in this, that the man overshadows the author; and therefore it is especially fortunate that we possess a biography which bears evidence of having been composed by some one who was well acquainted with Sarpi, and has handed down interesting personal traits of a man so well meriting immortality on all accounts. His heart to the last was in his work, and devoted to a country which so honoured and trusted him.

In 1580, James Crichton of Clunie, in Perthshire, who had arrived at Venice from Genoa in a destitute state, managed to introduce himself to the distinguished scholar and printer Aldus Manutius, and presented him with the manuscript of a Latin poem, which Manutius printed. To an edition of Cicero *De Officiis et cetera* which was then in preparation, (1) Crichton contributed two Latin odes and the printer a panegyric on his visitor. Aldus did his best to make the young Scot known, and the latter was at length commissioned to deliver a Latin oration before the Senate. On the 19th of August, the College, seeing that Crichton was in straitened circumstances, decided to give him 100 gold crowns, and he left the city where he had experienced such hospitality and munificence, to proceed with a good introduction to Padua.

(1)   Cicero, *De Officiis,* Venetiis, 1581, folio. In a copy before me
        there is a note on the fly-leaf, said to be in the hand of Bishop
        Butler, in which Crichton's Latinity is censured.

The Admirable had seldom had such good days as these; he was killed at
Mantua in 1582 by the young Prince of Mantua in a nocturnal brawl, and
Aldus published an obituary and memoir. But an earlier visitor, the
Neapolitan poet Sannazzaro, had had a yet more striking experience of
lavish Venetian bounty, when, for a hexastich on the Republic, he was
requited with six hundred ducats, or more probably than he had gained
for his literary works during his whole life. (1)

(1)   Lovelace inserted a translation of this eulogy in his *Lucasta,*
        1659, and a very poor one it is; but it is not worse than his satire
        on the gift, which is dull and prolix beyond measure.

The Scots appear to have found their way to Venice as well as other
Italian centres. Crichton printed some of his *opusculi* here and others at
Milan. The Keeper of the Library of Saint Mark's in the sixteenth
century was for some time John Dempster who died in 1571, and who
may have been related to George Dempster, Professor of Philosophy at
Pavia in 1495. A less favourable illustration of the tendency of the north
Britons to foregather abroad was the information supplied to the Doge
Donato by Sir Henry Wotton, that the assailant of Fra Paolo Sarpi was a
Scot who passed under a factitious name. In 1618, a rumour was current
that a Scotish engineer was, or had been, in Venice, purporting to have a
scheme for undermining Saint Mark's under pretence of erecting a
fountain in the Piazza. The poverty of the country under the Stuarts, and
its intimate relations with the Continent, explain the occurrence of
Scotish names in the Italian transactions of that epoch as adventurers
even of the most equivocal type. The assassin of Wallenstein, some years
later, was Gordon the Scot who appears to have been known as the
Marquis de Gourdon.

Very few branches of research were neglected by those who lived under
the old government; even in the colonies, we have from the pen of
Onorio Belli an account of the theatres and other remains in Candia,
drawn up in 1586 but not printed till 1854, when an English version by
Edward Falkener appeared as a supplement to his *Museum of Classical
Antiquities.* Belli was a native of Bergamo who had settled at Vicenza.
He acted as medical officer under the Venetian Governor-General of

Candia. He was a well-known antiquary, physician and botanist, and a correspondent of Pigafetta and other learned contemporaries, and, in the course of his stay in Candia, made notes and sketches of many buildings long since destroyed.

Besides the accumulation during ages of literary productions in manuscript form, of which not a few at last found their way into type, there was, from a remote date, the same body of traditional and oral learning common to all other regions, more or less varied by local circumstances and experience. More than one collection of early popular rhymes peculiar to districts in Lombardy, Venice inclusive, have been published; some of these yet current within the limits of the old Republic partake of the nature of charms and invocations. We perceive that different classes of superstitions, not dissimilar from those recorded in the folk-lore of more westerly countries, prevailed among the lower orders of Venetians, and that there was the same credulous faith in the efficacy of prayer to cure diseases, to heal wounds, to staunch blood, to secure a passage to heaven, and even to redeem souls from purgatory.

It has been incidentally noted that a belief in the virtues of the magical art was part of the popular faith here from the Middle Ages, and that, among other forms which it assumed, it led serfs to ingratiate themselves with their employers and proprietors by means of philtres and charms. A manuscript. of the fourteenth century, elsewhere quoted, furnishes actual texts, not of these incantations, which were never probably committed to writing, but of some of those to which reference has just been made, and which were fortuitously preserved by some well-meriting antiquary of the fourteenth century. Others have been more recently recovered from the lips of the people, a more or less treacherous source, which becomes after protracted neglect the sole one at our command. It has been affirmed that these remains of ancient folk-lore are still remembered and repeated. (1)

(1)   (compilation) *The Antiquary,* Volume XXXVIII page 266-267.

Here is a short formula of a particular type:

Chi la leze, chi la sa,	He who reads it, he who knows it,
In Paradise i ghe andara;	To Paradise shall go;
Chi no la leze, e chi no la sa,	Who reads it not, who knows it not,
A casa del diavolo i andara.	To the devil's house must go.

Others were more elaborate and difficult of execution, scarcely surprising, when it is considered what momentous fruits they in some cases bore. Subjoined is the spell for rescuing three souls from purgatory, which has to be repeated three consecutive times without a mistake in order to be effectual. It is one of those which is declared, rightly or wrongly, still to hold its ground.

1. *E una ... e una:*
    E una la luna.
    Chi a crea, sto mondo,
    L' e sti'l Nostro Signore.

    1. And one ... and one:
        The moon is one.
        He who created this world
        Was our Master and Lord.

2. *E do ... e do:*
    L'aseno e' l bo,
    El Bambin e la cuna,
    El sol e la luna.
    Chi a crea sto mondo
    L' e sta 'l Nostro Signore.

    2. And two ... and two:
        The ass and the ox,
        The Child and the cradle,
        The sun and the moon.
        He who created the world
        Was our Master and Lord.

3. *E tre ... e tre:*
    I santi tre Re Magi,
    L' asino e 'l bo,
    (et cetera).

    3. And three ... and three:
        The holy three Kings,
        The ass and the ox,
        (et cetera).

4. *E quatro ... e quatro:*
    I quatro Evangelista,
    I santi tre Magi,
    (et cetera).

    4. And four ... and four:
        The four Evangelists,
        The holy three Kings,
        (et cetera).

5. *E cinque ... e cinque:*
    Le cinque piaghe del Nostro Signor,
    I quatro Evangelista,
    (et cetera).

    5. And five ... and five:
        The five wounds of our Lord,
        The four Evangelists,
        (et cetera).

6. *E sie ... e sie:*
    I sie gali di Galilea,
    Le cinque piaghe del Nostro Signor,
    (et cetera).

    6. And six ... and six:
        The six cocks of Galilee,
        The five wounds of our Lord,
        (et cetera).

7. *E sete ... e sete:*

    7. And seven ... and seven:

Le sete alegrezze della Madonna,
I sie gali di Galilea,
(et cetera).

The seven joys of our Lady,
The six cocks of Galilee,
(et cetera).

8. *E oto ... e oto:*
   Li oto portoni di Roma,
   Le sete alegrezze della Madonna,
   (et cetera).

8. And eight ... and eight:
   The eight gates of Rome,
   The seven joys of our Lady,
   (et cetera).

9. *E nove ... e nove:*
   I nove cori de Anzoli,
   Li oto portoni di Roma,
   (et cetera).

9. And nine ... and nine:
   The nine choirs of angels,
   the eight gates of Rome,
   (et cetera).

10. *E diese ... e diese:*
    I diese commandamenti de la
    *   Lege di Dio,*
    I nove cori de Anzoli,
    (et cetera).

10. And ten ... and ten;
    The ten commandments of the
         Law of God,
    The nine choirs of angels,
    (et cetera).

11. *E undese ... e undese:*
    Maria Vergine,
    I diese commandamenti de la
    *   Lege di Dio,*
    (et cetera).

11. And eleven ... and eleven:
    Mary Virgin,
    The ten commandments of the
         Law of God,
    (et cetera).

12. *E dodese ... e dodese:*
    I dodese Apostoli del Nostro
    *   Signore,*
    Maria Vergine,
    (et cetera).

12. And twelve ... and twelve:
    The twelve Apostles of our
         Lord,
    Mary Virgin,
    (et cetera).

13. *E tredese ... e tredese:*
    Le tredese grazie di Sant
    *   Antonio,*
    I dodese Apostoli del Nostro
    *   Signore,*
    (et cetera).

13. And thirteen ... and thirteen:
    The thirteen graces of Saint
         Anthony,
    The twelve Apostles of our
         Lord,
    (et cetera).

14. *E quatordese ... e quatordese:*
    Le quatordese stazioni,

14. And fourteen ... and fourteen:
    The fourteen stations of the
         cross,

(et cetera).

(et cetera).

15. *E quindese ... e quindese:*
   I quindese misteri del Nostro
      Signore,
   Le quatordese stazioni,

   Le tredese grazie di Sant
      Antonio,
   I dodese Apostoli del Nostro
      Signore,
   Maria Vergine,
   I diese commandamenti de la
      Lege di Dio,
   I nove cori de Anzoli,
   Li oto portoni di Roma,
   Le sete alegrezze della Madonna,
   I sie gali di Galilea,
   Le cinque piaghe del Nostro
      Signor,
   I quatro Evangelista,
   I santi tre Re Magi,
   L'aseno e' l bo,
   El Bambin e la cuna,
   El sol e la luna.
   Chi a crea sto mondo
   L' e sta 'l Nostro Signore.

15. And fifteen ... and fifteen:
   The fifteen mysteries of our
      Lord,
   The fourteen stations of the
      cross,
   The thirteen graces of Saint
      Anthony,
   The twelve Apostles of our
      Lord,
   Mary Virgin,
   The ten commandments of the
      Law of God,
   The nine choirs of angels,
   The eight gates of Rome,
   The seven joys of our Lady,
   The six cocks of Galilee,
   The five wounds of our
      Lord,
   The four Evangelists,
   The holy three Kings,
   The ass and the ox,
   The Child and the cradle,
   The sun and the moon.
   He who created the world
   Was our Master and Lord.

These and similar superstitions yet linger in their early homes; but they will suffer the common incidence of such primitive ideas throughout the world. It is in the outlying districts, where they more than equally prevail, that they will survive the longest.

CHAPTER LXII

The Venetian Drama — Gregorio Corraro and His Progne — Private Theatricals — Japanese Envoys in 1585 — The First Theatre — Coryat's Comparison ff Venetian ad English Theatres — Theatre of San Cassiano — Evelyn Visits the Opera — Private Theatres of the Nobility — Popular Representations — Female Writers; Christine de Pisan, Cassandra Fedeli, Veronica Franco, Gaspara Stampa, Elena Coruaro — The Marcian Library — Depredations of Napoleon — Bibliographers — Origin of Printing; the Spiras, Jenson, Valdarfer, the Aldi — Provincial Presses — Literary Academies — Press Censorship — Collectors — Marino Faliero — The Vendramin Museum — An Old Bookseller — The Correr Museum — Bookbinding.

The Venetian drama, in its origin and character, closely resembled the same class of institution throughout Europe. In the capital itself there is no trace, however, of the Mediaeval mysteries and miracle plays, although it is difficult to suppose that so conspicuous an element in the religious and social life of the remainder of western Europe can have been actually deficient here, more particularly as at Padua in 1243 we meet with representations of the *Passion* and the *Resurrection*, and in Friuli in 1304 with one of the *Creation*.

It is certain that at Venice the Compagnia della Calza, which originated in the early years of the fourteenth century, was influential in promoting and refining, as well as in secularizing, the theatrical shew, and in rendering it, instead of the rude popular spectacle elsewhere placed on the boards down to the fifteenth century, an entertainment at once more elegant, more costly, and less partaking of primitive superstition. In the beginning of that century, it was, about fifty years posterior to the actual occurrence when there might well have been many who recollected the facts and the man, that a Latin tragedy was produced at Padua by Albertino Mussato of that city on the story of Eccelino da Romano. Petrarch, in describing certain festivities at Venice in 1361, mentions Tommaso Babasio of Ferrara in a way which suggests that he was a theatrical performer of some kind, for he compares him with Roscius, while he speaks of him as a private and esteemed acquaintance.

As Babasio came to the city to bear a part in a tournament, he was perhaps an amateur actor or histrionic reciter — a fellow of some Ferrarese dramatic society. At the same time, some of the historians insist, and perhaps with reason, on the exhibition in the public squares of the city during a long course of years — during centuries, maybe — of those ingenuous dramatizations of scriptural subjects which delighted other capitals and nationalities, and when we perceive that the earliest official reference to the matter appears to be of the 29th of December 1509, we have to conclude that that contemplated the normal theatrical performance in some kind of building appropriated to the purpose, although very possibly *al fresco*.

It is singular that the father of the regular Venetian drama was a boy of eighteen. (1) In his college days, Gregorio, son of Giovanni Corraro by Cecilia Contarini his wife, and grand-nephew of the Cardinal Angelo, founded on the Ovidian tale of Tereus and Philomela a tragedy which he called *Progne*. Corraro was born in 1411 or thereabout; *Progne* appeared in 1429 or 1430. In a letter written to a noble lady of his acquaintance, he says that he shewed his achievement to his schoolmaster Messer Victorino da Feltre who kept a seminary at Mantua, and that Messer Victorino, when he saw it, did not quite despair of him; he adds, that he (Corraro) was so strongly affected by the pathos of the story, that hot tears rolled down his cheeks while he was reciting it. (2)

(1)   At Oppenheim, in 1516, appeared a Latin comedy entitled *Epirota* by Thomas Medius Venetus. It purports on the title to be of a very festive and humorous character, and was edited by Johann Kneller, but it was doubtless for the closet only.

(2)   Morelli, *Dissertazione Sulla Cultura della Poesia Presso li Veneziani.*

Progne was first printed anonymously in 1558 by the Accademia della Fama, and again at Rome in 1638. A manuscript copy, bearing the title *Tereus* and belonging to the fifteenth century, was discovered at a later period in Germany, and was put into type in 1790. The merit of the treatment rendered the subject popular. In 1561, three years only after the appearance of the original Venetian edition, Lodovico Domenichi published at Florence a drama entitled *Progne* and purporting to be of his own conception, but it was chiefly borrowed from Corraro. The subjoined extracts may not be unacceptable:

CORRARO (Diomedes is speaking).

Lucos et amnes desero inferni Jovis:
Ad astra mittor supeia convexi poli.
Neque enim inter umbras noxius visus furor
Est ullus aeque: Thiacia, heu! solus potest
Explere furiis corda Diomedes: nefas
Odisse liceat: crimini datum est satis,
Satisque sceleri: deprecor fontis plagas:
Amare liceat: Addite ad poenas meas,
Si quid potestis, dira Furiarum agmina:
Titana pubes exuat vinclis manus
Coelo rebelles: aeneis nodis prematur. (1)

(1)   Correr, *Progne*, sign. B.

DOMENICHI.

Io me ne vengo da l'oscure grotte
De l'empio Re de le perdute genti,
Et son mandato a riveder le stelle,
Et l'aer vostro luminoso: poi
Che fra l'ombre infernai non s'e veduto
Altro cosi maligno empio furore:
E i Thracii cuor puo Diomede solo
Empiere, oime, di furie, e di veleno.
Lecito sia quel che non lice odiare:
Che si son viste assai colpe, e delitti:
Et come reo mi prego ogni gastigo.
Lecito sia, che s'ami ogni peccato.
Et voi di Furie abominosa schiera,
S'alcuna e in voi possanza, a le mie pene
Aggiugnetemi pur pena, e tormento.
Sciolga le mani lovo al ciel rubelle
L'empio stuol de' Giganti. (1)

(1)   Domenichi, *Progne,* page 9.

But *Progne* was only one of the numerous works which are ascribed on
good authority to Gregorio Corraro. The dramatist dedicated to his
grand-uncle, Filippo the Procurator, a translation of fifty-three of the
Fables of Aesop and others from Greek into Latin; to his brother Andrea,
in 1466, (1) a didactic poem on the education of youth, (2) and to his
schoolmaster a volume of satires, (3) Sundry odes, epigrams,
miscellaneous lyrics and letters, (4) an Oration delivered before the
Emperor Sigismund at the Council of Basle in 1433, (5) and a letter to
Saint Cecilia (6) are also known, but all remain in manuscript.

(1)   Agostini, *Notizie degli Scrittori Viniziani,* Volume I page 149-
         152.
(2)   *Quomodo educari debeant pueri et erudiri, Liber didascalicus.*
(3)   The contents of this collection are:

         1.   Satire shewing why the author adopted this class of writing
              to the exclusion of every other,
         2.   Satire against avarice,
         3.   Satire shewing that men are led by venial faults to great
              vices,
         4.   Satire to his friend on the fear of death,
         5.   Satire shewing that a virtuous life alone can stop the tongues
              of the vulgar,
         6.   Satire upon himself and his servant David.

(4)   These are as follow:

         1.   A book of epigrams, dedicated to Martin V., the reigning
              Pontiff (who died in 1431).
         2.   A pastoral, entitled *Lycidas,* and commencing: *Pastoris
              Licidae dum (nos?) referamus amores.*
         3.   An ode in imitation of Horace, called *Dicolos Tetrastychos.*
         4.   A hymn to boys and virgins,
         5.   A sapphic ode against the Turks,
         6.   An epigram on the tomb of Gregory XII.
         7.   An epigram to a friend,
         8.   Two epigrams and a distich to Antonio Ricchi, sculptor,
         9.   A letter to a Carthusian novice on the advantages of a regular
              life,

10. Letters,
11. A soliloquy on the life and death of Antonio, Bishop of Ostia, of blessed memory.

(5)   *Oratio Gregorii Corrarii Veneti Romanes Ecclesiae Protonotharii ad Sigismimdum Imperatorem pro Concilio Basiliensi.*

(6)   *Epistola Ejusdem ad Caeciliam Virginem de Fugiendo Soeculo.*

In 1565, a free version of the *Oedipus* of Sophocles by Giovanni Andrea dell' Anguillara was published at Venice, and has been described as one of the best tragedies in the Italian language. About this time, it had been not unusual at private entertainments to present a sort of dramatic interlude or a poetical recitation, as in 1517, when Gasparo della Vedova, Secretary of the Council of Ten, gave a *fete* and supper, at which game, stewed fruits and other delicacies were served. In 1522, at an entertainment at the Ducal Palace, a comedy, the subject unnamed, was performed after dinner, and it casually transpires that, behind San Cassiano, there was a house in 1527 where comedies were recited, whatever that may mean, for, in that year, the premises were taken for a convalescent home. The date was not at all too early for Titian and his friends.

But a more widely appreciated form of spectacular amusement were the *momaria* or mummeries, otherwise known as *bombaria* from the Venetian word *bomba*, in which a good deal of licence was permitted, and which were in the first instance confined to marriage feasts, subsequently found their way into the houses of the great, and in the end were mainly relegated to the streets.

Dramatic pieces of simple construction, but of a more serious and conventional type, now began, however, to contribute to the diversion of the nobility and gentry. In 1514, the *Miles Gloriosus* of Plautus (a loan from a Greek source) was exhibited at the Casa Pesaro at San Benedetto by the Compagnia della Calza; (1) and, what is especially curious, we hear a few years later (1532) of the holy brethren of Santi Giovanni e Paolo organizing theatricals, termed comedies, at which no lay folk were allowed to be present. It may incidentally be noted that in 1517 a tragedy on the story of Alboin, King of the Lombards, by Giovanni Rucellai was performed at Florence in the Rucellai Gardens before Leo X. (2)

(1)   Ariosto adapted the *Rudens* of the same author, and bestowed on
        it the name *Ruffiano* or *The Pimp*.
(2)   Warton, *History of English Poetry From the Twelfth to the Close
        of the Sixteenth Century,* Volume I page 254.

The existence of more than one theatrical company in 1574 seems to be
conclusively established, by the engagement of a troop by Henry III. of
France in that year to play before the States of Blois, in consequence of
the satisfaction which His Majesty had derived from seeing them during
his stay at Venice.

There were presumably very few known types of dramatic exhibition of
which the knowledge and practice did not promptly reach the city, and
more particularly in the earlier and purer period, performances of a
religious cast were doubtless in favour and vogue. It seems somewhat
extraordinary, however, to find, so late as 1585, when the Japanese
embassy to Rome, which had disembarked at Lisbon, took the city on its
way, a series of spectacles presented by the schools, in which the
treatment was almost Mediaeval, and the mechanical part ostensibly of a
very rudimentary character.

The bodies which had prepared these shews were the six principal
confraternities of La Carita, Misericordia, San Giovanni, San Marco, San
Rocco and San Teodoro, and they went round certain parts of the capital
in procession, supporting scaffolds on which were arranged scenes in the
lives or histories of the saints with mottoes, while others carried
symbolical representations of the various portions of the Venetian
dominion. The author of the account of this shew assures us, after
entering into rather copious details, that he has not told us the thousandth
part of the story, and declares that the jewels and gold and silver were
worth millions of ducats. The stage or platform dedicated to the Patron
Evangelist was the receptacle of a richly attired maiden personifying
Venice, in front of whom were six children belonging to the schools, in
the supposed act of demanding what they ought to do, to which she
replies, through the medium of a label inscribed with large characters;
Servate proecepta. It was an interesting spectacle, and must have
enormously edified the oriental beholders, who saw all the leading
incidents of the Hebrew scriptures delineated by means of lath and
pasteboard.

But the distinguished and unusual visitors were, no doubt, highly
impressed by the eight demons with tridents in their hands, who danced

and leapt about to the general surprise and gratification. What report the Japanese carried home of their Venetian experiences might have been worth hearing. They had come from Ferrara to Chioggia by the Po, in the Duke's own barge which was built on the model of the Venetian *Bucentaur*. It was a journey which Sanudo the diarist reckoned in 1498 as occupying sixteen hours. The Duchess gave them several handsome presents to take back, as her Highness put it, to their mothers. (1) From Venice the strangers proceeded to Mantua. (2)

(1)   The term may have been intended in a sense not usual among us at present, to indicate friends or protectors, as the term appears to have been formerly understood in east Africa among the native chiefs.

(2)   See Volume Five, page 367. The visit of the Japanese to Venice forms part of a volume by Gualtieri entitled; *Relationi della Venvta degli Ambasciatori Giaponesi a Roma Sino alla Partita di Lisbona: con le Accoglienze Fatte Loro da Tutti i Principi Christiani per Doue Sono Passati.*

It seems difficult to understand how the School of San Rocco brought within manageable compass its manifold display ranging from the Creation to the Last Judgment, but it must have had more than one scaffold. The wide range of subjects comprised in the programme denotes an amount of scriptural scholarship which was hardly to be surpassed.

The first theatre at Venice was erected from the designs of Palladio who executed the work in 1565 for the Accesi, a branch of the Compagnia della Calza. It was of wood, and was almost contemporary with the house built at Verona by Sebastiano Serlio. Palladio subsequently adopted twenty years later some of the details for the Olympic at Vicenza, the place of his birth; the work was completed by his pupil Scamozzi.

Thomas Coryat deemed the Italian playhouses in 1608 "very beggarly and base in comparison of our stately Play-houses in England; neyther can their Actors compare with us for apparell, shewes, and musicke." But he saw women performers there, and he observes that the Venetian actresses shewed "as good a grace, action, gesture, and whatsoever convenient for a Player as ever I saw any masculine Actor." (1) The writer was under the impression that women had then sometimes appeared on the London stage, but such had only been the case at private theatricals or on special occasions.

(1)   Coryat, *Coryat's Crudities,* page 247.

On the other hand, John Florio, Coryat's contemporary and almost a naturalized Englishman, criticizes very adversely the treatment in England of Italian subjects or stories, instancing the *Merchant of Venice* and *Othello*. In point of fact the English playwrights made sad havoc of these foreign themes, and Shakespeare was by no means an isolated sinner in historical and local particulars, even while he wealthily atoned by methods exclusively his own.

But whatever the English traveller might have thought of the Venetian stage, a contemporary Venetian spectator at the performance of the *Merchant of Venice* or *Othello* in London would have wondered whence the dramatist obtained his models and his history, even while, in the case of the Moor, he might have appreciated the passion and have forgiven the violence. Nor would the *Blurt Master Constable* of Middleton, 1602, or the *Venice Preserved* of Otway, 1682, have been regarded as truer to historical facts or local colouring.

John Florio characterizes this class of English theatrical exhibition indeed as "perverted histories without decorum." In those days women were apparently unknown on the regular stage, but Coryat observed them on the platforms in the mountebanks' exhibitions, and some years later they qualified themselves as operatic singers. He probably signifies the former category, when he speaks of their grace, action, gesture and all other properties becoming players, and when the first theatre was built there was probably no deficiency of material for the formation of a company.

At the Theatre of San Cassiano, where in the time of Titian dramatic recitations seem to have been already given, we hear of the performance in 1637 of the musical play *Andromeda* by Benedetto Ferrari, which was placed on the stage with the most sumptuous appointments and dresses, and in which original dances, devised by Giovanni Balbi, a Venetian, formed *intermezzi*.

Evelyn, accompanied by his friend Lord Bruce, took tickets (1) for the opera in 1645 beforehand, and saw *Hercules in Lydia*, the scenes being changed thirteen times. The famous treble, Anna Rencia, whom the diarist subsequently invited to a fish dinner, sang; also a eunuch whom the Englishman almost preferred, and a Genoese, an incomparable bass. The performance lasted till two in the morning. Evelyn subsequently visited Vicenza, and in his pages describes the Olympic, but he does not seem to have attended any performance there. More than half a century later, in writing to his old friend and travelling companion Henshaw, in 1698, Evelyn recalled one of the songs which they had heard. (2)

(1)   These orders of admission became in the eighteenth century absolute works of art. See Molmenti, *La Storia di Venezia nella Vita Privata,* Liber III page 221.

(2)   At a later date, other singers attained celebrity, and have had their portraits transmitted to us. Molmenti, *La Storia di Venezia nella Vita Privata,* Liber III page 229.

In the later years of the century, the patrician Marco Contarini built for himself a theatre contiguous to his country house at Piazzola, near Padua, and connected with it by a long corridor. The same class of performance seems to have been in favour here. In 1679, a piece entitled *Amazzoni alle Isole Fortunate,* by Piccioli, the music by Carlo Pallavicino, was presented; the arrangements are described as of the most princely and expensive character, although not so many years had elapsed since the ruinous Candiot war.

The members of the aristocracy themselves composed some of these lyrical entertainments, and the Compagnia della Calza promoted such methods of diverting their female friends and displaying their own talent and profusion. But at the ordinary theatres, of which there were, it appears, at least twelve, the scenery and costumes were far more modest and frugal, and the programmes embraced a wide range of subjects, from the ancient comedies of Plautus and the contemporary productions of Ariosto or Machiavelli to the broadest and coarsest type of low domestic comedy.

The Cassetta de Burattini of Rome and Naples had its counterpart here in the puppet-shew, which embraced a popular survival of the old morality and mystery; the story of Judas Iscariot was a favourite performance on the scaffold erected for the purpose, and a collateral attraction of the streets was the itinerant magic lantern. All these popular entertainments owed much to the artists engaged, and alike here and in the street-song we miss in a mere narration the auxiliary virtue of gesture and grimace, where the intrinsic quality or merit is apt to be so slender.

The Venetian of the later and latest eras at all events, especially among the junior members of the lower class, was a tuneful character, and when he frequented the places at the theatre or opera let at the minimum tariff, was fond of humming in the thoroughfares the next day the airs which had struck his fancy overnight.

From this time down to the age of Gozzi and Goldoni, a succession of dramatists kept the stage supplied with pieces adapted to the local taste, and more capable of appreciation by Venetian than other audiences from their language and allusions. (1)

(1)   The memoirs of Gozzi (*Memorie Inutili*) afford a curious insight into the chequered personal and professional career of the writer, and the elaborate prolegomena of Mr. John Addington Symonds will be read with pleasure, for the view which they supply of the Venetian low comedy of the eighteenth century.

Independently of the acted dramatic literature, scarcely a public incident occurred which did not, at some later date, become the theme for treatment by national writers whose productions did not leave the closet. In the course of these pages, numerous plays of which the plots dealt with exploits performed by Venetian characters so far back as almost prehistoric days have been cited; some of them were of a lyrical cast, and others were unsuitable for representation.

At Venice, except before select academic audiences, the genius of the stage soon acquired a spectacular or operatic character when it did not descend to low comedy and farce, and the classic Muse was obliged to content herself with the smiles of scholars and patriots. But, within a measurable distance of time, compositions professing to depict the scenes and manners of the remote past appealed for sympathy and approval to Venetian readers, in whose minds the original *dramatis-personae* were as mythical and dim, as Romulus and Remus or Hengist and Horsa to the average Roman or the average Englishman.

About 1440, Antonio Nogarola of Verona and his two sisters Bartolommea and Isotta, resided at Venice. Isotta (1) developed literary tastes, and corresponded with many of the distinguished men of the day, who were unanimous in their encomiums on her accomplishments, but the brother and his sisters were charged by an anonymous contemporary with leading immoral lives. (2)

(1)   Her works were collected by Count Apponyi in 1866 (Nogarola, *Apponyi Rariora*) and her portrait, that of a very prepossessing woman, accompanies the volume.

(2)   Molmenti, *La Storia di Venezia nella Vita Privata,* Liber I page 300-301.

The Republic produced at least six female writers of celebrity, or women at least who enjoyed a reputation for culture, not all of whom, however, were strictly Venetians. One, Cristina Pisani, better known by her French name, Christine de Pisan, was born at Venice in 1363 of Bolognese parents. Her father, Tommaso Pisani, a renowned astrologer, left the city in 1368, and settled in France with his wife and daughter, and the latter never revisited the spot of her nativity.

All her productions are in French. The principal are:

1. *The Life of Charles the Wise, King of France*, her father's patron, written on commission for Philip the Good, Duke of Burgundy;

2. *The Feats of Arms and Chivalry*, a compilation from Vegetius' *De Re Militari*, printed in an English version in 1489;

3. *The Book of the City of Ladies*, translated by Bryan Ansley or Annesley, and printed in English in 1521;

4. *The Moral Proverbs of Cristine*, translated by Anthony Widville, Earl Rivers, and printed in 1478, which incidentally shews the familiarity of the more cultured Englishman of that day with her name;

5. A volume of amatory poems, printed at Paris in 1529;

6. *The Hundred Histories of Troy.*

Many of her compositions remain in manuscript, and are scattered over the public libraries of England and the Continent; she is said to have died very poor in or about 1420. The story runs that the Earl of Salisbury, when he visited France to arrange a marriage between Richard II. and Isabella, daughter of Charles VI., saw her, and being a man who delighted in ballads and light literature, offered to take Christine back with him; but she had become too warmly attached to her adopted country, and the reason which she gave the Earl, was "*Je ne puis croire que fin de desloyal viengne a bon terme.*" (1)

(1)   The most complete account of her life and writings is that
        furnished in the second volume of the *Memoires de l'Academie
        des Inscriptions*, and in a monograph published in 1838. See
        Agostini, *Notizie degli Scrittori Viniziani,* Volume II page 477-
        478, 485, 601.

A third lady, who belongs to the end of the fifteenth century, was
Cassandra Fedeli, a Venetian subject, but a native of the terra firma.
Fedeli enjoyed the esteem of many of her learned contemporaries;
Angelo Politiano terms her *Decus Italiae.* In 1488, on graduating as
doctor at Padua, she delivered before the university a Latin speech of her
own composition which was warmly admired. About the same time, at a
banquet in the Ducal Palace during the reign of Agostino Barbarigo
(1486-1501), the same fair personage improvised certain Latin verses
which she accompanied by the lyre.

A widow at fifty-six, Cassandra determined to embrace a religious life,
and died Lady Superior of the Hospital of San Dominico at Vicenza in
1567, at the more venerable than romantic age of one hundred and two.
Coryat saw a picture of her in 1608 in a shop in Venice, and it pleased
him, because he had heard so much of this *Fidelis Veneta Puella.*

Then there was the beautiful and famous Veronica Franco called the
Venetian Aspasia. Born in 1554, probably in the Street of Sant' Agnese,
she published at the age of twenty a volume of *terze rime* of an amatory
cast, and had the honour of being painted by Tintoretto. Veronica who
was left a widow at a very early age became the central attraction of an
intellectual and musical circle, and was distinguished by the brilliance of
her conversation and the charm of her voice. It was just when she was in
the rich bloom of early womanhood that Henry III. visited the city; he
was at once taken captive, and would not quit Venice before he had
personally visited her house to solicit her portrait. She subsequently sent
it to His Majesty, with two sonnets in her own handwriting which are
printed by Gamba. She was courted in her prime by the great, the learned
and the gay, and unhappily succumbed to the powerful temptations by
which she was surrounded. But, in 1578, when she had nearly completed
her twenty-fifth year, she sought to make amends for the errors of her
short life, by the institution at her own expense of a *soccorso* or
magdalen. The portrait of Veronica which has come down to us does
much to exculpate both her and her admirers.

A few years later — in 1580 — Veronica committed to the press her *Familiar Letters*, with a dedication to the Cardinal d'Este, and Montaigne came just in time to receive from her a copy fresh from the hands of the printer; he was extravagant enough to give the messenger who brought the dainty present two gold *scudi*.

Contemporary with Veronica Franco, but a person of totally different character and fortune, was Gaspara Stampa, member of a family distinguished by its accomplishments; for, besides herself, her sister Cassandra and her brother Baldassare achieved considerable distinction in the sixteenth century as writers of verse. Gaspara Stampa is believed to have been born at Padua about 1523, originally of Milanese stock, at an early age to have lost her father who was devotedly attached to her, to have spent the greater part of a very short life at Venice, and to have died there, not without suspicion of poison, in 1554.

Her closing years were saddened by a disappointment in love. The Count of Collalto, heir to an illustrious name, descendant of that Collalto who had served the Signory in the wars of the fourteenth century, and himself Captain-General of the armies of the Emperor Charles V. and of Henry II. of France, had inspired Gaspara with a flame which for some time wore the aspect of being reciprocal. But Collalto was frequently absent in the performance of his duties in the field, and eventually met with a mistress who supplanted the former in his affections and whom he married. This blow probably hastened the end of Gaspara who died in 1554 at the age of thirty or thereabout.

Her poems and letters, with those of Cassandra, Baldassare and others, were printed in 1554 under the care of her sister, and dedicated to the Archbishop of Benevento; a second impression, mainly founded on the first, appeared at Venice in 1738. Both editions are accompanied by a series of panegyrics on Gaspara Stampa by some of the most eminent writers of the age, and the metrical effusions of Collalto himself, who is described as a man of culture and a patron of letters — qualities which had, no doubt, contributed to enlist the sympathy of the authoress. There is a likeness of Collalto in the edition of 1738, forming part of a beautiful double print engraved by Sastori, after Bartoli and Sedelmeyer respectively, of Gaspara and her faithless admirer. They are half-lengths; she has the head laureated, and in her right hand holds a roll of music, her left leaning on books, while a harp lies at her side. Collalto is in armour, bareheaded, his left hand resting on his casque, and below each is an inscription commemorative of their virtues. (1)

(1)   Stampa, *Rime di Madonna Gapara Stampa; con alcune altre di Collaltino, e di Vinciguerra Conti di Collalto: e di Baldassare Stampa. Giuntovi diversi componimenti di varj Autori in lode della medesima.* In Venezia, MDCCXXXVIII, octavo.

Then Elena Cornaro Piscopia is cited as a prodigy of her sex, and Evelyn (1) says of her that she received the doctor's degree at Padua "for her universal knowledge and erudition, upon the importunity of that famous University prevailing on her modesty." She was the daughter of a Procurator of Saint Mark, and had been sought in marriage by many great persons, but she preserved her celibacy, and when she died at Rome, shortly before the date of Evelyn's letter, her obsequies were performed with every mark of honour and appreciation.

(1)   In his well-known letter to Pepys, 12th August, 1689.

In the last days of the Republic lived Giustina Renier Michiel, authoress of a well-known book on the Venetian festivals; this high-born lady, the descendant of doges, survived to witness the closing scene, and to look back sorrowfully on the past.

The Public Library, which is most, familiarly known under the designation of the Marciana, was originally a very small collection, and boasted, perhaps, little more than the few volumes presented by Petrarch in 1362, with some later additions. (1) Of this parent nucleus of the public or national library, which was stated in 1882 to contain 120,000 books, it is questioned whether any vestiges whatever be extant. It is stated to have comprised some interesting manuscripts, and a few Books of Hours.

(1)   Romanin, *Storia Documentata di Venezia,* Volume IV page 501.

The Latin poem on the Marian Games by Pace del Friuli, written about 1300 and dedicated to the Doge Gradenigo; a Latin version of the *Therapeutica* of Galen; and a French missal of the twelfth century, which there is an inclination to identify among a few others as memorials of the liberality and goodwill of Petrarch, are not of undoubted authenticity. The same must be said, it is to be feared, of the treatise by Riccardus de Mediavilla In *Secundum Librum Sententiarum*, a folio manuscript on vellum with an engraved inscription at the foot of the first leaf, which apparently does not belong to the book, "*Fragmentum Bibliothecae*

Petrarchae", although the manuscript's notes are said to resemble his handwriting. Neither the Dante which Boccaccio presented to his friend, nor the copy of Quinctilian *De Institutione Oratoria* which the poet himself discovered at his birthplace in the winter of 1350, is known to exist. But the Republic was literary heir to the poet only in a limited sense, and between 1362 and the date of his death Petrarch had opportunities of making additions to his shelves. Such books as remained at Arqua or elsewhere, when he died ten years later, were publicly dispersed at Padua.

Morelli (1) seems to establish that, in point of fact, the number of books which actually came to Venice was exceedingly small, and that many volumes, after passing through various hands, at length found their way into the public collections of Rome and Paris. Yet we are bound to credit the Republic, at this tolerably early date, with the spirit and feeling for letters and culture which received such a powerful stimulus in the succeeding centuries.

(1)   Morelli, *Dissertazione Sulla Cultura della Poesia Presso li Veneziani,* Volume I page 7.

During the temporary ascendancy of the Albizzi party at Florence, that illustrious patriot and statesman, Cosimo de' Medici, sought an asylum at Venice in 1434, and appears to have taken up his quarters at San Giorgio Maggiore, while members of his family resided in other parts of the Venetian territories. It occurred to the exile to requite this hospitality in a manner characteristic and worthy of his tastes, and he engaged his personal friend and fellow exile, the architect Michelozzo, to enlarge and partly rebuild the old Abbey library, to which he presented books and works of art. (1) This seems to have been intact in 1713 when the Elector of Saxony visited it and admired the bindings of some of the volumes.

(1)   See Romanin, *Storia Documentata di Venezia,* Volume IV page 501.

Again, thirty-four years later, in 1468, the Greek manuscripts, and other valuable books of Cardinal Bessarion, Archbishop of Nicaea, which had cost the owner 30,000 ducats, came as a donation to the Republic. The piece of good fortune, which was cordially accepted by the Doge in a letter of the 10th of August, was attributable to the intimacy which the Cardinal had contracted with several of the more cultivated patricians, especially Paolo Morosini. In his communication announcing the gift,

His Eminence had observed: "I should regard all my care as inadequate, if I did not take measures to provide that the books collected by myself with such great pains should be placed where, after my death, they will be secure from loss or dispersion, in order that they may be at the service of Greek and Latin scholars. Of all the towns of Italy, your illustrious and flourishing city appeared to me to answer most completely my views. What country could offer a safer asylum than yours? Actuated by equity, submissive to the laws, and governed by integrity and wisdom." The donor concluded with a hope that Venice would wax greater day by day in power and fame, and in the time to come be recognized as a second Byzantium.

In 1526, in order to gratify Cardinal Wolsey, then a valuable ally of the Signory, some of the Greek manuscripts appear to have been presented to him for the college which he had founded at Oxford, as well as some of those of Cardinal Grimani. (1) By various gifts and purchases, the national institution gradually assumed an importance and extent which encouraged the government to employ the architect Sansovino to erect a building for the reception of these accumulated stores — too late, however, to save the precious Sanudo Library of 6500 volumes, (2) which the owner had dearly wished in 1536 to leave to his country, and for which there was then no adequate accommodation.

(1)   (compilation) *Calendar of State Papers Relating to English Affairs in the Archives of Venice,* Volume III page 515. It appears that there had been a greater number, but some were sold in the lifetime of Grimani to meet incumbrances.
(2)   Sanudo, *Diarii,* Volume VI page 281.

A list of the librarians of the Marciana is an impressive record, because it establishes the solicitude of the Signory to select individuals who had rendered themselves conspicuous by their attainments and public services. It at the same time illustrates the catholicity of the Venetian functionary;

1485.	Marco Barbarigo, afterward Doge.
1486.	Agostino Barbarigo (his brother), afterward Doge.
1486.	Marcantonio Sabellico, the historian.
1486.	Andrea Navagiero, the historian.
circa 1530.	Pietro Bembo, afterward Cardinal.
circa 1530.	Giorgio Battista Ramusio (assistant librarian).

1543.	Benedetto Ramberto.
1547.	Andrea de' Franceschi, Grand Chancellor.
1547.	John Dempster (a Scot).
1547.	Bernardino Loredano.
1575.	Luigi Gradenigo.
1584.	Luigi Pesaro, lecturer on philosophy.
1588.	Benedetto Giorgio.
1601.	Nicolo Morosini.
1601.	Girolamo Soranzo.
1635.	Giovanni Nani.
1650.	Angelo Contarini.
1659.	Battista Nani, the historian.
1678.	Silvestro Valiero, afterward Doge.
1693.	Francesco Cornaro.
1716.	Girolamo Veniero.
1736.	Lorenzo Tiepolo.
1742.	Marco Foscarini, afterward Doge
1762.	Alvigi Mocenigo, afterward Doge.
1763.	Girolamo Grimani.
1763.	Alvigi Contarini.
1763.	Girolamo Ascanio Giustiniani.
1763.	Zaccaria Valaresso.
1763.	Francesco Pesaro. (1)

(1)   The last was in office in 1797.

The French, the Italians, the Spaniards, and even the Germans, soon learned to look toward Venice for the means of obtaining for their own institutions transcripts from valuable or even unique codices, particularly after the installation of the Bessarion bequest in 1468. Sansovino relates how the Duke of Ferrara and Henry III. of France, in 1574, spent an entire day in inspecting the literary and bibliographical stores of the Grimani family.

After the surrender to the French Republic in 1797, a large number of valuable books and manuscripts., in addition to works of art, were appropriated by Bonaparte, not only from Venice itself, but from Padua, Verona, Treviso and Udine in Friuli. Among them were many of the most precious examples of the parent presses of Venice itself, including the *Rationale* of Durandus of 1459 on vellum, as well as an extensive assemblage of important codices, a considerable proportion of which belonged to the Bessarion library. (1) The selection has the air of having been made by a person or persons conversant with bibliography and the relative importance of literary antiquities. It was in this respect that Bonaparte proved himself an Attila to the Republic, for his system of plunder was alike merciless and shameless, and was characteristic of the arrogant brutality of the ascendant power. The municipal authorities, in the face of these and other exactions, could only say: "Since right cannot resist force, it lies with you to do as you please."

(1)　　　Romanin, *Storia Documentata di Venezia,* Volume XI page 389-446.

The ardour of bibliographical research, the earnest spirit of literary inquiry, and the desire to become acquainted with the best classic models, which began toward the middle of the fifteenth century to animate her patricians and merchant princes, had the natural effect of securing to Venice the finest and largest assemblage of manuscripts. in the world. Giovanni Aurispa who travelled in the east, and is said to have sold part of his wardrobe at Constantinople to secure some literary prizes, formed a library of 238 manuscripts, among which were the works of Plato, Procopius, and Callimachus. Many others followed the example of this enthusiast, and formed similarly choice and precious cabinets; the Venetians became the highest bidders for autograph or unique codices.

Bibliomania was here seen in its wealthiest aspect, and the passion was productive of the most salutary results. But the generous thirst for knowledge, and the ever-growing appreciation of ancient masterpieces soon led to an increased demand for those compositions which rank among the noblest efforts of human genius, and a gigantic revolution was to be wrought in the course of time in the character of literature and the history of books.

The Republic, though not the cradle of typography, shewed herself almost at the outset one of its most magnificent patrons; in fact, the Venetian territory on the terra firma is not without its pretensions to the still somewhat doubtful claim of priority in that most valuable of discoveries. For Pamfilio Castaldi of Feltre is alleged to have acquired, in 1440, the art of committing characters to typo, and to have associated himself with Fust to whom he imparted the secret, the latter through Gutenberg forestalling him, however, in its practical application; but Castaldi failed to take any definite steps to carry out the use of movable types at home.

That Castaldi conceived the idea of such an advanced stage in the science is little more than an assumption from his alleged contact with Fust, and it is quite possible that he did not go farther than an essay in xylography which Fust developed. But, inasmuch as, within the same region at a comparatively short distance, so unusual and novel a conception is hardly likely to have simultaneously presented itself to two persons, the question arises whether Sabellico the historiographer, in his *Epitome*, 1487, in signalizing the unique distinction conferred on the reign of the Doge Pasquale Malipiero (1457-1462) by the introduction of the art, has not confused two distinct or successive events, for he proceeds to tell us that Jenson whom he thought to be a German was the founder of the Venetian press — of course, an absolute and absurd error.

It seems fairly clear from the accidental survival of a block book illustrative of the Passion, admittedly of Venetian origin and belonging approximately to the time of the Doge mentioned, that the invention noted by Sabellico was simply xylography. It was probably, though not necessarily, prior to the use of movable types, limited to works susceptible of being treated by such a process, engravings with letter-press inclusive. It is therefore submitted that the aforesaid Castaldi may have found a patroness in the consort of the Doge Malipiero, for, on the back of a *Cavallo di Spade* belonging to a pack of cards printed in 1681, occurs the inscription "*Arte della Stampa introdotta in Venetia dalla Dogaressa Dandola Malipiera.*" This, if true, is certainly a remarkable tradition to be preserved, after more than two centuries, by the draughtsman of a playing-card. But the Venetians were singularly tenacious of such reminiscences, and, until superseded by movable types, xylographic examples would perhaps answer to the term "*arte della stampa*"; in fact, the two systems were for a considerable period concurrent.

Sabellico, the Venetian historiographer, (1) who may be regarded and respected as a contemporary witness, tentatively assigns the commencement of operations at Venice itself to "about 1462." Thus the parentage was not Venetian or even Italian, but German — the same which had already yielded in the Fatherland several productions which are well known, as well as more than probably some which are lost or are subject to recovery. Within a measurable time, so much has been added from unsuspected sources to our stock of information, that, not Venice perhaps, but the peninsula may yet have some hidden surprises for us. Looking at the terms of the concession of 1469 to Speyer, there is a disposition to suspect, or even conclude, that any antecedent typographical operations, which can scarcely have been unknown to the government, were in the nature of block books. (2)

(1)   Sabellico, *Decades Rerum Venetarum,* Liber XXVIII. The copy on vellum presented to the Doge Marco Barbarigo is still extant, and is described in the *Hoe Catalogue,* 1912.

(2)   Certain manuscript records of an ancient Venetian family speak of xylographic editions of Donatus the grammarian about the middle of the fifteenth century, and the grammar was printed at Subiaco in or about 1465. The *Missoe Speciales* and any other similar opuscula issued by Gutenberg seem to be ascribable to a date prior to that of his first Bible, 1455. See Brown, *The Venetian Printing Press,* page 2.

On the 18th of September, 1469, the Senate, seeing "that this peculiar invention of our time, unknown to those former, is in every way to be fostered and advanced," accorded to Johann zu Speyer for five years the right of printing books; and, of course, the Republic enjoyed the advantage of Speyer's experience in his own country. In the same twelvemonth, which, according to the old chronology, did not expire till March, 1470, Speyer or Spira produced two editions of the *Familiar Letters of Cicero,* as well as the *Natural History* of Pliny, of both of which a few copies were struck off on vellum. The two successive impressions of the Cicero on paper consisted of 300 copies, both completed in four months; several vellum copies of each survive.

The concession granted to Johann zu Speyer was not extended to his brother Vindelin, and the monopoly was only of a few months' duration. The former had finished an edition of the *Decades* of Livy and part of Saint Augustine's *De Civitate Dei,* when he died suddenly, and left the unfinished book to be brought out by his brother, (1) who for some time carried on the business single-handed, and produced an edition of the *Annals* of Tacitus without date, said to be the earliest printed book with catchwords. The call for copies on vellum had a steady duration; in 1486, Antonius de Strata printed a limited number of an edition of the *Annals* on this material; a copy formerly belonged to Saint Leonard's Monastery at Venice. As a casual illustration of the wide distribution of books, even at a very early stage, we may cite the fact that a copy of the Livy of 1470 was bequeathed a few years later to a school at Castres in Languedoc.

(1)   This fact is expressly intimated in the completed book.

In common with those of other early states, especially where the constitution was aristocratic, the Venetian proto-typographers could look for no public support, either within or outside the dominion, and their sumptuous productions appealed exclusively to wealthy and generous patrons. When they were not service-books of the Church or copies of official papers, they were limited to classical or patriotic masterpieces. As a rule, the parent presses of Italy under the old governments do not seem to have met with more than local encouragement. The feeling and demand for their outputs were seigniorial or sentimental rather than literary, and the veritable incunabulum almost equalled in rarity the work in its manuscript form.

The exclusive concession of 1469 was broken by a second grant to Nicolas Jenson of Sommevoire, who inaugurated his work here in 1470 by an impression of the *Rhetoricorum Libri Quatuor* of Cicero, of which there are copies on vellum. The colophon was in verse and presumably from the pen of the printer who was less proficient as a Latinist. In his folio collection of Diomedes and other grammarians and in an Italian version of Pliny, 1476, he describes himself as Gallus or Gallicios. In 1471, he reprinted Caesar's *Commentaries* from the Roman edition of 1469, and produced the *Bibbia Volgare* which was reprinted at Turin.

Prior to his death in September, 1480, Jenson had entered into partnership with a printer named Zuan da Cologna, and by his will his plant was to be valued and his own share of it offered to the firm. In the preceding year, however, Jenson had furnished the father-in-law of Aldo, Andrea de' Torresani, with a certain set of matrices, and the latter is found, in 1482-1483, producing a book professedly executed with these types; this so far constitutes an interesting link between what may be termed the first and second era of Venetian typography.

It is noticeable that, among the earlier examples, there is an error in date analogous to that in the Oxford *Saint Jerome* of 1478. The *Decor Puellarum*, issued by Jenson in 1471, is misdescribed in the colophon as having appeared in 1461, but the evidence in favour of the later year is quite conclusive. (1) That the demand for the printed book quickly grew remunerative, there is some indication in the circumstance that Jenson, one of the earliest labourers in the field, succeeded after a ten years' career in accumulating a handsome fortune, notwithstanding the costliness of material, the slow process of completion, the necessarily high price of the finished product, (2) and the inevitable residue left on hand, all bespeaking the need of capital. A copy of the Pliny of 1472 was not, it appears, rubricated till 1474 — perhaps when a customer was found.

(1)   The same printer issued also, in octavo, the *Gloria Mulierum;* Romanin, *Storia Documentata di Venezia,* Volume X page 401.

(2)   William Morris owed to Jenson the suggestion of his so-called Golden Type.

Nor was it long before others entered so apparently profitable a field; of these the most famous were Christoph Valdarfer from whose press proceeded the first edition of the *Decameron* with a date, a later Johann zu Speyer who was in business as late as 1493, Theobaldo Manutio (commonly called Aldo), the house of Sessa, and that of Giolito. The two latter survived down to the middle of the sixteenth century and executed much good work.

From a monograph on the typographical annals of Venice we perceive that the early printers long continued to belong to several nationalities. Apart from theology and the classics, their productions will be found to embrace a copious assortment of contributions to history, lyrical and dramatic poetry and folk-lore.

The literary committee of Aldo included many distinguished names, and goes back to 1482, when Alberto Pico, Count of Carpi, and his uncle the accomplished Signore of Mirandola, are said to have concerted with the printer at Carpi the place for the establishment of the Aldine Press. He employed, among others, the learned Petrus Morinus (1) and Marcus Musurus, the renowned collector and student who edited Aristophanes for him in 1498, and to such co-operation is due the accuracy of these lasting monuments of erudition and technical skill. In 1499, the elder Aldo was enabled by the munificence of a lawyer, Lionardo Crasso, to produce the celebrated *Hypnerotomachia* of Francesco Colonna of Treviso, Crasso reserving all rights.

(1)   A copy of the Naples edition of Pontanus, 1505, has the autograph of Morinus, and may be the very book from which the Aldine edition was derived.

Linacre the grammarian was another adviser. In 1501, our printer produced in script type an edition of the *Cose Volgari* of Petrarch, and, in 1502, a folio Herodotus — a very appropriate homage by such a state to such a man. We seem entitled to believe that both Erasmus and Holbein were professionally associated with Aldo, the former in an editorial capacity, the latter as a designer of bindings. The distinguished Dutch scholar certainly superintended the issue of the *Hecuba* and *Iphigenia* of Euripides in 1507, and added a Latin ode in eulogy of Henry VII. of England and his family, and, in the ensuing year, he published here his own *Adagia*. Aldo and he, however, subsequently quarrelled, and the former contemptuously alluded to the great Hollander as "*Transalpinus quidam homo.*" The acute troubles attendant on the war between Venice and the League of Cambrai (1508) interrupted the operations, more particularly those devoted to elegant literature; and there was no important revival till the appearance of the Plato of 1513, under the joint care of the printer and Musurus, and the patronage of Leo X.

At a comparatively early stage, the Venetian printers adopted the principle, not only of accepting proposals from patrons of literature to defray the cost of certain works, but undertook such as were committed to them by private individuals, for issue at their expense and under their responsibility. In 1496, an edition of the *Metaphysica* of Albertus Magnus came from the press of Bonetus Locatelli of Venice, "*jussu et expensis nobilisviri domini Octaviani Scoticiencis Modoetiensis,*" and, in 1503, we find the *Commentaries* of Duns Scotus on the *Metaphysics* of Aristotle similarly printed "*iussu domini Andreae Torresani de Asula.*"

Venice cannot be supposed to have been behind its Italian neighbours and other European states in the art of typography, but we are unquestionably in imperfect possession of a large number of products of the Venetian press, which may securely be presumed to have started, in common with other countries, by issuing humble and inexpensive tracts, or official ephemerides, before its founders launched into undertakings of a wider scope and a more costly character. It is by no means unlikely that thousands of tracts and broadsides have perished without leaving a trace.

In the course of these pages, allusion has repeatedly been made to proclamations and a variety of other notices relevant to the periodical acts of the Republic, for the existence of which we are almost exclusively indebted to contemporary registers or diaries. An almanac of 1488 has survived by an accident, and the employment of pasteboard for such literature has as frequently led to its destruction as to its transmission to us.

We meet with numerous evidences of the activity and enterprise of printing-houses in nearly all the provincial centres; Padua, Treviso, Verona, Vicenza, Bergamo, Brescia, in the last of which Angelus and Jacobus Britannicus were in business in the closing years of the fifteenth century. Pierre Maufer of Rouen was at Padua from 1474 to 1479, removed to Verona in 1480, was at Venice in 1483, and at Modena in 1491.

Of course, as time proceeded, typographical adventurers, Germans, Belgians and French, distributed themselves and moved from one place to another. In one instance, a printer came from Bologna to Venice and migrated in 1481 to Florence, in consequence of the already severe competition. An enormous output accumulated in the fifteenth century at Venice, in the provinces and even in Dalmatia. Gregorio de Gregoriis and his brother went from Forli to Verona about 1486, and transferred themselves to Venice where the firm existed during many years. Verona, under the sway and influence of the Signory, is entitled to the distinction of having produced in 1472 the earliest dated volume from an Italian press, with engravings by a native artist — the treatise of Valturius *De Re Militari*; a folio volume, honourable to the local typographer, Johannes de Verona, and to the reputed artist, Matteo Pasti. In another case, the Italian version of the account of Hispaniola by Cortes, 1524, was printed by a Venetian from Vercelli for a firm at Brescia. Jenson of Sommevoire himself was followed at a short interval by Jacques le Rouge, who published in 1476 an edition of the *Historia Florentina* of Leonardo Aretino. He there gives his name as Jacomo de Rossi, and describes himself as of the Gallic nation. At a later date, a Venetian, Johannes Antonius or Gianantonio, was in business at Paris, where he issued two editions of the *Bucolics* of Publius Faustus Andrelinus in 1501, venturing to pronounce them not inferior to those of Virgil and Calpurnius.

The printing fraternity seems to have gradually concentrated itself in the parish of San Paterniano, whither Aldus himself removed from Sant' Agostino. It is shown by official records that, in 1514, Andrea de Axolla occupied a house here belonging to the Trono family at a rent of sixty ducats a year, and that a second typographer, Lazzaro de Soardi, and his partner carried on business at another, paying only thirty-one ducats. The inducement to settle in San Paterniano very probably was the more moderate rental, and an aim at more popular prices; but the typographer was to be found almost everywhere, and the aggregate output became enormous, while the quality of the work often not unnaturally, as it appealed to the community at large and not almost exclusively to a limited number of patrons, exhibited a decline.

We find a considerable assortment of printers' signs specified by the authorities; (1) but it is not made very clear when the printing office and the bookseller's shop became independent institutions in separate premises, as, at first, the firm which produced the work also offered it to the public. We find the famous house of the Giunti introducing a popular novelty in the shape of a pocket edition of the *Officiolum* of Roman use. (2)

(1) Brown, *The Venetian Printing Press,* page 100.
(2) Molmenti, *La Storia di Venezia nella Vita Privata,* Liber II page 310, where a facsimile occurs.

A practice to which occasional recourse was had, both at Venice and in the provinces, was the introduction into the imprints of books, not only of the customary particulars, but of the regnal year of the Doge. An edition of Platina *De Honesta Voluptate,* printed in Friuli in 1480, expressly mentions the Doge in office, Giovanni Mocenigo, and, in a second case, a copy of the *Ortus Sanitatis* from the press of Quantel at Cologne, 1497 or thereabout, bears a contemporary inscription by a purchaser, presumably a Venetian, in the Low Countries or in Germany, *Anno Domini MCCCCLXXXXVII. Kalend. Novembris regnante inclyto Principe Angus. Barbarico z. 2. emptus 11 Guild. 10dnii.*

In connexion with the pursuit of the typographical art, it is proper and necessary to introduce a notice of the two literary academies, the Accademia della Fama and dei Pellegrini, which not only afforded facilities in the form of libraries and assembly rooms for the promotion of knowledge and culture, but undertook the publication of works for which there was not sufficient public encouragement. The Accademia della Fama was founded on a princely scale in 1558 by Federigo Badoer, a distinguished statesman and a personage of the most illustrious descent. It was composed of about one hundred members, and lectures were delivered on every branch of polite and technical learning; it accumulated a fine library for the use of all who chose to resort to it; it had its own chapel and ministers, and there were periodical festive or hospitable gatherings.

Bernardo Tasso held the office of Chancellor with a salary of 200 gold ducats, and the President was Paolo Manutio, son of the celebrated

Theobaldo or Aldo. Manutio borrowed or procured from the printer Bevilacqua the type used in printing some of the publications, of which there are about sixty on record. This magnificent scheme came to an end in 1561, and the Badoer family was almost ruined by the profuse expenditure. A revival took place in the same year under the auspices of Paolo Paruta the historian, but it resembled the original institution in name only.

The Pellegrini held their meetings at each other's houses or in the gardens of Giudecca, Murano or San Giorgio, where they read aloud the poets and prose writers of ancient and modern times; they extended their programme to educational and charitable purposes, and to the payment of due honours to departed colleagues; it was a fusion of the club with the guild. There were also Academies Degli Imperfetti, established by the legist Count Marino Angeli, Dei Peripatetici, for the promotion of the study of natural history, l'Accademia Geografico-Storico-Fisica instituted in 1681, the Argonauti of which the patron was the Doge Giustiniani; outside the capital were others, including the Separati at Murano, which instructed the young in the fine arts, philosophy and theology, and finally, the Accademia Italiana, established by Venetians at Paris under the auspices of Cardinal Mazarin.

These two features in the life of that period may be said to have sprung from the more or less informal gatherings which assembled at the house of the elder Aldo at San Paterniano, at first for purposes of consultation with that learned and accomplished man on the most suitable authors to be undertaken for his press. Among those to whose scholarship and counsel the world may be more or less indebted were Cardinal Bembo, the historians Sanudo, Sabellico and Navagiero, and Ramusio the cosmographer. These and other personages not only tendered their advice to Aldo, but lent their aid, as we see, in revising the texts and even in reading the proofs.

An interesting account has been given of the meetings at the Nani palace in Giudecca of the Academy of the Filaleti instituted by the historian, and where Nani and his friends discussed questions in the garden on a variety of topics, especially botany. A member of the club was Ambrogio Bembo, a young man of three and twenty who had served two years in the Candiot war, and spent four more in travelling in the east, collecting rarities and making notes till he was qualified to take his seat in the Great Council.

The provinces of terra firma followed the precedent of the mother city in instituting academies for all the branches of learning and accomplishment — at Padua the Ricovrati; at Verona the Societa Filarmonica and the Constanti, the latter composed of forty gentlemen who paid professors. Vicenza had its Olympian Society for the encouragement of the dramatic art in Italy.

The patronage of the press, the protection alike of printers, authors and buyers, and the safeguard of the community against the mischievous fruits of publications of an immoral or offensive character, appear to have engaged, from the outset, the serious and steady attention of the ecclesiastical authorities, of the College and of the Ten; a system of limiting books for a term of years, or even during the life of the writer, soon became a tolerable substitute for copyright. On the one hand, there was the principle of accepting a manuscript recommended by some competent authority, and, on the other, of requiring a certificate in the case of every volume intended for educational purposes, that it was in all respects accurate and trustworthy. Among the distinguished men who offer themselves as applicants for privileges are Ariosto who acquires for his *Orlando Furioso* a life interest under the date 1515, a twelve-month prior to the first appearance of the poem at Ferrara; Francesco Berni and Bernardo Tasso, whose rights are similarly acknowledged in 1531; and Aretino, Trissino, Straparola and Parabosco who brought out his *Diporti* in successive impressions a little later.

The immediate motive for the institution of a censorship of the press in the Republic, when the authorities had for some time allowed tolerable latitude, even toward printed matter of a highly equivocal type, was the scandal occasioned by the appearance, in 1526, of a volume in *terza rima* by a certain Venetian doctor named Alvise Cynthio degli Fabritii, who dedicated it to the Pope under the title *Della Origine delli Volgari Proverbi*. The author bore some grudge against the monks of San Francesco della Vigna, who had inflicted on him a serious commercial injury, and one of his forty-five proverbs; *Ciascun Tira l'Acqua al Suo Molin*, with an accompanying triplet, gave great offence to the brethren and led to an official inquiry of which the most notable outcome was the censorship.

There is an odd account of the seizure of the edition by the holy fraternity at the printer's, of an order obtained from the executive for restitution to the author, and of the refusal of the printer to surrender possession till his bill had been settled. The monks are supposed to have destroyed a considerable number of the copies while they were in their custody, but there is no ground for the statement that the book was burned. (1)

(1)   Brunet describes this book as "*ouvrage dans lequel l'auteur explique par des contes orduriers, ecrits en vers, l'origine de 45 Proverbes.*"

The new official jurisdiction over the press was more apt to be enforced in cases of alleged impiety or sacrilege than in cases of licentiousness. A few years later, some of the writings of Alessandro Caravia were proscribed on the former account, notably, his *Dream*, published at Venice in 1541, but very few instances of effectual suppression are within our knowledge. A few copies almost invariably escaped — a sufficient number to satisfy modern demands, and yet confer the piquancy of uncommonness.

Previously to the revival of culture and the introduction of typography, the scope of the connoisseur was necessarily much restricted. Yet he might have, if he chose, manuscripts of the classics, of more recent authors, and of the Scriptures — books of hours and missals which, in the thirteenth and fourteenth centuries, displayed a beauty of style and a chaste grandeur of design not degraded by popularity and cheapness; oriental porcelain of fine paste and workmanship; medals and coins of innumerable types and periods; paintings in the hard and frigid manner of the first Italian masters, and remains of ancient sculpture. But the antiquary, as we know him, was a somewhat later creation; the earliest private collections were probably not formed prior to the fourteenth century, when we meet with the ill-fated Doge Faliero (1) as a dilettante with a taste and an eye for what struck him as curious or valuable; but an even anterior case is quoted by Count Papadopoli, in which a private individual signalized himself by forming an assemblage of books, bronzes and coins about 1335. (2)

(1)   (anonymous) *Bulletino di Arti e Curiosita Veneziane,* 1880.
(2)   Papadopoli, *Le Monete di Venezia Descritte ed Illustrate,* page v.

The Mediaeval Venetian was more disposed, however, to invest his capital in ships and cargoes, counters and houses at home and abroad, or in government stock which, if it was less advantageous, was more secure. It is curious to consider that, with the now reigning and almost tyrannical love of what is old, the furniture, the kitchen utensils and the money in daily use by that same Venetian, if he was a housekeeper of fair resources and taste, and they by some miracle had descended to us in an unimpaired state, would be prized at more than their weight in gold ducats, while similar illustrations of the domestic life of the Greeks and Romans would probably have possessed in his eyes a more subdued interest. An omnivorous study of bygone ages was reserved for men and for times whereof he had formed no conception.

The term *studio* bore at Venice a twofold signification. It meant a university, and it also stood for the repository where a collector arranged his books and other possessions of an artistic or archaeological character; it was the modern study with a somewhat wider application. It was a room in which literary monuments in print or manuscript merely constituted a section, and which might embrace paintings, bronzes, sculpture, majolica, porcelain, armour and all kinds of miscellaneous antiquities.

The inventory made in 1355 after the death of the Doge by Johannes Presbyter of Santi Apostoli, of the artistic and ornamental effects in the Red Room of the Casa Falier at Santi Apostoli, has been preserved, (1) and merits particular notice, partly because many items of value had in some way passed from the hands of Marco Polo into the possession of the Falieri — perhaps of the Doge himself who must have personally known the great explorer.

(1)   (anonymous) *Bulletino di Arti e Curiosita Veneziane,* 1877-1880.

The most prominent objects were:

> A painting (*tabula*) with the effigy of Saint George.
> Another executed by Magister Thomas Pictor, with figures of various nationalities.
> A couch (*triclinium*) of rosewood (*lignum rubeum*), with carved work.
> Objects in glass and alabaster.
> A cabinet with fifty coins "*mirae antiquitatis.*"
> Another with rings and jewels, two given to the family (? of the late Doge) by Marco Polo.
> An antique sword with an inscription.
> Two heads of barbari or foreigners, brought from Africa by Jhacobello, a seaman.

Costumes of various peoples.

A curious berretta.

A copper (? bronze) sword found at Padua.

Two manuscripts, one with animals painted in gold and colours,
the other containing Lives of Saints with their effigies.

Three engraved silver cups.

A gold statuette of Santa Marina.

Two cases of white leather, with various objects in gold and
silver, given to Marco Polo by the Khan or some other
foreign king.

A three-edged sword belonging to Polo, and carried by him in
his travels.

A brazen *Sphoera Mundi*, which formerly belonged to Master
Antonio the astrologer.

Painted Indian cloths, formerly the property of Polo.

A manuscript of Polo's travels.

De locis miribilibus Tartarorum, said to be in Polo's autograph.

Several astrological and physical treatises and other books in red
and white leather.

Thus the house of Falier clearly seems to have come into possession, by
gift or otherwise, of many of the curiosities which Marco Polo brought
back with him to his native city, on his return from his strange and
romantic experiences in regions then previously unknown. The present
document, transmitted to posterity by the systematic care of the Venetian
archivists, exhibits one of the most familiar names and characters in the
story of the Republic, as a pioneer in the pursuit and preservation of
antiquarian remains and works of art.

The Venetians signalized their zeal in the formation of libraries and in a
diversity of allied pursuits. A long list of names gradually accumulated,
commemorating those distinguished and meritorious citizens who
became owners of literary treasures, both before and after the invention
of the printing press, and of whom some generously bequeathed their
possessions to the Republic.

Quite a long catalogue might be drawn up of the men who followed in
the footsteps of Faliero down to the end of the eighteenth century, and
Cardinal Domenigo Grimani who died at Rome in 1523, (1) and brought
together at Santa Maria Formosa that princely collection which included
the famous *Breviary*, stands nearly foremost; Sansovino enumerates
many others.

(1)   Sanudo, *Diarii,* Volume VI page 281.

Bibliomania dated from an even anterior period. Let us assist in commemorating as many as possible of those distinguished book-lovers in the days of Italian and Venetian splendour. Venice itself was on the one hand a gainer, on the other a loser, by the incidence of devolution in this way. For instance, the libraries of Saint Mark and San Giorgio Maggiore were enriched by the donations or otherwise of Cosimo de' Medici, Cardinal Bessarion and the Vespucci family, while the books of Cardinal Bembo passed to the Vatican, and the original collections of Consul Smith to England.

> Andrea and Francesco Odoni.
> Jacopo Foscari, son of the Doge Francesco, a phil-Hellenist, obit 1457.
> Bernardo Trevisano.
> Giovanni Grimani, Patriarch of Venice.
> Pasquale Cicogna, Doge from 1585 to 1595.
> Gabriele and Andrea Vendramino.
> Marino Sanudo.
> Benedetto Dandolo.
> Antonio Calbo.
> Andrea Loredano.
> Cardinal Bembo.
> Girolamo Donato.
> Jacopo Contarini.
> Leonardo and Alvigi Mocenigo.
> Francesco and Domenigo Duodo.
> Giambattista Erizzo.
> Simone Zeno.
> Giovanni Gritti.
> Francesco Bernardo.
> Giorgio Paolo Cornaro.
> Apostolo Zeno.
> Marco Foscarini, Doge (1762-1763).

The Foscari family at one period undoubtedly owned a more or less considerable number of the class of books then in vogue. A Cicero of 1502 preserves evidences of the former proprietorship of two members of this distinguished and ancient house: "*filippi foscari et amicor[um],*" and "*Aloysii Foscari & Amicor[um].*"

The catalogue of the Museum of Andrea Vendramino (1400-1478), which Sir Henry Wotton officially visited in 1619, occupied sixteen large volumes. Of Cardinal Bembo many of the acquisitions found their way to Parma and Turin. The books of Francesco Barozzi, a Venetian nobleman of the sixteenth century, were purchased by the Earl of Pembroke, who presented the bulk to the Bodleian Library at Oxford — the remainder, it is generally thought, were subsequently acquired and given by the Protector Cromwell. Andrea Odoni was a connoisseur on general lines, including books and coins; he acquired the assemblage of antiquities formed by his uncle Francesco — in the painting of him by Lotto he is contemplating some of them; this was in 1527; he was one of the Titian coterie, and is thought to have befriended the great artist, although no likeness from that source has been identified. There is one, however, by Lotto at Hampton Court, in which he is represented seated at a table, a dark, bearded man, surrounded by ancient statuary. (1)

(1)   Molmenti, *La Storia di Venezia nella Vita Privata,* Liber II page 378.

The libraries of Jacopo Contarini and Apostolo Zeno came to the state; that of Marino Sanudo was unhappily scattered. Apostolo Zeno, the eminent man of letters, who is said to have amassed 30,000 volumes, bequeathed them to the Jesuits College whence they were transferred to the Marciana.

The Venetians in the days of prosperity were in the field whenever any great collection was announced for sale, either at home or abroad, and there is collateral testimony to a fact which is itself eminently probable, that portions at least of the library of the celebrated Matthias Corvinus, King of Hungary, found their way to the shores of the Adriatic. This was about 1490 when the purchasing power of the subjects of the Republic was in its zenith.

The books of Corvinus, which it has been erroneously stated Lord Arundel purchased in 1636 at Nurnberg, were, in fact, gradually dispersed. The most important had disappeared in 1520, when the Venetian representative at Buda saw the remains of the once noble and extensive collection, and wrote to a literary friend to say that there was next to nothing left worth carrying away. He mentions a Virgil, a Cicero *De Legibus*, and a Pliny as desirable acquisitions. The greatest treasures had already been abstracted by the ministers of Maximilian, and the shelves were apparently open to every comer.

There were cases in which personages of rank and influence became recipients of gift or dedication copies, of a special character as regards the material on which they were printed and the sumptuous bindings which the donor bestowed on them. An interesting copy on vellum, with illuminated initials and the arms of the ducal family of Barbarigo, of Sabellico *Rerum Venetarum Decades*, 1487, still exists, but has long left its Venetian home, and has parted with its original vesture; there are many such memorials of former magnificence and taste.

Other favourite lines of collecting were arms, armour and ancient musical instruments. We have the names of some of those who made such objects their speciality, and the extent to which prodigality of decoration on weapons of more or less recent manufacture was carried is familiar to later generations. The Doge Faliero who died in 1355 seems to have been one of the earliest enthusiasts in numismatics, and left behind him a cabinet of Roman coins; he had numerous followers, particularly Sebastiano Erizzo (1522-1585), a public servant, lecturer and archaeologist, who published at Venice in 1559 *A Discourse on the Medals of the Ancients, on the Consular Money of Rome, and on the Medals of the Emperors.*

Other connoisseurs were Domenigo Pasqualigo whose treasures came to Saint Mark's, Giovanni Soranzo, Onorio Arigoni who published a description of his fine collection of coins in 1741, and finally the founder of the Correr Museum. But a member of the Correr family, apparently a different person, formed a cabinet of Roman medallions, which seem subsequently to have passed into the hands of the Pisani, by or for whom a catalogue was printed at Venice in folio with 92 plates.

The multiplication of printers and books naturally led, as elsewhere, to the rise of a class which made it their special calling to distribute in retail and sell at second-hand. There is in the Marciana the ledger of an anonymous dealer of this kind, who flourished in the last twenty years of the fifteenth century, and who seems to have been quite miscellaneous in the character of his stock. He must have been one of the leading members of the trade, and his place of business was somewhere near the Rialto. His entries extend from May 1484 to October 1485. He sometimes gave books in exchange for household requisites; sometimes he sold a lot at an agreed price, as when he lets sixteen various works go

W. CAREW HAZLITT

"*in massa*" to Messer Alvise Cappello for two ducats and one *lira*. In one instance, he makes a present to a corrector, probably of the press.

Popular literature at the period fetched comparatively nothing; indeed, many of the classics and many books with fine engravings were estimated in *soldi*. Plutarch's *Lives* are thought worth two ducats, or about a sovereign, and for nearly the same money a customer might have had Plato, Dante, Petrarch and Diogenes Laertius. The *Geography* of Ptolemy, however, is invoiced at 3 ducats 4 *lire* 18 *soldi*. The owner of this unique day-book recognized the principle of allowing credit, perhaps only to regular and safe clients, and pursued the modern method of always keeping in hand surplus copies of articles in constant demand, such as school books, the *Satires* of Juvenal, *Itineraries to Jerusalem* and the letters of His Holiness Pius II.

The winter months constituted, according to the returns for the period comprised in the account, the busiest part of the year; from September to December, 1484, the takings were 318 ducats. Not only the season, but current circumstances, influenced custom, for, in the case of the lawyer Leonardo Crasso, an extension of copyright was conceded in 1509, because the *Hypnerotomachia* of Colonna, 1499, of which he defrayed the heavy cost, had proved unsaleable by reason of the wars. In the previous May, the dealer in question took stock, and found that he had 1337 volumes on hand. A list attached to the ledger enumerates the nine holy-days, mainly occasions of state ceremonials and processions, on which he was obliged to close his premises wholly or partly, and to refrain from exposing goods for sale outside or "on the balcony."

The restriction was not very exacting and was perhaps indulgently interpreted, the expression "*aperto a mezo*" being susceptible of loose solution. He does not state whether the regulation was generally applicable. As a record there are few things approaching this Venetian memorandum book in antiquity and curiosity, since for the date it is unusually full, and presents a refreshing leaven of books of human interest. (1) At the Frari in Venice, there is a second relic of a similar kind belonging to a much later epoch, 1596 to 1603, but such manuscripts are almost necessarily of peculiar rarity, as they are objects long deemed unworthy of preservation or notice.

(1)   Brown, *The Venetian Printing Press,* page 37-39, 432-452, The earliest Scotish if not British ledger is that of Andrew Halyburton, 1612.

The collection of antiquities implies indeed the existence of sources whence the acquirers furnished themselves, and where such things were stored pending the arrival of a buyer. The records of this class are both scanty and intermittent. So far as books are concerned, we learn that such as Petrarch left behind him at his death in 1363 were sold at Padua. Anton Kressen of Nurnberg bought in that city a copy of the poet's works, printed at Venice in 1501, and caused it to be bound for him in his own home in 1505. In the first half of the sixteenth century, the members of one of the Councils were supplied with copies of Aesop to fill up vacant time; each of the forty-one Councillors had one, and they were all brought to light in a short space of time from local depots. In 1536, the dispersal of the extensive library of Marino Sanudo must have flooded every emporium and private study in Venice.

We know that Paolo Sarpi was for years a daily frequenter of the shop of Bernardo Secchini, and that many others resorted to it, both Venetians and foreigners; it was there that Sarpi fell in with the French Jew. He is said to have known Secchini as early as 1586, and his biographer speaks of the latter as having his place of business at the sign of the Golden Ship. (1) There were not only shopkeepers, but stall-holders who exposed their goods in the public thoroughfares where space allowed, and, in 1774, we meet with the hawker who traversed the streets in search of clients.

(1)   Michel et Fournier, *Histoire des Hôtelleries, Cabarets, Courtilles, et des Anciennes Communautés et Confréries d'Hôteliers, de Taverniers, de Marchands de Vins,* page 297, where, however, Secchini is described as an innkeeper. Perhaps he kept his stock on the first floor over a tavern or hostelry.

Evelyn was much struck, on his visit to the city, by the museum of curiosities which had been formed by Signor Rugini, a noble Venetian, who occupied a fine and richly-furnished palace. The collection was of the type then admired in England and associated with the names of Ashmole and Sloane; but Rugini counted among his acquisitions many costly and splendid specimens of ornamental furniture and, according to the diarist, some valuable cameos. It is worth noting, in immediate reference to a bedstead inlaid with agates, crystals, carnelians and other stones, estimated at 10,000 *scudi,* that at that time gilt-iron bedsteads were commonly used in Italy, on account of the liability of wood to harbour vermin.

Many private collections of more or less notable character existed down to the last years of the Republic, and a few survived the fall in 1797. It was in those families which had retained their wealth, or had been willing to sacrifice other considerations to their heirlooms, that relics of the past were to be sought. The contents of aristocratic mansions and palaces were of a sumptuous, varied and more or less casual description; the middle-class or bourgeois connoisseur was long unknown in a state where even merchants were patricians, and one of the most recent cases under the old regime was that of Teodoro Correr or Corraro (1750-1830), who formed and carried out, on an ambitious scale, the design of accumulating all available remains which served to illustrate the Venetian annals and life from the earliest period.

This noble undertaking resulted in the Correr Museum, bequeathed by the owner to his native city and country. It embraces archaeological examples of every kind; unique state-papers, weapons, bronzes, coins, medals, and the entire world of culture cannot be too thankful to such a man for his invaluable legacy. Correr was on the ground, of course, when such things were procurable, more especially in the last dark days when a vast amount of property was cast adrift, and few, if any, besides himself were at hand or disposed to secure it. The Museum is consequently the sole repository of a large number of historical and personal memorials, which might have perished in the absence of those affectionate eyes and hands. It has received some later accessions, particularly the Molin bequest.

Of a native school of binding and gilding we find no actual vestige before the fifteenth century, beyond a casual mention, which is of course suggestive, of two manuscripts bound in 1321 for Marino Sanudo the traveller, one in red, the other in yellow, and it is not certain that these were done in Venice. The multiplication of books, after the establishment of the Aldine Press in or about 1494, probably encouraged the institution of a binding department which may, as in France and England, have been under the same roof, and there is ostensible evidence that the appliances for gilding covers of volumes were even exported to Germany at an early date. The dedication copy of a book of poems, printed at Vienna in 1529, has been decorated on the sides in gold with Venetian tools, and exhibits, moreover, gauffred edges. The most likely explanation, however, appears to be that the sheets were transmitted to Venice, to be clothed in the rich morocco vesture which is still in its faded glory recognizable.

The extant specimens of Venetian work in morocco can hardly be referred to an earlier period than the first half of the sixteenth century; the Venetian leather, which was doubtless of Levantine origin, became celebrated, and modern English artists long followed the practice of attiring, not only the productions of Aldus and Asulanus in this vesture, but any choice volume committed to their care. But the expression Venetian binding is very loosely and vaguely employed in catalogues, to denote morocco liveries which have no perceptible connexion with Venice, and may not even be of Italian origin. It is extremely probable, however, that many of the Grolieresque bindings, found on the productions of the Aldine Press between 1520 and 1540, may have been locally executed; they are sufficiently abundant, but seldom occur in a high state of preservation.

Although the Petrarch of 1501, (1) noticed above as purchased at Venice, was carried back home to receive a German cover, there is no doubt that, even before the time of the Aldi, Venice had a school of biblio-pegistic art which, starting with oaken or other wooden boards covered with plain or stamped leather (2) as elsewhere, alike in Italy and France, gradually developed through the stages of pigskin and limp vellum into Levantine morocco, gilt, tooled and otherwise decorated to meet an ever-growing variety of tastes. A Strabo, printed at Venice in 1472, yet exists in a nearly coeval binding of stamped leather over oaken boards, exhibiting a curious oriental interlaced knot-work design; it may originally have belonged to the Barbaro family, as on the last page is a manuscript. epitaph on Ermolao Barbaro who died in 1493. On the other hand, many books of course parted with their first clothing, and were reattired in a less becoming and dignified manner. Such we can scarcely doubt to have been the case with a copy of Cicero's *Orations*, attributed to the Milanese press about 1478, in which the former ownership of the Venetian house of Moro is established by the shield of arms on the first page, but the covers are of relatively modern calf.

(1)   Now in the British Museum.
(2)   The Huth copy of the *Hypnerotomachia Poliphili*, 1499 (by Colonna), appears to be in its original vesture of oak boards with a leather back, and the paper has not suffered from the process of rebinding.

Some rich examples occur among the *Ducals* of a more or less early period. There is one of the Doge Andrea Gritti, directed in 1531 to Andrea Gradenigo who was proceeding as Governor or Proveditor of

Monselice. It is in the original gilt red morocco, with the name of the recipient on the upper cover. A second, in its old red velvet binding with ties, was delivered by the Doge Priuli in 1561 to Giovanni Soranzo on his appointment as Captain of Brescia, an office which he was to hold for sixteen months and until his successor arrived. A *Ducale* delivered to Zuan Battista Pasqualigo, proceeding Podesta to Cresignana in 1593, affords an uncommon example of Venetian morocco binding of the time. It is a manuscript on 170 leaves of vellum, in Italian; the covers are designed in the oriental style, and decorated with gold tooling, the Lion of Saint Mark being impressed on the obverse and the Pasquialigo arms on the reverse.

The grants of arms to new families were similarly preserved in sumptuous Turkey leather covers, with religious or other symbols on one side and the shield or medallion on the other, accompanied by the Doge's leaden seal. There is an example appertaining to the Moro family, dated 1608, in magnificent red morocco binding, enriched with elaborate scroll-work and embellished with the Crucifixion and the Moro coat on either side.

The fashion among persons of means and taste, both among the aristocracy and in the religious houses, for painted book covers and edges set in even before the sixteenth century, for the Piloni family of Belluno formerly possessed a marvellous assemblage of volumes, (1) so decorated by no less a personage than Cesare Vecellio. A Florentine visitor to the Monastery of San Giorgio Maggiore in 1713, in company with the Elector Friedrich August of Saxony, records that they saw there a collection of books with richly embellished bindings, but at Florence itself the earlier Medici caused their books to be treated in this manner, whether they were from a local or from a foreign press. The painted edge has the air of having been an outgrowth from the gauffred style of decoration not uncommon on examples of works from the Venetian press.

(1)   The collection was sent *en bloc* abroad.

CHAPTER LXIII

The House — Its Various Apartments — Household Articles — Chimneys
— Ovens and Wells — The Water-Supply — Domestic Objects; Musical
Instruments, Birds, Flowers, Cats, Dogs, Gardens — The Curfew —
Conflagrations — Torchbearers — Use Of Charcoal — Venice, a Busy
Resort — Liberty of Strangers — Guides — Hotels — Police Supervision
— Pilgrims To The Holy Land — Plagues and Famines — Details of the
Population at Various Dates — Sanitary Precautions — Punishment For
Adulteration — Board Of Health — Quarantine.

The houses of the early Venetians, subsequently to that primitive epoch
when the city presented an assemblage of low and undecorated timber
tenements, roofed with thatch and pierced with unglazed port-holes,
exhibited some points of resemblance to the Roman buildings at
Pompeii. This may be another way of saying, that the models of building
transmitted by the Romans were followed by their successors, who may
have had some of them still fairly preserved under their eyes in the
Middle Ages. But a unique piece of testimony survives, in the form of a
reference to certain judicial proceedings in the second half of the
eleventh century, to indicate that, in some of the ancient dwellings of the
aristocracy, a spacious covered portico or porch constituted a feature; for
a suit at law is said to have been heard before the Ducal Court in these
circumstances, at the residence of a member of the Candiano or Sanudo
family. This perhaps corresponded with the later *loggia*, which was
reached by a flight of steps and constituted an open-air apartment where,
as in the *altana* and *liago*, the family might meet in suitable weather. It is
perceivable that in some instances, more especially perhaps in earlier
times, a mansion occupying a more than average area was designated by
the term *corte*, the prototype of the modern court.

Coryat observed the peculiar way in which some of the foundations of houses bordering on the canals were made, and states, probably as something which he had immediately heard, that the preliminary process represented a third of the total cost. He then describes the process of damming the water and driving in the piles, and says that it was the same as that followed at Amsterdam and Stockholm. At a later date, it was the plan pursued in building Saint Petersburg. It is traceable in Venice back to the fourteenth century.

Fir, larch and elder were the descriptions of timber in principal use. The house, which was not uncommonly one-storeyed, (1) seldom exceeded two storeys exclusive of the *liago* (*heliacum*) or solarium; namely, the basement or *terreno*, on which were the kitchen offices and the armoury, and the upper storey which contained the reception rooms and dormitories. (2)

(1)   Zanetti, *Dell'Origine di Alcune Arti Principali Presso i Veneziani,* page 78-79.

(2)   Molmenti, *La Storia di Venezia nella Vita Privata,* Liber I page 66 et seqq.

On entering a house of the better class through the ample portico, of the ancient employment of which as a court of justice in eyre mention has already been made, (1) the first object which met the eye was an outer court, leading into a vestibule (*atrio*), from which a staircase conducted to the second storey. The latter, in addition to the dormitories, contained the principal sitting-room, along the walls of which were ranged curiosities of art, armour, weapons and other family relics — the sword which a Michieli used at Jaffa, or the spurs which a Dandolo wore at Constantinople. It was a quadrangular apartment, usually not very spacious, the sides of which were covered with leather embossed with gilt arabesques; or, if the family was particularly wealthy and extravagant, with silken tapestry brocaded with silver. The more private portion of even palatial dwellings was not adapted for the accommodation of festive assemblies.

(1)   It was the same in France, at all events in regard to gateways, and also among the Hebrews. Fosbroke, *Encyclopaedia of Antiquities,* page 140.

From the sitting and sleeping apartments you ascended to the *liago*, which was closed on three sides, and open only on that which had a southern aspect and enjoyed the morning sun. The roof was flat and supported by rafters, instead of being vaulted like that of the Roman edifices, and on it was sometimes raised the *altana*, which was absolutely open. But the settlement of details, where there was in former times at least no municipal control, depended on individual taste and discretion. A singular attic belonging to the Palazzo Contarini in the fifteenth century is illustrated by Molmenti. (1) Round the roof they gradually learned to place a stone gutter, which received the rain water, and conveyed it by pipes into the wells; the means of filtration were a still later improvement.

(1)   Molmenti, *La Storia di Venezia nella Vita Privata,* Liber I page 90.

Wherever we look, flat roofs appear generally to have been preferred, as they are still in many places, either for safety where the cyclone is an habitual visitor, or for use and enjoyment where it is often possible, as in the tropics, to sleep in the open air. At Venice the inmates of the house could here inhale the evening breeze during eight months of the year, after a sultry summer's day, and here even the processes of the female toilette were occasionally performed. Nor was such a structure by any means unknown in more northerly latitudes, though the nature of the climate in England and elsewhere made such an architectural feature comparatively unserviceable. Coryat was agreeably impressed by the verandahs or little galleries of pleasure, as he terms them, projecting from the main building, and affording a prospect of the whole city in the cool of the evening.

It was in the hall that entertainments were usually given, especially those on a large scale. Meetings of interest to the various branches of a family were held in it. As long as the Ducal Court was one of circuit, and the Doge himself presided over it, this part of the house was often devoted to the hearing of suits, as it yet continues to be in Morocco and other parts of the east, if the weather or other circumstances precluded the use of the porch. It was here, perhaps, in residences of pretension, that the bronze fire-dogs, as time proceeded, were placed, of which a very few magnificent examples, executed by famous sculptors and worth many times their original price, have come down to us.

In the better sort of houses, as now (at the Palazzo Papadopoli, for instance), the hall was sufficiently spacious for convivial purposes, and on or against its walls were placed paintings, arms and armour. The trophies of the chase also found a place, so long as forest land within a reasonable distance afforded ample facilities for sport, and hunters or hunting parties frequented the neighbouring terra firma in quest of the boar, the wolf, the deer and the fox, nearly all once found within the confines of Venice itself.

In the hall of the Casa Polo, the great explorer received his friends and kinsfolk at a banquet on his return in 1295. Out of it a series of doors opened into the various offices and the apartments intended for reception or for family use. The *terreno* generally contained the store-rooms. Above, in the second storey, besides the dormitories and study or library, was a private chamber used as a withdrawing room for the ladies. But there was, of course, at no time a precise uniformity in the distribution of the apartments or their application. Of beds and bedrooms we should know less, had it not happened that they casually enter into the details of ancient illuminations and musaics, in which we are able to trace, so far as important dwellings are concerned, the evolution of the universal sleeping-recess into modern forms, and to note the long prevalent usage of dispensing with night-clothes. The bed, as a detached article of furniture, is found in paintings of the fifteenth century, and was infinitely varied in its style and appurtenances.

A study of the forms used in the construction of the staircase, alike external and internal, must lead to the natural conclusion that personal taste or local circumstances governed the fashion and details, and Molmenti supplies us at different points with the means of judging the range of choice and style, where the spiral or cylindrical staircase, as within the Casa Contarini at San Bovolo, is the most characteristic and conspicuous. (1)

(1)   Molmenti, *La Storia di Venezia nella Vita Privata,* Liber I page
         91, 376, 404, Liber II page 120, 466.

Existing remains of the fifteenth and sixteenth centuries sufficiently demonstrate the growth of plastic and decorative art, not only for ornamental purposes, but even for the normal service of all parts of the dwelling. Objects in pottery and bronze, the commercial value of which is now enormously enhanced, owing to the naturally limited survivals, especially those in fine preservation, were once, and indeed long, utensils or appliances in common vogue among householders, dealers and professional practitioners. Entries in the catalogues of modern collectors, among which *chefs-d'oeuvre* by renowned masters of other days meet the eye and change hands at stupendous figures, are not instantly recognizable as having formerly, for a modest consideration, been acquired as ordinary furniture, or as part of the fittings of an apothecary's or grocer's shop.

They belong to an age anterior to machinery and competition, to one appreciative of beauty of feeling and form for their own sakes, without a side-look to emulation and to the auction room. Our museums have become treasuries of countless articles of infinite variety, instruction and charm, of which the honour is unequally apportionable between the genius which created them, and the sentiment which promoted their development. It might not be a difficult task to replace, on the ground, an old Venetian residence of the better class with all its sumptuous embellishments, from examples which are in our hands, and the same may be said of the contemporary place of business, where the appurtenances were viewed, not with our eyes, but with the eyes of those who had bought them from the maker.

The usual receptacles for apparel, and even the chamber-fittings, were those large carved chests or coffers of oak or cypress which the Venetians exported in Plantagenet days to England and other countries, and which are described in numerous ancient inventories and writings. They received, as time proceeded, artistic embellishment, and occasionally served as trunks for travelling purposes; it appears that a particular sort, known as a *bisacca*, was employed to hold books, as, in a trial which took place in 1549, certain heretical works are described as kept by the owner in *"un per de bisacche."*

At a later period, Flanders competed with the Republic in this as in other things, and examples of Flemish work are still to be seen in museums and private collections. The use of cypress-wood at Venice was recommended by its presence close at hand in earlier times, when so large an area was still forest and coppice. For ordinary travelling purposes, other kinds of trunks and handbags were gradually introduced, and soon attained such a degree of efficiency as to answer without material change the requirements for centuries, even of the most exalted personages. (1)

(1)   In Humphreys, *The Illuminated Illustrations of Froissart,*
         Number 27; Gascoigne, *The Complete Poems of George
         Gascoigne,*   Volume I page 233. The mail or trunk is
         distinguished from the cap-case which a traveller probably
         carried in his hand.

It was probably the occupation of the Guild of Casemakers to construct
these receptacles, indispensable for household use and for journeys by
land or sea. The romantic episode of the Brides of Saint Mark in the
tenth century reveals to us the existence of this body, and it was then by
inference in a flourishing condition. It responded to a large and incessant
want, and the followers of the vocation appear, from a casual allusion, to
have extended their labours to the manufacture of umbrellas.

In the dwellings of the poor, the floor of the room consisted of common
paving-stones, strewn with sand or rushes; but the remains of cement
pavement which have been exhumed shew that that material was often
applied to a similar use in more fashionable residences; marble and
musaic were also largely employed.

Buildings of an antique and patriarchal type were still to be seen in the
eighteenth century — some the original structures abandoned to the
humbler classes, others reproductions of old tenements of an
unpretending character on the former lines.

It is capable of proof that chimneys were to be found here and there
during the reign of Domenigo Contarini (1043-1071), even in the
habitations of the middle classes. (1) In a document of the year 1048, in
which a house is sold by one of the Morosini family, with a specification
of its contents and character, the chimney is one of the features named.
There was evidently not more than one, although the premises have the
undoubted air of having been of considerable importance for the period,
and even to have been in part of stone.

(1)   Filiasi, *Ricerche Storico-Critiche da Giacomo Filiasi,* page 163.

The earthquake of 1282, which committed the most terrible damage in
many quarters of Venice, was fatal to a very large number of chimneys in
the metropolis. The Venetian *cammini,* which were generally in the
kitchen (1) of the residence, were, in the first instance, of the rudest
possible structure, especially in the humbler abodes, where the inmates
contented themselves with the hollowed trunk of a tree or even with a

bamboo. Nevertheless, their existence must be treated as a mark of superior civilization, for elsewhere such appliances, in any form, continued till the fourteenth century to be of the rarest occurrence, (2) and it is hardly an exaggeration to say that, during a very long course of years, a larger number of chimneys might have been counted in the Dogado than in all the rest of Italy.

(1)   Zanetti, *Dell'Origine di Alcune Arti Principali Presso i Veneziani*, page 78.
(2)   Zanetti, *Dell'Origine di Alcune Arti Principali Presso i Veneziani*, page 79. They were not introduced into Rome till 1368.

It was to the faulty structure and inflammable material of the chimney which, prior to the great fire of 1106, was formed, like every other portion of the house, entirely of timber or bark, that the origin of many of the innumerable conflagrations which desolated the metropolis between the fifth and sixteenth centuries was due. In the view of the Piazza as it appeared in or about 1494, the chimneys are particularly conspicuous from their funnel-like form, but other authentic sources of information lead to the view that there was no fixed plan or rule, and that, in the same thoroughfare, each owner pursued his own pleasure or taste. The great fire at the Palace in 1574 was thought to have originated in the kitchen chimney-flues during the preparation of an inaugural banquet.

In 1355, an apartment or saloon at the Ducal Palace, supposed to belong to the private portion of the building reserved for the sovereign, is designated *sala camminorum* or the chimneyed room, as if the feature were then sufficiently exceptional to be thus distinguished; and we know from various authorities, as well as from actual experience, that the Venetians, even in modern times when the weather not infrequently demands artificial warmth, content themselves with a stove. The *sala camminorum*, however, may have been a species of hall where the chimneys of the building converged. It is difficult to speak or feel with certainty where it is a question of a structure no longer extant. (1)

(1)   Molmenti (*La Storia di Venezia nella Vita Privata*, Liber I page 72, 75) furnishes some early examples of chimneys of varied forms.

It is deserving of mention that, in the *Cries of Venice*, 1785, a posthumous work probably calculated for a much earlier period — the artist was born in 1698 — a chimney-sweep is represented at the top of a building, pushing a long broom down one of the chimneys, and a second figure in the foreground is plying for hire, his implement on his shoulder. It is a primitive contrivance consisting of a couple of poles fastened together, and at the end of each a bundle of twigs; it had perhaps been in use for centuries. The same set of prints shews that the supply of fuel for wood-fires formed a distinct industry — a man is delivering bundles from a boat at the door of a dwelling-house — and that the use of bellows was general, as a dealer figures elsewhere. They are not dissimilar from the modern type.

But in connexion with the same era and the same personage — the unhappy Doge Faliero — it is mentionable that, at his private residence at Santi Apostoli, the room which held his library and antiquities was known as the Camera Bossa, and not improbably it grew customary thus to distinguish apartments in important and stately houses by their decoration or upholstery. While of the books and manuscripts with which Venice was formerly adorned we have fairly copious particulars, we do not learn much of the older type of bookcase which superseded the chest or ran parallel with it. We casually hear of a bookcase in which certain archives were kept by the executive in 1574.

Every good establishment was provided, not only with a kitchen, but with a well and an oven — the two great essentials among all Mediaeval communities. The former is one of the features specified in the deed of sale in 1048 of premises belonging to the Morosini, but the oldest monument of this kind is probably the great Nuns' Well, dating back to a period of unknown antiquity and situated in what was once part of the garden of the Abbey of San Zaccaria, but had long formed, when it came to light in 1888, a central spot beneath the Piazza.

We are all aware of the stress laid on the possession of a well in the *Old Testament*, and of the principle on which it was regulated. In the *Second Book of Samuel*, the well of Bethlehem is represented as by the gate of the city, but this, like our own parochial wells, was for public use. At Venice, on the contrary, if a well was sunk, it belonged to the person who owned the property and his tenants or clients; it was usually sunk, as at Pompeii, in the outer court, and near at hand was sometimes a cistern, in which a sufficient quantity of rain was preserved for use. The water from the cistern was allowed to filter into the well, it being thought that pure filtered rain-water was an improving ingredient in that which was derived from the subsoil or the river.

One or two of the shocks of earthquake, which so often visited the Republic down to the end of the thirteenth century, inflicted serious damage on these valuable contributions to comfort and health, and, until the Brenta was brought into service, the supply of fresh water was always in danger of interception or deterioration by natural agencies. Temanza proposed to himself a dissertation on this subject, but it does not seem that the idea was carried into execution. The 24th of the *Cries of Venice* portrays one of these wells, from which a woman has been just drawing two buckets of water; she is allowing a boy to quench his thirst. Many of the well-heads in private dwellings were elegantly carved, and became in modern times objects of attention to connoisseurs.

In 1540, the Venetian envoy at the court of the Emperor Ferdinand sent to his government a report of the system then followed at Bruges by which the city was supplied with water brought by leaden pipes from the nearest river, and the ambassador, Tommaso Contarini, intimated that at Venice they might get at no great cost, by a similar expedient, superior water from the Brenta; this was done at a later date. (1)

(1)   Romanin, *Storia Documentata di Venezia,* Volume VII page 246-247.

The English traveller Thomas, who was at Venice about 1548, testifies to the care and cost undertaken in constructing these essential contributions to health and comfort, in order to preclude the contamination of the fresh water by that of the lagoon, and he apprises us that, although water to the value of 20,000 crowns a year was also brought into the city in boats, complaints were often heard of a scarcity among the poorer classes. There seems to have been a special service of boats for this important purpose, with a station on the Rio dell'Acqua Dolce, and the water-sellers were to be found in the adjoining Campo de San Baseggio, where they characteristically enough had their own chapel.

The conveniences to which they were accustomed at home the Venetians are naturally found seeking in their colonial settlements, and even in the ports where they merely enjoyed trading rights, since the employment of those common to the inhabitants was apt to prove a source of disagreement.

Molmenti (1) has very serviceably refurnished for our inspection and study the early Venetian kitchen, including that of the Ducal Palace —

the pantry, the dinner-table, the banqueting apartment with all its sumptuous accessories; and that agreeable writer has, in common with others, been largely aided by the painters of the national school, who ingenuously made the domestic costume of their own day subservient to the immediate object.

(1)   Molmenti, *La Storia di Venezia nella Vita Privata,* Liber I page 162-166, 169-175, 472-483, 485.

The violence to consistency was universal, and in a picture of the Supper at Emmaus, a place of which the exact identity is unsettled, Christ is seated at a primitive table on trestles, and has on one side the Venetian nobleman for whom the work was executed, and, on the other, a Turk. We see the same thing when our eyes fall on representations by Veronese or Tintoretto of the Marriage at Cana or the feast in the house of Levi. The treatment and colouring are transparently local and casual, and bear the appearance of having been borrowed from Venetian analogues; the incongruity has to be balanced with the gain.

Modern familiarity with the houses of antecedent ages might have been far less considerable in the absence of incidental illustrations, even when the material asks for editorship. When the dwellings of the respective classes have been realized, the process of supplying their arguable or average contents has to follow, and the pages of the illustrated edition of the *Vita Privata* are wealthily enriched by examples of furniture and articles of daily use among different orders of the community at successive epochs — the tables and chairs, the mirrors, the arras, the chandeliers, the beds, the kitchens and kitchen-utensils, the pantry, the dairy, the fireplaces and the staff employed in dressing and cooking the food, in serving and carving the meats, and the inferior servants whose functions were discharged in the scullery. Of all these details the means of enabling us to form a connected idea are in a certain measure extant. There are even vestiges of the old ducal culinary apartment, as it existed in the later days of the independent Republic, when it had beyond question undergone constant restoration, and preserved few traces of its aspect in grander times; when it not only prepared all that was required for public entertainments, but for the private table of the Doge, where His Serenity was entitled to freedom from intrusion by any beyond his family and personal friends.

Research and curiosity have been perhaps too exclusively confined to the habits and environments of the rich and fashionable class in the community, and we have to study all works dealing with this branch of the subject, with the steady recollection that they not only concern relatively modern times, but a social minority more restricted than under more popular governments. The archaic domestic and personal costume of Venice, in greater measure than that of states differently constituted, lacks material for its elucidation, even when we regard the higher levels, and the lives and homes of the population at large have merely here and there a gleam of light shed upon them by some accidental and indirect allusion, or by the permissible inference that conditions in so conservative a society differed but little from century to century.

Amid their graver callings, the Venetians were distinguished by a passion for music, birds and flowers, and few houses were without a garden and an aviary, in the former of which flower-beds and avenues of fruit-trees were agreeably diversified with shrubberies of cedar, cypress, larch, pine and laurel. In the *Cries of Venice*, 1785, a flower-seller, exhibiting a basketful before two women, is made to say that, in summer, spring, autumn and winter, he has always these things on sale, so that at Venice you may have a perpetual garden. Cages filled with singing-birds formed part of the pageant at a ducal coronation in 1268, and such birds are also a feature in the *Cries*. We remark that, in another engraving in the series, a woman is represented at a window holding a cat in her arms, because such domestic pets were presumably common long before. The printing house of Sessa placed a cat on its title pages in the fifteenth and sixteenth centuries, and the great Doge Francesco Morosini, who died in 1694, carried with him in all his campaigns a cat, of which the skeleton is still, or was till lately, preserved.

One of those incidents, of which the main importance for posterity and the historian resides in their indirect bearing, was the loss, about 1212, of a Doge's son through the injuries sustained while he was bathing, from the savage dogs kept by the monks of San Giorgio Maggiore, and this circumstance may be allowed to stand sponsor for the existence of the practice at Venice of employing watchdogs, as the Romans had done, while the pursuit of the chase, even within the limits of the Dogado in early times, must have involved the use of more than one species of hound. But we fail to trace back the dog as a domestic pet; those which were attached to San Giorgio were probably mastiffs, a breed apparently familiar to the Gauls of ancient Venetia, and found as a type on the coinage of the independent Dukes of Mantua, There was also a breed which was known as the Dalmatian — the modern carriage dog.

In the gardens which belonged to the wealthier class, exotic plants became not uncommon, when the Crusades had rendered Europeans familiar with oriental botany; and a crystal fountain, which sometimes was to be seen playing in the centre, completed the picturesque effect of the landscape. The orchard of San Giorgio Maggiore, the vineyard of San Zaccaria, the olive-yards of Amiano and the aviary of San Giobbe enjoyed during the Middle Ages peculiar celebrity. Among private grounds, those of Tribuno Memo at San Marcuola in the ward of Cannaregio, were most famous at the close of the tenth century.

The Venetians, in common with other Mediaeval societies, had the curfew, an almost unavoidable safeguard in an age of timber and thatch, but at what hour of the evening it rang does not appear. That there was at least one exception to its provisions seems certainly to be shown by a law (1) of 1306-1307, granting to the Guild or Company of Barbers the privilege of keeping fires after dusk in the Barbieria; in the Rialto generally lights were permitted, it appears, till an hour after midnight. If at Venice, as in England, it was the case that the barbers were also professors of surgery and dentistry, and were, in fact, prior to the rise of the regular physician, the only medical men outside the monasteries, we can more readily understand the grant of such an indulgence to them.

(1)   Gallizioli, *Delle Memorie Venete Antiche, Profane ed Ecclesiastiche,* Liber I Capit 10.

But a free resort to links and the use of oil as a lighting medium, especially when its employment was extended to public and other buildings, almost necessarily formed a fruitful source of casualties, even with the strictest enforcement of the curfew and the exercise of the utmost care. Marco Polo had brought back with him in 1295 information of the means which, in some parts of China or Cathay, they then employed for the extinction of fires — means not dissimilar from those still in use in the north of Europe; but no explicit account reaches us of the machinery, if any, adopted in Mediaeval Venice.

The general operation of the curfew restricted, perhaps, the enjoyment of indoor recreations after nightfall, but at certain seasons, and, in the case of the aristocracy, at the dispersion of festive parties on the approach of dusk and a retirement to the dormitory, the rule was evidently subject to many modifications. It was certainly a law for which, beyond the excessive danger of locomotion by night in a labyrinth of dark alleys and canals, and the inconceivability of an adequate illuminating medium for general purposes, no actual necessity existed, and in its origin was rather political than social or domestic, while, in the poorer or less populated quarters of Venice, silence and gloom probably prevailed when daylight waned and the night was moonless. In London, at the close of the seventeenth century, it was usual to retire to rest at an early hour for reasons analogous to those which governed society elsewhere, and the hour of rising was also earlier. Arrangements were adapted to existing conditions of life. (1)

(1)   Human remains, periodically exhumed from the banks of the Thames below London Bridge, have been supposed in some cases to belong to persons who had lost their way in the dark or had been murdered.

There is sufficient testimony that nocturnal entertainments and late hours among the higher classes were by no means unfamiliar, even in the presence of the old Decemviral ordinance passed some time about 1310, that no one must be seen traversing the streets after the third bell of the night. (1) Of lighting appliances there was (in a rude and barbarous way) a tolerable profusion. The giver of a ball or masquerade, a concert or a birthday supper, might have his oil lamps and candelabra for waxen tapers, or, as at the fatal masquerade when, in 1393, Charles VI. of France was nearly burnt to death, the host might line the saloon with flambeaux.

(1)   At Forli, in the time of the Riario government, no one was permitted to walk abroad when the great bell had sounded, with or without lights.

When the moment came for breaking up the party, the guests could proceed home on foot or by water, attended by torch bearers for protection against the darkness, and furnished with weapons for defence against still more dangerous enemies. Here, again, the phlegmatic conservatism of the Venetian comes to our assistance, for, with all the riches of modern invention at his elbow, he still contents himself at night with the occasional glimmer, shed over the canals and over all but a few leading thoroughfares by the lights of the hotels and public offices.

Those who have in quite modern days travelled abroad, as well as those who are familiar after nightfall with the open country in England in the immediate suburbs of London, will not be surprised to learn that a vast space of time elapsed before any attempt was made in the direction of lighting Venice when daylight failed. The appliances were long absent, and nocturnal locomotion necessarily became limited. Within living memory in old Antwerp, almost unbroken darkness prevailed at night in the minor thoroughfares, except where, in a niche appropriated to an image of some saint, a candle or small oil lamp burned, not for the public convenience, perhaps, but for devotional ends.

Centuries earlier the conception of the illuminating medium occurred to the Republic (1117-1128), and appears to have arisen in a similar way and spirit. Small oil lamps, called *cesendeli* and fixed in *capitelli*, were distributed over the thoroughfares of the metropolis, and indirectly helped to indicate where water-lanes terminated in a canal. The remedy was, of course, extremely imperfect, and the new reform did not accomplish much, it is to be apprehended, in the way of checking robberies and acts of violence.

The cost, it appears, was, at the outset, met by intrusting the clergy of each parish with the execution of the work, and authorizing the levy by them of a local rate for its maintenance; (1) and it may be supposed that the religious aspect of the usage tended to reconcile the taxpayer with this particular burden. The devotional side long continued to be prominent. In 1178, the Doge Ziani left funds to a monastery to maintain a *cesendelo* outside its gates in honour of Saint Stephen. This was the *lampas ardens* of Mediaeval England, for which rents or funds were left by pious persons at different times. (2)

(1)   Gallizioli, *Delle Memorie Venete Antiche, Profane ed Ecclesiastiche,* Liber I Capit 8 Section 19; Mutinelli, *Del Costume Veneziano Sino al Scolo Decimosettimo Saggio di Fabio Mutinelli,* page 49.

(2)   Kennett, *Parochial Antiquities,* Glossary under Luminare.

At a comparatively late period, when the influx of strangers desirous of visiting all parts of the city and of attending places of entertainment after nightfall was greater and more continuous than in earlier times, when business was more exclusively the aim of those arriving in the city, a special institution arose to facilitate the more secure transit from point to point of those unacquainted with the unique topography, and it was the *codega,* a person of approved character, who was stationed, lantern in hand, at certain places to conduct passengers to their destinations. No precautions were neglected to render the thoroughfares at all hours reasonably safe, and De la Lande went so far as to express the opinion that, in spite of the defective lighting, one might traverse the place at night without risk. It is, at any rate, beyond doubt that life was safer at Venice than in the Papal States, where, almost concurrently under the pontificate of Clement XIII. (1758-1769), 11,000 murders of which 4000 occurred in Rome itself were recorded.

An incidental help is given to us in respect of the usages of this in common with other Mediaeval capitals, when daylight failed and some extraordinary occasion demanded artificial illumination, by a passage in the historian Sabellico. He informs us that, during the famous Carmagnola tragedy in 1430-1432, the Senate sat from the first lighting of the torches to the break of day. The torch yet plays its part on the same ground, but is no longer required for the same or any kindred purpose. Let us imagine, however, an august body of about two hundred legislators, engaged under such conditions for several hours, in deliberating on a public question of the most momentous consequence, the Doge Foscari one of them, with the natural incidence of reading and examining papers, registering propositions and taking notes! At the same time, the wax-candle was at first, perhaps, dedicated to religious ceremonies, and even clothed with a sort of sacred character, as the term ceremony has its root in the Latin *cera*.

The custom was, in many places where the torch was charged with wax, to mix with the latter a proportion of resin to prolong its duration. The wax chandler was a known vocation in England in the middle of the fourteenth century, and must have been so in Italy, but the torch bearer is an inevitable figure in all the scenes and transactions of the old time after nightfall. Shakespeare introduces them into the *Merchant of Venice* (1) and in 1641 we hear of the exportation of bees-wax from England to Ireland for the tapers employed in churches. The case of 1430-1432 above cited may securely be taken to be a typical one, and a sample of what occurred for centuries at repeated intervals on emergencies. An identical experience must undoubtedly have attended the deliberations of the Senate or the executive during the War of Chioggia, the League of Cambrai, the Spanish conspiracy of 1618 and numerous other vital junctures. The practice was so familiar to those who pursued it, that the reference to it by a contemporary or early writer may be treated as purely fortuitous and a sponsor for a general principle.

(1)   Shakespeare, *The Merchant of Venice,* Act II Scene 4.

The *Cries of Venice*, 1785, portraying and renewing many aspects of the earlier life and customs, introduces a public lamp-lighter, whom we observe on his round at dusk, kindling the oil lamps thinly scattered up and down the back lanes and at the doorways of certain houses. It is elsewhere noted that, in the time of Annibale Caracci who died in 1609, sulphur matches were in use at Rome, and doubtless co-operated in multiplying disasters. The fifteenth illustration in the *Cries* introduced to us a highly curious and serviceable piece of knowledge. An old woman is chaffering with a boy for the commodities which he carries in a couple of baskets; in one hand she holds a pan to receive her purchase, and in the other a lamp of antique type, which might have been modelled on one from Pompeii. This receptacle for the oil was doubtless the utensil in general use by night, and suggests by its construction a tributary to the periodical fires which visited the city.

It yet remains a difficult and hazardous undertaking to approach and enter, when daylight has failed, any harbour in the world with all the advantages of modern improvements; but, when the sun went down and the night was moonless, Venice was as unreachable as if it had been surrounded by a wall of brass; one of the busiest and most wealthy capitals of Europe lay in silence and darkness. In 1380, when Carlo Zeno, on whom the existence of his country hung, reached Lido in the middle of a winter's night with his prayed-for fleet, he does not seem to have ventured to proceed to Chioggia till daybreak. There seems to be no record of a lighthouse even at Lido in those days, and if such a safeguard existed, it is not difficult to guess how rudimentary it would be. Leghorn is credited with the possession of one in 1303, but the supply of a clue to a port, where there were no adequate appliances for nocturnal protection against an enemy, might have been regarded as a dubious advantage.

Another and cognate respect, which was unquestionably an element in rendering conflagrations more frequent, was the recourse for warming and cooking purposes to wood and charcoal, before oil was introduced as a heating medium. Wood was long employed in open fires, surrounded by the same material on all sides except the floor; charcoal seems, in the eighth century (742), to have been deposited in braziers or pans, and served a variety of uses, including the deprivation of a few early Doges of their eyesight as an expedient for rendering them incapable of farther mischief, which, as in so many other cases, doubly serves us, since we thereby see the antiquity of the practice, and are able to recognize the application of an ordinary domestic item to judicial purposes as they were understood in former days.

The brazier, at least, continued to be a method of torture down to a comparatively late date, and when we first hear of it as a punishment, it had long, no doubt, served as a household convenience. The most modern provision on this ground for mitigating the severity of winter is inadequate enough to persuade us that, in former times, especially in the beginning of Venice, the condition of affairs was even less supportable. Utensils were introduced for blowing the fire when a pan or other receptacle of charcoal was employed, but the earliest and rudest have naturally disappeared. A pair of Venetian bellows of comparatively late date is carved in oak in high relief, having, on the upper side, the arms of the Doge supported by angels and surmounted by the ducal berretta, a head of Saint Mark above and a grotesque one below; on the lower side is a demoniac mask. This example probably resembled those to be seen in noble houses; the poor had their own humbler equivalents.

Venice was almost from the beginning a place of universal resort. Here was to be purchased every article of use, luxury or ornament. Here might be found shopkeepers, manufacturers and contractors of every class, who were ready to execute orders of any description. On her quays or at outlying points, captains of vessels were continually waiting to receive cargoes and passengers. In those streets, sailors and mechanics, the workmen at the glass-furnaces and the operatives at the Arsenal, busy townsfolk and curious strangers, were to be seen at all times hurrying to and fro in a confused throng from the break of day, when the bell at the Campanile (beneath which were the counters of the money changers) summoned the artificers in the employment of government to their labours till sunset.

Evelyn tells us as the fruit of his personal observation in 1645: "Nor was I less surprised with the strange variety of the several nations seen every day in the streets and piazzas; Jews, Turks, Armenians, Persians, Moors, Greeks, Sclavonians, some with their targets and bucklers, and all in their native fashions, negotiating in this famous Emporium." It is to be much suspected that the handsome young Persian, whom he met at Bologna in a rich vest of cloth of tissue and decorated with ornaments according to the fashion of his country, had been supplied by a Venetian tailor.

Referring to the liberty of strangers, an English eyewitness of the sixteenth century remarks that all men have so much freedom at Venice that, though they may speak very ill of the Venetians, there is no interference with them so long as they refrain from political allusions or criticism; and, in their carnival, the same writer says that all sorts may disguise themselves, and deliver with impunity under the very noses of the authorities views derisive of the customs, dress and even misery of the people. (1) He emphasizes the universal religious tolerance, and declares that it signifies nothing if a man be a Jew, a Turk, a Gospeller, a Papist or a believer in the Devil; nor does any one challenge you, whether you are married or not, and whether you eat flesh or fish in your own home. The freedom which appeared everywhere, both in the case of residents and strangers, struck Fynes Moryson who was in Italy some years before he published his *Itinerary* in 1617.

(1)   Thomas, *The Historye of Italye,* folio 85.

The general toleration of Venetian institutions, outside the political government of the Signory itself, attracted hither some of the Catholic recusants during the reign of Elizabeth, particularly from the northern parts after the rebellion of 1569. In 1581 and later years, we find Richard Collinge or Cowling of York and his brother Thomas at Venice, and the former, after his return home, in correspondence with one of the friends he had known there, Signore Giulio Piccioli, and from a letter addressed to that gentleman about 1599, there comes the interesting information that at this time Guy or Guido Fawkes, the writer's cousin-german, was resident at Venice in a state of great poverty. In 1591, Martin, son of Edward Turner, also of York, was sent by his parents beyond seas in order to be educated at Venice or Padua, where the tone was then said to be absolutely Jesuitical; and the exodus from the country under pretence of enabling sons to acquire languages was so considerable at this juncture, that the Council of the North directed the authorities at York to make an inquiry into the matter and report the facts. (1)

(1)   Davies, *Pope; Additional Facts Concerning his Maternal Ancestry,* page 32-35.

The floating population of such a city, where the number of permanent dwellers never reached 200,000, was of course very great. Multitudes were constantly arriving or leaving. (1) Whether the visitor to Venice was a pilgrim who desired to take his passage in a vessel bound for the Holy Land, or a foreign merchant who had come to attend the fair at Murano, or some devout person who wished to join in the celebration of the Feast of Corpus Christi, it mattered little. On landing at the Piazza of Saint Mark, he was sure of meeting with one of the commissionaires (*tholomagi, sensali* or *messeti*), (2) who were bound to be in constant attendance on that spot, and whom he engaged to provide him with a lodging, to change his money, and to perform any other service which he might require. It was the business of the commissionaires, of whom there were twelve under a *gastaldo*, to protect their employers against fraudulent innkeepers, and to caution them against the deceitful practices of sea-captains; if they were detected in an act of dishonesty, or in a dereliction of duty, or if they were charged with a misdemeanour of any kind, they were liable to a penalty of not less than half a ducat. The *tholomago* delivered such fees as he had received during the week to his *gastaldo* on Saturday, and the latter at once, or on the Monday, handed them to the *cattaveri*, who made a monthly distribution of the funds in hand.

(1)   Sanudo di Torcello, *Epistolae;* (general note); Bongars, *Gesta Dei per Francos,* Liber II page 304.
(2)   Marin, *Storia Civile e Politica del Commercio dei Veneziani,* Volume V page 181.

It was the province of a particular department of the public service (Messetaria) (1) to take cognizance of the proceedings of this body of officials, as well as to examine and regulate the charges of hostelries, to check mercantile agreements, and, generally, to see that no imposition was practised on unsuspecting travellers. The *tholomago* was under oath to accept or solicit employment only at the hands of strangers or of members of the Venetian clergy and nobility.

(1)   Marin, *Storia Civile e Politica del Commercio dei Veneziani,* Volume V page 181.

There were many posts which were less lucrative than that of *tholomago.* Not a single day elapsed without witnessing the landing of a large number of persons at the Piazza on business of various kinds. Sometimes it happened that an ambassador and his suite came and wished to secure berths in a vessel about to leave for Constantinople. From time to time, a royal or pontifical visit, or a coronation, or a ducal wedding, was the means of providing profitable employment for every member of the calling in the city.

But the cause, which more than any other contributed to swell the floating population, was the periodical recurrence of holy festivals, as well as secular diversions, when the gathering of strangers from every part of the adjoining terra firma was beyond all belief. As many as

100,000 visitors were reckoned among the company at the annual fair of the Ascension (*Sensa*), at a time when the entire urban population did not approach double that number. One year, during the reign of Pietro Tradenigo (860), was recollected, when the frost was so severe, that the visitors to the annual fairs were able to cross on foot or come in carriages, instead of employing boats. (1)

(1)   The only other occasions when the ice on the canals was sufficiently firm to allow free transit and to suspend navigation were 1378, 1491 and 1709.

There is an extremely graphic account of a lodging-house kept by Diana Palermitana, in which in 1618, during the Spanish conspiracy, about 300 men of different nations were domiciled together, and had no landing-permit as required from the Uffizio della Biastema, yet, in 1647, when matters were so much less critical, the omission to procure this voucher was declared to be capital. (1) Diana averred that the English ambassador connived at the admission of lodgers without obtaining the licence, and she lets us conclude that there prevailed a degree of laxity almost incredible in dangerous circumstances.

(1)   Raymond, *An Itinerary Contayning a Voyage, Made Through Italy, in The Yeare 1646, and 1647,* page 186-187.

The Venetian hotels or *alberghi* were very ancient and very celebrated. The leading establishments of this kind in the fourteenth century were the Moon, the White Lion and the Wild Savage. The first-named was flourishing in 1319, the second was the resort of distinguished visitors in 1508. The Wild Savage was a famous house for travellers who could afford to pay well, in the time of the Doge Andrea Contarini (1368); in 1769 when the Emperor Joseph II. visited the city in strict incognito, he put up at the White Lion on the Grand Canal, possibly the same house. In the fifteenth century, the Pilgrim, the Little Cap or Cappello and the Rizza are mentioned in the books of the Procuratie of Saint Mark. The Black Horse on the Piazza of Saint Mark and the Sturgeon at Rialto, with their hanging signs, have come down to us as details in paintings by Bellini and Carpaccio. Montaigne does not name the house at which he stayed in 1580; he merely informs us that it was "*trop publique et assez mal propre,*" but then he adds that he was making only a brief stay. Lithgow the Scotish traveller put up, he tells us, at the Cappello Rosso; this was about 1614. When Evelyn was here in 1645, he selected the Black Eagle, near the Rialto, proprietor Paolo Rhodomante, whom the visitor describes as honest; we may therefore conclude that his charges were reasonable; Evelyn does not say what they were. From Rome hither his expenses had been "seven pistoles, and thirteen julios." It will be recollected that it was at the Luna that Silvio Pellico stayed, both when he was a free man, and when he returned to Venice a prisoner in 1820. At a short distance from the capital, we come across the Campana or "Bell" at Mestre, where Casanova stopped when he had effected his escape from prison in 1786.

After 1280 and perhaps earlier, it became the business of the police to take care by special inspection that hotel keepers provided proper beds and clean sheets and coverlets, and duly attended to the comforts of their visitors. (1) In 1484, the concourse of strangers at a tournament held in that year was so vast, that all the hotels were filled, and permission was given to private householders to let their apartments furnished.

(1)   Romanin, *Storia Documentata di Venezia,* Volume IV page 492.

The practice of inscribing the names of visitors in a register for reference and security had been known to the Romans, and Marco Polo found it in force in China. At Paris an official ordinance of 1407 imposed such a regulation on all innkeepers, and probably it was the same at Venice. In the declining years of the Republic, some of the palaces were let to various tenants, and some were converted into warehouses or inns.

We meet with no ancient guide-books to the city, analogous to the *Mirabilia Urbis Romae,* of which the edition published at Treviso within the Venetian territories in 1475 may not be the first, or to the *Guide to Rome* published at Venice in 1588, but Rome had, of course, a peculiar degree of attractive sanctity independent of local and commercial requirements. It is extremely curious and interesting to meet with a second type of publication of this kind, written by an Englishman who calls himself Scha Kerlay (Shakerley), and who published his manual at Rome in 1562, as he tells us, without expectation of praise or gain. (1)

(1)   Shakerley, *La Guida Romana.*

The polyglot vocabularies intended to assist travellers on the continent were issued from the first half of the sixteenth century from numerous presses in Germany, Switzerland, France and Italy itself, and there are two bearing the Venetian imprint in 1541 and 1549. A manual in a pentaglot shape was printed at Venice in 1526, and embraced Latin,

Tuscan, French, Spanish and German in parallel columns. The contents are ranged under the subjects, and were, of course, calculated for the use of those desirous of entering into conversation or of ascertaining the equivalents for articles in daily use. The volume is constructed on the same principle as the later and more familiar works which comprise the English language.

Sufficiently copious particulars have descended to us of the experiences of travellers who made it their aim to pay a visit to the Holy Land. The earlier pioneers naturally had their lessons to learn, and, even in the fifteenth century, there were those who could by practical observation afford to later pilgrims the benefit of their own discoveries and errors. The persons who, from a variety of motives, desired to behold with their own eyes and tread with their own feet the very ground which had been the scene of the labours and sufferings of Christ and his Apostles, belonged to different classes of society, and embraced both the clergy and the laity; even great soldiers who had spent their active lives on battlefields amid all the horrors of war devoted some of their fortune to this pious and meritorious object.

At first the hardships and the cost were alike formidable; not less than 200 gold Venetian ducats sufficed to convey a passenger to the desired spot and bring him back, and in any circumstances the rough seas and scanty accommodation proved more trying to the veteran condottiere than the hardships and privations of long campaigns. The unchronicled mortality must have been enormous; the descriptions in some of the itineraries are appalling.

It was a strange infatuation, yet not more so than the modern devotional visits to Lourdes and other shrines. Even Casola, himself a churchman, cynically remarks in 1494: "Each one who goes on the voyage to the Sepulchre of our Lord has need of three sacks — a sack of patience, a sack of money and a sack of faith." (1) We appear to get nearer to him and his ship, when he speaks of the terrible storm off Zante, and of the cries on board of "Jesus" and "Miserere," of his pious reflections on the just anger of God, and of the propitiatory engagement of the passengers to undertake on their safe arrival three pilgrimages — to Loreto, Padua, and Venice itself.

(1)   Casola, *Canon Pietro Casola's Pilgrimage to Jerusalem in the Year 1494.*

The great Loyola, who began as a courtier and a soldier, walked from Rome to Venice, there took ship for Cyprus and the Holy Land, and returned by way of Venice in 1524 to Spain. The accomplishment of the scheme when funds were limited involved almost insurmountable difficulties, but arrangements were gradually made for pilgrimages on a more popular basis, in which a number of travellers occupied one vessel, and a fixed inclusive tariff was established for the double journey.

There are numerous accounts of early visits to Palestine by way of Venice, and the process was facilitated as far as possible from time to time; printed guides were soon forthcoming, setting forth what each passenger required in clothes, food and conveniences; a warm overcoat, a sea-chest, a barrel of wine and another of fresh water, cheese, sausages, junk, preserved sweetmeats, syrups and a close-stool, and, if he was not accustomed to the sea, he was recommended to secure a place amidships.

It is not difficult to perceive that, during all the years the fashion of engaging in these remote expeditions lasted, the Venetian government found it necessary to organize a special machinery for protecting its own subjects on the one hand and their customers on the other, and the traffic, on the whole, was doubtless highly remunerative, looking at the heavy charges levied on the owner by the authorities, who might feel that the clients were exceptionally wealthy.

Toward the close of the fourteenth century, women began to brave the dangers and discomforts of the enterprise, and occupied places on board side by side with the other sex. This marked the point of time when it was decided to select a department to manage and control, subject to the sanction of the Senate, the licences to owners and contracts between the pilgrims and the shippers. The earliest registers of the cattaveri, the *Pilgrims Book* included, have apparently perished, but the office had been in existence since 1280 for the safeguard and recovery of communal property. It subsequently superintended all matters relative to pilotage, and its duties were extended, agreeably to a decree of the Great Council in 1392 when the movement took more definite shape, to the conduct of the often troublesome and intricate details arising out of pilgrimages; the extant records constitute part of the colossal system by which the Republic bequeathed to future ages the materials of its history.

It is equally characteristic of Venetian temperament that, stringent as the law in this immediate respect might be, the Senate seldom refused to concede special terms to royal and noble applicants for passages. During a certain course of years (about 1442), the licences to take pilgrims were sold by auction, and the buyer enjoyed a monopoly of the voyage, the proceeds of the sale being devoted to the purchase of timber for the Arsenal.

It is a small detail, but we incidentally learn that, at stopping points on voyages, the departure was notified by men who landed and sounded trumpets to warn laggards, and sometimes even guns were fired to reach more distant wanderers.

Those who, in the course of centuries, made Venice their port of departure for the Holy Land and the Sepulchre, naturally arrived from different points and, as a rule, on horseback, as whatever baggage they proposed to carry was purchased when they reached the place of embarkation and found what was requisite. According to circumstances, they rode as far as Mestre, Padua, Pavia or Treviso, and then parted with their horses, proceeding by boat the remainder of the way. Casola, in 1494, came from Milan in this way, and embarked for Venice at Padua. It is characteristic that the horse was left in charge of the innkeeper till its owner returned; sometimes the animal disappeared, sometimes the owner.

On the journey from Mestre to the city, *sbirri* met the gondolas bearing travellers from various points, and examined their luggage, but, as a visitor about 1714 apprises us, (1) "not very strictly, and if you have any thing prohibited, on giving them a small matter they will take no notice." Such a statement is to be received with caution; these officers were probably not the official police, but rather custom-house functionaries who levied on dutiable goods or property.

(1)   Chancel, *New Journey Over Europe,* page 101.

A passport of health was, as already has been stated in connexion with a political episode of 1607, absolutely imperative — probably down to the close. Chancel mentions that those who had omitted to procure one were detained forty days, were very poorly accommodated, and paid high prices for their food, which was handed to them on the end of a long pole as a precaution against contagion. (1)

(1)   Chancel, *New Journey Over Europe,* page 99.

In the *Itinerary* of William Wey, of Eton College, 1456-1462, we are apprised that he set out for Jerusalem from Venice with nearly 200 other pilgrims, and that it was then customary to purchase the necessaries for the voyage at a depot near Saint Mark's. The bedding cost three ducats or about 28s., and was taken back by the vendor on the return into store at half-price, even if the articles were more or less deteriorated by use. This outfit comprised a feather-bed, a mattress, two pillows, two pairs of sheets and a quilt.

Way and his companions occupied two galleys. The freight and commissariat from Venice to Jaffa amounted to about forty ducats, but this sum did not include many extras indispensable for an English gentleman, medicine among them. (1) It is easy to see that, at the place of call, passengers who were at all fastidious took the precaution of buying certain provisions for themselves. Even those who had made a stay at Genoa, bound for Palestine, proceeded, it appears, to Venice to take ship for Alexandria. (2) Judging from the case of Casola in 1494, pilgrims, on their return from the east, disembarked at Sopra Porto, Malamocco, where there was good anchorage, and performed the rest of the journey by boat.

(1)   Jusserand, *La Vie Nomade et les Routes d'Angleterre au 14e Siecle,* Page 241-244.

(2)   (anonymous) *Romance of Paris and Vienna,* page 69.

There is a contemporary narrative of the journey of Sir Anthony Shirley to Persia in 1600, by way of Venice, where he was honourably entertained by the Signory. He had crossed from England to Flushing, and had proceeded to Cologne, Frankfort, Nurnberg and Augsburg, and thence across the Alps to the Adriatic (1)

(1)   (anonymous) *A True Report of Sir Anthony Shierlie's Journey Overland to Venice, &c.*

Chancel, a traveller of the early part of the seventeenth century, (1) specifies Mestre as the best place of accommodation for such as intend to travel into Germany by Tyrol and Carinthia, or into Austria by Friuli, and likewise for those who intend to make the tour of Italy. He speaks of it as about two miles from Venice.

(1)   Chancel, *New Journey Over Europe.*

From those twin scourges of the Middle Ages, plague and famine, which were largely due to an ignorance of agriculture, to the slowness of intercommunication, and to the stagnation of trade, Venice did not enjoy an exemption. Her experiences, however, though severe, were not more so than those of Milan and Florence. It was only as the spirit of commercial enterprise, which the Italian republics fostered and to which the Crusades gave an undoubted stimulus, was gradually developed in Europe, that those frightful visitations of pestilence and hunger with the recitals of which the pages of history abound, when men forgot their humanity and blasphemed their Creator, sensibly diminished in frequency and horror.

There can be slight doubt, however, that epidemics largely influenced the permanent population of Venice which was at all times abnormally limited. It has been supposed that, in the tenth century, the numbers were about 40,000; in 1170, they had only reached 64,000; in 1339, 40,000 able-bodied men were counted, and the Black Death of 1348 is said to have been fatal to 100,000 persons — an almost undoubted exaggeration. From 1422 to 1593, the figures are quasi-officially given as follows:

1422	190,000
1509	110,000
1540	131,000
1552	158,000
1563	174,201
1574	195,863
1581	134,800
1586	151,296
1593	155,722

But these particulars are receivable with allowance. The plague of 1575 swept away about 50,000; that of 1630-1631 nearly 47,000; and when the day of thanksgiving was held, the crowd is said to have been enormous; this may prove nothing, yet it does not suggest, at all events, a decline in the numbers. Lassels, the travelling tutor, mentions 180,000; this was about 1670. In 1795, the official figures were; for the city itself, 137,240; for the entire dominion, 2,921,011. At the period of the extinction of independence (1797), the urban statistics shewed 149,476.

In former days populations were scantier, with heavier death-rates, and the Republic, apart from casual visitors at fairs and festivals, shewed a chronic disposition to render accessions to actual citizenship at least difficult, since fifteen years' residence and fulfilment of civil obligations were required, before an alien could be admitted to an equality with a person of Venetian birth. In circumstances of exceptional emergency, the qualification was occasionally relaxed, and, of course, honorary citizenship stood on a distinct footing. Political decadence, however, operated more powerfully and permanently than any other cause in the shrinkage of numbers, and parts of the Dogado which were once thickly inhabited are at present occupied by market-gardens or are absolutely desolate.

The city, although placed in a situation which naturally suggests extreme humidity and insalubrity, has been considered healthier and drier, even than Milan, in consequence of the beneficial influence of the east and south-east winds, while the saline exhalations from the lagoons have been recommended to sufferers from phthisis, scrofula and tuberculosis; (1) yet Montaigne is heard in 1580 to complain of the effluvia from this source, although he says nothing about the dirt which might have offended his nostrils in Paris at that time.

(1)   Compare Molmenti, *La Storia di Venezia nella Vita Privata,* Liber II page 66.

But in summer there was always danger of contracting malaria or enteric fever from the wide areas of marsh and brackish shallow bordering on the Adriatic and Mediterranean. In 1782, a foggy and wet spring followed by a very dry summer involved Venice, in common with nearly the whole of Europe, in an epidemic of Russian catarrh. This malady could be traced back to the fourteenth century, and in 1731 it spread as widely as in the later year; it was supposed to emanate from North America. At the present time, in certain states of the tide, the canals omit an odour as unpleasant as unwholesome. The mist which is apt to rise from the lagoons is known as the Mermaid.

The government was perpetually adopting some fresh precaution against epidemics. During the plague of 1348, a Committee of Three Sages had been deputed to concert all necessary and possible measures for arresting the evil; and in 1423, the first Lazzeretto was established on part of the site of the modern Armenian convent. The successive developments which this novel and admirable institution received greatly helped to improve the health of the capital, and to diminish the rate of mortality. In 1467, larger accommodation for afflicted persons having been demanded, a hospital with 100 wards was built at the public expense, in a vineyard belonging to the Abbey of San Giorgio Maggiore, and this building became known, as the New Lazzeretto. (1) During the plague of 1527, the convalescent home already existing at Santi Giovanni e Paolo was enlarged, and three others behind the Hospital of the Incurables, at San Cassiano and at the Giudecca respectively, were established; the patients received gratuitous rations of bread, soup and wine.

(1)   Romanin, *Storia Documentata di Venezia,* Volume IV Capit 6. A remarkable account of the lazar-houses established in England and elsewhere may be found in a paper by Dr. Cookson in the Lincolnshire Topographical Society's *Transactions*, 1841, page 29 et seqq.

In the same spirit, every species of commercial roguery was brought within the pale of the law. A heavy penalty attended the exposure for sale, or even the attempted introduction into the city, of meat unfit for human food; justice had its terrors for the vintner who endeavoured to palm upon his customers some nondescript compound as the finest growth of the Marches or as undoubted malmsey. One ground of complaint and trouble in respect of wine was the habit of the shippers of adulterating foreign wines with the brackish water of the lagoons when they had tapped the casks at sea. It went hard with any confectioner who was detected in putting chalk into his sugar-plums or adulterating his maraschino or even diluting it.

Of her project of sanitary reform the Signory never allowed herself to lose sight. In 1459, the Board of Health, which had been already organized from time to time as occasion required, was virtually rendered (1) a permanent branch of the administration, although it was not officially declared to be so till 1485; somewhat later, a species of Highway and General Police Act, in the shape of regulations for keeping the thoroughfares in a state of cleanliness, and the clearance of all offal, putrefying substances and rubbish from the footpaths was promulgated.

(1)   Malipiero, *Annali Veneti,* page 655. The printed copy in Vieusseux, *Archivio Storico Italiano,* Liber VII page 137, was abridged, and there the passage does not occur.

No expedient which tended to add to the general safety and comfort was neglected. During the prevalence of an epidemic in the neighbouring cities, no meat, fish or wine was admitted into Venice, until it had undergone a regular process of disinfection. The most tender care was exhibited to secure for metropolitan use the sweetest and most wholesome water, and subsequently to the fifteenth century the entire supply was derived from the Brenta. No impurities were suffered to offend the eye or the nose; smoky chimneys, as well as noxious smells, were prohibited; and it was illegal to pollute the canals, which were periodically dredged to check the stealthy accretion of mud and slime from the continuous deposits of the Brenta, the Adige, the Piave and the Po itself.

In 1501, the lagoons were placed under the special superintendence and control of three Savii or Sages, and in 1542 the department engaged the permanent services of a professional adviser. Two bulky quarto volumes by the engineer Zendrini attest the energetic and unremitting efforts to keep the waterways open. These regulations were framed with such extraordinary attention to the minutest and most trifling details, that they acquired in process of time European celebrity, and furnished a model so recently as the eighteenth century for the Dutch Republic. The malodorous condition of the minor foot-ways and back lanes under Austrian and Italian rule would hardly have been tolerated in the old days, in the face of the more general distribution of wealth and the abundance of splendid and luxurious private habitations.

One of the most memorable visitations of Asiatic cholera or Black Death, subsequent to that of 1348, was that experienced at Venice in 1447. So powerful was the dread of contagion, that altars were erected in the streets, and mass was celebrated in the open air. Fires were kept continually burning to purify the atmosphere; braziers of scented woods were employed with a similar object; processions were formed in every quarter; every effort was used to deprecate the supposed wrath of the Almighty, and a hymn was composed, which the people sang aloud in the streets and on the canals:

> *Alto re della gloria*
> *Cazzi via sta* (1) *moria*
> *Per la vostra Passion*
> *Abbiane misericordia.* (2)

(1)   i.e. *questa.*
(2)   *Cronica Erizzo*, manuscript in the Marciana. Quoted by Romanin, *Storia Documentata di Venezia,* Volume IV page 482.

The plague of 1447, with the customary deliberation and delay characteristic of all proceedings when urgency was not deemed imperative, led to the introduction, about the same period as the admittance of the Board of Health in 1485 among the permanent executive bodies, of the principle of quarantine, in which, as in so many other matters of police, the Republic took the initiative, and which yet remains a feature in all European systems. Its wisdom and efficiency are not to be judged at present sanitary needs and views, but by those of the time, as well as by the special precautions imposed on a city which had such constant intercourse with the east.

CHAPTER LXIV

Hospitals and Other Charitable and Pious Institutions — Scuola della Carita — Asylum for Destitute Children — Misericordia — Magdalens — Poor-Relief — Monastic Institutions Employed to Accommodate Prisoners of War — Manners and Costume of The Earlier Period — Testimonies of Foreign Writers (940-1494) — Dress of the Humbler Class — Character and Attire of Ladies — Their Personal Appearance — The Chopines or Zilve — Their Long Prevalence and Ultimate Abolition — Pietro Casola at Venice in 1494 — His Description of a Noble Lady's Lying-In Apartment — Architecture — Dom Pedro of Portugal At Venice In 1428 — Other Distinguished Guests from Italy and Other Parts of the World — Three Great Ladies Visit the City Incognito — The Conti Del Nord — The Drawing Rooms — The Procurator Trono and His Wife — Sumptuary Laws — Their Inefficacy — The Sigisbeo or Maestro di Casa — Lady Arundel's Maestro in 1622 — Parsimony — Gallantry — The Gondoliers — Gloves — Burials — Popular Marriage Ceremonies.

From the opening of her independent career, Venice abounded with pious and charitable institutions which were broadly classifiable into hospitals or *hospitia*, *scuole* and guilds. By his will, made in 977, Orseolo the Holy left funds for the erection of a hospital — a term and thing of wider application in its origin than is at present understood, and, no doubt, comprising the graver or more chronic types of insanity. A Scuola della Carita was established before 1310. The Doge Marino Giorgio founded an asylum for outcast or destitute children. In 1392, was erected the Scuola dei Zoppi or Zotti, in a lane which yet preserves the name, and it was restored in 1533; it was exclusively for the benefit of the lame and their dowerless daughters. (1)

(1)   It is said that the Scuola was annually entertained in April at the
         Contarini Palace, and that members of the aristocracy served the
         tables. Such a usage would be in keeping with ancient Venetian
         bonhomie.

The growth of these philanthropic and beneficent institutions was steady
and almost incessant during the fourteenth and two succeeding centuries.
The government erected in 1474, as a thanksgiving for the recovery of
Scutari, the Jesus Hospital at Castello, which at Easter and Christmas
dispensed generous alms to the poor, and took measures for the perpetual
replenishment of the public granaries. Official zeal and benignity vied
with private munificence in meeting all legitimate claims and needs. In
1498, one of the Morosini family built in the Street of the Holy Trinity
thirty-six dwellings for impoverished patricians, and, in 1535,
Bartolommeo Nordio, a timber merchant from Bergamo, established the
Fraterna, which distributed relief to decayed nobles, to indigent
gentlefolks, and to young married women who were in need of aid.

Even after the fall of the Republic, under the will of the Doge Manin
who died in 1802, 110,000 ducats were devoted to the establishment of
an orphanage and an asylum for persons of weak intellect. A building,
known as the Misericordia, was endowed successively by Giacomo
Moro, Bartolommeo Verde and Veronica Franco for poor women and
penitent females. During the reign of Bartolommeo Gradenigo (1339-
1342), the Foundling, or La Pieta (1) had its rise, four centuries prior to
the appearance of such a thing in London, and, in 1349, an orphanage
was to be seen at San Giambattista, at the Giudecca. A Hospital for
Incurables for the particular use of victims of the venereal disease
followed, as we have seen, very closely on the discovery of America; it
was established there in 1522 by Gaetano Thiene, a Vicentine, and was
the earliest of its kind.

(1)   A large contributory element to the foundling institutions was
         the illegitimate offspring of courtezans of humbler rank. Such as
         belonged to the Veronicas and Margaritas, if they were indiscreet
         enough to bear any, were brought up and educated at their
         parents' expense, and such was equally the case in regard to all
         children who were left till they were too big to pass through a
         narrow grating in the wall, and whom their mothers were then
         obliged to take back home. If the infant answered to the
         regulations, no questions were asked, and the woman was

discharged for ever from her parental obligations. As they grew up, the boys were drafted into the naval or military service, or other public employment, but the girls too often trod in the maternal footsteps. The Venetian institutions incurred slight risk of lacking tenants.

Both the founder and Girolamo Miani who, after leading an active and free life, devoted the whole of his fortune to the endowment at San Basilio in 1524 of an asylum for the children of poor artificers, where they were fed and clothed and taught a trade, were after their deaths almost canonized. (1) Miani extended his noble benefactions to Padua, Vicenza, Verona, Brescia, Bergamo, Como, Milan and other places.

(1)   Miani was actually placed in the calendar by Benedict XIV. in 1747. There is a portrait of this enlightened and estimable man in Molmenti, *La Storia di Venezia nella Vita Privata,* Liber II page 57.

Well might Ritio in his book on Italian place-names, 1585, say:

> "*Gentil huomini e ricchi sono*
> *Venetiani populo bono.*"

The system of establishing schools such as the Carita seems to have attained great development in the sixteenth century, when we meet with two classes, *maggiori* and *minori*; these were mainly supported by voluntary contributions or endowments, and occasionally took part in public ceremonies and processions. They were partly charitable, partly educational, in their objects. Moreover, periodical distributions of alms and poor-relief took place, both on the part of the government and on that of individuals. At the same time, by a law of the Great Council passed in 1300, street-begging was interdicted; the officers of the Signori di Notte were ordered to take all mendicants, and to convey them to the hospitals.

A peculiar appropriation of the monastic establishments under stress of circumstances was their share in housing prisoners of war, for whom the government had no means of providing in the ordinary places of detention. Venice has been usually regarded as a spot remarkably rich in gaols, but, as a matter of fact, its resources in that respect were always scanty and when pressure arrived, special arrangements were compulsorily made.

Pope Gregory VII., the immortal Hildebrand, is said to have remarked that the spirit and liberty of ancient Rome survived in the Republic, and assuredly, in comparison with the state of the rest of Italy including Rome itself at that period (1073-1085), the Venetians might well have seemed to be what this great man described them. But long before his time, a Lombard envoy, who was at Venice in 940 on his way to Rome, animadverted on the politeness as well as the rich attire of the citizens, and compared these traits with the social condition of his own countrymen and of the Franks.

"The City of Venice," writes Ferretus of Vicenza, (1) "deserves to be called free, for it is governed by the counsels of good citizens, and not by the dictates of an absolute King; it was a saying, when the ducal authority threatened to grow too over-bearing, 'It is no king that we want.'" Nicholas Bonotriensis, who accompanied Henry VII. of Germany during his Italian journey in 1310-1314, complains of the discontented and restless spirit of the Venetians of his time. "They will have," says the Bishop, "neither God, nor the Church, nor the Emperor. Neither the land nor the sea satisfies them!" (2)

(1)   Ferretus, *Historia Rerum in Italia Gestarum ab Anno MCCL ad Annum Usque MCCCXVIIIin* Muratori, *Annali d'Italia,* Volume IX.
(2)   Bonotriensis, *Iter Italicum Henrici Septimi, A.D. 1310-1313;* Muratori, *Annali d'Italia,* Volume II folio 895.

A similar stricture is passed by Froissart, however, on the Lombards generally, and Cardinal Wolsey, in a conversation with the Venetian Resident at London in 1516, somewhat inconsiderately declared that, if the Republic aimed at grasping so much, it would end by making enemies all round. The Duke of Milan had said much the same thing as far back as 1466. In the *Chronicle of Muazzo,* the Islanders are accused of being incurable ramblers. "The villas, the gardens, the castles of the Venetians," remarks this writer, "are Dalmatia, Albania, Romania, Greece, Trebizond, Syria, Armenia, Egypt, Cyprus, Candia, Apulia, Sicily and other countries, where they find advantage, recreation and security, and where they stay ten years at a time with their sons and their nephews." (1)

(1)   Filiasi, *Ricerche Storico-Critiche da Giacomo Filiasi,* page 163.

It is the rather optimistic remark of Sansovino that, in times of the highest antiquity, the citizens of the Republic judiciously adopted a style of attire which harmonized with the simplicity of their manners and the soberness of their carriage. "Originally," he continues, "the Fathers (*i Padri*) (1) being strongly attached to religion on which they based all their actions, and anxious to educate their children in the observance of virtue, the true foundation of all human affairs, as well as in the love of peace, had recourse to a species of costume suitable to their gravity, and such as might indicate modesty and respect. They were filled by a solicitude to do no wrong to any man, and to live in quiet with all; and they desired to make this solicitude apparent, not in their manner only, but in their garb also."

(1)   Filiasi, *Ricerche Storico-Critiche da Giacomo Filiasi,* page 163.

But there were doubtless departures from this puritanical sobriety of costume. At the entertainment which Marco Polo, his father and his uncle gave at the Casa Polo in 1295 on their return from their travels, the three explorers appeared, successively, as we have seen, at table in long gowns of crimson satin, crimson damask and crimson velvet. These transformations were part of a preconcerted expedient, but Ramusio, writing in 1553, seems to speak of such a class of dress as usual at that period. In short, much depended on circumstances and the taste or resources of the wearer.

"I have considered," writes Pietro Casola of Milan in 1494, (1) "the qualities of these Venetian gentlemen. For the most part they are tall, handsome men, astute and very subtle in their dealings, and whoever has to do business with them must keep his eyes and ears well open. They are proud — I think this is on account of their great dominions — and when a son is born to a Venetian gentleman they say themselves, 'A Lord is born into the world.' They are frugal and very modest in their manner of living at home; outside the house they are very liberal. The city of Venice preserves its ancient fashion of dress — which never changes — that is, a long garment of any colour that is preferred. No one would leave the house by day if he were not dressed in this long garment, and for the most part in black. They have so observed this custom, that the individuals of every nation in the world — which has a settlement in Venice — all adopt this style, from the greatest to the least, beginning with the gentleman, down to the sailors and *galeotti.* Certainly it is a dress which inspires confidence, and is very dignified. The wearers all seem to be doctors in law, and if a man should appear out of the house without his toga, he would be thought mad."

(1)   Casola, *Canon Pietro Casola's Pilgrimage to Jerusalem in the Year 1494,* page 142-143.

We are sent to Cesare Vecellio (1) for the fullest and perhaps best account of the male and female attire of all classes at Venice, in and just antecedent to his own time. His volume is extremely well known, and some of the Venetian section has been ineffectively copied. He has patriotically devoted more than a just proportion of space to the Signory, and the work is lavishly embellished with engravings, of which some may have been derived from drawings by Titian himself. It is a compilation unequal in its graphic value, but we are concerned only with that section which is most likely to have owed its pictorial illustrations to the great artist. The figures purporting to represent the more ancient dress are neither more nor less authentic, however, than those supplied elsewhere. Vecellio helps us only where he furnishes the results of personal or quasi-personal observation.

(1)   Vecellio, *De gli Habiti Antichi e Modérni di Diversi Parti di Mondo.*

Lassels (1) observes: "The men Themselves here, who looked like men indeed; and as a Philosopher anciently sayd, that when he came from Corinth to Sparta, he seemed to come from horses to men; so me thought, when I came from France to Venice I came from boyes to men. For here I saw the hansomest, the most sightly, the most proper and grave men that ever I saw any where else. They weare alwayes in the towne (I speake of the noblemen) a long black gowne, a black cap knit, with an edgeing of black wooll about it, like a fringe; an ancient and manly weare, which makes them looke like Senators. Their hair is generally the best I oversaw any where; these little caps not pressing it downe as our hats do; & Perywigs are here forbid. Under their long gownes (which fly open before) they have hansome black sutes of rich stuffs with stockins and garters, and spanith leather shoos neatly made."

(1)   Lassels, *The Voyage of Italy,* Part II page 377-378.

At the same time, allowance has to be made for the individual taste or fancy of unofficial persons, and for the humours of such bodies as the Company of the Stocking or of such as took part in masquerades and the carnival. The tailor of Casanova brought home a doublet of taffeta, with a fringe of silver lace designed by the young lady with whom he had arranged to breakfast at Castello, and the same eccentric character orders not so long after a pair of very wide boots, lined with bearskin to keep him warm in the *Piombi* during the winter. Before his troubles, when he could press the fine pavement of Venice at his pleasure, he says that he found little shoes sufficient.

The dress of the men among the common classes was merely a sky-blue (*Veneto colore*) frock with narrow sleeves confined at the wrist, those wide breeches which went under the name Venetians, and close-fitting hose; their head-gear with the rest of their habiliments was probably of a no less simple character, and subject to little variation. In a climate where a warm temperature prevailed during eight months of the year, there was a limited call for thick clothing. (1)

(1)   For the gala dress of the working women compare Chapter 66 ad finem. As to the Venetian colour, see Morgan, *Romano-British Mosaic Pavements,* page 86-87. There is a monograph by Calogera on the subject.

Signor Tessari has depicted for us, and an English lady has described, the workwomen and the maidens of the lower class at Venice, as they now are, (1) and it is perfectly safe to assume that their appearance and dress have not materially changed since the days of the old Republic. They retain their aristocratic figures, graceful carriage and fine heads and features, but with these go a certain languor and sadness, in harmony, as it might seem, with the fallen national fortune. The fishermen and gondoliers rarely expended any considerable sum on their attire. A coarse blouse, pantaloons and a tasselled cap went far toward the completion of their outdoor wardrobe, the hosier and the cordwainer were infrequent creditors, and, if an organ-grinder is seen in the streets, he is less Italian in aspect than the same professional person in a London thoroughfare.

(1)   Pearson's Magazine, September 1905.

The Senators (1) usually appeared in a long robe with ample folds, and furnished with open sleeves which were variously termed *dogaline* and *ducali*; the colour chosen, if not black, was azure (*turchino*), of which the Venetians were passionately fond. In wet or cold weather, it was customary to fasten the large sleeves round the wrist with strings, which

was called wearing them *a comeo*, but the younger men, who disdained
this effeminate precaution, perhaps, and never used strings, were said to
wear them *a dogalina*. The sleeve was generally ornamented with a
double row of buttons, one of which, running in a transverse direction,
made with the other a species of cross. The cap, which was most
frequently composed of black or red velvet, was in form triangular, with
two silken fillets as strings, meeting cruciformly in front across the
forehead. There were temporary fashions. A favourite general won over
the young aristocrats to his particular way of wearing his bonnet; within
a few years (1430-1441) it had been in succession *alla Carmagnola* and
alla Sforzesca.

(1)   Mutinelli, *Del Costume Veneziano Sino al Scolo Decimosettimo
         Saggio di Fabio Mutinelli*. The practice of wearing the hair
         unkempt on the part of men in high stations, though long usual in
         other parts of Italy, does not seem to have prevailed at Venice; it
         may have originated in a fear of foul play during the operations
         of the barber. The Venetian of rank let his hair and beard grow at
         seasons of mourning or trouble.

Not satisfied with raising memorials of the Crucifixion in their churches
and their dwellings, the Venetians carried such memorials also on their
persons; they symbolized the Passion in the sleeves of their dresses and
the ribbons of their hats, and a Doge in the fourteenth century wore a
cross in his corno, as a concession to his father who would not uncover
in his presence, unless such a subterfuge was provided. We are reminded
of Sir Thomas More.

Above the inner robe was ordinarily thrown a long mantle or cloak which
descended nearly to the feet. To this cloak was in most cases attached a
hood which might be drawn at pleasure over the head, or allowed to hang
down the back or over one shoulder. The waist was commonly encircled
by a wide band of velvet or other material (in mourning black or violet
velvet), which served the twofold purpose of a girdle for the dress, and a
belt for the weapon which long formed an indispensable part of the
costume. High leathern shoes conspired with the flowing vest to hide the
red stockings, and completed the description of a Senator or nobleman of
the twelfth and thirteenth centuries.

The dress varied according to the seasons (1) as well as the personal taste
of the wearer, and its elegance and costliness had a tendency to increase.
At the same time, the mantle was very seldom seen without a fur lining;

in summer, ermine, in winter, furs of fox and squirrel, were preferred, and the number of skins of animals of this kind, preserved in the dwellings of the rich, was barely credible. Apart from external accessories, of which the minor varieties were infinite in either sex, there were the masculine types of feature, almost in equal measure liable to differentiation. A reference to Molmenti (2) will shew at a glance the wide diversity of face and pose among members of the nobility and followers of liberal professions.

(1)   See Folgore, *Sonetti de' Mesi,* Volume II page 172 in Alfani, *Poeti del Primo Secolo,* Volume II page 172,

(2)   Molmenti, *La Storia di Venezia nella Vita Privata,* Liber I page 202, 243-247, 401, 404, 464, 490-495. In a picture of the Last Supper by Paolo Veronese, Christ has on one side a Turk and on the other a Venetian patrician — probably the patron of the artist.

The modes were naturally governed by the practice of personages in high society, whose influence was capable of introducing changes and modifications of costume. At one time scarlet superseded blue; and that was again replaced by red. The cloak was an inseparable adjunct of outdoor dress, and even the beggar liked to imitate his superiors by throwing over his shoulder some rag which did duty for this appendage.

As the Shylock of the *Merchant of Venice* is represented to be a subject of the Republic and a Levantine Jew, (1) it may be permissible to remark that such persons usually wore yellow turbans or, in the words of Bacon, orange-tawny bonnets, whereas their Italian co-religionists were commonly seen in red hats.

(1)   Hazlitt III, *Shakespear, Himself and His Work,* page 449. But in a unique tract of a date near the period of the play, we have a Jew named Caleb Shilocke who was serving in the army, or was at least attached to it as a follower.

It is true that, in the nearly contemporary series of engravings by Giacomo Franco, we get the *Mercante* of the day — as the artist could see and portray him in 1609, but it is open to question, whether this personage is not to be construed into the equivalent of the French Marchand rather than into the opulent and influential proprietor of argosies, the capitalist, Jew or Gentile, who had his representatives and correspondents, and who, if he gained much, was content to risk much, especially in unsettled times.

Habito di mercante

MERCHANT'S DRESS
(Photograph by Donald Macbeth, London)

The ladies were distinguished by their intelligence, the sprightliness and vivacity of their wit, their fondness for music, their talkativeness, their coaxing ways and their love of spruce clothes. "Ladies of Venice," says Gianni Alfani, a Tuscan poet of the thirteenth century, (1) "I wish to sing with you of my mistress, because she is adorned by every virtue and charm which are resplendent in you."

(1)   Alfani, *Poeti del Primo Secolo,* Volume II page 420.

In person, the ladies were graceful and comely, though rather low in stature and with a slight inclination to fulness of bust, ascribable, perhaps, to the warmth of the climate and the prevalence of indolent habits, but also in part due to the prevailing fashion in attire, as we are best able to judge when a modern Englishwoman adopts on a special occasion the same style. A traveller, writing in 1714, assured us that "here is a greater number of lovely women than in any place in Europe." (1) They are said by Sansovino to have enjoyed a pre-eminence among the Italian women for the whiteness of their linen and for their skill in sewing and embroidery.

(1)   Chancel, *New Journey Over Europe.* Molmenti (*La Storia di Venezia nella Vita Privata,* Liber II page 500-510) furnishes some interesting types of Venetian female beauty from pictures by Titian, Giorgione, Veronese et cetera, but it is possible that we should allow for idealization.

Their costume underwent numberless changes at successive periods. (1) Originally it consisted of a robe of gay colour, generally blue unless they were in mourning, and of simple pattern descending in loose folds to the instep, with a mantle of azure tint which could be thrown, at the wearer's option, across the shoulders, or be drawn close to the person by a clasp. In a drawing which probably belongs to the thirteenth century, appears a Venetian lady in this kind of drapery, with those peculiar shoes, resembling pattens, then in vogue, and with a small cap, perhaps of velvet, from which her hair escapes in careless ringlets down her back. Her sleeves are straight and fitted tightly to the wrist. The outer garment seems to be lined with a warm material, and the whole aspect of the figure indicates that it is designed to represent a female of the better class in the winter garb of the period.

(1)   Filiasi, *Ricerche Storico-Critiche da Giacomo Filiasi,* page 144; Molmenti, *La Storia di Venezia nella Vita Privata,* Liber II page 408 et seqq., where this subject is copiously illustrated.

A second drawing (1) which is ascribed to the fourteenth century exhibits a lady, in indoor and perhaps evening apparel, who, from her mien and deportment, may be pronounced without much hazard to be a member of the aristocracy. Her hair is elaborately arranged and parted, and is combed off her brow; her head-dress is a species of turban. The robe which, though fitted with a high body, leaves the neck exposed, is confined at the waist with a narrow zone; the sleeves are of the simplest description. The hand which is not concealed by the drapery is gloveless; the arms are bare considerably above the elbow, and a bracelet encircles the right wrist. The feet are quite hidden from sight; pattens were employed in traversing the kennels and alleys, and were replaced in the house by easy slippers, or, on formal occasions, by shoes of more elegant workmanship.

(1)   Mutinelli, *Del Costume Veneziano Sino al Scolo Decimosettimo Saggio di Fabio Mutinelli.*

When Pietro Casola was at Venice in 1494, the pattens or *zilve*, as they were called, were worn so monstrously high, that ladies in the streets were obliged to save themselves from tumbling by leaning on the shoulders of their lacqueys. (1) Yet he says explicitly it was a well-kept and clean city, and that, whatever rain may fall, there is no mud. The same writer archly observes that they did not seem to spend much on shawls to cover their shoulders. The chopine was still in full fashion in the time of Coryat; they were frequently made of the Lombardy poplar. They have long been discarded, (2) although they were almost essential till the thoroughfares were improved; but while they prevailed, they were among the numerous sources of worry to the authorities who regulated their dimensions, as women of low (3) stature adopted exaggerated patterns to cover their natural deficiencies.

(1)   See Hazlitt III, *A Select Collection of Old English Plays,* Volume X page 367. When Lady Jane Grey made her state entry into London in 1553, she disguised her short stature in this way; but when she proceeded to her execution she dispensed with this artifice.
(2)   Romanin, *Storia Documentata di Venezia,* Volume IV page 495.
(3)   Raymond, *An Itinerary Contayning a Voyage, Made Through Italy, in The Yeare 1646, and 1647,* page 201.

The daughters of the Doge Domenigo Contarini (1659-1674) are credited with having taken the courageous initiative, in revolting against this highly inconvenient and unbecoming feature in the outfit of women of quality, and emancipated their countrywomen from a mischievous fashion. An improved police had perhaps rendered it less needful, but they still remained in use when the Sieur de la Haye was here about 1660, and saw the ladies going abroad supported by female attendants.

An earlier traveller, John Raymond, who speaks of the fashionable promenade at Santi Giovanni e Paolo, calls them walking may-poles.

Coryat writes in 1608:

> "All the women of Venice every Saturday in the afternoone doe use to annoint their haire with oyle, or some other drugs, to the end to make it looke faire, that is whitish. For that colour is most affected of the Venetian Dames and Lasses. And in this manner they do it; first they put on a readen hat, without any crowne at all, but brimmes of exceeding breadth and largeness; then they sit in some sunshining place in a chamber or some other secret roome, where having a looking-glasse before them they sophisticate and dye their haire with the foresaid drugs, and after cast it backe round upon the brimmes of the hat, till it be throughly dried with the heat of the sunne; and last of all they curie it up in curious locks with a frisling or crisping pinne of iron, which we cal in Latin, Calamistrum, the toppe whereof on both sides above their forehead is acuminated in two peakes."

The author saw the operation, he says, performed by a Venetian lady who had married an Englishman.(1)

(1)   Coryat, *Coryat's Crudities,* page 262-263.

Casola describes the lying-in chamber of a member of the Dolfini family; we propose to stand aside and let him tell his story:

> "The aforesaid royal Ambassador [Philippe de Commines] said truly, that neither the Queen of France nor any French noble would have displayed so much pomp in similar circumstances. The ducal Ambassador said the same, and declared that our most illustrious Duchess (1) would not have such ornamentation on a similar occasion.

(1)   Beatrice, wife of Lodovico il Moro. She was herself at Venice in this year.

> "As the room was not capable of holding many persons, the aforesaid ducal Ambassador chose me specially to enter with him so that I might see and also report what I had seen elsewhere. While we were standing in the room he asked my

opinion several times, now about one thing, now about another. I could only reply with a shrug of the shoulders, for it was estimated that the ornamentation of the room where we were and where the invalid was — I mean the permanent structure — had cost two thousand ducats and more, although the length of the chamber did not exceed twelve *braccia*. The fireplace was all of Carrara marble, shining like gold, and carved so subtly with figures and foliage that Praxiteles and Phidias could do no better. The ceiling was so richly decorated with gold and ultramarine and the walls so well adorned, that my pen is not equal to describing them. The bedstead alone was valued at five hundred ducats, and it was fixed in the room in the Venetian fashion.

"There were so many beautiful and natural figures and so much gold everywhere that I do not know whether in the time of Solomon, who was King of the Jews, in which silver was reputed more common than stones, there was such abundance as was displayed there. I had better not try and describe the ornaments of the bed and of the lady — that is, the coverings and the cushions, which were six in number, and the curtains — as I fear I should not be believed. They were in truth most wonderful.

"I must tell about one other thing, however, which is true, and yet perhaps I shall not be believed, though it is certain that the ducal Ambassador would not let me lie. In the same chamber there were twenty-five Venetian damsels, one more beautiful than the other, who had come to visit the invalid. Their dress was most decent, as I said above, in the Venetian style. They did not show, however, less than four or six fingers' width of bare skin below their shoulders before and behind. Those damsels had so many jewels on the head, neck and hands — that is, gold, precious stories and pearls, that, in the opinion of those who were present, these must have been worth a hundred thousand ducats. Their faces were very well painted, and so was the rest of the bare skin that could be seen." (1)

(1)   Casola, *Canon Pietro Casola's Pilgrimage to Jerusalem in the Year 1494*, page 339-340.

Our Milanese conductor cannot have discovered all these matters while he was in the room, but must have collected his statistics outside. Nevertheless, his description is, considering the time, instructive enough.

It is only by intermittent glimpses that an insight is obtained into this class of history, and even Molmenti cannot yield us sensible assistance till we have reached comparatively modern days. A much earlier observer than Casola, Petrus Damianus, who was at Venice in the eleventh century, has drawn a picture of the Dogaressa of that day, a Greek by birth, whose luxurious habits excited mingled astonishment and displeasure in the mind of her biographer, although the intimate relations between the Greek capital and dynasty and the Italian republics, and even occasional intermarriages, should have familiarized western Europe, and especially careful observers, with Byzantine habits and tastes, for, almost precisely a century prior, the German Emperor Otho II., by his union with Theophano, daughter of the Greek Basileus, Romanus II., had introduced at his court the ideas and refinements of that of Constantinople.

It seems that every morning, when the consort of the Doge Selvo (1070-1084) rose, her cheeks were bathed with dew, which was found to impart to them a beautiful sanguine colour. Her ablutions were performed in rose-water; her clothes were scented with the finest and most delicate balsams; her hands were always gloved. Her chamber was saturated with essences and aromatic perfumes, insomuch that her attendants could scarcely refrain from fainting during the tedious process of the toilette.

The lady was a Greek; and this was a personal trait — especially at so early a date. Yet it is observable that, in the coronation oath of 1229, balsam and rose-water are expressly mentioned as articles which might (with plants, flowers and sweet herbs) be offered as gifts to the ducal family. There is too slight ground for apprehending that, on the European continent at least, habits of personal cleanliness were, down to relatively modern times, incredibly rare among both sexes and all classes. The case of Diana of Poictiers (1499-1566) has been adduced as an illustration of the prevailing tendency, as it was treated in the light of eccentricity or idiosyncrasy on her part, that she preserved her health and physical charms by the assiduous use of the bath. It was even insinuated that she had recourse to artificial restoratives, such as crushed gold in the water, although a contemporary assures us that she refrained from the use of rouge or paint.

Casola was an eyewitness of the splendid pageant of the *Corpus Domini* on the Piazza in 1494, and can scarcely find words to describe the splendour of the cloth-of-gold and velvet costumes, the richness of the decorations, the profusion of flowers and wax-tapers, the prodigality of colour; the scene survives for us all to-day in the well-known painting in the Venetian Academy.

This observant traveller continues to give an account of the life of the period. He tells us that the elderly ladies and the young matrons used in his time to walk abroad closely veiled, (1) but that the unmarried women were, on the contrary, liberal rather to excess in the display of their charms, and painted a good deal. Perhaps the latter practice was followed to hide their bad complexions, which, according to a contemporary of Casola, Marino Sanudo the younger, (2) they spoiled by their artificial way of living. Casola himself observes: "These Venetian women, especially the pretty ones, try as much as possible in public to show their chests — I mean the breasts and shoulders — so much so, that several times when I saw them I marvelled that their clothes did not fall off their backs. (3) Those who can afford it, and also those who cannot, dress very splendidly, and have magnificent jewels and pearls in the trimming round their collars. They wear many rings on their fingers with great balass rubies, rubies and diamonds. I said also those who cannot afford it, because I was told that many of them hire these things. They paint their faces a great deal, and also other parts they show, in order to appear more beautiful."

(1)   It may be that the author of the *Decor Puellarum*, 1471, supposed to be Zuan Corner, intends the married women, when he speaks of them going veiled according to the custom of Venice. See Brown, *The Venetian Printing Press,* page 2.

(2)   Sanudo, Marino, *Edificazione della Citta di Venezia* (Cicogna manuscripts. 920), quoted by Romanin, ubi supra.

(2)   Sanudo, *Edificazione della Citta di Venezia,* Volume I page in Cicogna, *Manuscripts,* page 920, quoted by Romanin (*Storia Documentata di Venezia,* Volume IV page 495).

(3)   Casola, *Canon Pietro Casola's Pilgrimage to Jerusalem in the Year 1494,* page 144-145. Equally in Great Britain, in the time of James I., ladies of position went so *decolletees,* that it was suggested, as a discouragement to the practice, that female offenders should be hanged with naked bosoms and backs. Amos, *The Great Oyer of Poisoning,* page 47.

Long before the time of Titian, (1) in whose portraits we recognize the characteristic, they powdered their hair with gold-dust or with some preparation of wood-ash, to lend it an appearance more attractive to the other sex than that which nature had bestowed. Nor was this practice confined to women, for the beau and the dandy also followed it. It had been common among the Romans, and prevailed in Spain in the beginning of the sixteenth century, if not earlier. Alike in the case of the Spaniards and Italians, the fashion strikes us as out of harmony with the normal Venetian complexion.

(1)   Fournier, *Le Vieux-Neuf: Histoire Ancienne des Inventions et Decouvertes Modernes,* Volume II page 215-216.

At Venice, the process of dyeing the hair occupied a considerable time, and it was common to the hetairae. These artificial methods survived down to much later days, in fact to the close of the independent life; (1) Mrs. Thrale who was here in 1784, speaking of the Venetian ladies, says: "Few remain unmarried till fifteen, and at thirty [they] have a wan and faded look," She quotes "Madame la Presidente" for the remark: "*On ne goute pas ses plaisirs ici, on les avale.*"

(1)   The mode is described by Byron in a letter to Hobhouse as in vogue in 1821.

At the same time, while the writer notes that the female members of the better classes did not concern themselves with housekeeping cares or maternal duties, she pays a high and warm tribute to the fascinating address of the ladies whom she encountered. "A Venetian lady has in particular," she tells us, "so sweet a manner naturally, that she really charms without any settled intent to do so, merely from that irresistible good-humour and mellifluous tone of voice which seize the soul, and detain it in spite of Juno-like majesty or Minerva-like wit. A woman of quality, near whom I sat at the fine ball Bragadin made two nights ago in honour of this gay season, inquired how I had passed the morning. I named several churches I had looked into, particularly that which they esteem beyond the rest as a favourite work of Palladio, and called the Redentore. 'You do very right,' says she, 'to look at our churches, as you have none in England, I know — but then you have so many other fine things — such charming steel buttons, for example,' pressing my hand to show that she meant no offence; 'For,' added she, '*Chi pensa d'una maniera, chi pensa d'un'altra.*' All literary topics are pleasingly discussed at Quirini's Casino, where everything may be learned by the conversation of the company ..." (1)

(1)   Seeley, *Mrs. Thrale, Afterwards Mrs. Piozzi,* page 236-238.

Mrs. Piozzi carried away the impression that Venice was a very delightful place, and quitted it at the end of five weeks with regret; but she thought the general mass of the people ignorant. She mentions having seen an exhibition of a stuffed horse, for which people paid a penny or its local equivalent, and she believed a statement made to her, that large numbers lived and died in the capital, without knowing or caring to learn how the milk brought for their consumption from the mainland was produced.

In 1201, when the rest of Europe was unable to shew any sensible advance in domestic architecture, we meet with a passage, connected with the share of the Republic in the Crusades, in which a great French soldier and a man of baronial standing, who may be accepted as a competent witness, Geoffroi de Villehardouin, emphatically commends the exceptionally spacious accommodation at the Ducal Palace, and the testimony possesses the distinctive value of being the earliest allusion of its kind.

The same writer enters at considerable length into the architectural improvements spreading over centuries, which gradually brought the abode of the Doge and the contiguous block of buildings to the condition and aspect familiar to the eye of the later traveller, and, indeed, to all of us to-day. There is veritably no European site, no area of such limited extent anywhere, which has been trodden by such a succession of feet, which has echoed to such a diversity of accents, representing all the nations of the earth, bound on missions in their nature so infinitely various — from Dante, Petrarch, Boccaccio, Albrecht Durer and Montaigne, to William Beckford, Mrs. Piozzi, Byron, Goethe and Ruskin.

As early as 1304, before that power had acquired any sensible measure of importance, the son of the King of Portugal paid a visit to Venice, and received every mark of distinction. The Arsenal and all the other attractions of the capital were shewn to him, and the demonstration of public enthusiasm or curiosity is described as extraordinary. The Doge met the prince at Malghera, and escorted him at his departure as far as Malamocco. His country had considerably advanced in power and rank when, in 1428, at a ball given in honour of the heir of a much later ruler, there were 120 ladies entirely enveloped in robes of cloth-of-gold, blazing with jewels, and 1300 others attired in crimson silk studded with pearls and precious stones. The noble visitor intimated a desire to see some of the private residences of the patricians, and pronounced them as less like the dwellings of citizens than the palaces of princes. Elsewhere we have a statement, almost a complaint, that, while crowned heads used wooden platters for their food, the Republic dined and supped off silver.

It was not long posterior to the visit of Dom Pedro, that the singular case happened — about 1441 — in which the Emperor Frederick III. of Germany presented himself, and, the Doge Foscari being reported indisposed, the reception devolved on his consort; the august pair — the Empress, a girl of fifteen, Eleanora of Portugal — remained a fortnight. Her Majesty had a surfeit of sight-seeing, and perhaps the Signory and the Dogaressa were not sorry when the guests took their leave. The latter were in command of the situation. To have given umbrage would have been out of the question; the experience was unique.

One of the earliest notices of the Sensa or Feast of the Ascension, to which persons of all ranks, conditions and nationalities were in the habit of repairing, is associated with a signal historical episode, for, in 1347, Isabella de' Fieschi, wife of Luchino Visconti, Duke of Milan, was among the visitors; a very beautiful and attractive woman of cultivated taste, but of a susceptible and licentious disposition; there is a tradition which seems to be fairly supported, that the Serenissimo Andrea Dandolo became enamoured of his guest.

Scarcely a year elapsed without some incident necessitated by political, commercial or other motives. In 1422, had come Francesco Sforza and his bride Bianca Visconti; in 1438, Johannes Palaeologos, Emperor of Constantinople, visiting Italy to attend the Council of Constance; in 1476, the Marquis of Mantua, (1) and in the same year a Tartar delegation from the Khan, of the stay of which in the city the Milanese envoy at Venice furnishes the Duke Galeazzo Maria with a narrative, shewing the profuse outlay on the representatives of a country in which the Republic had every desire to preserve and extend its reputation for wealth and power. Not only rich vestments and precious stones, but armour, weapons and horses, were offered as a testimony of the great affection and loyalty of the Venetians toward the Great Khan, and the travelling expenses of His Highness's diplomatic agents on their return home were handed to them, as a crowning proof of friendship and of indifference to money.

(1)   Compare Chapter LVI. The Gonzaga family was associated with the Signory during the fifteenth and sixteenth centuries on

several occasions in a military capacity. Giovanni Francesco II. (1484-1519) even inscribed on his coins his dignity as Captain-General of Venice; indeed he did the same in regard to the Holy See. The Marquis experienced many vicissitudes of fortune, and lived to become the friend and opponent, the generalissimo and prisoner of Venice.

There is a detailed coeval account of the mission of the Lord and Lady of Forli and Imola, Girolamo Riario and Caterina Sforza Visconti, in 1481, at the instance of Pope Sixtus IV., in connexion with a design for the partition of the Duchy of Ferrara between Venice and the Holy See. Madonna di Forli and her husband were met even at Ravenna by Venetian noblemen, and at Malamocco were welcomed by forty of the leading citizens. When they reached San Clemente, the Doge and 115 noble ladies appointed to attend on Madonna Contessa — a girl of eighteen — were waiting in the *Bucentaur* to offer their salutations, and to conduct them to the city. Among the suite was the daughter-in-law of His Serenity habited all in gold.

When Riario paid a visit of honour to the Doge, the latter met him at the foot of the Palace stairs. One day he was taken to the Arsenal, and another to the Great Council, where he was made a Venetian citizen by acclamation, and where, when he had designated Bernardo Bambo Podesta of Ravenna, his choice was forthwith confirmed without a ballot. On Sunday, the 9th of September, a ball was given in the great hall of the Palace, at which, says an eyewitness, 132 noble maidens, resplendent in gold, gems and pearls valued at 300,000 gold crowns, were present; the throng was so great, that the narrator declares he had never seen such, except at Rome at the time of the Jubilee. The Doge sat between his two guests; owing to the multitude the dances were rather confused; the banquet took place at sunset, and wax candles made the night like day.

A very unusual occurrence took place in 1485, when the Venetian executive apprised by circular the governors of Padua, Vicenza, Verona and Brescia, that the Grand Master of Rhodes might be expected their way, and that they were to neglect no means of doing him honour.

"Watch for his arrival; meet him on the way, well accompanied; receive him with every mark of love and respect, and accompany him to his lodging, where you will have his expenses and those of his retinue paid from the moneys of our Signory. On his departure, in like manner you will accompany him with tokens of honour, making the usual offers, and in such bland form of speech as of your prudence you will know how to do."

In a letter from the Doge to Richard III. of England, written on the same day, the 2nd of May, His Serenity refers to a visit paid to Venice by the Lord Prior of Saint John's, Clerkenwell (Sir John Kendal), three months before. (1)

(1) (compilation) *Calendar of State Papers Relating to English Affairs in the Archives of Venice,* Volume I page 154.

In 1493, Beatrice d'Este, wife of Lodovico il Moro, Duke of Milan, is found coming with a numerous retinue of kinsfolk, attendants and her husband's diplomatic representatives, to ratify the defensive treaty between Milan and the Signory against Charles VIII. of France, and was received with due homage; but when the Duke was taken prisoner and sent to Loches by Louis XII. in 1500, bonfires were lighted on the Piazza of Saint Mark to signalize the event. Sanudo the diarist writes under the 14th of April in the latter year: "This year they had a bonfire on the Place of Saint Mark. Yesterday the Signory caused to be brought thither thirty cart-loads of wood, and the French ambassador who arrived to-day also purchased a quantity, and had it set alight, together with the boat in which he came."

Philippe de Commines has been elsewhere noticed, as having been accredited by Charles VIII. of France to the government of the Doge, with a view to a stricter alliance between the powers in connexion with the French projects in the Peninsula. This was in 1494. The historian reports that he was met by an escort, comprising five and twenty gentlemen richly attired, and by a salute of drums and trumpets at Lizzafusina, which he transforms into Chafousine and describes as five miles from the city. He left at that point the boat which had brought him from Padua, and entered with his suite into certain small covered barks furnished with carpeted seats.

The visitor, whose first experience of the place this was, was astonished by the peculiarity of the site, by the number of clock-towers and monasteries and blocks of building, all rising, as it were, out of the water, and by the vast collection of boats, the only class of vehicles to be seen, which he set down at 30,000. Venice itself, when Commines reached it, impressed him as the most triumphant city he had ever seen; where the greatest honour was done to strangers and ambassadors; which was governed by the wisest methods; and which paid the greatest homage to God. The illustrious Frenchman was conducted to the principal sights, and was much gratified by the splendour of the Treasury of Saint Mark, and by the magnitude of the Arsenal, which he characterizes as the finest spectacle and the best regulated institution of the kind then extant. A curious and unexpected occurrence was his meeting at the Milanese embassy with Pietro Casola on the return of the latter from the Holy Land. A comparison of notes between these two notable individuals must have been mutually interesting and instructive. (1)

(1)   Commines, *Les Memoires de Philippe de Commines,* Book VII Chapter 15; Casola, *Canon Pietro Casola's Pilgrimage to Jerusalem in the Year 1494,* page 339.

Beyond the admiration of an unusually intelligent Frenchman for the amenity of Venice, the beauty of its buildings and the excellence of its policy, there was the tendency of the noble countrywomen of Commines, to pay homage in their own way to the Signory, by imitating its female aristocracy in their dress, which underwent a marked change, subsequently to the expedition of Charles VIII. to Italy at the end of the fifteenth century.

An unprecedented episode is referable to 1502-1503, when, on the 17th of February, three noble ladies, the Marchioness of Mantua, the Duchess of Urbino and the Marchioness of Cotrone, arrived incognito and were lodged at the Trevisano Palace at Sant' Eustachio. They received a private visit from a high government official, who offered them handsome gifts and placed himself at their disposition. In the course of the same year, a much more serious outlay was involuntarily and unexpectedly incurred by the arrival of Anne de Candalles, accompanied by the Marchioness of Saluzzo, on her way to Hungary to be married to King Ladislaus VII. The Hungarian commissioners were there to receive her, but her dowry of 40,000 ducats, promised by her cousin Louis XII. of France who had negotiated the alliance, did not accompany her, and she was obliged to remain till the money was forthcoming, as the representatives of Ladislaus would not leave without it.

The august young lady, who is described by the diarist Sanudo as seventeen years of age, short of stature, handsome and gentle of speech, was lodged at the palace of the Dukes of Ferrara, and is stated to have cost her hosts about 4500 ducats a week for some time; but a Senator observed that "he who drinks the sea may drink a river." The future queen did not embark till the 21st of July, when one of the Masters of the Arsenal, "the discreet and handsome Piero Lando," says Sanudo, was appointed commander of the galley which conveyed her to Segna. She retained a grateful recollection of her kind Venetian entertainers, and took an opportunity of conveying, through the ambassador at Buda, her acknowledgments to the Doge and the Signory, to the authorities at Brescia and to the aforesaid Lando. Her Majesty does not name the diarist himself, who states that he did the honours at Verona where he was then treasurer.

The visit of the lawyer, Anton Kressen of Nurnberg, to the city in or about 1505 is noticed in connexion with his purchase of a Petrarch there. It was in the same year that a more distinguished man than Kressen found his way to Venice, in the person of Albrecht Durer, who remained there or in Italy a full twelvemonth. In a letter to the magistrates of Nurnberg, he states that the Doge had once written to him, offering him a home and a yearly honorarium of 200 ducats; and, in a most interesting correspondence with his intimate friend, Wilibald Pirkheimer, (1) the scholar and collector, he shews to some extent how he employed himself during his stay, and what his opinion of the Venetians was. He evidently combined business with pleasure, for we hear of his laying out 100 ducats in colours. In a communication to Pirkheimer in September 1506, he says that the Doge and the Patriarch have called to see one of his paintings, and in another he announces his intention to pay a professional visit to Bologna before he leaves.

(1)   Narrey, *Albert Durer a Venise et Dans les Pays-Bas.*

Durer met with agreeable society here — artists, musicians, men of letters, persons of prepossessing address and extensive information. He formed the acquaintance of Giovanni Bellini, who recommended him to several, and expressed a desire to possess one of his works for which he would gladly pay a good price. He conversed with a printer whom he does not name, but does not suggest that he executed any artistic commission for him or any other member of the calling, or for any bookbinder. He certainly designed and engraved two book-plates for Pirkheimer, and decorated several of the books themselves, chiefly with slight marginal sketches, but in one instance at least with a finished painting. The book was a Theocritus printed at Venice in 1495, and apparently acquired by Pirkheimer in or about 1524, the date of the inscription in which Durer commemorated this testimony of affectionate regard for his friend.

In one passage of the correspondence, he declares that he is becoming by degrees a veritable Venetian signore. The letters of Durer to Pirkheimer almost lead us to infer that the prices realizable for his productions were not so high as in Germany, or at least at Nurnberg. We perceive that he made numerous purchases for his friend — rings, tapestry, fans, paper, glass. He reports to him the difficulty of obtaining sapphires, and the high tariff for emeralds, but says that amethysts of medium quality in white and green might be had at prices ranging from 20 to 25 ducats. As to the latter, he merely professes to repeat what the experts have told him, knowing nothing about precious stones. He had bought some wool or woollen goods on his own account, and the parcel was lost in a fire, as well as, he fears, a cloak, which loss altogether puts him out of humour. It was in the course of the present visit, that Durer executed a still extant plan of Venice as it then appeared.

This sojourn was quite independent of previous overtures of the Signory, and the event merits commemoration, looking at the singular eminence of the individual and the rarity of notices of the resort of his countrymen to Venice, notwithstanding the long existence of a local German guild, and the antiquity of diplomatic relations. It seems improbable that Durer and Kressen met on Venetian ground, for the latter was back at Nurnberg in the course of 1505, and his Petrarch was sent home by the binder.

Pirkheimer himself was no stranger to Italy, having spent a good deal of time in the last decade of the preceding century at Padua and elsewhere; and he undoubtedly knew Venice. His Aldine Martial of 1501 was given to him by a Venetian nobleman Andrea Cornaro.

There is a mention in Sanudo, under the 16th of May, 1507, of the visit of a Scotish bishop (supposed to be Robert Blackader, Bishop of Aberdeen and of Glasgow) to the city on his way to the Holy Land, and of his gracious reception by the Doge. He entered the presence-chamber with attendants dressed in purple camlet. He was invited to occupy a seat near the Doge. He brought letters of introduction from the Kings of Scotland and France, and delivered a Latin oration in praise of the Signory. The diarist thought that his income was 2000 ducats, and tells us that accommodation was found for him at the Ca Frizier at Cannaregio. He was still at Venice on the 1st of June, and was invited to join the party, when the Doge went in the *Bucentaur* as usual on Ascension Day to bless the sea beyond Santi Andrea and Nicolo. He at length took his passage on the Jaffa galley and died on board. (1)

(1)   (compilation) *Calendar of State Papers Relating to English Affairs in the Archives of Venice,* Volume I page 329-331.

We meet, in his badly dated autobiography, with an account, of a short stay at Venice, some time before 1548, of Benvenuto Cellini who saw there Titian, Jacopo Sansovino the sculptor whom he had known in earlier life at Rome and Florence, and Lorenzino de' Medici with whom he became acquainted during his residence at Paris, while Lorenzino was staying under the roof of Giuliano Buonacorsi. Cellini was strongly importuned to prolong his visit, but he hastened back to Tuscany. About twenty years later. Miles Blomefield of Bury Saint Edmunds, a well-known book-collector, appears to have been here, as he has inscribed in a copy of *The History of Italy,* by William Thomas, 1549: "Myles Blomefylde in Venice, A° 1568."

A very elaborate affair was the visit in 1572 of Alfonso II., Duke of Ferrara, of which an eyewitness has transmitted particulars. Seven palaces were engaged to accommodate him and his suite, and the crowd of gondolas on the Grand Canal was such that there were some fatal collisions. The reception of Henry III. of France some years later was attended by great display, but the Cappello and another mansion sufficed to lodge His Majesty and those who accompanied him.

In 1574, we meet with a distinct vestige at Padua, so near to Venice, of Sir Philip Sidney, who brought away with him a reminiscence of his visit in the shape of a copy of Guicciardini's *Storia d'Italia,* printed at Venice in 1569, and inscribed at the top of the title-page: "*Philippo Sidneio, Patavij, 20 Junij 1574.*" Is it not probable that he extended his journey to the Lagoon, if indeed he had not previously landed there, and beheld the city in its unfaded splendour? (1)

(1)   Hazlitt III, *Roll of Honor,* page 214, where a facsimile of the inscription may be found.

Montaigne, who had been here in 1580, furnishes a recollection of his feelings, where, in the enlarged impression of his famous book in 1588, he added a paragraph, noting his opinion that Venice was a good place in which to spend the declining years of life.

When the Duc de Rohan was here in 1600, the Arsenal was described by him as being in a high state of efficiency, and as having 100 galleys fully manned and equipped. The Duke says that it contained the means of arming 20,000 infantry, and that 2000 hands were employed in various branches of work. He saw the Palace, or rather, he says, the prison of the Doge, and speaks highly of the paintings by Titian and other masters, and was charmed by Saint Mark's Basilica. Although we collect that his stay at Venice and Padua extended over two months, his account is meagre, but he visited the greater part of Europe as well as Great Britain, and his book of travel is a small one. (1) He admits that Venice was so wonderful, that scarcely any length of stay was sufficient to exhaust its beauties and its treasures.

(1)   Rohan, *Voyage du Duc de Rohan, Faict en l'an 1600, en Italie, Allemaigne, Pays-Bas-Vnis, Angleterre & Escosse.*

Evelyn has left his impressions of the Sensa as it appeared to him in 1645, and takes the opportunity of describing the ladies at that period and their attire.

"It was now Ascension-week," he writes, "and the great mart, or fair, of the whole year was kept, every body at liberty and jolly; the noblemen stalking with their ladies on choppines. These are high-heeled shoes, particularly affected by these proud dames, or, as some say, invented to keep them at home, it being very difficult to walk with them; whence, one being asked how he liked the Venetian dames, replied, they were *mezzo carne, mezzo legno*, half flesh and half wood, and he would have none of them. The truth is, their garb is very odd, as seeming always in masquerade ... They wear very long crisp hair, of several streaks and colours, which they make so by a wash, dishevelling it on the brims of a broad hat that has no crown, but a hole to put out their heads by; they dry them in the sun, as one may see them at their windows. In their tire, they set silk flowers and sparkling stones, their petticoats coming from their very arm-pits, so that they are near three quarters and a half apron; their sleeves are made exceeding wide, under which their shift-sleeves as wide, and commonly tucked up to the shoulder, showing their naked arms, through false sleeves of tiffany, girt with a bracelet or two, with knots of points richly tagged about their shoulders and other places of their body, which they usually cover with a kind of yellow veil, of lawn, very transparent."

The diarist proceeds to mention that the courtezans and citizens did not wear the high shoes, and covered themselves with a long taffeta veil, out of which they cast glances at passers-by; but he presently discriminates between the women of pleasure and the *cittadinanza*, by informing us that the former went unveiled.

Evelyn mentions one or two matters immediately after his arrival which are worth transcribing: "June, 1645. The next morning, finding myself extremely weary and beaten with my journey, I went to one of their bagnios, where you are treated after the eastern manner, washing with hot and cold water, with oils, and being rubbed with a kind of strigil of seal's skin, put on the operator's hand like a glove. This bath did so open my pores, that it cost me one of the greatest colds I ever had in my life, for want of necessary caution in keeping myself warm for some time after." He presently dwells on the abundance of excellent and cheap provisions which had been observed by previous visitors.

Sir Andrew Balfour, a Scotish physician who visited Venice about 1668, (1) arrived there by water from Bologna in a vessel which made the voyage twice a week. He was advised to go to the English Consul for information as to lodgings. At that time, Giles Jones filled the position and entertained lodgers, and Balfour speaks of him as an honest fellow who sent his purchases on to London. Sir Andrew considered three or four weeks not too long to gain a thorough knowledge of the place.

(1)   Balfour, *Letters Written to a Friend by the Learned and Judicious Sir Andrew Balfour, M.D.*, page 223-226.

Speaking of Murano, he observes: "They have likeways a great Art of whitneing Wax, which is observed to succeed better in this Island than any other place in or about the city."

> He presently adds: "You cannot miss to meet with a great many Curiosities here, both Natural and Artificial, because of the great resort that Strangers have to this Place, especiallie from the Levant; you will find Medals, Intaleos, Chamaeos &c. amongst the Goldsmiths. I have seen severall Curiosities to sell in the place of Saint Mark, and sometime within the Court of the Palace, and in many other corners throughout the city. You may meet with many Curiosities of Glass, that are both usefull and delightfull. It will be worth your while to visit the Book-sellers' Shops, for besides many Curious Books, that you may light upon

here, and particularly of Botany; you may likeways find verie many Books, that are prohibited in other places of Italy."

The writer was pleased to meet with the brother of Antonio Donato, a botanical authority, who had published in 1631 an account of certain natural objects found in the *lidi* of Venice, and who shewed him copperplates of them. He adds: "There are many Virtuosi in the city, that have great collections of fine things, which you may be pleased to inquire after and see."

Richard Lassels, an English tutor, who, after paying several visits to Italy in his professional capacity, published his experiences in 1670 at Paris, has devoted a considerable space to an account of what he saw here.

> "The Habit of the Doge," he writes, "is ancient, and hath something of the Pontifical habit in it. His Pompe, Train, and Lodgeing, are all Princely; and in publick functions he hath carried before him the eight sylver trumpets, the great Umbrella of cloth of tyssue, the cusshen, the Chair, the guilt sword, and a tvhite wax candle carryed by a child. All letters of state are written in his name."

Lassels left very little unexplored, but he says nothing of the prisons. He remarks in one place:

> "We went after diner one Satturday, to see the Jews Synagogue. Among other things I heard here a Rabbin make a Homily to his flock. He looked like a French Minister, or Puritanical Lecturer, in short cloacke and hat. The snaffling through the nose made all the edification that I sawe in it; It was in Italian, but the coldest discourse that I ever heard in any language. Indeed it was their Sabboth day, and they eat no other meat that day, but cold meat."
> (1)

(1)   Lassels, *The Voyage of Italy,* Part II page 371-372, 422-423.

William Acton, somewhat later, (1) set down a few passing impressions about the place to which he appears to have devoted a three weeks' stay; but he is not so minute in his description as in the case of Rome. He visited the Arsenal, where he states that arms for 400,000 men were stored — a probable exaggeration or slip of the pen. The Treasury of Saint Mark struck him as inferior to that at Loreto. He ascended the steeple of Saint Mark's, apparently meaning the Campanile, from which he saw, he tells us, a larger number of buildings than in Rome. In the choir of the Church of Sant' Antonio were twelve brass tablets engraved with Scriptural subjects, and in the cloisters he observed "a little black marble stone that covers the bowels of the old Duke of Norfolk, father to the supposed mad Duke, that we saw confined at Padua." The writer must refer to Thomas, Duke of Norfolk, who died unmarried at Padua in 1677; but the marble stone seems to belong to a much earlier date, and probably to the story related in these pages of a Duke of the Plantagenet period. (2)

(1)   Acton, *A New Journal of Italy.*
(2)   Chapter LIV.

In 1688, Cosimo III., Grand Duke of Tuscany, came to attend the Carnival, or at any rate in Carnival-time. A regatta was arranged in his honour. (1) There was no cessation of visits of illustrious personages of all countries, so long as the Republic lasted, nor was there much abatement of extravagance. They came from a variety of motives; but the Carnival and Regatta, and the unique city, with so lengthened and brilliant a history, were the prevailing inducements, although the Duke of Brunswick, of whose stay there is a coeval narrative, brought with him in 1685-1686 the troops with which he proposed to operate in the Morea, and was consequently quartered at Lido.

(1)   An account of it appeared at Venice in a folio volume with fourteen folded plates. Compare Romanin, *Storia Documentata di Venezia,* Volume VII page 552.

It had been the intention of Peter the Great of Russia to call at Venice on his way back home in 1698, but his return was accelerated by political events, and he sent forward one of his favourites to learn particulars of Venetian naval construction and to study the Italian language. When he next met this person at home, he bad him get out of his sight as he was only fit to play the fool, inasmuch as he confessed that he had spent all his time in Venice in his rooms, smoking and drinking brandy. In 1755, the Elector of Cologne met with a friendly and hospitable welcome, and a public banquet was arranged for him at the Nani Palace at the Giudecca. The contemporary painting in the Museo Civico exhibits the quests seated round the tables in the form of a horse-shoe, in an apartment of noble dimensions lighted by candelabra suspended from the ceiling.

In 1769, the Republic had notice from the Cavaliere Trono, Superintendent of the Government Posts, that the Emperor Joseph II., after visiting Florence, Mantua, Turin and Milan, proposed to come to Venice in strict incognito as the Graf von Falkenstein. His Majesty arrived on the 22nd of July about midnight with a very small retinue, and was taken by Trono, whom the Signory had selected to attend upon him during his sojourn, to the White Lion at Santi Apostoli on the Grand Canal. The lateness of the arrival did not prevent him from going to the Opera at the San Benedetto Theatre, where he paid his respects to the great ladies in their boxes and had his visits returned.

The next day, he visited all the objects of interest, especially the Arsenal, but declined all publicity and state, and excused himself to the Senate, through Trono, for not attending the festivities and diversions which had been prepared in his honour, observing that he did not care for such matters, and that, during all his travels as a young man, he had followed the same principle. The Cavaliere, however, prevailed on His Majesty to go to a *conversazione* at the Casa Rezzonico, (1) it being understood that the meeting had not been arranged on his account, and that he was not to be received with the slightest ceremony.

(1)   The card of invitation was as follows: "*Resta avvertito V.E. figli e consorte per parte degli eccellentissimi Savii, cassiere attuale ed uscito, che nella sera di martedi, sara li 28 luglio alle ore 24, vi sara una publica conversazione in ca Rezzonico a cui resta supplicata d'intervenire. Sono invitati li nn. hh. in vesta nera, e le eccell. dame in andrien nero con cerchio e barbole.*" Romanin, *Storia Documentata di Venezia,* Volume VII page 191.

There were present one hundred and twenty ladies splendidly dressed and blazing with jewels, and upward of six hundred patricians. The Emperor arrived when the music had already commenced, and entered unnoticed without torch bearers and footmen, attended only by his major-domo. He attended a sitting of the Great Council, and insisted on occupying one of the ordinary benches set apart for strangers, where the Cavaliere Mocenigo explained to him the course of procedure.

The Emperor subsequently heard a cause before the Quarantia, and, although he considered all existing judicial systems liable to a charge of inconvenience, he pronounced the Venetian forms the purest and most conducive to equitable results which he had seen.

He conversed with Trono upon the objects and benefits of commerce, of the inevitable tendency of powers to commit acts or adopt measures prejudicial or obnoxious to their neighbours, but observed that such things ought not to produce a breach of friendly relations. To the Procurator, touching on Trieste, and mentioning that others, who had studied commercial questions more than himself, had remarked that millions might be spent in that city without any adequate fruit. His Majesty replied that that might be so, but that he intended to go there, and judge with his own eyes what the real facts were.

His Majesty left Venice after the *conversazione* on the night of the 25th of July, full of admiration of all that he had seen. Trono informed the Senate that Joseph spoke German, French, Italian, Latin and a little Hungarian; he gave him a very high character. The Emperor was again at Venice in 1775, and was then accompanied by the Archdukes Leopold, Maximilian and Ferdinand. The whole party was in strict incognito, and remained eight days, witnessing the Sensa and the Regatta.

This certainly was one of the most remarkable experiences of the kind, and the city had never been honoured by the presence of an exalted guest so unassuming in demeanour. The Venetians must have regarded His Majesty with speculative wonder, as a type totally distinct from those to whom they had been immemorially accustomed; perhaps as one meeting half-way the new democratic spirit to which Venice itself was not by any means a stranger toward the last.

The preparations for the Imperial visitor, in addition to fireworks, illuminations and a regatta, included the formation of an artificial lake in front of the Piazzetta, set off with fruit trees to represent the Gardens of the Hesperides, and, on this sheet of water, fishermen dressed as tritons plied their craft, and went through all the forms of their pursuit by torch-light. The Emperor acted at Venice in no exceptional manner in declining the honour due to his rank; His Majesty had done the same in Paris and elsewhere. Peter the Great of Russia had set the example, so far as crowned heads went, though the practice of travelling incognito was no novelty even in the sixteenth century; it went back to the Middle Ages, and farther.

A very different person from Joseph II., William Beckford of Fonthill, author of *Vathek*, speaking of the appearance of the streets in 1780, mentions the unusual number of orientals, and the polyglot conversation heard by him; here, some talking in a Slav dialect, there, some in a Greek argot or jargon. If the Church of Saint Mark, he says, had been the Tower of Babel, and the square in front of it the principal street of that city, the confusion of tongues could not have been greater. The numerous Jews, both Italian and Levantine, in their gabardines and red hats or yellow turbans, contributed to render the scene more impressive and dramatic.

There was scarcely any interruption of this sort of incident, or limit to the variety of guest who sought, in these late days, the hospitality of Venice, and found it not less generous and thoughtful than in times of infinitely greater prosperity and power. In 1782 and the succeeding year, came His Holiness Pius VI., the Grand Duke Paul of Russia and his wife travelling as the "Conti del Nord," (1) and Gustavus III. of Sweden who adopted the name Count of Haga; all were received with splendour and politeness. The visit of their Imperial Highnesses had been expected for some months, and their near approach was indicated by the appearance one evening at the Opera of the Duke of Wurtemberg, brother of the Grand Duchess.

(1)   Wynn, *Del Soggiorno dei Conti del Nord a Venezia in Gennaro del MDCCLXXXII. Lettera della Contessa Giustiniana degli Orsini, e Rosenberg a Riccardo Wynne, sue Fratello, a Londra. Dal Francese Recata in Italiano.* octavo, 1782, with portraits of the Duke and Duchess. page 78; *Descrizione degli Spettacoli, e Feste Datesi in Venezia per Occasione della Venuta delle LL. AA. II. il Gran Duca, e Gran Duchessa di Moscovia, Sotto il Nome di Conti del Nort Nel Mese di Gennajo 1782. Seconda Edizione corretta, e ampliata. Octavo, Venezia 1782.* Plates, page 20.

The Procurator Francesco Pesaro, a Savio of the Council, and Signore Giovanni Grimani, Savio di Terra Firma, were delegated to attend upon the new-comers, to salute them on their arrival, and to forestall all their wishes. The Duke of Wurtemberg, accompanied by Pesaro and Grimani, proceeded to Conegliano where the Duke and Duchess appeared toward the evening, and the next day the whole party set out for Venice, a portion of the Russian retinue having gone before.

The narratives of this episode admit us to a fuller acquaintance with the particulars of the reception, and the pains taken to propitiate and impress the distinguished and unusual visitors. On the first evening, there was a grand assembly at the Palazzo or Casino dei Filarmonici, and the Cavaliera Andriana Foscarini, wife of a former ambassador at the court of Vienna, was introduced to the Russian princess by Pesaro, as the most suitable personage to wait upon her during her stay.

The two strange guests were conducted through the city, preserving a strict incognito, and were even attired in Venetian costume. The most signal feature in the whole affair was probably the superb and brilliant spectacle at the Theatre of San Benedetto, where, from the absence of any public hall of adequate capacity, a banquet was given to the visitors, and where we perceive in one of the contemporary engravings (1) the tiers of boxes from floor to ceiling, filled by members of the aristocracy arrayed in the height of the prevailing fashion, many with opera-glasses in their hands, to enable them to command the scene beneath and around them.

(1)   See the large illustration in the "pocket" of Volume II. of this work. [not available for this edition].

There was also a grand dance at the Filarmonici, when the Grand Duchess gave her hand in a minuet to the Procurator Pesaro, taking occasion to tell him that that was only the third time she had consented to dance since leaving Saint Petersburg, her two previous partners having been the Emperor and the King of Poland. Pesaro officially acted as proxy for the Doge.

For the Pontiff there were religious ceremonies and a special cantata written by Gasparo Gozzi, with music by Buranello; Pius visited all the public buildings and the Arsenal. The shews prepared in honour of the Russian *incogniti* necessitated a temporary enlargement of the Piazzetta; the crowd of spectators is described as enormous. Yet, to the infinite astonishment of the Grand Duke, perfect order was preserved by the head of the police in his red robe, assisted by five *uscieri* of the Council of Ten. His Highness may have appreciated the contrast between Venetian and Russian institutions, but Casola in 1494 was equally struck by the maintenance of perfect order during the festival of Corpus Domini under precisely similar conditions. Russian acquaintance with western affairs had improved since a Duke of Muscovy imagined that Venice was a province of the Apostolic See.

Still another class of witness is the Spanish Abbot Juan Andres, who travelled in Italy in 1789 and took Venice in his way. He appears to have been a bookman, and was struck by the large number of book sellers in the place, in comparison with Rome, Naples or any other Italian city. Such commodities, according to him, were exposed for sale, not only in regular shops, but on stalls and benches, by those who lived by dealing in nothing else.

One of the last guests of distinction seems to have been the Comte d'Artois, who presented himself here in 1791 on behalf of the Royalist cause in France, and was received with royal honours, as the progress of the French revolutionary movement was still uncertain, and the king still reigned; shortly after, the Queen of Naples and the Emperor Leopold arrived on a similar mission. The object appears in both cases to have been to obtain the friendly neutrality and advice of Venice, rather than an active support, although the exploits of one of its naval commanders at this juncture in Africa, against the corsairs of Tunis and Algiers, may have led some of the continental powers to exaggerate the belligerent resources of the Signory. These two episodes were quickly succeeded by the fall of the French Bourbons, and, when we next hear of the Comte d'Artois, he has been desired by the government to quit the Venetian territories where he had taken up his residence.

The drawing-room or salon had its history and development, if it had been practicable to trace with any amount of consecutive precision the gradual stages through which it passed, till it assumed the form which it is described as wearing in the eighteenth century by correspondents, diarists and play-wrights. The peculiar rigour of the official system survived to a great extent to the close of the Republic, but even at Venice the tribunals, more especially the Senate, grew at last more pliant to those influences which are mixed products of the drawing-room, the theatre and the fashionable promenade or the *ridotto*.

As the corruption of manners tended to increase, there were cases in which important political preferment was decided by the wife of some statesman, more ambitious, more indomitable, perhaps more attractive, than himself. Maria Quirini Corraro desired in 1756 to obtain for her husband, then filling one of the embassies, the post of Bailo of Constantinople, and at first failed; but the Signora canvassed everybody likely to be of service, exhausted all expedients, even procured a private interview with the Doge, and ultimately gained her point at all risks.

There were several others equally celebrated and equally intrepid in the pursuit of their aims. But, partly owing to the rare personal capacity of her husband in the diplomatic service, and his extraordinary predominance in the last days, Caterina Giacobba Dolfin Trono or Tron acquired a social position and influence probably unsurpassed. The Procurator Tron (1702-1762), whose features and dignified presence have been preserved to us in the portrait by Longhi, had, from his special prominence and his selection to discharge any function in which unusual tact and dexterity were needful, received the popular sobriquet el Peron (*il padrone* or the governor). He belonged to a family which had given a Doge to the Republic in the fifteenth century, and had popularized itself by its munificence, and the salon of his beautiful and imperious wife was the favourite resort of all who aspired to be in the inner circle, who had a taste for hearing or talking scandal or who had a suit before the councils or the courts.

La Trona was in her time the central figure of the most distinguished, the most influential, and the most brilliant society in Venice — the Venice of Gozzi and Goldoni, of feverish gaiety and ubiquitous intrigue, of the masquerade and the card-table. According to the descriptions of her which have descended to us, she must have been a highly fascinating woman, who had a wide circle of friends both in and out of Venice, (1) but she had two faults — a daring and insolent indiscretion and a want of self-command. She committed herself both by what she said and what she did; she sometimes lost her temper and sometimes left room for unfavourable criticism. One of her retorts is preserved. When some one said, "*La Trona vendeva il palco piu caro dela persona,*" the lady rejoined, "*Gave razon, perche questa al caso lo dono.*" Her connexion with the Gratarol affair, however, was the most serious blow to her prestige, and is supposed to have been immediately instrumental in excluding her husband from the Dogeship when a vacancy occurred in 1779. Pier Antonio Gratarol, Secretary to the Senate, was compelled to quit his office and his country, and ascribed his disgrace to her machinations. In his *Apology* (2) printed in 1779, he has drawn the character of the "Venetian princess" with a pen dipped in gall, imputing to her the gravest improprieties, and at the same time insinuating that she employed the Senate as a medium for publishing her decrees.

(1)   "*D'apres le portrait que nous en a laisse un de ses adorateurs, elle avait les cheveux blonds, le front serein, les yeux d'azur, la bouche de roses, la gorge opulente et d'une blancheur de neige,*

les mains et les pieds tres-petits." Molmenti, *La Vie Privee a Venise,* Liber II page 463.

(2)   Molmenti, *La Vie Privee a Venise,* Liber II page 437.

Her husband the Procurator and Postmaster-General (Deputato alle Poste) was a really eminent and valuable public servant, and his wife and himself were perhaps the most distinguished couple of their time. Andrea Tron in 1772 rendered a signal service to his country, by promoting the suppression of a considerable number of the monastic institutions with which the city swarmed. A noble kinsman wrote: "Six and twenty monasteries suppressed! what a consolation!" These establishments (1) had gradually acquired the character of fashionable resorts for the ordinary friends and acquaintances of the inmates, men and women alike, and the *parlatorio* was, at certain appointed or understood times, a general rendezvous where gaily-attired ladies foregathered, where Punchinello was admitted to amuse the children of visitors, and where boys sold refreshments.

(1)   Compare Chapter XLV, and see Molmenti, *La Storia di Venezia nella Vita Privata,* Liber III page 412-415. Many of these monasteries, nunneries, and even churches, were at intervals removed, and the sites utilized for secular purposes — to enlarge the Arsenal, form a public garden, or lay out a cemetery.

Modern research has admitted us behind the scenes, and placed us within view of the high social life at Venice in the seventeenth and eighteenth centuries. We are familiar with the toilette, the *conversazione,* the concert, the ball and all the accessories indispensable to persons of rank and fashion. The innumerable diversities of head-dress, the preferences in jewellery, the changing sentiment in boots and shoes and the multifarious ideas legible in the rich historical fan, which even the inmates of some of the religious houses were at liberty to use out of devotional hours; the artistic visiting card (1) and the book-plate are at our disposal. Both sexes partook of the same capricious and wavering humour, and were perhaps more or less, as they have always been, under the tutelage of their caterers and leaders. The modes of Padua and Milan became not dissimilar from those of the Adriatic metropolis.

(1)   See a note in Molmenti, *La Storia di Venezia nella Vita Privata,* Liber III page 412, and facsimiles of two eighteenth century examples (pages 458 and 459). He also furnishes an elegantly engraved plate of an invitation to a wedding, addressed to a guest

by the mother of the bride (page 361). The business card (pages 76 and 77) had been in vogue, at all events elsewhere, in the seventeenth century, and, in the eighteenth, assumed more ambitious proportions, and demanded the hand of the engraver when it became a medium of advertisement for goods on sale.

The sumptuary laws which were promulgated as early as the last year of the thirteenth century, in order to restrain extravagant expenditure on dress, personal ornaments and household living, dated from a political crisis, when the government discovered that the resources demanded for public objects were squandered on luxury and ostentation. Practically, the observance of statutory precepts was never in this respect very rigidly enforced. On the day after the issue of one of these edicts, so to speak, a magnificent ceremony or pageant necessitated a revival of the old splendour and profusion; and when, not a constitutional, but a social principle was involved, the authorities were singularly lenient, or granted on application a special grace. Vast sums of money, no doubt, were wasted, but the community at large was entertained and propitiated.

The wars with Genoa (1353-1355) and Hungary (1356-1358) had superinduced a scarcity of money and a rise in prices, and the times were pronounced to be bad. Yet this distress was insufficient to check the progress of luxury among the higher classes who were less sensible of the pressure, and it was thought necessary in 1360 to impose restraints on this costly tendency. The measure, which had been preceded by one of a similar character in 1334, (1) was the third known step which the Senate had actually taken in that direction, for, in 1299, an ordinance appeared in the wake of the Genoese troubles to repress extravagance. The effect of the new legislation (2) on the 21st of May was to limit the amount of marriage presents, to keep within more moderate bounds the taste for jewellery and the extravagant love of personal decoration, and to forbid parents to take their sons and daughters of tender age to parties and wedding-suppers, where the young ladies more especially imbibed precocious notions respecting pearl earrings and jewelled head-dresses; at a later date, it was not permissible for girls under eight to attend marriages, unless they were near kinsfolk of the parties.

(1)   Romanin, *Storia Documentata di Venezia*, Volume III page 347.
(2)   Romanin, *Storia Documentata di Venezia*, Volume III.

Spinsters were not unreasonably asked to restrict themselves to thirty pounds' worth of ornaments, and they received an encouragement to marry at the earliest opportunity, by the privilege which they thus acquired of more than doubling their stock. A father was responsible to the state for the observance of the law by his family and dependents, and if his authority failed, it was. for him to report the matter to the proper quarter, and leave the rest to the magistrates; the latter had no sinecure.

One conspicuous source of trouble was the wide and embroidered sleeve. When that was banned, the milliners or tailors concentrated their art on the lining, and there was a second official pronouncement. From these rather harassing rules and restrictions, the Doge, the Dogaressa and the Ducal family were expressly exempted, and their operation extended neither to esquires, judges nor medical practitioners, who were permitted to dress themselves as they pleased. (1) Yet the dearer furs such as ermine were denied to men under five and twenty, the age at which they were qualified to take their seats in the Great Council.

(1)   *"Item licet cuilibet militi, judici, vel medico conventato posse portare quicquid voluerint in suis personis propriis."*

Nowhere, indeed, were regulations laid down for the government of society outside the executive with more minute precision, and more audaciously disregarded. In the fourteenth century, entertainments involving late hours and the presence of women, unless they were relatives, were prohibited from the month of September till the last day of the Carnival, and no one was to be permitted to keep his doors open to guests of either sex after the third evening bell from Michaelmas till the commencement of Lent.

In 1450, the authorities conceived the notion of limiting private dinners or suppers to half a ducat a head, and they carried their paternal interposition to the extent of prescribing the quality or quantity of table-linen, gold and silver plate, and other accessories to be displayed on festive or ceremonial occasions. The waiters and cooks at forthcoming banquets were required under penalties to wait on the Proveditori alle Pompe, and furnish full particulars of the programme. This, to be sure, was in 1512, when the Republic had scarcely rallied from the exhaustion of the wars of the League of Cambrai. In the case of a wedding, the parties were expected to notify to the authorities eight days in advance all the details, the outlay to be incurred, and the names, ages and relationships of those who had been invited. The subject of dowries was one for which the state provided. Under a law of 1420, the amount was fixed at 1600 ducats, or, if the bride was a plebeian, 2000, of which a third seems to have been allotted to the outfit.

In 1523, when the Marquis of Mantua was staying at Venice, he desired to give an entertainment at his own house to the ambassadors, and to invite twenty-five Venetian gentlewomen. He applied for leave for the ladies to come in -cloth-of-gold and jewellery, the Act notwithstanding, and the Proveditori alle Pompe were authorized accordingly. But the latter pleaded their inability to comply, and a special leave to gratify the Marquis was granted on their suggestion in the College.

These injunctions were almost uniformly inoperative, for the state itself was the greatest offender, and set the worst example. When Beatrice, Duchess of Milan, came to Venice in 1493, there was a grand reception at the Palace, with music and an infinite number of torches, and the guest of the day describes in a letter how there were 300 objects in gilt sugar and fine drinking-glasses, the tables extending the entire length of the hall. The display of costly subtleties in sugar became a favourite and constant feature at these princely celebrations. When Henry III. of France was similarly feted in 1574, all the appointments of the table were formed of sugar, and when the King proceeded to take up his napkin it broke in his hands. The dish placed in front of His Majesty represented a queen seated on two tigers, the breasts of which presented the arms of France and Poland; to the right of the royal table, there were two lions with figures of Pallas and Justice, and to the left, figures of Saint Mark and of David. (1)

(1)   Sugar refineries are not officially or specifically mentioned till 1612.

The provincial governors and proveditors lay under the same nominal disabilities as those at home, but not improbably the letter of the law was similarly set at defiance. Nor were the official ordinances respecting personal attire and ornament more practically successful. Decrees were periodically launched against the unseemly and extravagant excess in clothes and in jewellery, which was proclaimed an abomination in the sight of God; yet the alleged abuses and contempt of heaven remained in full vigour. The fashions might change, but, whether they were oriental or French or Italian or Spanish, or even English, they were always splendid, always ruinously costly. It was not only so here, but after a time at Milan and at Florence; even Dante lived to behold and regret the disappearance in the Tuscan capital of the chaste and simple manners familiar to him in his youth.

It is almost amusing to scan some of the drastically worded ordinances of the Senate, respecting ladies' dress and ladies' preposterous extravagance in changing, at short intervals, the fashion, and incurring enormous expense at their milliners' or *modistes*. One of 1504, just before Cambrai, enters into all sorts of particulars, and probably received as much attention as its predecessors and those which came after. But one cannot forbear to speculate, who sat down at the council table to formulate such libels on the fair sex, and how it went with him if he was known, when he next appeared in any of the drawing-rooms.

The sumptuary laws were probably the least happy and successful efforts of the government, and they were so because powerful private influence was ever at hand, behind the scenes or otherwise, to neutralize their effect or procure their repeal. But they have for us a practical value and interest, as contributions to our acquaintance with the history of Venetian costume and fashion among both sexes, and are auxiliary to the literary and pictorial records which we possess, while they realize in a measure the aspect of those parts of the city in its days of independence, where the rich classes purchased their costly dresses and mantles, their fine and elegant underlinen, their head-gear, their trinkets and their jewellery. These regulations admit us to the salon of the dressmaker, to the premises where the furrier displayed his attractive goods, and where other vocations, patronized by either sex, long brought handsome profits to the proprietors. The modes were constantly changing; French patterns and models, themselves liable to variation or supersession at short intervals in obedience to the leaders of society and their advisers, may be said to have prevailed for centuries; but German costumes were discountenanced by the government.

The passion for dress was common to all classes, and the lower orders were particularly partial to bright hues set off on holidays with beads and counterfeit stones, and, among those above them who could not afford to purchase jewels and other finery, it became a practice to hire them for the occasion or even for a term, as twenty-five ducats a year was judged by the functionaries charged with these delicate matters sufficient for a necklace or a ring.

The paternal principle in these sumptuary affairs, however, almost exclusively, as may be concluded, touched just that class which commanded the means of evading its incidence, whether such a result was attained by favouritism, or by transgressing the ordinances and paying the penalties. The latter alternative became sufficiently frequent to render proverbial the phrase *pazar le pompe*. Looking back, as we may do, at such experiments, it cannot fail to impress us with the feeling that the old Venetian executive might well have spared itself these additional sorrows, by letting things find their own level, especially when so many instances are recorded, and of course infinitely more occurred, in which the influential personages at whom in fact the regulations aimed habitually defied them, and at most, if challenged, paid the fines. It is thoroughly characteristic of the Venetian genius, that offenders became involuntary benefactors to the state, inasmuch as, not only did the payments into the bureau swell the revenues, but those who exceeded legal bounds were presumed to be capable of meeting a higher scale of fiscal assessment.

The same spirit, however, was almost universal in Europe down to the nineteenth century, and must on no account be understood or received as indigenous or peculiar to Venice, It may perhaps be regarded as a survival from patriarchal days, with such refinements as time and progress appeared to necessitate.

The most curious aspect of the present burning question is perhaps the occasional interposition of the Church, when the civil authorities found their measures insufficient, and the appeal from the Church to the Holy See, of which the initial sumptuary enactment of 1299 was the product. The petitions of Cristina, daughter of the late Andrea Correr, who has splendid jewels, and is not to be permitted to wear them, and of Felice and Benedetta Donata and others, were granted in consideration of a pecuniary fee for three years. But, through the centuries, it was to be a never-ending struggle between the offenders and an executive organization competent to grapple with all other problems, yet all but powerless, when the laws and female prejudice and influence were in conflict.

It may be taken for an eminent probability, that the restrictions on the length of ladies' skirts were instrumental in promoting unpleasant episodes, if the officials insisted on verifying measurements, and especially if the husband appeared on the scene and joined the Signora in abusing or even belabouring the unwelcome visitor. But both these indulgences were enjoyable at a tariff; hard words cost five and twenty ducats, blows double. There is a sort of insinuation in the ordinance of

1441, that there were such things as excess of zeal and breaches of decorum on the part of inspectors.

The aggrieved and over-governed ladies in 1437, when the Primate of Venice had interdicted certain extravagances of attire or embellishment, went to the length of approaching the Holy See, and the Pontiff decided in their favour. But, at the coronation of the Doge Andrea Gritti in 1523, His Serenity's niece, presenting herself at the Palace in a robe of cloth-of-gold contrary to regulations, was sent back home to change it.

Two other directions, in which the Magistrato delle Pompe found abundance of employment, as well as rather invidious experience, were weddings and mourning; and within the former category fell the extravagant outlay, gradually incurred in connexion with the Festa delle Marie, or the anniversary ceremony of the Brides of Saint Mark, dating from the tenth century. The law of 1299 and its successors dealt with the number of guests at a wedding, the dresses to be worn and their embellishments, presents to be offered and the expenditure on the feast. One privilege was accorded to the bride on her nuptial day — it was the right to wear as long a train as she pleased.

The inquisitorial phrenzy extended to interrogatories put to parties shriving themselves. Fathers of families were asked whether they allowed their daughters to wear superfluous ornaments; the tailor, if he has ignorantly cut garments or wasted the material supplied or introduced novelties of style; the shoemaker, if he has made his goods conformably with rule or has exceeded the official limit for *zocoli* or clogs.

The same generosity of option was extended to the black toga, which with the berretta constituted normal mourning attire; it might even trail in the mud, so that the wearer brought it by successive curtailments to a more moderate length before it was cast aside.

There does not appear to have been, in the matter of fashionable mourning, the diversity found elsewhere. In England and France, white, black and white, and yellow were employed; at Venice we hear only of black and violet.

In the time of Louis XIV., the ladies appear still to have copied the French modes which had come into vogue in the commencement of the fifteenth century, and, in 1512, they are described by the diarist Priuli as firmly established, as, at an anterior period, the subjects of Charles VIII.

had been influenced by those of the Peninsula, Venice included. An eyewitness tells us that when Madame du Plessis Besancon was at Venice about 1670, "they most industriously imitated her in all the fashions she brought with her out of France." (1)

(1)   De la Haye, *The Policy and Government of the Venetians: Both in Civil and Military Affairs,* page 68.

Late in the next century, an instance occurs in which a Venetian diplomatist at Rome in August, 1796, sends a lady a gown, of very inconsiderable value, he confessed, and merely wool, but made in the prevailing style, and, he thinks, with some taste. The recipient is to bear in mind that the dress should be worn, as he is informed, a little over the bosom, the sleeves gathered up to the shoulder with ribbon, and the bodice fixed with pins over the little white favours, says he, which you will see — a costume which will suit either town or country, and serve both for ceremony and every-day use. (1) This pretty little attention from the representative of the Most Serene Republic at the court of the Vatican to his sweet friend Caterina Cornaro was, no doubt, just at that moment the top of the fashion in the Eternal City.

(1)   Molmenti, *La Vie Privee a Venise,* Liber II page 435.

Venetian householders of the higher class, as time proceeded and luxury increased, did not concern themselves with domestic details, and both the master and mistress of an aristocratic establishment were accustomed to engage a *sigisbeo,* who had his analogue in other parts of Italy, but was, and is, only imperfectly represented elsewhere by such officers as stewards, treasurers and bailiffs. (1) He was a kind of factotum;. he transacted all kinds of business for his employers, acted as an escort for the lady or ladies of the Palazzo, and settled accounts.

(1)   But the French have in this connexion the term *sigisbeisme.* See Fournier, *Le Vieux-Neuf: Histoire Ancienne des Inventions et Decouvertes Modernes,* Volume II page 298. Indeed, in modern France and even England, although the character of the functionary may have undergone modification, the thing widely survives. When Hazlitt was in Italy in 1824-1825, the practice still prevailed, but was thought by him to be on the decline.

Sometimes the Signore and his consort had independent functionaries; it was a question of means and tastes. But it is easy to perceive how mischief and disaster might accrue from this anomalous relationship, when the *sigisbeo* presented himself at an early hour, was at liberty to proceed to the lady's private apartment, sat chatting at the bedside, assisted her in completing her toilette, conversed with her on the same sofa while the hairdresser attended to her wants, took chocolate with her, accompanied her to her place of worship, and, later on, to the theatre or the promenade, and relieved her, in short, of all trouble. He even organized the dinner parties and soirees, and if his mistress was invited to another house he was her chaperon. The *sigisbeo* was thus something between a major-domo and a gentleman in waiting, but of a type which only Italian manners and ideas were capable of regarding with tolerance, although we discern an approach to the same sort of cavalieresque gallantry at the courts of Charles II. and Louis XIV.

Among the most distinguished houses, the selection of the *sigisbeo* was a task of difficulty thought to demand careful consideration. A not too fastidious abbe frequently accepted the post, and the by-name *abbatino* was coined to describe this equivocal type of ecclesiastic. In former days, a noted beauty passed through the streets, veiled or masked, attended by several male admirers or *cavalieri serventi*, to two of whom she gave an arm to support her in her clogs, while the others carried her fan or her cloak.

The *sigisbeo*, who was by no means an exclusively Venetian institution, may be taken to have developed gradually from the *maestro di casa* (1) of whom we hear at a comparatively early period, when manners had not yet acquired so lax a tone, and when establishments of a certain rank already found it convenient to allow the management of household details to devolve on such an official. In the opening years of the seventeenth century, it casually transpires from a political correspondence that Signore Francesco Vercellini of Venice had been acting in this capacity at the Casa Barbarigo, and that he subsequently entered the service of the Earl and Countess of Arundel, who had residences at that time both at Venice and in the country. A notary of the Chancery, writing to the Council of Ten at the end of April, 1622, states that he had been acquainted with Vercellini ten years. He was apparently an ordinary steward.

(1)   For the important and multifarious functions of this officer, see Liberati, *Il Perfetto Maestro di Casa di Francesco Liberati Romano.*

But, side by side with the external splendour of life and the sumptuous embellishment of private interiors, we hear from early observers (1) that the Venetian gentleman was almost parsimonious in his expenditure and domestic economy, and that the possessor of eight, nine or ten thousand ducats a year contented himself with two or three women servants, and a, man, or perhaps two, to row his gondola. He would go to market himself, and lay out as little as possible. He deemed it more than enough if, out of his thousands, he bestowed three or four hundred on his house. When it was a question, however, of the dress of his wife or his mistress, or of a dowry for a daughter, it was a different affair; in such directions he was lavish, and he always had a handsome sum in reserve when a public loan was announced at 10, 12 or 15 per cent.

(1)   Thomas, *The Historye of Italye,* folio 84.

The same authority states a case for the defendant. "Admit," says he, "this report to be true. If I am proud, I have good cause, for I am a prince and no subject; if I am economical, it is because my commonwealth allows no pomp, and moderation is wholesome; if I keep few servants, it is because I need no more; if I buy my meat myself, it is for the reason that I wish to get what I like; if I am hard to my tenantry, it is because they live by me; if I gain, I gain on my own money, and do not hide my talent in the ground," and so forth. But the writer was possibly a little unfortunate in his personal experience, although there is evidence that Venetian notions of expenditure must at all times have struck an Englishman or even a western European with surprise.

The Sieur de la Haye speaks of the gallantries of the ladies in church, where on saints days they went under pretence of public prayer, and returned the glances of the young gentlemen behind the pillars. Both De la Haye and his son served the Republic in a military and diplomatic capacity, and his account belongs to the second half of the seventeenth century, but this licence in church was by no means of recent origin or an exclusive characteristic of later and more corrupt manners, for, in the official records of the fourteenth century, occur numerous convictions for indecent assaults on ladies and their female attendants. A trace of such libertinism is visible in the incident which brought to pass the Faliero tragedy in 1355, the obscurity of which is partly owing to the loss of the registers for the years 1355-1367.

At that date, no less than when Montaigne was at Venice about 1580, (1) the precision of the gondolier was as noted as it is at the present day; the boatman whom we happen to engage utters a peculiar cry when he is on the point of reaching some sharp turning where another gondola may be meeting yours; he has uttered that very vocable, with the least possible variation, since gondolas and canals first existed; and he has likewise equally been from time immemorial an accomplice in intrigue. Nowadays, he is in touch with all the frail sisterhood, and is prepared to convert his deck-cabin into a place of meeting at a slightly augmented tariff.

(1)   Montaigne, *Essais,* Livre III Chapter 5.

De la Haye testifies to the dexterity with which he threaded his way through the infinite number of boats, as well as the unerring manner in which he would follow a gondola containing a lady whom his own freight was desirous of keeping in sight. Early in 1646, when Evelyn and his friends were escorting a lady home after supper, they heard shots from two carbines just as they approached the landing stairs, and these had been fired at them by men in another gondola in which a nobleman and his mistress were entertaining each other, and did not wish to be disturbed or reconnoitred.

It was estimated that, at this time, there were 40,000 gondoliers at Venice, (1) but these figures strike us as too high, looking at the total population of 200,000 or thereabout. In the middle of the eighteenth century, a collection was made and harmonized by Signor Hasse of the ballads in vogue among this class, and published in London with a dedication to the Earl of Middlesex. Even to-day, the evening serenades on the canals are among the most pleasant and recallable experiences of visitors to the city. In 1714, the charge for a gondola by the day with two men was seven *lire.*

(1)   Raymond, *An Itinerary Contayning a Voyage, Made Through Italy, in The Yeare 1646, and 1647,* page 197.

The first explicit reference to the haberdasher in London is under 1311, (1) and, under 1378, we are supplied with the contents of the shop of one who had relinquished business. It does not ostensibly include any items of Venetian origin; a counterpart illustrative of a similar depot in the Republic is much to be desired. From the appropriation of the term *milliner* to the city of Milan, it has been inferred that that place was in ancient times an important centre of the trade. In England, the business was known as early as the fifteenth century, and was then in the hands of the haberdasher or dealer in small wares, but, in the sixteenth, we occasionally meet with the milliner as an independent trader of considerable importance. Venice must have been furnished with keepers of such emporia as soon as any European capital. But while there is for our use and edification so extensive an assemblage of works of art, shewing the modes in which the Venetians of both sexes attired their persons, history has failed to transmit the names of their tailors, their dressmakers, their coiffeurs and their hatters, as much as it has those of their great masters in cookery, pastry and sweetmeats, in which the world never beheld such triumphs.

(1)   Hazlitt III, *The Livery Companies of the City of London,* page 115. In Fairholt's *Costume in England; A History of Dress to the End of the Eighteenth Century,* page 457, is a notice of the stock of a French maker of the thirteenth century, in which occur purses, readily saleable, it is said, at fairs.

Gloves had been introduced into France at a period of high antiquity, and were in use in that kingdom in the beginning to the ninth century (814). Johannes de Garlandia in his *Dictionary* (thirteenth century) speaks of the glovers of Paris as cheating the scholars by selling them gloves of inferior material. He describes them as of lamb-skin, fox-fur, and rabbit-skin, and he refers to leathern mittens. (1) To the Greeks this article of apparel was familiar at a prior epoch, it being extremely probable that their knowledge of it had been transmitted to them through the Romans from the ancient Athenians. It therefore seems perfectly irrational to suppose that the Republic, which traded with both countries at least so far back as the Carolingian era, and which had already become the great vehicle of communication between the eastern and western worlds, was otherwise than conversant with a usage which she was perhaps the first to introduce to the latter.

(1)   Wright, *A Volume of Vocabularies,* page 124.

Political circumstances were about that time fortuitously instrumental in improving, to a material extent, the commercial relations of Venice with the two leading European powers of the day. Even in the time of Charlemagne himself (768-814), Venetian fashions had found their way into the Imperial palace no less than into the mansions of the nobility. So far is it from being likely that the Venetians of the ninth century were strangers to the practice of covering the hand, that the probability rather is that the great annual fair at Pavia, which was frequented almost exclusively by their traders, formed the sole mart for the gloves which are represented to have been worn to such a pitch of extravagance by the subjects of Louis le Debonnaire.

The entertaining narrative of Petrus Damianus bears, however, the earliest allusion of an explicit nature to the employment of gloves among the Venetians, and if the evidence just adduced was not strongly contradictory of such an hypothesis, it might have been supposed that the fashion in question was much rarer than it is proved to have been at that time (1071), and that the Dogaressa Selvo was guilty of innovating upon the manners of the period to an extent which scandalized Damianus.

At what point of time the kid-glove found its way to France, where it subsequently became so great a speciality, is not at present known to me; but, in 1622, James Howell, writing to his intimate friend Daniel Caldwall from Poissy, near Paris, desires him to forward from London "a Dozen Pair of the whitest Kid-Skin Gloves for Women." (1)

(1)   Howell, *Familiar Letters,* Book I, Section 2, Letter 20.

Marcel (1) does not commend the washing arrangements, as he observed them in 1714. He says: "The Washing is pretty dear, and spoils the Linen much; for if you don't pay a great Price, they will wash with Salt Water to save the buying of Fresh."

(1)   Marcel, *Travels,* page 105.

The burials at Venice in the time of Coryat impressed him as different from any that he had elsewhere beheld, for the corpse was borne to the church with the face, hands and feet exposed, and wearing the same apparel as during life, or some dress in which the departed had expressed a desire to lie; and so it was deposited in the ground. Of course, there were constant exceptions to such a form of interment, when it was a question of any notable personage. Coryat, however, was even more struck by the committal to the earth of vicious and licentious characters in the habits of monks, which, it was explained to him, was a supposed means of procuring them partial remission of their sins. The author of the *Crudities* was not aware that the same superstition prevailed in ancient times in his own England.

The funeral customs at Venice seem almost to await an historian. At the deaths of certain distinguished personages, including a few Doges, there are incidental references to customs observed in times of mourning, and to the colours adopted in commemoration of the dead; indeed, a casual passage or remark is all that assists us to an acquaintance with many other interesting features of social life. In the accounts of the obsequies of eminent Venetians in early times, which form part of the present narrative, slight glimpses are afforded of this side of the subject, as, for example, where Sanudo in his *Diary*, under the 18th of May, 1498, records the return of Andrea Trevisano, knight, ambassador to Henry VII. "with beard" and in mourning for the death of his father and mother. (1)

(1)   See (compilation) *Calendar of State Papers Relating to English Affairs in the Archives of Venice,* Volume I page 268.

It entered into the oligarchical bias of everything at Venice, that the preponderance of interest, publicity and reminiscence in respect of social observances and functions was on the side of a slender minority of the population. In such a community, the bulk or mass came into the world, and passed through it and out of it as best they might, and where accounts have been transmitted of births, marriages and funeral rites, they are found to bear an almost exclusive relation to the governing class. Minute particulars are incidentally preserved of transactions and occurrences in the life of the people, but they amount to no more than casual anecdotes.

As regards nuptial usages, till the sixteenth century a contract or betrothal before witnesses sufficed, and the parents or relatives completed the ceremony. (1) Burial of the poor was a process not less summary and informal than elsewhere; the common pit was for centuries the allotted destination, (2) and the Venetian soil probably covers millions of human beings to the resting-places or dates of whom there is not the faintest clue. The stately monument, the elaborate inscription, the proud or affectionate record, were for a few patriots and heroes who had served well the state, or for a few devout or repentant persons, even courtezans, who had fattened the Church.

(1)   Molmenti, *La Storia di Venezia nella Vita Privata,* Liber I page 296-297.
(2)   See the case of Bianca Cappello, supra.

Here and there it happens that a few circumstances have been put on record, less for the purpose for which posterity immediately values them than from some current official motive. We have, in this way, one or two glimpses of the marriage ceremonies among the common people. On an October day in 1443, a certain Pietro di Trento, a broom seller, passing along the Street of Santi Gervasio e Protasio, stopped in front of the house of Cattarina, widow of Giovanni Bianco, and, seeing the lady at the window, the following dialogue took place;

> *Madonna, catenare qualche fante per mi*
> *Bruto mato, me vorrestu niai far messela?*
> *Io non dico cussi, io dico per mia muyer.*
> *Ben cussi si ...*"

The lady had at first charged him with taking her to be a procuress, but it turned out that he was in quest of a girl whom he could marry, and she bethought her of a likely candidate. So she tells him that she thinks she can supply him, if he comes again the next day, when *"una bella fanciulla, di nome Maria"* presented herself, and the whole business was accomplished.

Ten years later, two fellow lodgers in the house of Lazzaro Tedesco at San Luca fell in love with each other, namely Giovanni da Crema and a certain Chiara, and they, on a certain day, invited a witness before whom Giovanni says: "Chiara, I take thee for my wife." The latter replies: "And I take thee for my husband, and am content." He gave her a ring, and they became man and wife in the eye of the law.

In a third case (1456), Beatrice Francigena, on her return home from Treviso, repaired to the house of a female relative and there met one Falcon, to whom she had apparently engaged herself by giving him her hand, but who suspected her of having been inconstant. Both, however, in the presence of the said witness, ultimately arrived at a happy understanding. He says to Beatrice: "Thou knowest that thou art mine," and she replies: "Madi." He touched her hand and said: "And I will take no other wife but thee," and she made answer: "And I will take no other spouse but thee."

CHAPTER LXV

Meals — Diet and Provisions — Character of Cookery — Confectionery — Beef and Veal — Game and Poultry — Fish — Fruits — Wheaten and Millet Bread — Shambles and Fish-Market — Food of the Lower Classes — Wines — Liqueurs — Coryat on the Food — Sobriety — Forks — The Knife — Evening Amusements — Games — Music — Singing — Dancing — Painters — The Benches in the Piazza — The Social Circle of Titian — His and Other Men's Pictures Offered for Sale at the Sensa Fair — Pietro Aretino — His Intimacy with All the Great Folks of the Day — Giorgione and His Friends — The Bellini — Tributes of Titian to Fellow Artists — Paolo Veronese and the Holy Office — Rosalba Carriera — Canova.

The science of cookery had of course passed its rudimentary stage, modelled on Italian and even Roman tradition, and on local prepossessions, before the printing-press rendered the production of manuals on the subject in all its branches feasible, although here, as elsewhere, collections of recipes for individual use were doubtless drawn up in manuscript form. From the earlier half of the sixteenth century, a regular and voluminous series of such guides, comprising instruction in the arts of cooking, serving, carving and the making of confectionery, was published at Venice itself and throughout the Venetian dominion, and offer in their contents a striking monument of taste, ingenuity and social luxury and refinement.

Two meals in the course of the day ordinarily sufficed then, as at present. The first (*pranzo*) was originally taken at or even before noon. The other, a repast the character of which depended on circumstances and tastes, followed at seven or eight in the evening according to the season. At the

Palace in ancient times, the *pranzo* was served in the principal hall, and the Doge and his ministers who resided under the same roof ate in public. (1) His Serenity usually supped in his own apartment with his private circle. Councils were held in the forenoon, and, if the business was lengthy and urgent, were adjourned at a certain hour to reassemble "*dopo pranzo.*"

(1)   At Hampton Court there is a very interesting picture by Van Bassen, in which Charles I. and his Queen are dining in public. It was painted in 1637. *Law's Catalogue*, 1881, page 212. Evelyn, under the 3rd of August 1667, records the resumption of this practice by Charles II.

The Kings of France are represented as similarly dining in public in the twelfth century, and as being entertained during the repast by some sort of theatrical spectacle. The more travelled Venetians were of course conversant with the social habits of other countries, but adhered to their own traditions. We find in 1515 the ambassador at the court of England, during the May celebrations at Greenwich and Shooter's Hill, partaking of what he designates "*un Brecafas a la Polita*," which Mr. Rawdon Brown renders "a proper good breakfast;" but this was, it seems, at a fairly early hour. (1)

(1)   Warton, *History of English Poetry From the Twelfth to the Close of the Sixteenth Century,* Volume II page 225.

In cookery, oil, garlic, onions, sugar and all sorts of condiments and spices were used. Beans, peas, cabbages and other vegetables were well known, and, after the first course of soup (*grasso* and *magro*) and meat, fruit, wine, pastry and confectionery, (1) of the last of which the ladies were particular patronesses, were frequently placed on the tables of the more affluent.

(1)   John the Deacon, Da Canale, Chinazzo, et cetera, *locis supra citalis.*

The keen national taste for sweetmeats displayed itself in different forms at a very early date on a variety of public occasions. In 1268, an industrial exhibition was organized by the trading companies at the Palace, in honour of the Dogaressa who was presented by the masters with comfits. In 1390, the Duke of Austria, as a distinguished guest, received on his departure thirty ducats and a parcel of sweetmeats. At the reception of Henry III. of France on his passage from Poland to take possession of the French throne, the most elaborate and splendid artifices in sugar were placed on the table in the banqueting-chamber, even the napkin of His Majesty, when he handled it, proving to be of that material; and a few years later (1597) when the Dogaressa Morosini was crowned, three hundred baskets filled with objects in gilt sugar were a feature in the solemnity.

Old English banquets were similarly diversified with forms of men, animals, houses, and castles made of sugar and almonds. But perhaps the most notable and curious articles of consumption in this way was the *fava*, a recollection of the very ancient religious observance of beans, which in England assumed the shape of a Twelfth Night merriment, and among the Venetians was still farther modernized by a popular confection of flour, sugar and honey, a speciality on All Souls Day. These small delicacies were originally actual beans eaten or offered to the spirits of the departed at funeral feasts or on special occasions, but subsequently replaced by bonbons, on the principle, which became general, of supplying commodities of this description in an infinite diversity of forms.

Excellent beef was procurable, and the veal of Chioggia, the hams of Friuli and the sausages of Bologna were renowned. All kinds of game, peacocks, pheasants, partridges, hares, boiled or roasted, were eaten; pigeons and other birds were common. The Polesine of Rovigo and the extensive marshes bordering on the Adige supplied a never-failing store of poultry, and wild fowl must have long abounded in the Dogado. Eggs were always plentiful, and were brought down the rivers to the lagoon in little barges of light build especially devoted to this service.

Among fish, salmon, (1) trout, mackerel, lampreys, crawfish and eels, both fresh and salted, were favourite delicacies;, but, above all, were the turbot eulogized by Boccaccio in his letter to the Prior of Santi Apostoli at Florence, the superb and too seductive red mullet, and the fresh sardine designated the ortolan of the Adriatic. Oysters and mussels were obtained, the larger oysters being served as made dishes; at Murano, Coryat tasted a very small variety resembling the Wainfleet kind, as green as a leek and (as he puts it) "*gratissimi saporis & succi.*" Red mullet has been served up at the breakfast table time out of mind, and is so to-day; it is obtained from the canals. Another dish of the same class is a sort of plaice found off Lido. Shrimps were caught at Gambarere.

(1)   Folgore, *Sonetti de' Mesi* in Alfani, *Poeti del Primo Secolo,*
         Volume II page 168.

The grapes of San Zaccaria and of Comanzo in Chioggia had a special
reputation. Large importations of apples and cherries were made from
various parts of Lombardy and the Marches and from Dalmatia. Oranges,
lemons, citrons, medlars, figs and melons were found nearer home. Of
the melon there were three varieties, yellow, green and red, the red the
most toothsome, but all, according to Coryat, apt to produce dysentery if
eaten to excess in the hot weather.

Wheaten bread, in ordinary times, was not uncommon among the poorer
classes, but millet was also used. During the war of 1413, the pressure of
high taxes obliged many to submit to the latter, but it is said to have been
regarded as a hardship. The Republic procured its wheat for the most part
from Apulia and the Levant, from Egypt and from Barbary. In the famine
of 1268, Venetian ships penetrated as far as the Crimea in search of
grain. The ever-increasing uncertainty of political events and the
imprudence of relying on supplies from home markets led, in 1493, to
the institution of the Fondaco della Farina, where flour was stored under
the control of the government. In old times, the shops of the bakers were
mainly concentrated at the Rialto and the Campanile. Forty-four depots
are mentioned as existing for the sale of different kinds and qualities.

Mattheolus, in a note on Dioscorides, acquaints us that, in later times, the
flour of the prickly root called water-caltrop, growing freely in the
lagoons, served as bread when roasted in the hot embers, and that this
product was commonly on sale in the market. (1) There were also
biscuits (*scalete*) which, like the British muffin, were manufactured by
specialists. They were said to owe their name to the horizontal bars
impressed upon one side, and might have been originally introduced
from Verona where the House of La Scala once ruled.

(1)   Saint John, *The History of the Manners and Customs of Ancient
         Greece,* Volume III page 108.

It is through one of the tragical occurrences which so largely entered into
the earlier annals, that we make our first acquaintance with a shambles in
976; the remains of a dead Doge and his murdered child were deported
thither in that year in a boat as food for dogs; it was ostensibly at some
little distance from the centre of the city. The coronation oath of 1229
refers to a shambles as well as a fish-market, both licensed by the

executive. In 1339, the butchers' quarters were removed from the neighbourhood of San Giovanni in Rialto to the Casa Quirini which was popularly known as Stalon; this, again, afterward became the poultry market. In 1649, it was estimated that 520 bullocks were slaughtered weekly. The emporium for sale of the article, however, seems (judging from much later times) to have been unrestricted in its habitat; for, in 1565, Jost Amman depicts a meat-shop on the Molo itself under the very nostrils of the Doge, and similarly a sort of bread-market impinged on the Campanile. In 1597, the Butchers' Guild took a prominent part in the coronation of the Dogaressa Morosini-Grimani.

The gastronomic wants of the Mediaeval Venetian were circumscribed by his experience, and his diet was governed by the climate and by local conditions. Fish, bread, oil and fruit formed the staple food of the lower class. Oil was an article in universal demand; it was obtained from Lucca, and was allowed even to prisoners, who preferred it to season their salad, and were prepared to defray the cost. To the Mediaeval Italian, as it does still, oil stood in the same relation as honey or butter to his Anglo-Saxon or Anglo-Norman contemporary. Pork and poultry were more or less plentiful, but of beef and mutton the oldest documents do not speak, beyond the general indication of a taxed shambles. The art of improving the breed of sheep and oxen had still to be learned, and the bullock was principally reserved for the plough and the wain; nor had many of the fruits and vegetables, which are now regarded as among the necessaries of existence, been introduced into Europe.

Still we learn something of the culinary resources of Venice, at the end of the fourteenth century, from the details of prices of various articles of food during the War of Chioggia in 1379. Everything had at that crisis become frightfully dear, however. Corn was selling at nine *lire di piccoli* the small or sixteen the large measure; millet, ten *lire* the measure; barley, five; beans, from eight to twelve; peas, twelve. Salt meat was fetching eight *soldini* a pound, oil the same. Two *soldi* were given for an egg or a cabbage; a *lira di piccoli*, or the third of a ducat, for a rope of onions; and, for a hundred head of garlic, two *lire*.

Wine was not to be bought under six *lire* a quart; the choicest vintages produced double that amount; and (the winter coming on) firewood was eleven *lire* the boat-load. It is one of those cases in which indirect or collateral evidence has to suffice in relation to the diet of the humbler classes. In the *Cries of Rome*, 1646, a various assortment of domestic necessaries occurs, in company with cheese, curds, chestnuts and cakes, as well as "fine tripe" which doubtless importantly entered into the poorer Venetian cuisine, but of which a choice sort was produced at Treviso.

The Venetian chefs do not seem to have included the sweet-potato or yam in their menu. Andrea Navagiero, the ambassador of the Signory, saw it in Spain in 1525, and in his *Diary* at Seville, on the 15th of May, he mentions that he met in that city with many things from India or the Indies, and among them a root, called *batatas*, which he ate, and thought in flavour like a chestnut. (1) It is remarkable that Evelyn the diarist expresses a similar judgment on the potato of his day, which appeared to him to taste "like an old bean or roasted chestnut." This seems in both cases to have been the sweet-potato (*batata edulis*) of Java and other regions, and not our common vegetable which was a later European acquisition. There is the somewhat parallel case of the introduction of tobacco into Europe so long after it was noticed by Columbus in the Bahamas in 1492.

(1)   (compilation) *Calendar of State Papers Relating to English Affairs in the Archives of Venice,* Volume IV page xxiv; Evelyn, *Memoirs Illustrative of the Life and Writings of John Evelyn,* Volume IV page 364.

At a later period, no refinements in luxury were omitted by the Venetian gourmet and epicure. Every article of food was procured from the locality which enjoyed the principal celebrity for its production or preparation — the *mortadella* or rich sausage of Cremona, those of Bologna, Milan and Modena, the cheese of Piacenza, the lampreys of Binasco, the sturgeon of Ferrara, the thrushes of Perugia, the geese of Romagna, the quails of Lombardy. In their sauces the chefs put sugar and even gold, as the latter was supposed to exhilarate the heart.

Wines of all vintages were obtainable, and were brought, not only from Hungary, the Rhine, the Moselle and Austria, but from the east. That made from the muscat grape was much esteemed; it was this kind which the Doge offered to the Fruiterers' Guild in 1618, with other equivalents in kind for their customary oblation to him on his accession, and which the physician of Sarpi sent from his own house for the use of the patient, when that great man lay on his death-bed in 1622. Liqueurs were already in vogue, and the cherries of Zara were thought to produce the finest maraschino. All these articles of consumption must have been costly, while heavy duties were charged alike on all imports and exports. Yet the

German traveller or observer, who wrote the semi-mythical account of the life of Faust published at Berlin in 1587, makes his hero particularly struck by the cheapness of food at Venice in the sixteenth century, even in the absence of immediate sources of supply.

Coryat many years later says precisely the same thing, and enters more at large into the infinite conveniences and facilities afforded by the city under such apparent disadvantages. He remarks: "Amongst many other things that moved great admiration in me in Venice, this was not the least, to consider the marvellous affluence and exuberancy of all things tending to the sustentation of mans life. For albeit they have neyther meadows, nor pastures, nor arable grounds neare their city ... yet they have as great abundance ... of victuals, corne and fruites of all sorts whatsoever, as any city (I thinke) of all Italy." (1)

(1)   Coryat, *Coryat's Crudities,* page 256.

But a Venetian representative at the court of Henry IV. of France implies that the art of dressing food at Paris surpassed that at home. He seems to have lodged in the Rue de la Huchette, and after his return recalled the excellent table kept there with affectionate regret, describing the roast meat as a *cosa stupenda.* (1)

(1)   Michel et Fournier, *Histoire des Hôtelleries, Cabarets, Courtilles, et des Anciennes Communautés et Confréries d'Hôteliers, de Taverniers, de Marchands de Vins,* page 93.

A French traveller (1) of the last years of the eighteenth century describes the Venetians as abstemious in their habits at table, and as soberer than other Italians. They drink little wine or liqueur, he says, and are not partial to ragouts; but they care more than we do for rice, *pates,* chocolate and ices. It is to be suspected that the prevailing tenor of the diet of the poor, and their general habits of life, were frugal to excess. Tripe, fish, fruit, bread, farinaceous substances and the cheaper wines entered into the plebeian cuisine, and those who had not the means or desire to cook at home probably resorted to public eating-houses.

(1)   Lalande, *Voyage d'un Francois en Italie,* cited by Romanin, *Storia Documentata di Venezia,* Volume IX page 10 note.

The Riva degli Schiavoni became famous for these establishments, as we learn from the local proverb:

"Sulla Riva degli Schiavoni
Si mangiano bei bocconi."

At the tables of the common people, the method of eating was ever primitive enough, but, among the better classes, the food was conveyed to the mouth by a fork with one prong, which represented an evolution of the oriental chopstick. Forks were known in England and France in the thirteenth century, but they were of gold or crystal inlaid with precious stones, and were laid up among the jewels of crowned or noble personages; Piers Gaveston is described as the possessor of three implements of silver for eating pears. The Greek princess, Theodora Ducas, who married the Doge Selvo (1071-1084), was thought to be guilty of an almost sinful refinement in making use at meals of a double-pronged fork of gold. It is not improbable that this exalted personage merely introduced into the land of her adoption a practice to which she had always been accustomed at home.

Doubtless, the very early and constant intercourse between Venice and the Mediaeval Greeks contributed to Hellenise at once the sentiments, manners and language of the western power. It has been pointed out that the Republic derived from this source the common name *piron*, for a fork in her local dialect, whereas the Italians around her employed a wholly different word, *forchetto*, to signify the same thing. But the Italian *prone* (*pirone* or lever), which presents a strong appearance of relationship to the Greek term, was perhaps at the outset a tool with a single prong, and acquired by degrees a secondary meaning in the vocabulary in which it was incorporated.

The double-pronged development may have been suggested to the moderns by the pronged trident observable on many early coins, and known as a weapon among the Tartars; it is illustrated in the *Cuoco Sacrato di Papa Pio Quinto*, by Bartolomeo Scappi, published at Venice in 1598, and is there termed a *furcina*. We are all aware that a third prong was eventually added and completed the resemblance.

It was not till recently that remains of Mediaeval domestic utensils have been on view in our museums, while those in fashion among the ancients are rendered abundantly familiar by descriptions or actual examples. The material was probably stone at the outset, then bronze, and finally copper. In the will of Richard de Plumpton, 1443, mention occurs of a pair of silver *forpices* in immediate association with one of carving-knives; (1) these were perhaps tongs. But a fork of silver, weighing three ounces and valued at 12s., was presented to Henry VII. in 1500, and the purchase of a pair of carving knives occurs in that prince's privy purse expenses.

(1)   Plumpton, *Plumpton Correspondence. A Series of Letters, Chiefly Domestick, Written in the Reigns of Edward IV. Richard III. Henry VII. and Henry VIII*, XXXIV.

A steel double-pronged fork which is said to have belonged to Henry IV. of France was long preserved at Pau, his birth-place, as a curiosity. But the fork was, for the most part, limited to helping purposes during centuries, even in Italy, and, curiously enough, its employment was justified there by the prevalence of unclean hands. When Thomas Coryat was at Venice in the opening years of the seventeenth century, the fork was still sparingly used at table, but it was far more uncommon in England, and, when the traveller returned, he acquired from the circumstance that he brought some specimens with him and habitually ate with one, the sobriquet *Furcifer*, to which his friends may or may not have intended to apply a double sense.

Coryat intimates that the general habit was to employ a single fork at a table to keep the meat in position while it was being cut, and not for each person to have one. The object was to preclude the fingers of those present from touching the food, since, as the writer observes, everybody's hands are not always clean. But he had his own implement which he doubtless carried about him in a case. It appears that it was Lawrence Whitaker who quipped him on the point, but he assures us that it was only Whitaker's fun. Jonson, in *The Devil is an Ass*, performed in 1616, makes one of the characters say:

> "The laudable use of forks,
> Brought into custom here, as they are in Italy,
> To the sparing of napkins."

But it was a custom long very much neglected, judging from a passage in Lovelace's *Lucasta*, 1649. (1) The information may have reached Jonson through Coryat's book.

(1)   Lovelace, *Lucasta,* page 77.

We gain very slight explicit information about the knife, an implement everywhere in vogue from the most remote times, but we know that Venetian cutlery gradually became celebrated, and was exported to other countries. At the great fairs of Europe, England included, it was a staple commodity, and our universities were supplied with Venetian knives purchased at the nearest fairs. There had been a period, however, when all refinements of this class were rare in western Europe, and when travellers found it necessary to carry their knife, fork and spoon on their persons in leathern cases. Chaucer introduces us to the Sheffield whittle.

Till recently, there was no collection of ancient cutlery at Sheffield, but at present they have one in the Central Park Museum. Besides the cutlery from Venice, a good deal was made in Germany and in the Chatellerault district in France. The specimens which have come down to us, marked with a pine, appear to be attributable to Augsburg. The Venetians, no doubt, imported and reshipped, as well as manufactured; but the cutlery the hafts of which terminate in a Doge's bonnet are of unmistakably local origin.

The evening amusements were varied. There were dancing and singing; and for those who did not dance or sing there was instrumental music, while for such as did not care for the viol, the guitar, the cittern or the lute, there was a chess table or a backgammon board, both in full force in the thirteenth century, the latter an inheritance from Rome; at a later time basset was a favourite form of gambling. To some of the pastimes out of doors, by which the wealthier Italians beguiled their leisure, a nation of islanders was necessarily a stranger. It is not known that the earlier Venetians were addicted to the winter diversion of snowballing the ladies, which was so much in vogue on the mainland, but hunting, fowling and fishing, at first within the alluvial confines, and eventually throughout the continental territories in Lombardy, were pursued with regularity and enjoyment by those who had the time and the means, or who found in those occupations a source of subsistence.

Convivial meetings, concerts, balls and serenades were soon introduced. In Siena the musical instruments chiefly used came from Germany, but the song and the dance were contributed by Provence, as described by the old poet, Folgore da San Geminiano, who admirably paints in his sonnets the life of his day: (1)

> *Cantar, danzar alla provenzalesca*
> *Con instrumenti novi d'Allemagna*

(1)   Folgore, *Sonetti de' Mesi,* Volume II page 168 in Alfani, *Poeti del Primo Secolo.*

San Geminiano relates that in his own town Monday was the day for serenades, and Wednesday for receptions and balls:

> *Ogni Mercoledi corrido grande*
> *Di lepri, starne, fagiani, e paoni,*
> *E cotte manze, ed arrosti capponi,*
> *E quante son delicate vivande*
> ...
> *Vin greco di Riviera e di vernaccia,*
> *Frutta, confetti, quanti li e talento*
> ...
> *E donzelenni gioveni garzoni*
> *Servir, portando amorose ghirlande!*

This picture, which refers more immediately to the manners of Siena, may by analogy afford some insight into the contemporary aspect of Venetian society, of which it is to be lamented that no similarly graphic illustrations exist.

An Arezzan poet, Cene della Chitarra, who flourished concurrently with San Geminiano, has also left *Sonnets of the Months.* They shew that the life of Arezzo, Ancona, Florence and other places had many features in common with that of Siena, and we know enough of the intimate life of Cosimo de' Medici in the Via Larga and at Mugello to satisfy us that, in high society in the Tuscan capital in the middle of the fifteenth century, instrumental and vocal music and the dance formed habitual resources after the employment of the day. The verses of Cene are indeed less rich in colour than those of his fellow bard, but this circumstance may partly be explained by the fact that one was an advocate of abstinence, while the other was not only fond of his glass of wine, but goes even farther than Jean le Houx, author of the *Vaux de Vire,* and counsels intoxication:

> *Bevete del mosto, e inebriate;*
> *Che non ci ha miglior vita in veritate;*
> *E questo e vero come il florin giallo.* (1)

(1)   "The Florin of Gold." Alfani, *Poeti del Primo Secolo,* Volume II page 181, 196 et seqq.

Speaking of his mistress, Albertuccio della Viola, a third poet of the same epoch, writes:

> *Ali danza la vidi danzare,*
> *L' Amorosa, che mi fa allegrare.*
> *Cosi, come danzava, mi ferio —*
> *Vestut' era d'un drappo di Soria,*
> *La Donna mia, e stavale bene.*

The most ancient vestige of the employment of musical instruments at Venice appears to be the incidental notice by the Greek Exarch Longinus, when he was there in 568, of the presence and use of the flute and cittern, both equally, no doubt, of Hellenic origin, and importations from the Italian terra firma. The culture of music appears, from an allusion in the *Chronicles of San Giorgio Maggiore* under the date 790, to have found affectionate promoters among the members of this holy fraternity at that epoch. The knowledge of instrumental harmony made such rapid progress, that a Venetian priest (Fra Gregorio) was invited into France, about 826, to superintend the construction of an hydraulic organ for the king.

In the beginning of the fourteenth century, one Mistro Zuchetto is mentioned as filling the appointment of organist to the Chapel of Saint Mark, but it is not to be supposed for an instant that Zuchetto was the first who had served in that capacity. In 1498, the government granted a monopoly for twenty years to Ottaviano de' Petrucci da Fossombrone for the printing of all figured song and tablature for the organ and the lute; this was the starting point of that enormous volume of musical literature which claims Venice as its source. (1)

(1)   Brown, *The Venetian Printing Press,* page 41.

In 1515, in a letter from the secretary of the Venetian embassy at London to a friend at home, the writer begs his correspondent to send him some compositions by Zuan Maria, as he had been speaking very highly of him in London, and had been requested to obtain specimens of his music; he also desired a few more ballads.

The fame of Venetian musicians reached, as a matter of course, the ears of a prince who, like Henry VIII., was so passionately fond of this art and recreation, and Giustinian acquaints us that Henry was greatly struck and charmed by the performance of Fra Dionisio Memo, who was introduced to him and played to His Majesty's high satisfaction, as well as that of Catherine of Arragon and Margaret of Scotland. On another occasion, the King made Memo play before the German and Spanish ambassadors. (1)

(1)   Vowell, *The Life and Times of Sir Peter Carew,* page 38-39.

Giuseppe Zarlino, born at Chioggia in 1517, composer of *Orfeo,* has been called the modern restorer of music. He harmonized the hymns used in the thanksgiving of 1577 after the cessation of the plague, and in 1589 his name and repute were sufficiently powerful to warrant a collective issue of his professional works in four folio volumes. (1) Not only in Venice and the Venetian territories and in Italy, but throughout Europe, the works of Zarlino were appreciated; and they found a place even on the shelves of English libraries in the eighteenth century, when the English nobility and gentry paid so much homage to literature and art, as, at all events, to collect the masterpieces on those subjects in the course of their travels abroad.

(1)   Zarlino, *De Tutte l'Opere del R.M. Gioseffo Zarlino da Chioggia, gia separatamente poste in luce; hora di nuovo corrette, accresciute, et migliorate insieme ristampate.*" with musical notation and diagrams. The *Dimostrationi Harmoniche* appeared in 1571, but the series had appeared separately from 1558.

In the days which immediately succeeded and down to the close, Venice was the centre and the soul of all that was agreeable, gay, bright and seductive. In the seventeenth century, according to De la Haye, there was no want of music; it was so disposed into several apartments, that one was sensible only of a single melody. In one chamber there was a theorbo, in another a lute, in a third a viol, in a fourth a violin, and at a later date the harpsichord (*clavicembalo*) grew into favour. Montaigne, his countryman, notices precisely the same fusion of sound in the musical entertainments of his time in France. A hundred years before, there is a notice that the Lady of Forli, Caterina Sforza Visconti, engaged two drummers to play while her ladyship was at table. (1)

(1)   Pasolini, *Caterina Sforza,* page 63.

Down to a period not very remote from the close of the independent life of Venice, the love and culture of music had a steady succession of votaries, and public officials of high grade gave their leisure to the study of social accomplishments and humanism. Benedetto Marcello (1686-1739) has transmitted to us an interesting body of musical compositions of various classes, with which he occupied some of his spare hours during the performance of his functions as a member of the Civil Quarantia, and as the holder of important posts at Pola and Brescia.

The naval and commercial glory of Venice was all her own, and her literature and drama were, to a large extent, of local origin and complexion, but with her typography and schools of painting and architecture it was not altogether so. The men who worked for her earlier Doges were, like the Lombard engineer Barattiero, neither her citizens nor her subjects. They executed commissions for the first comer, or, like the soldier of fortune, for the employer who paid best. Of her great painters nearly all belonged to the Venetian terra firma, and adopted the city as a residence. They created a school whose triumphs in form, ornament and colour are recollected when the commerce of the Republic is extinct, and her victories by sea and land are more obscure, and seem scarcely less remote, than Marathon or Salamis. They were settlers on that soil from choice; there was the sense of freedom and the assurance of security.

This may possibly strike as a fanciful distinction the professional man who, destitute of sentiment and indifferent to history, visits Venice to-day to study work produced under conditions of life wholly different from his own; produced, not as speculations, but with the whole feeling and might of a generous affection for the art which they pursued. The Venetian painters were not all Titians, but they had, in the middle of the seventeenth century, become a numerous and respectable school, and with their names were then, and are even still, associated many meritorious and characteristic performances. (1)

(1)   In 1648, biographies and portraits of the more eminent members of the school were published by the Cavaliere Ridolphi.

A primitive survival which strikes dwellers in a harsher climate as strange and refreshing, and, apart from the question of conventional dignity, affords a curious aspect of alfresco life in the middle period, must have been the painters' benches in the Piazza, where they were suffered to sit and make their sketches at will, and where for a time they had as an associate a dyer's son named Tintoretto. But these rude appliances made way, even in the time of Titian, for studios where the artist, if he did not desire to use his private residence, could accommodate pupils and see clients, or even place works on view; Titian himself found it necessary to have such a central convenience in Rialto. But in simpler and greater times, the merchant also condescended to occupy a bench in a prominent situation, where he would be most likely to come into contact with customers or acquaintances, and hear the latest news. The Cheapside street counters in the London of Edward III. were very similar.

The circle which gathered round him at his successive residences in Venice itself and in the country included, during some years, the famous Aretino, who made his society acceptable and serviceable by his eulogistic notices, in his extensive correspondence, of the works which his artistic comrades had from time to time in progress. This strange character doubtless promoted the sale of many a canvas which might otherwise have remained on hand, for his acquaintance among the rich and influential was considerable, and he deserves to be regarded, among his manifold qualifications, as the founder of an ingenious literary mechanism not generally thought to have so distinguished or so remote an origin.

Messer Aretino could have told us the Venetian word for tip. The mention of paintings by masters of the Venetian school, now accounted almost priceless, among the ordinary objects exposed for sale at a fair, necessitates a word of suggestion that, at and long after their original production, these works were regarded with an admiration and respect much more qualified than ours. The charm which perspective bestows was wanting; the canvas was fresh and damp (so to speak) from the easel, and if the purchaser or patron was dissatisfied, the artist might be summoned from his own residence a few streets or a few miles away to put in the required touches.

The probability is, that at the Sensa the landscape and the flower or fruit-piece were more usually to be seen and bought, either new or second-hand, than the portrait, which, being a direct commission from a wealthy personage for his gallery or salon, was protected from the humiliation of being offered at a stall, side by side with objects in glass and hardware. Titian, in the course of his long career as an artist, must have had an abundant and constantly growing amount of patronage. The Marchese del Guasto has often been mentioned as one of his customers and friends, and he painted the Marquis more than once. Of course this great man had rivals who shared with him the favour of sitters, such as that consummate master Lorenzo Lotto of Bergamo who settled at Venice in 1527, and, in the same year, executed a likeness of the eminent collector Andrea Odoni. Rubens, during his visit to Italy in 1600, spent some time at Venice, in order to study the work of Titian and Veronese on the spot, but it was doubtless long after Titian's death, that his works were appreciated at anything like their veritable worth, for, in his will (1637), Sir Henry Wotton, in leaving to Charles I. four portraits, by Odoardo Fialetti, of Doges contemporary with him, adds as an object of inferior consequence, "the Picture of a Duke of Venice by Titiano or some other principal hand long before my time."

It is strikingly significant of the difference between the views entertained of some historical characters in their own time and among their own people, and those with which we have been taught to look at them, that, in the case of such a man as Aretino, the relict of the great Correggio, Veronica Gambara, herself a person of literary taste and achievements, (1) not only ranked this celebrated personage among her real friends, but addresses him in a letter as "*divino signore Pietro mio.*" It almost makes us pause to reflect whether we look at these famous actors of the past from the true point of view, when we remember those lines in which Ariosto couples Lucrezia Borgia with her Roman namesake — the Lucrece of Shakespeare.

(1)   In 1537, after Correggio's death, she published at Perugia a small volume of poems. Her husband's picture, *La Zingarella*, has been supposed to be her portrait.

There is a letter from Aretino to the Cardinal of Ravenna, dated from Venice on the 29th of March, 1549, in which he takes occasion to remind His Eminence of his promise to assist him in providing a dowry for his daughter. With Titian who painted him twice, Sansovino the architect and all the choicest and most spiritual society of the day, the author of the *Sonetti Lussuriosi* was on terms of the closest intimacy; they constantly exchanged visits, and partook of the best of good cheer. Nor did a stranger of distinction come to Venice without paying his respects to Aretino. He was one of the select group of men and women of culture which gathered round Titian, and made his musical *conversazioni* so delightful.

It is a pleasant point in connexion with Aretino, and a tribute to his social standing and weight, that, when his friend Sansovino was involved in trouble through a professional mishap, he exerted his utmost efforts in contributing to allay the official resentment and to obtain his pardon. In a case in which he was unlikely to obtain any benefit by interference, he also interceded for a poor galley-slave, who had been, as he deemed, more than sufficiently punished for committing an offence under strong temptation. (1)

(1)   Letter to Ferrante Gonzaga, 6 January 1556-1557, quoted supra.

Many of the stories about this strange, whimsical, many-sided man may be inventions or extravagances. It has been said that he boasted — perhaps only that — of being able, with a pot of ink and a quire of paper, to conjure a handsome income out of the pockets of those (Imperial majesties not excluded) who did not desire to have their weak points brought out in relief in his next Rabelaisian lampoon.

Other notable rendezvous in the *cinqicecento* era were the houses of Giorgione, Lorenzo Lotto, one of whose portraits was long ascribed to Correggio, Sebastiano del Piombo, Tintoretto and Veronica Franco, where all the artists and men of letters met, and where Aretino was in exceptional form. Both Giorgione and del Piombo were skilful musicians, and the former sang; but under the roof of Tintoretto the evenings were rendered especially attractive by the accomplishments of his daughter Marietta, and the presence of Giuseppe Zarlino the great composer. Gentile Bellini, who lived at Rialto in a handsomely decorated house where he was surrounded by places of business, seems to have less courted miscellaneous society, and to have preferred a select intercourse with the members of his own profession. Altogether, there can have been no deficiency of means, during all the best period, of making life even more than endurable; in fact, the members of these pleasant circles seldom lived to be old. If they were not all so intemperate as Aretino, they did not spare themselves.

The masters of the Venetian school counted among them many whose manly and frank independence we admire and appreciate. They were, in their way, aristocrats, and they sometimes played the part with effect and success. Tintoretto advised an intending sitter who prescribed scrupulous fidelity in rendering his habiliments, his lace and his jewellery, to go to Bassano, an animal painter; and when a distinguished party of senators and prelates once visited his studio, and remarked that he worked less carefully than one of the Bellini, the dyer's son retorted that perhaps that artist was not interrupted by such company.

Several touching personal traits of Titian and his contemporaries belong to Venetian ground, but they must be left to the biographical specialists. Such sweet and tender reminiscences, however, as that of Titian meeting Tintoretto on the Piazza, and hailing him as an honour to his art, and his exclamation on seeing the works of Correggio at Parma, "Now at length I behold a painter," are something more than common biography, and linger in the mind for ever.

Much in the private social life of this grand coterie has of course been forgotten or lost. In the *Diporti* of Parabosco, printed here before 1552, it is casually stated that Aretino and some of his friends were accustomed, at a certain time of the year, to hire huts or shanties erected at a short distance from the city, for the purpose of indulging in angling, and that, in consequence of the fact that the weather on one occasion proved inauspicious, the party decided on employing their time in the narration of a series of tales. This alleged source of the *Diporti* is a familiar invention among the earlier Italian romanticists, but for the existence of the usage it may be received as adequate authority. What a vision it raises up! In estimating the high tide of Venetian vital energy, the local atmosphere, the general costume, the hereditary training, have to be admitted into account.

At a time when the Republic was politically decadent, and had abdicated its position and pretensions as a European power, the interest in literature and the arts was still fostered both at home and abroad. A demand came from all quarters where any measure of culture existed, even for such bulky publications as the *Views* of Canaletto, and the two atlas folio volumes of 1720 containing engravings from the masters of the Venetian school.

Among the archives of the Holy Office, occurs under 1573 the *viva voce* examination of the very distinguished Venetian painter Paolo Cagliari, detto Veronese, then residing in the parish of San Samuele, on account of certain alleged improprieties in a picture of the Last Supper, which he had just executed on commission for the refectory of the Monastery of Santi Giovanni e Paolo. The particulars are curious and piquant, looking at the chief person concerned, (1) and the case is one almost standing alone.

(1)   Yriarte, *La Vie d'un Patricien de Venise au Seizieme Siecle,* page
        161.

The Holy Office usually consisted of the Metropolitan of Venice, the
Papal Nuncio, an ecclesiastic, termed Father Inquisitor, who represented
the Holy See, and three laymen on the part of the Republic, denominated
Savii all'Eresia. These are the particulars:

> "Proces-verbal of the Sitting of the Tribunal of the Inquisition,
> Saturday, the 18th of July 1573."

> The painter was, first of all, formally asked what his name was,
> and what his employment, and then the interrogatories
> commenced, by the Father Inquisitor pointing out, as a strange
> circumstance, that one of the attendants in the picture had his
> nose blood-stained, and carried a bandage on his face; and,
> farther, an explanation was solicited of the men-at-arms in
> German costume, with halberds in their hands and in a state of
> intoxication. The tribunal invited his attention to Saint Peter
> carving a lamb, and another apostle holding a plate or dish to
> receive a slice, while a third is picking his teeth with a fork.

> "We painters," rejoined Veronese, "take the same liberties as
> fools and antics do, and I have represented these halberdiers, one
> drinking, the other eating, at the foot of a ladder, both prepared,
> at the same time, to perform their duties, for it appears to me
> proper and possible that the master of the house, a rich and
> magnificent signore, as they tell me, should have such
> attendants."

> "Has some one directed you to paint Germans, buffoons and
> nude figures in this picture — one buffoon with a paroquet on
> his fist?"

> "No; but I had instructions to put in ornamental accessories, as I
> thought fit, and when in a canvas I have some spare room, I
> embellish it with inventions."

> "Is it not the case that the decorative details, which you painters
> are accustomed to introduce, have to offer some direct relation to
> the subject, or are they left wholly to your fancy and discretion?"

"I execute paintings with full consideration of the spirit which seems to belong to them, and to be necessary to make them intelligible."

"Do you not know," put the Father Inquisitor, "that in Germany and other places, where heresy is rife, they have a way, by painting pictures full of fooleries, to expose to ridicule the practices of the Holy Catholic Church, and spread false doctrine among the ignorant and senseless?"

"I agree that it is a bad thing to do; but I must tell you, that I have ever deemed it my duty to follow in the steps of my instructors," — and the speaker cited Michael Angelo and the Sistine Chapel. — "No," said he, "most illustrious lords, I do not pretend to prove that my work is decent; but I did not think that I was doing any harm. I had not reflected, and I did not foresee so much irregularity."

The tribunal deliberated; and the upshot was that the great artist was requested to make alterations, for which purpose three months were allowed him. It is remarkable that this work was intended for the Convent of Santi Giovanni e Paolo; and Veronese had already treated the same subject for other religious fraternities in Venice, apparently without comment. It was a large canvas, 39 feet by 7, and is now in the Louvre, having been presented by the Signory to Louis XIV. It exhibits the result of the citation before the Inquisitors in 1573; Veronese signs the changes made with a protest as to their impropriety, for which he would give his reasons on a future occasion. Where a harrier was in the original design, he has inserted a Magdalen.

We remember that the Roman authorities overhauled in a somewhat similar manner the *Essays* of Montaigne, which they found among that author's luggage, and ended by leaving the revision of passages to which they objected to his own discretion.

Giambattista Tiepolo (1696-1770) has been regarded and described as the last of the long series of artists of the Venetian school, and he resembled his predecessors, at least, in his versatility, for we have from his hand memorials or records of his genius in many classes of work indicative of a successful and prosperous career. He was at once an art decorator, etcher, engraver and portrait-painter, (1) and there is a considerable survival of his labours in all these departments. His engravings and etchings embrace secular and scriptural subjects; he executed a series of eighteen prints from the works of Marco Ricci, and, as in this undertaking he assisted another artist, it may have been an early effort.

(1)   There is in the Maidstone Museum a portrait in oils by him of Antonio Riccobuono.

A later painter of Venetian origin was Rosalba Carriera of Chioggia, who was famous for her crayon miniatures which conferred on her a European reputation, and who also succeeded in portrait. To her we owe the charming likeness in the Dresden Gallery of La Moceniga alle Perle, and in the same collection that of Caterina Sagredo Bragadino in which similar accessories are conspicuous. Nor should we overlook the portraits by Pietro Longhi, including those of the Cavaliere Tron, Matilda da Ponte Quirini, and her daughter Maria Quirini Benzon.

When the English traveller Joseph Spence was at Venice about 1740, he saw La Signora Carriera, or Signora Rosalba as he calls her, and records a conversation which he had with the lady. He makes her say: "The eyes are everything. When some one observed to me, that a picture was like in everything but the eyes; my answer was; 'then it is not like at all.' Everything I do seems good to me just after I have done it, and perhaps for seven or eight hours afterwards. I have been so long accustomed to study features, and the expressions of the mind by them, that I know people's tempers by their faces. I was always imitative in everything, as far back as I can remember. As to painting, in particular, I began with miniature; and it was a good while before I drew any portrait the size of life. That Magdalen is a very fine one! If you observe it, 'tis not only her eyes that cry; she cries all over. (*Jusqu'au bout des doigts*, were her words). I pray in German, because that language is so energetic and expressive. The German painters are not so genteel (*valenthuomini*) nor so good as the French. I have seen but very little of Sir Godfrey Kneller's. There is a Mocenigo, done by him here at Venice; that is a very good piece ... I concluded he could not be religious, because he was not modest." (1)

(1)   Spence, *Observations, Anecdotes, and Characters, of Books and Men,* page 185-187.

These English renderings of the sentiments of the Chioggian painter have their interest, and may add something to the narrative of her career as given by Italian biographers.

A name which has been mentioned more than once, and is more intimately associated with sculpture than with painting, is that of Antonio Canova (1757-1822), a native of the village of Possagno on the Venetian terra firma, who owed the completion of his course of study and his earliest success to the discernment of Giovanni Faliero, who had observed the dexterity of the boy as a modeller, and who sent him successively to Bassano and Rome, to develop his genius and extend his experience and observation. The representative of the Signory at the Vatican at that time, the Cavaliere Zuliano, was, fortunately for the young man, a distinguished patron of art, and under such auspices Canova speedily acquired confidence and made progress in his profession.

During his protracted and brilliant career as a sculptor, which he occasionally diversified with painting as a sort of by-play, much of his time and thought was absorbed by his important undertakings in Rome, Paris and elsewhere. He evinced in many cases, however, his Venetian patriotism, and was a man superior to merely pecuniary considerations, applying his Roman pension of 3000 *scudi* to the relief of poor artists in that capital, and offering his gratuitous services when a great public object was in view, or even when it was a question of private friendship.

After his death, two governments claimed the honour of perpetuating his memory, and a statue was erected to him at Venice in 1827 and at Rome in 1833. Canova may perhaps be regarded as the last of the long and illustrious line of men of genius of the old school and type, whom the Venetian soil and atmosphere yielded, and who, so frequently in a commercial state, rose by a fine instinct above commercial considerations. Another opportunity will be taken to refer to his romantic and almost affectionate association with the famous restaurateur Florian.

CHAPTER LXVI

Luxury of the Later Venetian Life — Indulgence of the Government Toward Popular Amusements — Profusion of Public Holidays — The Regatta — Athletic Sports — Andate — Abandonment of Some of Them — Religious Ceremonies — Casini — Clubs — Theatres, Opera-Houses — Prodigality — The Carnival — Mountebanks — Masks — Gaming-Tables — Dice — The Ridotti — The Cafe Florian — Outdoor Sports — Fencing — Street-Music — Evening Resorts and Resources of the Working Classes — Theatrical Life — Sior Antonio Rioba — Magic — Country-Houses — Popular Excursions — The Garanghelo or Women's Holiday.

When we look at the profligacy and exuberant gaiety of the later and feebler Venetian life, we conceive surprise at the princely display and exorbitant disbursements of an aristocracy which no longer possessed the old channels of wealth and the former financial elasticity. The amounts expended on entertainments in the eighteenth century, especially when we take into account the higher value of money, strike us as very large, with all our own modern proneness in a similar direction in special circumstances. The municipal splendour of London appears to be eclipsed by that of a private Venetian nobleman who had fifty retainers at his call. The secular and religious *fetes* — the ball, the masquerade, the regatta, with the pomp and expense attendant on marriages among the upper classes, tended to promote trade and to popularize the government — at a cruel and a serious cost. Those were days never to return throughout the world's whole history, when the wife of a Contarini, dancing with a king, let her priceless pearl necklace fall, and her husband, stepping forward, crushed it beneath his feet, lest it should disturb the harmony of the proceedings, or induce the suspicion that the loss of a few thousand ducats was a matter of the slightest consequence. It was the intoxication of vanity.

The severest political tension and peril — the crisis when half Europe was in arms against them in 1509 — did not hinder the Venetians from organizing the most sumptuous and costly pageants in celebration of some marriage or other important event. The oligarchical government seems to have shrunk from restraining the love of splendid gaiety among the younger aristocrats, while the funds so squandered might have proved of essential public utility.

One of the points of policy, indeed, observed more and more by the government under the oligarchical principle, was the extension of indulgence to the subjects of the Republic in all matters relating to recreations and amusements, if no constitutional question was involved or implied; and, as time went on, pleasure was pursued on this ground in every conceivable form. But, apart from private entertainments which often, in the middle and later periods, acquired a degree of sumptuous splendour elsewhere unparalleled, both in the appointments of the table or salon and in the apparel and decorations of the guests, there were manifold diversions open either to the richer and more fashionable members of the community or to the people at large. For the former, the regatta, the masked ball, the opera, the theatre, the puppet show and the pantomime gradually constituted an ample opportunity of bestowing hours of leisure. For the latter, there was a tolerably frequent recurrence of popular festivals and sports, characterized by coarse and boisterous humour, and by the barbarous and brutal temper yet incidental to such matters, but here advisedly left unmolested by the police unless there was the strongest cause to the contrary.

Several historical anniversaries furnished the opportunity for popular holidays, which helped to reconcile the mass to the loss of their voice in the direction of public affairs, and, among pastimes in which all classes more or less joined as spectators, were tournaments on the Piazza of Saint Mark, and bull baitings, prize fights, wrestling matches, acrobatic feats (*forze d'Ercole*) and equestrian exhibitions on two or three other public squares, all subject to official permission. During the intense frost of 1491, there was an equestrian joust on the Grand Canal, in which certain Estradiots took part, and which the ex-queen of Cyprus, Caterina Cornaro, honoured by her presence. (1)

(1)   Molmenti, *La Storia di Venezia nella Vita Privata,* Liber I page
        205-218.

The public regatta, one of the most important of Venetian pastimes, is of
unascertained antiquity, but it may safely be referred back to the middle
of the thirteenth century. A regatta and a water *fete* were among the
festivities which attended the coronation of Lorenzo Tiepolo in 1268. In
the Latin poem on the Marian Games, written about the year 1300, (1) it
is said that two boats propelled with oars were then usually appointed to
run a course along the Grand Canal, and that whichever won the race or
received honourable mention gained a prize. On the 14th of September,
1315, a decree of the Great Council ordered that an annual regatta should
henceforth be held on the Feast of the Conversion of Saint Paul (the 25th
of January), with vessels of fifty oars, and the superintendence of the
necessary arrangements was committed to the Masters of the Arsenal.
The boats generally employed on these occasions appear to have been
galleys, but it may be collected from the wording of the Great Council
minute, that the rule in this respect was not strict.

(1)   Letter of E.A. Cicogna to Cleandro, Count of Prata, respecting
        certain Venetian regattas, public and private. Prata, *La Regata di
        Venezia: Composizione Poetica in Dialetto Veneziano,* page 17.

The plausible notion that the canal races were instituted for the first time
in 1300 by the Doge Gradenigo, as one of the methods of reconciling the
people with the recent loss of their political liberty, is disproved by the
manifestly superior antiquity of the custom. It is highly probable indeed
that the regatta was originally nothing more than an occasional recreation
or a grand holiday entertainment, and that the earlier experiments were as
rude as they were intermittent. But it seems to be barely likely that the
Republic remained long a stranger to a class of spectacle which was so
thoroughly congenial with the national instincts, and which was so
admirably calculated to excite and gratify the emulation of the seamen
and gondoliers. (1)

> *"El Decreto xe sta quelo,*
> *Che le Feste ha comandae*
> *Per le spose de Castelo*
> *Che xe stade rescatke.*
>
> *"Su le prime no ghe gera*
> *Chi la pompa avesse in cuor:*

Tuto stava in dar bandiera
A chi gera vincitor.

"Ma col tempo sta spetacolo,
Che xe pur original,
Deventa xe assae magnifico,
Veramente nazional."

(1)   Prata, *La Regata di Venezia: Composizione Poetica in Dialetto*
         Veneziano.

The regatta was accompanied by athletic sports and other games,
including water polo, in which the populace divided themselves into two
parties, the Nicolotti and the Castellani, a dim and vague recollection of
an old feud which arose in the fourteenth century, by reason of a disputed
claim for mortuaries from the Bishop of Castello. In 1764, the
anniversary was observed on the 4th instead of the 1st of March, on
account of the weather. A letter from Venice describes what occurred:

> "On the 4th of this month the Doge and Senators repaired to the
> balcony of the Ducal Palace in the square of Saint Mark; which
> place was crowded with spectators, most of them masked; and
> there was performed the usual ceremony of striking off the heads
> of three bulls at one blow. After this operation, a man, mounted
> on a sort of dragon, rose from the sea, and flew along a rope to
> the gallery of the Tower of Saint Mark, throwing *sonate* among
> the people as he passed. From thence he made a rapid progress,
> by means of another rope, to the balcony of the Doge, to whom
> he presented a nosegay and some verses; he afterwards mounted
> by the same rope to the cupola, and then returned to the sea. The
> two factions of the Castellani and Nicolotti afterwards amused
> the people with feats of balancing, morris dancing &c." (1)

(1)   (compilation) *Willis's Current Notes,* March 1856.

But they also had their yearly sport on the Ponte dei Carmini, where the
two opposing forces struggled to cross the bridge, and a certain number
on either side were inevitably ducked. All these manly and healthy
exercises, in which foreign visitors were not debarred from joining,
helped to form a nursery for the stout fellows who were engaged for the
navy and marine. Among the aquatic diversions introduced at the
splendid coronation of the Dogaressa Morosini-Grimani in 1597, was a

tilting-match with lances between certain Englishmen who happened to be in the city.

THE CASTELLANI AND NICOLOTTI GAMES
(Photograph by Donald Macbeth, London)

The system of anniversaries and *andate* became so frequent and onerous, that two or three celebrations were gradually blended. It was judged, no doubt, that such later episodes as the Battle of Lepanto, and the heroic achievements of the Venetian commanders in the Greek and Turkish waters, as well as by land, were not merely deserving of honourable and grateful commemoration, but that the displays of patriotic enthusiasm, renewed from season to season, contributed to foster a public spirit and encourage emulation. The day of Lepanto, for which the silver *giustina* in its several varieties was specially struck, continued to be held in remembrance for some time; all classes took part in it, and the Merceria was roofed from Saint Mark's to Rialto with blue cloth spangled in imitation of stars. It was a kind of grand bazaar and *fete* at which the usual diversity of amusements and religious observances was to be seen, and where a multitude of objects was on sale, from a string of beads or a bunch of grapes to a Titian or a Tintoretto.

Of all these joyous spectacles, two only survived the Austrian occupation — that of the Redentore on the Giudecca (the third Sunday of July), and that of the Salute on the Grand Canal. Both of these were of comparatively recent origin, the churches themselves having been erected in 1578 and 1630, respectively, as tokens of gratitude for deliverance from attacks of the pestilence. There were a few other periodical ceremonies and processions, but there was ever a drift into increased languor and insignificance.

Even the purely religious ceremonies, which were of sufficiently frequent recurrence, attracted a vast concourse of spectators, and formed part of the general plan for occupying the public mind in its hours of leisure or relaxation. "So long have I lived," says Martino da Canale, whose very precious chronicle extends only from 1267 to 1275, "in beautiful Venice, that I have seen the processions which Messer the Doge makes upon high festivals, and which he would not on any account omit to make each year." He proceeds to depict that celebrated on Easter Day, when the Doge, holding a waxen taper, went with his suite to Saint Mark's, and his attendants held over his head the umbrella which had been given to him by Monsignor the Apostle, or in other words the Pope, and carried the sword of state at his side. This particular celebration was before 1268, in the time of Reniero Zeno, who was probably unaware that observant eyes were carefully registering whatever he did or said worth noting.

The Festa delle Marie appears to have been among the earliest to drop. It was the celebration of the rescue of the Brides of Venice from the pirates of Narenta in the tenth century. At first the usage was probably observed with a moderate degree of display and expenditure, but, in 1008, the Doge Orseolo II. left rather ample funds for the continuance of the anniversary. Da Canale relates that, in his time, the Brides of Venice were accustomed to wear robes of cloth-of-gold, and gold crowns or coronets set with jewels, and that all the guests were regaled with wine and sweetmeats. Perhaps it was then that the oranges were added and that malmsey was introduced, but neither could very easily have made part of the original oblation by the Casemakers Guild.

The discontinuance of the festival did not interfere with the yearly visit of the Doge to Santa Maria Formosa. But the costly character which the pageant itself had assumed combined with the grave aspect of public affairs about 1378, to induce the government to suppress it. Probably the step was partly recommended by a fatal casualty in the year just mentioned, when one of the barques containing the girls foundered near Murano.

As recently as 1902, the anniversary of the translation in the eleventh century of San Gherardo Sagredo, a Venetian by birth, and Bishop of Csanad in Hungary, to the Church of our Lady at Murano, was celebrated by a festival upon the water, but the proceedings were comparatively formal and ineffusive, as unlike those of the old time as the whole of the environing costume.

The Republic had, in 1408, instituted at Padua what was termed a *Casino*, which was in reality a social club to enable men of the better class to meet and converse. We do not hear of any anterior recourse to this sort of provision, but such establishments multiplied at a later period, and their designations sufficiently indicate their distinctive character and aim. There were the *casini* for the nobles, for merchants, for literary men, for philosophers; the house for consular representatives domiciled at Venice; the *filodrammatico*, the *filarmonico*, of the *intraprendenti*, the Casino of the Hundred denoting the limit of membership, and the Casino de Vecchij. These manifold resorts evince phases of life in the city, even when certain enervating agencies had lowered the moral tone, outside and above the doubtless too prevailing elements of frivolous and profligate gaiety, and deserve to be taken into account when we estimate the general tenor of the Venetian life and thought of the seventeenth and eighteenth centuries. It was in these more or less intellectual centres, in common with the institutes and academies devoted to the fine arts, and often founded and upheld by private subscriptions and open to the public, that we must suppose all the culture and taste, even down to late times, to have been fostered and promoted.

The clubs of Venice were, of course, like our own, viewed as lounges or occasional haunts. Some, as the Bragora, were used as resorts for public dinners or for entertainments which it was inconvenient to hold at home, or were political, like the Murazzi, instituted in 1774 to promote certain novel ideas imbibed from France and Germany.

The city was, in the more modern days, amply furnished with theatres, opera-houses and other institutions of a less exalted and classical type, for the performance of pantomimes, marionette shows, and other more popular diversions. At the regular theatrical establishments, the comedies of Gozzi and Goldoni long enjoyed a far more than local celebrity. The musical melodrama or spectacle founded on classical legends was constantly produced at the Grimano, Cassano and other houses in the seventeenth and following centuries, and was committed to the press under distinguished native or foreign patronage.

A state which had existed and flourished during so many ages, and which carried out the principles of civil government to approximate perfection, long survived, without conspicuous change, the debilitating effects of geographical discovery, of new political complications, and of new commercial ideas. Down to the middle of the eighteenth century, life among the aristocracy continued to be an almost interrupted course of splendid and licentious pleasure, contrasting with the soberer manners of happier and greater times. In the more fashionable quarters of the city, there was much that might be curious and instructive, yet much that pointed to the inevitable end of the decadent spendthrift, of the thoughtless, ostentatious prodigal.

The account is a *coup d'oeil* of what we may conclude to have been observable at Venice in the sixteenth and in the earlier half of the seventeenth century. Many of the great families had accumulated large fortunes, and some continued to hold their ground. There was altogether a vast amount of wealth, but the earning power began to fail when the Portuguese, Dutch and English successively, and to a certain extent concurrently, absorbed more and more the trade long enjoyed as a monopoly by the Italians.

In common with nearly all powers which have lived long enough to amass riches and their infallible incidence, Venice, in the last days of her independent existence, displayed, side by side with public pusillanimity and private degradation, some brilliant exceptions under both categories, as well as traits which wear the aspect of inconsistency and waywardness. We are supplied with several almost touching instances of the survival of the ancient heroism and dignity in private life.

Napoleon stigmatized the Venetians in 1797 as *polissons*; there were such as deserved the epithet, no doubt, and the great soldier could have found an abundance in Paris. Yet to the last there was an element of patriotism and pride, and the last of the Doges only removed his bonnet and gave it to an attendant, with "I shall need it no longer," when he saw that the force brought to bear was overwhelming; he was the uncle of that Manin who led the struggle for the recovery of freedom in 1848. The naval glory of Venice, after all, far eclipsed that of France, and her military achievements were not insignificant.

But if we desire to study an epoch when Venetian glory was yet uneclipsed, and when the history of the Republic is to be read in the biographies of a few of her citizens, we have to go back to the century preceding that of the French Revolution, to the days when the magnificent exploits in arms of Mocenigo and Morosini more than vied with the noblest and bravest achievements of the Dandoli, Zeni and Loredani of brighter times, and when the aristocracy, as a body, was yet sensible of the value of personal decorum and etiquette. The reply of the noble Contarini, descendant of Doges and of a house coeval with the first settlement in the lagoons, who, when the Duke of Savoy at a public reception in 1667 offered to salute her on the arm, repulsed him with the observation, that His Highness would not find such behaviour acceptable at Venice, though it might be at Turin, bespeaks a spirit aspiring to emulate at home the heroism of her countrymen fighting against the Ottomans, and striving to win back lost empire and ebbing renown.

Yet, in a narrative written by an English gentleman at the court of the Stuarts, it is said that, when some untoward incident occurred, disarranging his dress at a masque, the Venetian ambassador severely chastised his wife who laughed in common with other ladies, because, although such a matter might awaken mirth at Venice, it was not considered decorous in England to betray observation of a contretemps of that kind. (1)

(1)   Atkyns, *Vindication of Richard Atkyns Esq.,* page 14.

The ruinous expense of the war in Candia did not prevent the Carnival in 1646 from being observed with unabated licence and display. Evelyn, who describes the winter of 1645-1646 as very severe, went over from Padua to Venice at Shrovetide, as he says, to see the folly and madness: "the women, men, and persons of all conditions disguising themselves in antic dresses, with extravagant music and a thousand gambols, traversing the streets from house to house, all places being then accessible and free to enter. Abroad, they fling eggs filled with sweet water, but sometimes not over-sweet. They also have a barbarous custom of hunting bulls about the streets and piazzas, which is very dangerous, the passages being generally narrow. The youth of the several wards and parishes contend in other masteries and pastimes, so that it is impossible to recount the universal madness of this place during this time of license. The great banks are set up for those who will play at bassett; the comedians have liberty, and the operas are open; witty pasquils are thrown about, and the mountebanks have their stages at every corner."

Howell, writing on Ash Wednesday, 1654, to Richard Baker, tells a story of a Turkish ambassador who informed his friends on his return from Venice, that the Christian hath a kind of ashes, which he sprinkles over his head on that day to cure him of the madness which had taken possession of him the day before. Not only were shops and private dwellings liable to invasion by the maskers, but the floor of the Great Council saloon itself was thronged with them at this season.

An English traveller (1) of the early part of the eighteenth century lets us know that, during the Carnival, any woman found alone and masked might be solicited. Byron, writing to Hoppner from Ravenna, on the 31st of January, 1820, simply describes the Carnival there as "less boisterous."

(1)   Marcel, *Travels,* page 104.

The allusion of Evelyn to bull-baiting in the streets is confirmed by one of the plates of Giacomo Franco's book, (1) probably published in 1609, in which a lady in costume is represented as engaged in this sport, and a dog is fastening on him. The incident takes place in a particularly confined area. A second bull waits to be let loose, a lady and her male companion holding him in, while a second man keeps a dog in check till a signal is given.

(1)   Franco, *Habiti d'Hvomini et Donne Venetiane.* One of the plates is dated 1597.

We have, in the pages of Coryat, a volume prepared from notes made at Venice, an excellent account of the mountebanks (from *monta in banco*), who used to give performances twice a day, in the morning and afternoon, in two different parts of the city. They all mounted a stage, variously attired, some like fools, others like women, or in character; Coryat tells us that there were women among them. The exhibition was accompanied by music, vocal or instrumental. The chief actor delivered an address, describing the marvels which he had to offer. When our author was a spectator on one occasion, they had a viper which was the lineal descendant of that mentioned by Saint Paul. No description or form of charlatanry seems to have been overlooked, and the prices demanded were retrograde, sometimes descending from ten crowns to a few pence, like the clown's nine-pence. The chief commodities were oils, foreign waters, amorous printed songs, apothecary's drugs; the amorous songs remind us of Shakespeare's Autolycus. (1)

(1)   The adoption of the full Venetian breeches by the local low comedian was almost certainly the source whence the somewhat analogous artist on the English stage in the sixteenth century derived his wide slops.

It is a sort of accepted notion that the pantaloon of the comic stage germinated in Venice, and that the name is a derivation from San Pantaleone, a saint of local repute, who thus became the godfather, not of the individual, but of the strange breeches and hose in one, by which this *dramatis persona* has always been distinguished. The etymology is at least dubious; the liberty taken with the saint awakens distrust. (1)

(1)   Webb, *The Heritage of Dress,* page 212.

There is an account of the festivities in celebration of Saint Mark's Day in 1680-1681, which were attended and enjoyed by the Doge, the Senate, the Executive, the Imperial ambassador and about 50,000 spectators. Among other novelties, a butcher with a Persian scimitar cut off at one continuous blow the heads of three bullocks. But an even more marvellous exploit was that of a man, who ascended by a rope 600 feet long from the Quay to the top of Saint Mark's, mounted on a white horse, and twice saluted the Doge and company — once when he had arrived half-way up, and once while he sat on the golden angel at the summit, having left his horse in the bell-tower. This feat seems stupendous, yet the extant engravings of the Giuoco di Forze in its various early types shew a surprising degree of skill.

So inordinately bent on the anniversary were the great body of the people, and so commercially advantageous was the concourse of visitors from the terra firma, that, although the death of the Doge Renier occurred on the 18th of February, 1789, the event was not officially published till the second of the following month. Nothing came amiss at such a season.

SCENE AT A CARNIVAL
(Photograph by Donald Macbeth, London)

In 1751, the old rhinoceros, which had been brought to Europe in 1741 and had been exhibited in numerous places, was shipped hither, and was, no doubt, a leading attraction at the festival. The animal was said to weigh 5000 pounds. A medal was struck, commemorating so signal an occurrence, but the Venetians had had a previous experience of the kind, when a specimen was imported in the fourteenth century, perhaps for transit elsewhere. The daily rations of the later visitor must have proved a serious deduction from the profits of his exhibitors.

There is a curious illustration of the Carnival, as it was celebrated at a posterior date, in the unique series of coloured porcelain figures, so contrived as to be at pleasure united or separated, executed, as it is supposed, by Kandler for the royal china factory at Dresden. This singular production, now exceedingly rare in a complete state, extended to about one hundred pieces, and represented *Boeuf Gras* escorted by figures in the form of cupids, and intended to personify trades and professions. Two carts, each drawn by four horses and full of masked personages, accompanied the procession, and the central object, when the whole was in order, was a large clock with rococo scrolls. (1)

(1)   Chaffers, *Marks & Monograms on European and Oriental Pottery & Porcelain, 1903,* page 478.

The practice of disguising the features by the assumption of masks and fanciful costumes was evidently an old one, when restrictions were imposed on its use for improper purposes in 1339. It seems to have been more or less usual for disorderly characters to cause annoyance and scandal in this way, by pervading the city at all hours of the night and early morning. (1) But at a later period, and when Coryat was here, the mask was customary among the courtezans who occupied the galleries of the theatre, and no one dared to remove or raise it. Subsequently it became the rule even for ladies to go masked.

(1)   Romanin, *Storia Documentata di Venezia,* Volume II page 3 note. The same experience survives, to some extent, at the present day, as I have been informed, although I did not personally witness it.

De la Haye who was at Venice about 1660 remarks: "At their Masques they (the ladies] have a particular care of refusing their hand to no body, lest it should prove some Gentleman in Masquerade, which amongst them would be an inexpiable affront. At these meetings they place themselves all in a rowe, without speaking a word, and when they are taken out to dance, one must have a special care he does it not with his glove off; if he does, he not only runs a hazard of an affront, but to be pistol'd or stabb'd. Their Dance is nothing but a grave and stately motion from one room to another, till at last they return to the place from whence they were taken." (1)

(1)   De la Haye, *The Policy and Government of the Venetians: Both in Civil and Military Affairs,* page 70-71.

This description of amusement lasted down to modern times; but private entertainments were gradually superseded by the *Ridotti*, places for dancing, card-playing and so on, one of which was situated at San Moise, where public *bals masques* were formerly held so many times a week in the winter. In the *Cries of Venice*, the *codega* with a lantern is guiding two gentlemen with masks to an entertainment of this sort. It is some criterion of the growth of artificial life, rather than of the waywardness of official arrangements, that, in 1339, it was as illegal to wear masks abroad, as, toward the close of the scene, it became to expose the features in places of public assembly.

The mask also played a leading and indispensable part in the low comedy placed on the stage in the eighteenth century, and was indeed a far more influential feature in the performance and in comic action than it is in the modern theatre. It was found to be a valuable accessory to the broad and coarse humour relished by Venetian audiences and spectators. The government held, moreover, that it had the collateral merit of concealing identity, when ladies of family thought fit to frequent these performances, for, in 1776, (1) the Decemvirs interdicted women of rank and honest repute from going to the theatre unmasked.

(1)   Romanin, *Storia Documentata di Venezia,* Volume VI page 186.

It is therefore no matter for surprise, that the supply of these adjuncts proved, as time advanced, a large and profitable industry, and the shop of the dealer was stocked with an ample variety of masks adapted for all occasions and tastes. (1) Even beggars wore them; perhaps to disguise their identity or conceal their humiliation; and medical men thought them, with certain special appliances, safeguards from infection when they visited patients in a season of plague.

(1)   Molmenti, *La Storia di Venezia nella Vita Privata,* Liber III page 200, 202.

Evelyn, who had seen the ordinary masquerades at Venice when he went abroad in earlier life, remarks in his *Diary* under 1650, that that at Paris "was very fantastic; but nothing so quiet and solemn as I found it at Venice."

The Venetian was the forerunner of his fellows in modern Europe at the gaming table — nearly the most fascinating and most destructive of all recreations and passions. Venice was to the eighteenth century what Homburg and Monte Carlo are to this, and some of the casinos were entirely dedicated to the object. Visitors and victims from all parts flocked hither to make or leave their fortunes; certain Venetians sought amid these scenes to retrieve their fallen prosperity and affluence, and perhaps parted with the last wreck of their family estates. What is immeasurably sadder — there were to be seen, officiating as croupiers at the faro tables, descendants of men who had sat in the Doge's chair, and who bore the most illustrious names in the Republic. The public lottery was yet another form of speculation.

Dice appear to have been in vogue tolerably soon; in fact, all these conventional accessories must have reached the lagoon from one or other of the numberless sources of communication, while, in the absence of collateral references, their arrival and use are often apt, from their very familiarity, to be post-dated. This particular amusement, known all over the world, is by some supposed to have conferred a new name on the Ponte del Malpasso or dei Malpassi, subsequently called the Ponte dei Dai or dei Dadi, and by the historian Sabellico, Tesserarum Pons.

Under the earlier designation, it plays a part in the Quirini-Tiepolo conspiracy of 1310. The election of a Doge in 1229 was embarrassed by the equal division of the forty votes between two candidates, and the tradition is, that recourse was had to the law of chance. No particulars are given. Did the grave fathers toss the dice box? A good deal is heard in posterior times of rules and orders in regard to this pastime, which was forbidden within a certain radius of the Ducal Palace.

The *ridotto* is associated by the Sieur de la Haye with a place where cards and gaming as well as dancing were carried on. "They have," says he, "certain places on purpose which they call Redotti, where they meet, and dispose of several hours without speaking a word. Their success is never known by their behaviour, for they win and lose, receive and part with their money with the same temper and indifference." But he adds just after, that one of their chief places of meeting was at a Senator's house, where they always had one of their judges under their eye.

This was when De la Haye was at Venice about 1660. A little farther on he proceeds to observe: "You shall see fifty or threescore Ladies about a long Table, shuffling and managing the Cards with as much silence as they were Statues, and losing their money with as little concernment, as their Husbands. I was many times at these meetings on purpose to have learn'd the game, but they play'd so quick, and talk'd so little, 'twas impossible I should do it." (1)

(1)   De la Haye, *The Policy and Government of the Venetians: Both in Civil and Military Affairs,* page 65, 71-72.

Evelyn had previously noticed the same thing. He states that his party "went to the Ghetto di San Felice, to see the noblemen and their ladies at bassett, a game at cards which is much used; but they play not in public, and all that have inclination to it are in masquerade, without speaking one word, and so they come in, play, lose or gain, and go away as they please. This time of licence is only in Carnival and this Ascension week."

Chancel, who was at Venice about 1714, gives the following account:

> "When the Redotti, or Gaming-Houses, are open in Carnaval Time, prodigious Sums of Money are lost at Basset. None are admitted into these Houses but such as are mask'd. The Nobles keep the Bank, and relieve one another from Morning till Night, who seem but little concern'd when they lose a Thousand Shekins by one Card, no more than when they win but one by another. I have seen the Bank broke twice or thrice; but could never see the least Sign of Discontent in the unfortunate Nobleman that kept it. They will play with the Loser upon his Word to the Value of Ten Thousand Ducats, which are always punctually paid next Morning." (1)

(1)   Chancel, *New Journey Over Europe,* page 103.

The gaming-houses remained open till the early hours of the morning, and the jaded and pallid players, gainers and losers alike, instead of going home, would, says Casanova, stroll about the quays or into the market place, where the business of the day had perhaps already commenced, or where the boats bringing the produce from various directions were arriving. Everybody knew who they were, even if they desired to have it supposed that they had risen thus betimes to enjoy the freshness of the air and the busy scene. It was a morbid, feverish appetite, as potent, in its way, and as ineradicable, as that for opium or for absinthe.

But gambling was equally rife at the country villa, where the tables were always kept ready for players, and where the comparatively harmless game of tresette, on which Morello founded a poem in blank verse in 1756, was a favourite. Was this similar to the Old English One-and-Thirty and the modern Vingt-et-un, in both of which the ace is the best card and counts eleven?

In the country, as well, no doubt, as in town, chess was occasionally a means of relieving the monotony of suburban or rural life. It had been one of the resources of the less diversified existence in the Mediaeval and Renaissance eras, and men even brought their boards into the verandah or the garden-house, and passed in this way a pleasant hour, while the villa was wholesomely and appropriately restricted to its natural costume and appurtenances, and was exempt from licentious intrusions.

In 1704, the attention of the Decemvirs was drawn to the multiplication of these *ridotti*, frequented by both sexes and a source of disorder and scandal, and it was prescribed to the Inquisitors of State to take measures for their closure. Two establishments are specified; one at the Carmini, the other at Cannaregio, but, in a later edict of the same body, and on the secret file for the 28th of February, 1743, the *ridotto* at San Moise is stigmatized as the common haunt of men and women of all ranks, even of a Procurator of Saint Mark, and others which had started in emulation or rivalry are marked for suppression.

The two principal games were basset and faro. It is particularly noticeable that the Ten in their decree on the subject discriminate between these *ridotti*, commonly called *casini*, and the true casino as it was familiar to the Republic from the fourteenth century. At a more recent date, the San Moise house itself, as if the former report on it had not taken effect, was peremptorily and definitively ordered, in a very long and detailed minute of the Great Council on the 27th of November, 1774, to be shut up, as an institution which was productive of grave scandal in a state bred up in piety and good discipline.

Thousands and tens of thousands of gold *scudi* changed hands, and two ladies lost altogether 80,000, which their husbands thought proper to pay. The Abbe Nicolo Grioni staked the very clothes on his back, and another man who did the same stayed at home in the day, and left the house at night in a suit lent him by his father.

The antiquity of the cafe, so far as Venice is concerned, has apparently to be conjectured rather than ascertained. The origin of coffee houses elsewhere is traced to the Levant, where an English traveller. Sir Henry Blount, saw them in the earlier part of the reign of Charles I. Nowhere should such institutions have obtained an earlier footing than here. They have been sufficiently abundant since the middle of the eighteenth century, and no establishment in Europe ever acquired such world-wide celebrity as that kept by Florian, the friend of Canova, and the trusted agent and acquaintance of hundreds of persons in and out of the city, who found him an unfailing source of information about everything and everybody. Persons leaving the city for a time left their cards and addresses and a clue to their movements with him; others coming to it inquired under his roof for tidings of those whom they desired to see; he long concentrated in himself a knowledge more varied and multifarious than that possessed by any individual before or since.

Venetian coffee was said to surpass all other, and the article placed before his visitors by Florian was said to be the best in Venice. Of some of the establishments as they then existed, Molmenti has supplied us with illustrations, in one of which Goldoni the dramatist is represented as a visitor, and a female mendicant is soliciting alms. So cordial was the esteem of the great sculptor for him, that, when Florian was overtaken by gout, he made a model of his leg, that the poor fellow might be spared the anguish of fitting himself with boots. The friendship had begun when Canova was entering on his career, and he never forgot the substantial services which had been rendered to him in the hour of need.

In later days, the Cafe Florian was under the superintendence of a female chef, and the waitresses used in the case of certain visitors to fasten a flower in the button hole, perhaps allusively to the name; in the Piazza itself girls would do the same thing. A good deal of hospitality is, and has ever been dispensed at Venice in the cafes and restaurants, which do service for the domestic hearth.

There were many other establishments devoted, more especially in the latest period of Venetian independence, to the requirements of those who desired such resorts for purposes of conversation and gossip. These houses were frequented by various classes of patrons — the patrician, the politician, the soldier, the artist, the old and the young — all had their special haunts, where the company and the tariff were in accordance with the guests. The upper circles of male society — all above the actually poor — gravitated hither to a man. For the Venetian of all ranks, the coffee house was almost the last place visited on departure from the city, and the first visited on his return. His domicile was the residence of his wife and the repository of his possessions; but only on exceptional occasions was it the scene of domestic hospitality, and rare were the instances when the husband and wife might be seen abroad together, and when the former would invite the lady to enter a cafe or a confectioner's shop to partake of an ice. (1) The coffee-house to a large extent was the successor of the early casino or social club, which dated from the commencement of the fifteenth century, but it did not supersede the older and poorer institution, which survived to the last, and may be said to have run parallel with the period of pronounced decline. Yet both almost equally militated against the home and the family.

(1)   Havard (*Amsterdam et Venise*) has impressively contrasted the private life of the Hollander and the Venetian.

In the latter half of the eighteenth century, we find the Council of Ten laying their hands on alleged abuses connected with the coffee houses of the metropolis, which are charged, in decrees of the 18th of December, 1775, and the 28th of December, 1776, with fostering all kinds of corruption and immorality, by harbouring women and youths, and remaining open till outrageous hours. An indirect fruit of this mischief was that the principal thoroughfares were thronged all night with loungers of both sexes, (1) and that public morals were jeopardized; the Inquisitors of State were therefore directed to eradicate this social canker.

(1)   "*Una deambulazione notturna pratticata perfino nelle ore avanzatissime della notte per tutte le pubbliche strade di questa Dominante non meno dalle femmine nostre ma dagli uomini ancora ...*" Romanin, *Storia Documentata di Venezia*, Volume VI page 188.

Outdoor recreations for all were at hand; not only those with which Venice is more closely associated, but, as we perceive, the tournament, bull baiting, which Evelyn witnessed in 1646 and in which women took part, the game of pell-mell which used to be played on the Campo San Giacomo dall'Orio, rackets and *calcio pallone* or football. In this pastime, the young patricians, casting aside their ordinary costume, attired themselves in close-fitting suits for the sake of greater freedom. Coryat describes it as he saw it played on the Campo Santo Stefano, now the Campo Morosini, in the presence of hundreds of spectators on Sunday and holy-day evenings, but it was allowed in other open spaces.

The fencing academy attracted its share of patronage, and appealed to all such as might contemplate a calling in which the use of weapons is imperative, or the contingency of a duel with rapiers, and there was a special manual of instruction for pupils. Apart from any serious application of the art, it has always been a favourite diversion, and Byron found it in the hour of sorrow a distracting solace. There were schools for the promotion of this science at Padua, Verona and other cities within the dominion.

Many of the younger sort were addicted to the pugilistic art, and down to 1705, the Campo adjoining the Church of Santa Maria del Carmine was the scene of a yearly prize ring. As many as seventy horses used to be kept in the inclosed space used as an arena for jousts at Santi Giovanni e Paolo, outside the Church of the Mendicanti. In some of the engraved series of views by Giacomo Franco occur scenes of popular recreations, in which the play was sometimes excessively rough; a bull baiting is shewn with ladies participating in the sport.

So far back as 1548, street musicians and public bands were required to obtain a licence from the Messetaria, an official department which superintended a variety of minutiae connected with the general comfort and security. In summer, when Lassels was here about 1670, they had at night, he tells us, "a world of *Montibancks, ciarlatani,* and such stuff, who together with their drudges and remedyes, strive to please the people with their little comedies, puppet playes, songs, musick, storyes, and such like buffonnerie. Its strange to see how they finde dayly either new fooling, or new fooles, not onely to heare them but even the throw them money too for such poore contentments."

He proceeds to say: "We went after dinner to see the Evening Corso at Murano, where we saw those fine Gondolas and Piottas, which we had seen waiting upon the Doge in the morneing, now rowing in state up and downe the great Canale of Murano to the sound of Trumpets; and with all the force of the branny watermen that row them. Sometimes meeting too thick in the arches of the woodden bridge here, they crack one an others Gondolas, breack one an others oares, overturne their boatmen, and are stoppt for an houre together without being able to untangle.

Embassadors themselves of Forrain Princes appeare in Corso this evening with all their bravery (five or six Gondolas all in one livery) as well as all the gallants and gentry of Venice, who appeare here this evening at Corso." (1)

(1)   Lassels, *The Voyage of Italy,* Part II page 404, 414-415.

In the *Cries of Venice* (1785), three musicians are in some public thoroughfare, one with a violin, another with a guitar, a third a vocalist. They are preceded by a boy who extends his cap for contributions, and their aspect is sufficiently lamentable.

The resorts of the working classes in Venice itself, as well as in the suburbs and outskirts, were of two leading kinds; the *bastioni* or wine shops and the *casini* or taverns, where the glass or other measure of cheap wine was accompanied by a turn at cards or some similar diversion; there were, after a while, the puppet shews and marionettes. In some of the less aristocratic quarters, games, dancing and singing served to beguile the evenings of the worker. In the sixteenth century, in Murano with a dense and thriving population, only two *bastioni* existed; in the nineteenth, with a tithe of the former inhabitants and comparatively no local industry, there are twenty.

When Mr. Howells was at Venice in 1861-1862, he found the Venetian of that day easily satisfied and amused, and no part of his book is more entertaining than that in which he sketches the theatrical life of the middle of the nineteenth century, and the admirable performances at the marionette and other puppet exhibitions, so largely and numerously attended by persons of all ranks. These spectacles were, in their essence, of long standing, and dated back even to before the time of Goldoni. At the Grimani Palace, there was formerly a miniature marionette theatre, handsomely appointed and divided into three compartments with a curtain. It is now in the Civic Museum, and has been depicted by Molmenti.

The author of *Venetian Life* speaks of the rough-hewn statue of Sior Antonio Rioba, set in the corner of an ordinary grocery near the Ghetto. "He has a pack on his back and a staff in his hand; his face is painted, and is habitually dishonoured with dirt thrown upon it by boys. On the wall near him is painted a bell-pull, with the legend, Sior Antonio Bioba. Rustics, raw apprentices, and honest Germans new to the city, are furnished with packages to be carried to Sior Antonio Rioba, who is very hard to find;" there is always a crowd of loafers near to enjoy the hoax. (1) A comic journal during the Republic of 1848 bore his name; it was then a jest of long standing — a thin one. In estimating the dependence of earlier ages on resources outside daily labour, there is always one element in the calculation; it is the absence of artificial light after nightfall, which for centuries rendered outdoor excursions impossible.

(1)   Howells, *Venetian Life,* Volume I page 225-226. A nearly identical hoax was perpetrated on the man who was sent to Tiverton in Devonshire to obtain information from Mr. Abb.

Magic and sorcery in their various forms had been familiar from a very remote date, and were called into service in a wide diversity of ways, even in winning for female serfs the affections of their employers. So, again, the Republic was not behindhand when the supernatural was reduced by the progress of science in some cases to common physical laws. In 1665, we find a notice in the *Diary* of Pepys of a feat performed at Bordeaux, in which a man was raised from the ground with the utmost ease by four little girls, the latter and the burden concurrently inflating their lungs with air; and this at a later period was more than once the source of wondering curiosity at Venice on the part of all who were not in the secret. An instance is cited in which a heavy man was thus held up on the forefingers of six persons. Such a trick would probably become a standard institution, and have its independent booth at fairs.

The wealthier classes had their country-houses both in the immediate vicinity of the city and on the terra firma, and were at liberty, in the absence of official ties, to go whither they pleased. Toward the period of the fall, open house appears to have been kept by several of the owners of these pleasances, on which the playwright and the satirist did not omit to lavish derision. But the operative, the artisan and the shopkeeper's assistant had their relaxation, and periodically made parties to go with music and refreshments on boating excursions to various points within a reasonable distance.

Working women with a mind to forget for a moment their hard lot at home took a day in the year, and started in a body from one of the places of embarkation at a very early hour, with an escort of two neighbours of mature years and of the other sex. The expense was defrayed by a weekly payment of a *quartarolo* or *obolo* to the treasurer by each intending participator in the holiday, and this jaunt was called a *garanghelo*. The women presented a gay and bright appearance in their scarlet bodices and bombazine skirts or petticoats, their snow-white linen and muslin aprons set off with as much cheap finery or jewellery as they could command, or with bouquets of flowers.

Their male relatives and friends came to carry the provisions for the day, and to see them off; their usual destination was Mestre, Lido or some place which afforded facilities for a picnic and a dance, accompanied or followed by songs and instrumental music. In the evening, they returned with the barks (*peote*) illuminated, and with all sorts of enjoyment and fun; it was the women's own day; they left, not only the men, but the children behind them.

THE END

INDEX OF CITATIONS.

by.

David Mignery.
2020.

This index represents my best effort at identifying the many authors and works cited in Hazlitt's history, The works attributed to each author are only those which are referenced in this volume, Documents are listed with "anonymous" authors when the author's name is lost to history, "Compilations" are collections of documents assembled by compilers.

Author	Particulars.
(anonymous)	*A True Report of Sir Anthony Shierlie's Journey Overland to Venice, &c.,* quarto 1600; an account of the travels of Anthony Shirley (1565 to 1635).
(anonymous)	*Ars Numerandi*; published in 1482 in Cologne.
(anonymous)	*Bulletino di Arti e Curiosita Veneziane*; unidentifiable publication. Hazlitt refers to editions published in 1877 to 1880.
(anonymous)	*Casselina, Sive Compendiolum Sacre Scripture de Brevibus et Longis Syllabis Distinctis cum Suis Accentibus*; 1525 edition, ocatavo, Venetia.
(anonymous)	*Cronaca Magna;* unidentifiable source.
(anonymous)	*Gloria Mulierum*; an unidentifiable work published by Nicolas Jenson of Sommevoire in octavo form.
(anonymous)	*Hoe Catalogue*; unidentifiable source, published in 1912.
(anonymous)	*Law's Catalogue, 1881*; unidentifiable source.
(anonymous)	*Romance of Paris and Vienna;* unidentifiable work published in 1485, reprinted in 1868.

(anonymous)   *Treatise de Recto Regimine*; unidentifiable work.

(compilation)   *A Chronicle of London*; A collection of manuscripts in the British Museum for the period 1089 to 1483, published in London in 1827.

(compilation)   *Calendar of State Papers Relating to English Affairs in the Archives of Venice*; documents originally printed by Her Majesty's Stationery Office, London 1867.

(compilation)   *Catalogus Librorum Manuscriptorum in Bibliotheca d. Thomae Phillips, Bt.;* a catalogue published by Sir Thomas Phillipps (1792 to 1872) of his famous collection of manuscripts. Hazlitt refers to a 1908 edition of the catalogue.

(compilation)   *Letters Received by the East India Company From Its Servants in the East*; 1896.

(compilation)   *Notes and Queries;* a journal for academic correspondence, established in 1849 in London under the editorship of W.J. Thoms.

(compilation)   *Ordonnances, Statutz & Instructions Royaulx,* Paris, 1538.

(compilation)   *Pearson's Magazine*; a monthly periodical published by C. Arthur Pearson, which appeared in Britain in 1896. It ceased publication in 1939.

(compilation)   *Statuta Veneta*; presumably a collection of the laws of the Venetian Republic, 1729 edition.

(compilation)   *The Antiquary;* a monthly magazine published in London from 1879 to 1915.

(compilation)   *Willis's Current Notes;* a series of articles on antiquities, biography, heraldry, history, languages, literature, natural history, curious customs, et cetera, selected from original letters and documents addressed to the publisher G. Willis during the year 1857, published in London, June 1857.

Acton   William Acton, unidentifiable author of *A New Journal of Italy*, published in 1691.

Agostini   Giovanni degli, 1701 to 1755 Venetian writer, librarian, author of *Notizie degli Scrittori Viniziani.*

Alessandri   Alessandro Alessandri (Alexandri ab Alexandro), 1461 to 1523, Neapolitan lawyer, author of *Geniales Dies*, 1532, folio edition, Parisiis.

Alfani   Gianni di Forese degli Alfani, 13th century Florentine author of *Poeti del Primo Secolo,* Firenze, 1816, octavo, 2 volumes.

Allatius   Leo Allatzes (Leone Allacci), circa 1586 to 1669, Greek scholar, theologian, keeper of the Vatican Library, editor of *Poeti Antichi.*

Amos   Andrew Amos, 1791 to 1860, British lawyer, professor of law at London University, member of the council of the Governor-General of India, Downing Professor of the Laws of England at the University of Oxford, author of *The Great Oyer of Poisoning,* 1846.

Ariosto   Ludovico Ariosto, circa 1475 to 1533, Italian poet, author of *Orlando Furioso,*

Atkyns   Richard Atkyns, 1615 to 1677, English writer on printing, author of *Vindication of Richard Atkyns Esq.*

Balbi   Gaspare Balbi, 16th century Venetian jeweller, merchant, traveller to the east from 1579 to 1588, author of *Viaggio dell' Indie Orientali,* octavo 1590.

Balfour   Andrew Balfour, circa 1634 to 1694, Scottish doctor, botanist, antiquary, book collector, author of *Letters Written to a Friend by the Learned and Judicious Sir Andrew Balfour, M.D.,* octavo edition published in 1700.

Beazley Charles Raymond Beazley, 1868 to 1955, British historian, Professor of History at the University of Birmingham, author of *John and Sebastian Cabot*, 1898, and *Prince Henry the Navigator*, octavo edition, 1895.

Blondus Flavio Blondo di Forli, 1392-1463, Italian historian, secretary to the Papal Cancellaria Apostolica under Pope Eugene IV, author of *Italia Illustrata* (1481 edition), and *De Origine et Gestis Venetorum* (1481 edition).

Blount Thomas Blount, 1618-1679, English antiquarian and lexicographer, author of *Ancient Tenures of Land*, 1874.

Boerio Giusepi Boerio, 1754 to 1832, Italian author of *Dizionario del Dialetto Veneziano*, second edition, 1856.

Bonfinius Antonio Bonfinis, 1434 to 1503, Italian humanist and poet, court historian for King Matthias Corvinus of Hungary, author of *Res Ungaricara Decades Tres*.

Bongars Jacques Bongars, 1554 to 1612, French scholar and diplomat, author and editor of *Gesta Dei per Francos*, Hanover, 1611.

Bonotriensis Nicholas Bonotriensis, Bishop, unidentifiable author of a work called *Iter Italicum Henrici Septimi, A.D. 1310-1313*, in Muratori.

Borgi Piero Borgi, circa 1424 to circa 1494, Venetian author of *Qui Comenza la Nobel Opera de Arithmetica*, 1484.

Brown Horatio Robert Forbes Brown (H.F. Brown), 1854 to 1926, Scotish historian, Churchwarden of Saint George's Church in Venice, President of the Cosmopolitan Hospital in Venice, author of *The Venetian Printing Press*, 1891.

Burton	Isabel Arundell Burton, 1831 to 1896, writer, wife of sir Richard Francis Burton, editor of his famous translation of *The Thousand and One Nights*, published as *Lady Burton's Edition of Her Husband's Arabian Nights Translated Literally from the Arabic by Sir Richard Francis Burton*.
Calandri	Filippo Calandri, unidentifiable 15th century Italian author of *Trattato di Arithmetica*, 1491, Florence.
Calogera	Angelo (Domenico Demetrio) Calogera, 1696 to 1766, Italian, Camaldolese monk, librarian of San Michele di Murano, Prior of San Giorgio Maggiore, publisher of *Spiegazione della Moneta del Doge Domenigo Michieli in Soria*.
Camocio	Giovanni Francesco Camocio, 16th century Venetian cartographer, publisher and printer, composer of *Isole Famose Porti, Fortezze, e Terre Maritime Sottoposte alla Ser. Ma Sig. Ria di Venetia*, 1571 quarto.
Cantalicio	Giovanni Battista Valentini (Cantalicio), circa 1450 to 1515, Italian humanist, author, Catholic Bishop of Atri-Penne, author of *Summa Perutilis in Regulas Distinctas Totius Artis Grammatices et Artis Metricae*, 1508, quarto, Venetia.
Caracci	Annibale Caracci, 1560 to 1609, Italian painter and instructor, composer of *Le Arti di Bologna Disegnate da Annibale Caracci ed Intagliate da Simone Guilini*.
Casola	Pietro Casola, 1427 to 1507, Catholic Canon from Milan, Cardinal Deacon of the Duomo, author of *Canon Pietro Casola's Pilgrimage to Jerusalem in the Year 1494*, edited and translated by M. Margaret Newell in 1907.
Caussin	Nicolas Caussin, 1583 to 1651, French Jesuit theorist of the passions, supposed author of a *Life or History of Mary Queen of Scots*.

Cecchetti	Bartolomeo Cecchetti, circa 1839 to 1889, Italian paleographer, co-author of *Sommario della Nuininografla Veneziana Fino alla Caduta della Repubblica*, Venice, 1866, in collaboration with Vincenco Padovan.
Chaffers	William Chaffers, 1811 to 1892, English antiquary and writer of reference works on ceramics, author, with Frederick Litchfield of *Marks & Monograms on European and Oriental Pottery & Porcelain*, 1903; and *The New Chaffers: Marks and Monograms on European and Oriental Pottery and Porcelain with Historical Notices of Each Manufactory*, 1912.
Chancel	Alexander Doriack Chancel, unidentifiable author of *A New Journey Over Europe*, 1714.
Chaucer	Geoffrey Chaucer, circa 1340 to 1400, English poet, writer, author of *The Canterbury Tales*.
Cicero	Marcus Tullius Cicero, BC 107 to BC 43, Roman statesman and orator. Hazlitt refers to his *De Officiis*, Venice 1588 folio edition.
Cicogna	Emmanuele Antonio Cicogna, 1789 to 1868, Italian writer, scholar, and book collector, author of *Saggio di Bibliografia Veneziana*, 1847. Hazlitt also refers to an unidentifiable source he calls the "Cicogna Manuscripts."
Ciotti	Giovanni Battista Ciotti, 1560 to 1625, Italian publisher and printer of *Esequie Fatte in Venetia dalla Natione Fiorentina al Serenissimo D. Cosimo II Quarto Gran Duca di Toscana Il dì 25 di Maggio 1621*.
Colonna	Francesco Colonna, 1433 to 1527, Italian Dominican monk and priest, reputed author of *Hypnerotomachia Poliphili*, 1499.
Commines	Philippe de Comines, 1447 to 1511, Flemish writer and diplomat in the courts of Burgundy and France, author of *Les Memoires de Philippe de Commines*.

Cornelio	Flaminio Cornelio (Cornaro), 1693 to 1778, Venetian historian, author of *Creta Sacra, Sive, de Episcopis Utriusque Ritus Graeci et Latini in Insula Cretae*, 1755 quarto.
Corner	Zuan Corner, unidentifiable supposed author of *Decor Puellarum*, 1471.
Correr	Gregorio Correr (Corraro), 1409 to 1464, Venetian humanist and ecclesiastic, Patriarch of Venice, author of *Progne*, 1558, and other works cited on pages 186-187.
Coryat	Thomas Coryat, circa 1577 to 1617, English traveller and writer, author of *Coryat's Crudities,* London, 1611.
Dandolo	Andrea Dandolo, 1306 or 1307 to 1354, Venetian, law professor at the University of Padua, 54th Doge of Venice, author of *Chronica Venetorum,* compiled in Muratori's *Rerum Italicarum Scriptores ab Anno Aerae Christianae 500 ad Annum 1500.*
Davies	Robert Davies, 1793 to 1875, English lawyer and antiquarian, author of *Pope; Additional Facts Concerning His Maternal Ancestry*, 1858.
De la Haye	unidentifiable author of *The Policy and Government of the Venetians: Both in Civil and Military Affairs*, English edition, 1671.
Domenichi	Lodovico Domenichi, 1515 to 1564, Italian translator of *Progne,* by Correr, 1561.
Drake	William Richard Drake, 1817 to 1890, English lawyer and collector, author of *Notes on Venetian Ceramics*, 1868.
Dunlop	Madeline Anne Wallace Dunlop, unidentifiable author of *Glass in the Old World*, 1883.

Evelyn — John Evelyn, 1620 to 1706, English writer, gardener, historian, a founding member of the Royal Society, His diary was published in 1818 under the title *Memoirs Illustrative of the Life and Writings of John Evelyn*, 1858.

Fairholt — Frederick William Fairholt, 1814 to 1866, English antiquary, wood engraver, author of *Costume in England; A History of Dress to the End of the Eighteenth Century*, 1860.

Ferretus — Vicentinus Ferretus (Ferreti), 14th century, Italian historian from Vicenza, author of *Historia Rerum in Italia Gestarum ab Anno MCCL ad Annum Usque MCCCXVIII*, in Muratori.

Filiasi — Jacopo Filiasi, 1750 to 1829, Italian historian and physician, author of *Ricerche Storico-Critiche da Giacomo Filiasi*.

Folgore — Folgore de San Gimignano, pseudonym of Giacomo di Michele, 1270 to 1332, Italian poet, author of *Sonetti de' Mesi*.

Formaleoni — Vincenzo Antonio Formaleoni, 1752 to 1797, author of *Saggio Nautica Antica de' Veneziani*.

Fosbroke — Thomas Dudley Fosbroke, 1770 to 1842, English clergyman, antiquary, author of the *Encyclopaedia of Antiquities*, 1843 edition.

Foscarini — Marco Foscarini, 1696 to 1763, Venetian poet, writer, statesman, Procurator of Saint Mark's, Doge of Venice, author of *Della Letteratura Veneziana*, 1854.

Fournier — Edouard Fournier, 1819-1880, French writer, dramatist, historian, bibliographer, librarian, author of *Le Vieux-Neuf: Histoire Ancienne des Inventions et Decouvertes Modernes,* 1877; co-author with Francisque Michel of *Histoire des Hôtelleries, Cabarets, Courtilles, et des Anciennes Communautés et Confréries d'Hôteliers, de Taverniers, de Marchands de Vins*, 1859.

Franco

Giacomo Franco, 1556 to 1620, Venetian illustrator, publisher of *Habiti d'Hvomini et Donne Venetiane*, Venice, 1609.

Galibert

Leon Galibert, unidentifiable author of *Histoire de la Republique Venise*, 1847.

Gallizioli

Giovanni Battista Gallizioli, 1733 to 1806, Venetian philosopher, Hebraist, orientalist, historian, archaeologist, philologist, Catholic priest, author of *Delle Memorie Venete Antiche, Profane et Ecclesiastiche.*

Gamba

Bartolommeo Gamba, 1766 to 1841, Venetian writer and bibliographer, editor of *Raccolta di Poesie in Dialetto Veneziano d'Ogni Secolo*, 1845, and an unidentifiable duodecimo work, 1817, in 14 volumes.

Gascoigne

George Gascoigne, 1535 to 1577, English poet, soldier, author of *The Complete Poems of George Gascoigne*, compiled by W.C. Hazlitt.

Giovanelli

unidentifiable author of *Illustrazione delle Medaglie Denominate Oselle*, folio, 1834

Giustiniani, B.

Bernardo Giustiniani, 1408-1489, Venetian diplomat, member of the Council of Ten, Hazlitt refers to an unidentifiable work called *Epistole di Bernardo Giustiniano* (suo figlio), Venice, 1492.

Giustiniani, L.

Leonardo Giustiniani, unidentifiable publisher of *Canzonette e Strambotti d'Amore Composte per el Magnifico Miser Leonardo Zustignano di Venetia. Impressum Venetiis per Johannem Baptistam Sessa, Anno Domini MCCCC(C), die vero xiiii. Aprilis, in quarto, and Comincio il Fiore delle Elegantissime Cancionete del Nobile Messere Leonardo Justiniano.* 1482, quarto edition.

Gozzi

Carlo Gozzi, 1720 to 1806, Venetian playwright, author of *Memorie Inutili.*

Gualtieri — Guido Gualtieri, 16th century, unidentifiable author of *Relationi della Venvta degli Ambasciatori Giaponesi a Roma Sino alla Partita di Lisbona: con le Accoglienze Fatte Loro da Tutti i Principi Christiani per Doue Sono Passati*, 1586.

Havard — Henry Havard, 1838 to 1921, unidentifiable author of *Amsterdam et Venise*, 1876

Hazlitt III — William Carew Hazlitt, 1834 to 1913, English lawyer, bibliographer, editor and writer, author of *Blount's Tenures of Land*, published in 1874 as a revision and expansion of the original work by Thomas Blount (see Blount); *Shakespear, Himself and His Work; The Coinage of the European Continent with an Introduction and Catalogues of Mints Denominations and Rulers*, 1893. *The Livery Companies of the City of London*, 1892; *Roll of Honor*, 1908, editor of *A Select Collection of Old English Plays*, based on the work of Robert Dodsley, 1704 to 1764,

Howell — James Howell, 1594 to 1666, Anglo-Welsh historian and writer, secretary of the Privy Council, author of *Familiar Letters,* sixth edition, Jacobs, 1688.

Howells — William Dean Howells, 1837 to 1920, American novelist, literary critic, and playwright, editor of the *Atlantic Monthly*, author of *Venetian Life,* Edinburgh, 1883.

Humphrey — Henry Noel Humphreys, 1810 to 1879, British illustrator, naturalist, entomologist, numismatist, editor of *The Illuminated Illustrations of Froissart*, London, 1845.

John — John the Evangelist, circa AD 15 to AD 100, presumed author of *The Gospel According to Saint John.*

Jusserand	Jean Adrien Antoine Jules Jusserand, 1855 to 1932, French writer and diplomat, French Ambassador to the United States during World War I, author of *La Vie Nomade et les Routes d'Angleterre au 14e Siecle*, 1884
Kennett	White Kennett, 1660 to 1728, English Bishop, author of *Parochial Antiquities*, 1818 edition, originally published in 1695,
Lacroix	Paul Lacroix, 1806 to 1884, French author, journalist, author of *Les Arts au Moyen Age et à l'Epoque de la Renaissance,* 1869.
Lalande	Joseph Jerome le Francois de Lalande, 1732 to 1807, French astronomer, freemason and writer, author of *Voyage d'un Francois en Italie*, 1790.
Lassels	Richard Lassels, circa 1603 to 1668, English Roman Catholic priest and travel writer, author of *The Voyage of Italy*. 1670.
Lazari	Vincenzo Lazari, 1823 to 1864, Italian numismatist, archaeologist, historian, author of *Le Monete dei Possedimenti Veneziani di Oltremare e di Terraferma*, 1851, octavo edition.
Liberati	Francesco Liberati, unidentifiable author of *Il Perfetto Maestro di Casa di Francesco Liberati Romano*, octavo, 1658, Roma.
Litchfield	Frederick Litchfield, 1850 to 1930, British art historian, author of *Pottery and Porcelain*, 1900.
Lovelace	Richard Lovelace, 1617 to 1657, English poet who fought in the English Civil War, author of *Lucasta,* 1659, W. Carew Hazlitt's edition, 1864.
Lucas	F.W. Lucas, unidentifiable author of a monograph, published in 1898 disputing Nicolo Zeno's account of the voyage of Caterino Zeno to North America.

Machiavelli Niccolo di Bernardo dei Machiavelli, 1469 to 1527, Italian diplomat, politician, philosopher, humanist, writer and poet, author of *History of Florence and of the Affairs of Italy From the Earliest Times to the Death of Lorenzo the Magnificent*. English edition, 1846.

Malespini Celio Malespini, 1531 to 1609, Italian author of *Dvcento Novelle*.

Malipiero Domenigo Malipiero, 1445 to 1513, Venetian naval captain, Senator, governor of various provinces, author of *Annali Veneti*.

Manin Ludovico Leonardo Manin, 1771 to 1863, Italian Conte de Polcenigo et di Fanna, author of *Illustrazione delle Medaglie dei Dogi di Venezia Denominate Oselle: Edizione Seconda con Correzioni ed Aggiunte*, 1847.

Marcel unidentifiable author of an unidentifiable work called *Travels*, 1714. Hazlitt may be referring to Chancel's *New Journey Over Europe* also published in 1714.

Medius Thomas Medius Venetus (Tommaso Mezzo), unidentifiable 15th century author of the play, *Epirota*, 1483.

Michel Francisque Xavier Michel, 1809 to 1887, French historian, philologist, co-author with Edouard Fournier of *Histoire des Hôtelleries, Cabarets, Courtilles, et des Anciennes Communautés et Confréries d'Hôteliers, de Taverniers, de Marchands de Vins*, 1859.

Molmenti Pompeo Gherardo Molmenti, 1852 to 1928, Italian writer, historian, politician, Senatore and Deputato del Regno d'Italia, author of *La Vie Privee a Venise*, 1882, the French version of his *La Storia di Venezia nella Vita Privata*, Bergamo, 1905-1908.

Monacis Lorenzo de Monacis, 14th century, Venetian diplomat and historian, Grand Chancellor of Candia, author of *Chronicon de Rebus Venetis*, Flaminio Cornaro's edition.

Montaigne   Michel de Montaigne, 1533 to 1592, French statesman, philosopher, author of the collection, *Essais*.

Morelli   Jacopo Morelli, 1745 to 1819, Venetian ecclesiastic, antiquarian, librarian, author of the following works; *Delle Solennita e Pompe Nuziali Gia Usate Presso li Veneziani*, 1793; *Dissertazione Intorno ad Alcuni Viaggiatori Veneziani Eruditi Poco Noti; Dissertazione Sulla Cultura della Poesia Presso li Veneziani*, 1796; and *Operette Ora Insieme con Opuscoli di Antichi Scrittori*.

Morgan   Thomas Morgan, 1819 to 1892, unidentifiable British archaeologist, author of *Romano-British Mosaic Pavements*, 1886.

Muratori   Ludovico Antonio Muratori, 1672 to 1750, Italian priest, archivist and librarian at the Ducal Library in Modena, Provost of St. Maria della Pomposa, author of *Annali d'Italia*.

Mutinelli   Fabio Mutinelli, unidentifiable author of *Annali Urbani di Venezia dall'Anno 810 al 12 Maggio 1797*, and *Del Costume Veneziano Sino al Scolo Decimosettimo Saggio di Fabio Mutinelli*, 1831, and *Lessico Veneto*, 1851.

Nani   Giovan Battista Nani, 1616 to 1678, author of *Storia della Repubblica Veneta*, 1662-1679.

Narrey   Charles Narrey, 1825 to 1892, French writer and playwright, editor of *Albert Durer a Venise et Dans les Pays-Bas*, 1866, octavo.

Nogarola   Isotta Nogarola, 1418 to 1466, Italian humanist writer and intellectual. Her works were collected by Sandor Apponyi (1844 to 1925) and published as *Apponyi Rariora*, 1866.

Padovan	Vincenzo Padovan, unidentifiable Italian numismatist, co-author of *Sommario della Nuininografla Veneziana Fino alla Caduta della Repubblica*, Venice, 1866, in collaboration with Bartomlomeo Cecchetti.
Paganino	Alessandro Paganino, 16th century, Italian printer and writer, author of *Raccolta de Tvtti i Ritratti & Disegni di Ricchami*, quarto.
Papadopoli	Niccolo Papadopoli Aldobrandini, 1841 to 1922, Italian banker, politician, numismatist, author of *Le Monete di Venezia Descritte ed Illustrate coi Disegni di Carlo Kunz*, 1893; *Les Plus Anciens Deniers ou Carzie: Frappes les Venetiens pour Chypre*: 1515-1518, octavo 1900; *Una Tariffa con i Disegni di Monete Stampata a Venezia nel 1517*, 1899; *Le Monete Anonime di Venezia dal 1472 al 1605*. Large octavo, Milano, 1906; *Tarifs Vénitiens Avec Dessins de Monnaies du XVIe Siècle*, octavo 1900.
Pasolini	Pier Desiderio Pasolini, 1844 to 1920, Italian author of *Caterina Sforza*, London, 1898, translation by Paul Sylvester.
Petri	Nicolaus Petri, 16th century, Dutch mathematician, astronomer, author of *The Pathway to Knowledge*, 1596, translation from the Dutch by William Phillip.
Plumpton	Edward Plumpton, 1581 to circa 1654, author of *Plumpton Correspondence. A Series of Letters, Chiefly Domestick, Written in the Reigns of Edward IV. Richard III. Henry VII. and Henry VIII*, 1839.
Polo	Marco Polo, 1254 to 1324, Venetian merchant, explorer, and writer, author of *The Book of Ser Marco Polo*, published by Sir Henry Yule; 2nd edition, 1875, translation by John Murray, 3rd edition, 1903, edited by Henry Cordier.
Pontanus	Ioannes Iovanus Pontanus (Giovanni Pontanus), 1426 to 1502, Italian humanist and poet.

Prata	Cleandro Conte di Prata, 1789 to 1868, unidentifiable author of *La Regata di Venezia: Composizione Poetica in Dialetto Veneziano*, Venice, 1856.
Rafn	Carl Christian Rafin, 1795 to 1864, Danish historian translator, antiquarian, author of *Découverte de l'Amérique par les Normands, Rapports des Normands avec l'Orient*, 1854
Raymond	John Raymond, unidentifiable author of *An Itinerary Contayning a Voyage, Made Through Italy, in The Yeare 1646, and 1647*, published in 1648.
Rohan	Henri II de Rohan, 1579 to 1638, Duke of Rohan, Prince of Leon, French soldier, writer, and Huguenot leader, author of *Voyage du Duc de Rohan, Faict en l'an 1600, en Italie, Allemaigne, Pays-Bas-Vnis, Angleterre & Escosse*, duodecimo, Amsterdam, 1646.
Romanin	Samuele Romanin, 1808 to 1861, Italian historian, professor of history at the Ateno Veneto in Venice, editor of *Storia Documentata di Venezia* and *Gli Inquisitori di Stato di Venezia*, 1858.
Sabellico	Marcus Antonius Coccius Sabellicus, 1436 to 1506, Venetian scholar and historian, professor of eloquence at Udine, curator of the Biblioteca Marciana, author of *Decades Rerum Venetarum*, 1487; *De Situ Urbis Venetae*, 1488, and *De Venetiis Magistratibus,* 1488.
Saint John	James Augustus Saint John, 1795 to 1875, British journalist, writer, traveller, author of *The History of the Manners and Customs of Ancient Greece*, 1842.
Salmon	Thomas Salmon, 1679 to 1767, English historical and geographical writer, author of *Lo Stato Presente di Tutti i Paesi, e Popoli del Mondo Naturale, Politico e Morale*, Venetia, 1740-1762, duodecimo edition in 24 volumes.

Sanudo

Marino Sanudo (Sanudo the Younger), 1466 to 1536, Venetian historian and diarist, member of the Maggio Consiglio, senator, author of *Diarii, Itinerario per la Terraferma Veneziana,* 1847 edition; and *Edificazione della Citta di Venezia* in Cicogna.

Sanudo di Torcello.

Marino Sanudo di Torcello (Sanudo the Elder), 1260 to 1338, Venetian statesman and geographer, author of *Liber Secretorum Fidelium Crucis.* His letters (*Epistolae*), are contained in Bongars' *Gesta Dei per Francos.*

Sanutus

Livius Sanutus (Livio Sanuto), circa 1520 to 1576, , Venetian geographer, cosmographer, mathematician, author of *Geografia di M. Livio Sanuto Distinta in XII. Libri,* folio edition, 1588.

Schweitzer

Federico Schweitzer, unidentifiable author of *Serie delle Monete e Medaglie d'Aquileja e di Venezia,* 1848-1852.

Seeley

L.B. Seeley, editor and publisher of *Mrs. Thrale, Afterwards Mrs. Piozzi,* 1891.

Serristori

Luigi Serristori, 1793 to 1857, Florentine economist, politician, author of *Illustrazione di Una Carta del Mar Nero del 1351,* Firenze, 1856 octavo.

Seyer

Samuel Seyer, 1757 to 1831, English schoolmaster, cleric, author of *Memoirs Historical and Topographical of Bristol and It's Neighbourhood: From the Earliest Period Down to the Present Time,* 1821-1823.

Shakerley

(Sha Kerlay), unidentifiable author of *La Guida Romana,* Rome 1562, octavo.

Shakespeare

William Shakespeare, 1564 to 1616, English poet, actor, playwright, author of the play, *The Merchant of Venice;* and *The Comedy of Errors.*

Spence   Joseph Spence, 1699 to 1768, English theologian, historian, literary scholar, Oxford Professor of History, author of *Observations, Anecdotes, and Characters, of Books and Men*, 1858 edition.

Stampa   Gaspara Stampa, 1523 to 1554, Italian poet, author of *Rime di Madonna Gapara Stampa*, 1554, octavo.

Symonds   Margaret Symonds, 1869 to 1925, author of *Days Spent on a Doge's Farm*, 1893.

Tagliente   Giovanni Antonio Tagliente, circa 1460 to circa 1528, Italian calligrapher, author, printer, publisher. Hazlitt apparently refers to an unidentifiable work called *Libro Mistevole*, quarto edition, and *Libro d'Abaco,* octavo edition, Venice.

Tajir   Sulaiman al Tajir, 9th century, Arab merchant, writer, author of *Ancient Accounts of India and China, by Two Mohammedan Travellers Who Went to Those Parts in the 9th Century*, octavo, London, 1733. Translated from the Arabic by Eusebius Renaudot.

Taylor   Edgar Taylor, 1793 to 1839, British solicitor, writer, author of *The Lays of the Minnesingers*, 1825.

Thomas   William Thomas, died 1554, Welsh scholar of Italian history and language, clerk of the Privy Council of Edward VI, author of *The Historye of Italye*, 1549, 1561 edition.

Thomsen   Christian Jurgensen Thomsen, 1788 to 1865, Danish archaeologist, first curator of the National Museum of Denmark, author of *Les Monnaies du Moyen-Age*, Copenhagen, 1874

Tommaseo   Niccolo Tommaseo, 1802 to 1874, Italian linguist, journalist, writer, author of *Canti del Popolo Veneziano Raccolti (per la prima volta)*, 1848.

Trevisani   Zaccharia Trevisani de Venetiis, unidentifiable author of *Oratoris Illustrissimi Ducalis Dominii Venetiarum ad Gregorium XII, Pontificem prò Unione S. Ecclesia Dei Conficienda Oratio,* 1407, *Ejusdem ad Dominum Ariminensem pro Integratione Ecclesiae,* 1409; *Ejusdem in Refutatione Officii Capitanae Almas Civitatis Paduae,* 1406.

Vecellio   Cesare Vecellio, 1521 to 1601, Italian engraver, painter, publisher of *De gli Habiti Antichi e Modérni di Diversi Parti di Mondo,* 1590.

Vowell   John Vowell (John Hooker), 1527 to 1601, English historian, writer, solicitor, antiquary, civic administrator, Chamberlain and Member of Parliament for Exeter, author of *The Life and Times of Sir Peter Carew*, 1857 edition by Maclean.

Warton   Thomas Warton, 1728 to 1790, English literary historian, critic, poet, Poet Laureate of England, Professor of Poetry at Oxford University, Camden Professor of History, author of *History of English Poetry From the Twelfth to the Close of the Sixteenth Century,* 1871 edition edited by William Carew Hazlitt (see Hazlitt III).

Webb   Wilfred Mark Webb, 1868-1952, English lecturer on biology and nature study, writer, author of *The Heritage of Dress,* 1912.

Wheatley   Henry Benjamin Wheatley, 1838 to 1917, British author, editor, indexer, Assistant Secretary to the Royal Society of Arts, President of the Samuel Pepys, the Bibliographical Society, and the Sette of Odd Volumes, author of *London Past and Present: Its History, Associations, and Traditions,* 1891.

Wright   Thomas Wright, 1810 to 1877, English antiquarian, writer, author of *A Volume of Vocabularies,* 1857.

Wynne	Giustiniana Wynne, 1737 to 1791, Anglo-Venetian author, Countess of Orsini-Rosenberg, author of *Del Soggiorno dei Conti del Nord a Venezia in Gennaro del MDCCLXXXII*, Venice, 1782, octavo.
Yriarte	Charles Yriarte, 1832 to 1898, French writer, draughtsman, reporter for *Le Monde Illustre*, author of *La Vie d'un Patricien de Venise au Seizieme Siecle*, 1874
Zanetti	Girolamo Francesco Zanetti, 1723 to 1782, Venetian archaeologist, numismatist, author of *Dell'Origine di Alcune Arti Principali Presso i Veneziani*.
Zarlino	Gioseffo Zarlino, 1517 to 1590, Italian music theorist, composer, Franciscan monk, Maestro di Cappella of Saint Mark's, author of *De Tutte l'Opere del R.M. Gioseffo Zarlino da Chioggia, Maestro di Cappella della Serenissima Signoria di Venetia*, Venetia, 1789 edition, and *Dimostrationi Harmoniche*, 1571.
Zeno, A.	Apostolo Zeno, 1669 to 1750, Venetian poet, librettist, journalist, writer. Hazlitt cites *Lettere di Apostolo Zeno*.
Zeno, N.	Nicolo Zeno, circa 1326 to circa 1402, Venetian traveller, author of *Dei Commentarij del Viaggio in Persia di M. Caterino Zeno il K. & delle Guerre Fatte nell' Imperio Persiano*, 1558.
Zeno, P.	Pier Angelo Zeno, unidentifiable author of *Memorie de' Scrittori Veneti Patrizi Ecclesiastici e Secolari*, 1662 duodecimo edition.
Zompini	Gaetano Gherardo Zompini, 1698 to 1778, Italian print maker, engraver, composer of *Le Arti che Vanno per Via nella Citta di Venezia*, folio edition, 1785, and *The Cries of Venice*, 1785.

Zoppino

Niccolo Zoppino, 16th century, Italian engraver, composer of *Esemplario di Lavori, Dove le Tenere Fanciullealtre Donne Nobile Potranno Facilmente Imparare il Modoordine di Lavorare, Cusire, Raccamare, Finalmente Far Tutte Quelle Gentilezzelodevoli Opere, le Quali Po' Fare Una Donna Virtuosa con Laco [!] in Mano, con li Suoi Compassi, Misure,* quarto edition, Vinegia 1530.

Zurla

Placido Zurla, 1769 to 1834, Italian Camaldoese monk, Cardinal Vicar of Rome, writer on Mediaeval geography, author of *Di Marco Polo e degli Altri Viaggiatori Veneziani Più Illustri Dissertazioni del P. Ab. D. Placido Zurla,* 1818, two quarto volumes.

INDEX

Nigro, Francesco, Latin
  Grammar, 134.
Nismes, Bishop of, 114.
Noah, 112, 125.
Nogarola, Antonio, of Verona,
  194.
Nord, Conti del, 284.
Nordio, Bartolommeo, of
  Bergamo, 254.
Norfolk, 5th Duke of, Thomas
  Howard (died 1677), 281.
Norfolk, Duke of, 92, 281.
Normans (Northmen), 55, 65,
  111, 117, 142, 147, 153,
  307.
North America, 118, 249.
North, Council of the, England,
  240.
Northmen (Normans), 55, 65,
  111, 117, 142, 147, 153,
  307.
Norway, 122.
Novello, Francesco, 95.
Nuns' Well, 230.
Nuremberg (Nurnberg), 57, 149,
  216, 219, 247, 275, 276.
Nuremberg Egg, 34.
Nurnberg (Nuremberg), 57, 149,
  216, 219, 247, 275, 276.

O.

Odoni, Andrea, 215, 216, 318.
Odoni, Francesco, 215.
Oil, 145, 234-236, 238, 279,
  304, 307, 335.
Old Broad Street, London, 23.
Olivetan monks, 169.
Olivo, Camillo, 178.
Olympian Society of Vicenza ,
  211.

Olympic Theater at Vicenza,
  191, 193.
One-and-Thirty, a card game,
  341.
Ongania, Ferdinando, 116.
Ordelafi family, 143.
Orefici, Ruga degli, 13.
Oresi, Ruga dei, 13.
Organ-building, 24, 27, 30, 31,
  314.
Orii family, 143.
Orkney Islands, 117.
Orkney, Earl of, 117.
Orseoli family, 143.
Orseolo I, Pietro (Orseolo the
  Holy), Doge (976-978),
  253.
Orseolo II, Pietro, Doge (991-
  1008), 330.
Orseolo the Holy (Orseolo I,
  Pietro), Doge (976-978),
  253.
Orsi family, 147.
Oselle 85.
Osmanli House (Ottoman
  Dynasty), 110, 333.
Ostia, Bishop of, 189.
Otho II, Holy Roman Emperor
  (973-983), 267.
Ottoman Dynasty (Osmanli
  House), 110, 333.
Otway, Thomas, Venice
  Preserved, 192.
Ovid, 186.
Oxford, 149, 150, 175, 200,
  205, 216.

P.

Pace del Friuli, poet, 198.
Pacific Ocean, 33.
Paciolo, Fra Luca, 131, 164.

Vercellini, Francesco, 296.
Verde, Bartolommeo, 254.
Veriera, the, 13.
Verona, 39, 51, 64, 69, 77, 144,
176, 191, 194, 201, 208,
211, 255, 272, 275, 306,
344.
Verona, Johannes de, 208.
Veronese (Cagliari), Paolo,
painter, 165, 232, 261, 263,
318, 320-322.
Veronese, the (March of
Verona), 81, 173.
Vespucci family, 215.
Vetrai, Rio dei, 23.
Vezzi family, 38, 143.
Vezzi, Francesco, Giovanni amd
Giuseppe, potters, 38, 146.
Via Larga, 313.
Via, Pietro de la, 115.
Vicentino, Lodovico, 133.
Vicenza and Vicentines, 69, 77,
143, 170, 180, 191, 193,
196, 208, 211, 254-256,
272.
Victorino da Feltre, 171, 186.
Vienna, 80, 173, 220.
Vienna, court of, 285.
Villehardouin, Geoffroi de,
Marshal of Champagne,
Marshal of Romania, Prince
of Achaia, 270.
Vinci, Leonardo da, 125, 131.
Viola, Albertuccio della, poet,
314.
Virgil, 208, 216.
Visconte of Genoa, 116.
Visconti Forza, Bianca,
daughter of Filippo Maria
and wife of Francesco
Sforza, 271.

Visconti, Caterina Sforza, wife
of Giovanni Galeazzo, 272,
315.
Visconti, Filippo Maria, son of
Giovanni Galeazzo, 42, 65.
Visconti, Isabella de' Fieschi,
147, 271.
Visconti, Luchino, Duke of
Milan, 271.
Visdomini, da Mar, 43.
Volto Santo, Church of, 41.
Vulgate, the, 165.

W.

Wace, Robert, Anglo-Norman
chronicler, 153.
Wainfleet oysters, 305.
Wales, 28.
Wallenstein, Albrecht
Wenceslaus Eusebius, 180.
War of Chioggia, 15, 21, 117,
237, 307.
Wards, see Sestieri, 94.
Warwick, 55.
Water Carriers Guild, 14.
Water supply, 225, 230, 231,
251.
Weavers' Guild, 14.
Weights and measures, 25, 87.
Wells, 225, 230, 231.
West Friesland, 53.
Western (German or Holy
Roman) Emperor, 65, 256,
267, 271.
Western (Holy Roman or
German) empire, 101.
Westminster, 34.
Westminster Hall, 102.
Wey, William, his Itinerary,
247.
Whitaker, Lawrence, 311.

Printed by Ballantyne, Hanson & Co.
Edinburgh & London

INDEX OF AVAILABLE BOOKS

Chronicon Books is dedicated to the production of inexpensive high-quality editions of neglected, out-of-print history books and documents which are in the public domain, Below is a list of titles currently available, Ordering information can be found at chroniconbooks,com

A HISTORY OF THE ART OF WAR IN THE MIDDLE AGES by Charles Oman

    Volume I
    Volume II

A HISTORY OF THE ROMAN REPUBLIC by Cyril E. Robinson

A PHILOSOPHICAL ESSAY ON PROBABILITIES by Pierre Simon Laplace.

CHURCH HISTORY FROM NERO TO CONSTANTINE by C.P.S. Clarke.

ETRUSCAN RESEARCHES by Isaac Taylor

FIREARMS IN AMERICAN HISTORY — 1600 TO 1800 by Charles Winthrop Sawyer

HISTORY OF SWITZERLAND by Wilhelm Oechsli

HISTORY OF THE GATLING GUN DETACHMENT by John Parker

HISTORY OF THE INDIAN NAVY by Charles Rathbone Low.
    Volume I - 1613 to 1816.
    Volume II - 1811 to 1830.
    Volume III - 1831 to 1853.
    Volume IV 1852 to 1863.

HISTORY OF THE THIRTY YEARS WAR IN GERMANY by Friedrich Schiller

ORDER OF BATTLE — THE UNITED STATES ARMY GROUND FORCES IN WORLD WAR II — PACIFIC THEATER OF OPERATIONS by the Office of the Chief of Military History

RAILROADS, THEIR ORIGINS AND PROBLEMS by Charles Francis Adams

ROGER OF SICILY by Edmund Curtis

SKETCHES OF BUTTE by George Wesley Davis

STUDIES, MILITARY AND DIPLOMATIC by Charles Francis Adams

THE ART OF WAR IN THE MIDDLE AGES by Charles Oman

THE AUXILIA OF THE ROMAN IMPERIAL ARMY by G.L. Cheesman

THE CRISIS OF THE NAVAL WAR by John Rushworth Jellicoe

THE GRAND FLEET — 1914-1916 by John Rushworth Jellicoe

THE HISTORY OF ATLANTIS by Lewis Spence

THE HISTORY OF CHIVALRY by G.P.R. James

THE HISTORY OF ENGLAND by David Hume

   Volume I — Julius Caesar to King John
   Volume II — King Henry III to King Richard III
   Volume III — King Henry VII to Queen Mary I
   Volume IV — Queen Elizabeth I and King James I
   Volume V — King Charles I to the Commonwealth,
   Volume VI — Kings Charles II and James II,

THE HISTORY OF FRANCE by John Gifford

> Volume I — the Roman, Merovingian, and Carolingian periods
> Volume II — the Capetian period
> Volume III — The early Valois period
> Volume IV — The continuation of the Valois period, The reigns
> of Charles VII and Louis XI
> Volume V — The later Valois period
> Volume VI — The Bourbon period

THE HISTORY OF THE REIGN OF THE EMPEROR CHARLES V by
William Robertson

> Volume I
> Volume II
> Volume III

THE HOLY ROMAN EMPIRE by James Bryce

HE LATIN KINGDOM OF JERUSALEM by C.R. Conder.

THE LOMBARD COMMUNES by W.F. Butler

THE MAJOR OPERATIONS OF THE NAVIES IN THE AMERICAN
WAR OF INDEPENDENCE by Alfred Thayer Mahan

THE MEDIEVAL EMPIRE by Herbert Fisher

> Volume I
> Volume II

THE ORIGINS OF THE ISLAMIC STATE by Abu al Abbas al
Baladhuri

THE RISE OF THE DUTCH REPUBLIC by John Lothrop Motley

> Volume I — 1555 to 1567
> Volume II — 1567 to 1577
> Volume III — 1577 to 1584

THE VENETIAN REPUBLIC by J. Carew Hazlitt

      Volume One — AD 407 to AD 1205
      Volume Two — AD 1205 to AD 1365
      Volume Three — AD 1365 to AD 1457
      Volume Four — AD 1457 to AD 1797
      Volume Five — Government and Culture
      Volume Six — Government and Culture

WE THE PEOPLE — The Founding Documents